1000
MARKETS for
FREELANCE
WRITERS

1000 MARKETS for FREELANCE WRITERS

an A-Z guide to general and specialist magazines and journals

ROBERT PALMER

PIATKUS

*Thanks are due to the editors and other
members of editorial staff who provided so
much assistance in compiling the entries.
Most of all, thanks to Beverley for all the
stamp-licking, envelope addressing,
perseverance and patience needed to make the
book a reality.*

Copyright © 1993 by Robert Palmer

First published in Great Britain in 1993 by
Judy Piatkus (Publishers) Ltd of
5 Windmill Street, London W1

**The moral right of the author
has been asserted**

*A catalogue record for this book is
available from the British Library*

ISBN 0-7499-1288-X

Set in Compugraphic Times by
Action Typesetting Ltd, Gloucester
Printed and bound in Great Britain by
Bookcraft Ltd, Midsomer Norton, Avon

CONTENTS

Part 1

Introduction to
Freelance Writing

Introduction to Freelance Writing

The Freelance Market

There are many opportunities for the freelance writer. National newspapers, regional newspapers, radio stations, TV companies and others all accept material from outside contributors. However, it is not always easy to break into these markets. In most cases, you need considerable experience and good personal contacts to make any headway at all.

Fortunately, magazines represent a major exception to this rule. Some six thousand of them are published in the UK each year, and a substantial proportion of their output is bought from freelance writers.

More important, many of them are happy to take work from new contributors and to develop fresh talent. From mass-circulation weeklies to subscription-only professional titles, editors know that their future depends on keeping their readers interested. Any freelance writer who can come up with original ideas for informative, entertaining features will get a warm reception from even the busiest editor.

Flip through the pages that follow, and you will see that the range of publications covered is wide indeed. There is a huge diversity in style, content and readership and every title represents an opportunity for you to develop and extend your freelance career.

Armed with the information in these listings, you will be able to approach an editor with a strong, carefully-tailored suggestion that has an excellent chance of success.

At first glance, you might think that this does not apply to every publication listed. If you know little about cars, for example, can you seriously hope to contribute to motoring magazines? The answer is, emphatically, Yes.

Past experience of a subject is less important than an enquiring mind, the ability to research a new subject, and a talent for spotting opportunities. Perhaps you have a neighbour who is busy restoring an ageing sports car to its former glory. One of the classic car magazines might well be keen to run a feature about it. You can be sure that your neighbour will be only too willing to co-operate, providing you with all the technical information you need to write authoritatively. And if you can offer the editor photographs to accompany the story, success is virtually assured.

If you look hard enough, you will find feature opportunities all around you. What about that corner shop that has been doing booming business since getting a face-lift? *The Grocer*, *Convenience Store* and *Independent Grocer* all run features on successful shops; there is no reason why these features should not be written by you.

More specialised trade and professional publications offer a wealth of opportunity. I have contributed successfully to *Surveyor*, *Dental Laboratory*, *Retail Week*, *Fashion Weekly* and many other similarly esoteric titles without having any relevant professional experience. Again, the key to success lies in generating original ideas that will be of interest to the readership.

How To Use This Book

So, with 1,000 markets at your fingertips, how do you set about making the most of them? Essentially, there are two ways in which this book can help you.

1. If you have an idea for a potential feature, you can use the book to identify those magazines which may be interested. Let's say you discover that a colleague has developed some innovative computer software in his spare time: there are a number of possibilities here. One of the computer magazines may consider running a review. Look up COMPUTING & VIDEO GAMING in the subject index and you will find a list of relevant titles. By carefully studying the listings for each one, you can identify those which are worth approaching.

    If your colleague is starting his own company to launch the new product, you may be able to place a feature with one of the business magazines. A regional magazine that covers your area might also consider covering the story. And if the software is aimed at a particular market − such as design companies or photographers − you can offer the story to the appropriate specialist publications, too. In each case, all you have to do is use the subject index to guide you to the right magazines.

2. You can also use this book to generate ideas. If you don't have any specific projects in mind, try browsing through the listings − studying the requirements and comments sections in detail. It is surprising how often a simple phrase will spark off an idea. A half-forgotten experience or story may spring to mind as exactly the sort of thing an editor is looking for.

Presenting Your Proposal

Once you have identified a magazine which looks like a promising candidate for a particular feature, you will need to offer a proposal.

You may have noticed that, in this section, the emphasis is on generating ideas – not completing manuscripts. There is a very good reason for this; you only have to look through the A – Z listing that follows to see why.

The overwhelming majority of magazines today prefer not to receive unsolicited manuscripts. Many publications receive a flood of these every week, and the chances of them being used are very slim indeed. Even if you submit a feature that is of a high standard, it is unlikely to meet the editor's requirements at that moment. The magazine may have run a similar feature in a recent issue, or may wish to look at the story from a different angle – or it may be that the style and structure are just not right for that magazine's particular requirements.

All these problems can be avoided by making an initial enquiry. Look at the market listing to find out whom to contact, and the best way to approach them. In most cases, the magazine will initially want only a brief synopsis of the idea. Remember – this is your 'sales pitch', so it is worth investing some time and effort into getting it right.

You should make an effort to find out as much about each magazine as possible. Get hold of a sample copy and study it carefully. One freelance, David Bruce, believes you should know a magazine inside out before approaching with ideas. 'First of all, you need to know the house style,' he says. 'If you know when the magazine uses capitals and when it doesn't, for example, the editor can assume that you are a serious contributor. And if you can talk confidently about the sections and structure of the magazine, you are half-way to a commission.'

With this information at your fingertips, you will be able to present your idea in summary form. Keep your summary short and concise, while making sure you cover all the main points. You will need to explain the exact nature of your proposal, and why it would be of interest to your chosen magazine's readership. Discuss the way in which you would approach the subject, and the material you would include. If you have any special experience which qualifies you to write the piece, make sure you mention this. And make sure that your proposal is correctly angled for the magazine you are targeting. If you are aiming at a consumer magazine, you may need to stress the human element of the story; in a business magazine hard facts and figures may be more important.

Next comes the waiting game. Publications are notoriously slow at responding to potential contributors, although specific enquiries are usually dealt with more promptly than unsolicited submissions. If you are lucky, you will eventually get a firm commission from a magazine. Then you can get down to the hard work of writing the article, secure in the knowledge that your efforts will be rewarded.

Sometimes, however, a magazine will express interest in seeing an article 'on spec'. In other words, you will be expected to write the feature with no guarantee of acceptance or payment. Whether you accept this arrangement is entirely up to you. If you are a new writer, then it is understandable that the editor will be wary of making a firm commitment: your work may prove to be unsuitable, or completely unpublishable. By asking you to submit on spec, the editor is ensuring that you take all the risks. Even so, you may consider it worth working speculatively in order to develop a portfolio of published work for future use.

But if you already have an established track record as a writer, you should try to work to firm commissions wherever possible. Time is money in the freelance world, and you must ensure that your time is spent wisely and profitably. I have written several thousand articles over the years, all except two based on firm commissions.

No matter how good a writer you are, you cannot guarantee that all your ideas will receive an enthusiastic response. Even for experienced freelances rejection is a fundamental part of life. The law of averages ensures that for every idea that is eagerly accepted, another one – or two, or three – will come bouncing back at something approaching the speed of light. To succeed as a freelance, you need to be aware of this fact and prepare for it accordingly. Certainly you should not send off a lone proposal, sit back and wait hopefully for a commission. Proposals have the same properties as mud – throw enough of them and some are bound to stick.

That is not to say that you should send half-hearted and poorly-researched ideas to any magazine that seems remotely relevant; rather, you should concentrate on developing a number of strong ideas, then focus on a list of magazines which are likely to be interested in each. Prepare a proposal for the first publication on your list and send it off. Do this for each idea, so that you have a number of strong propositions circulating at one time. Each time you get a rejection, revise your proposal to suit the next magazine on your list and send it off once more. If you adopt this procedure, then the polite – or not so polite – negative replies become not so much rejections as stepping stones on the route to acceptance.

Writing Your Article

Whether you write on commission or on spec, your success will depend upon your ability to write publishable material on a consistent basis. To achieve this, you will need to master the craft of writing articles which are accurate, informative and entertaining.

First of all, you are going to need information. Once in a while, you will be able to write an article based on facts that you already know. But if you limit your writing activities to the familiar, you will soon run out of material. To write knowledgeably on a broad range of subjects you need to master the skills of research. Some of your information will come from published material such as books, periodicals and even computer databases. This can be a valuable way of gathering background, but is no substitute for talking to people. Interviewing skills are essential. Whether you are talking to someone about their personal experiences, or gathering statistics from an acknowledged expert, you must be able to obtain information effectively and efficiently. Remember Kipling's 'six honest serving men' – the questions Who? What? Why? Where? When? and How? Prepare for your interview well in advance and make sure you cover every question thoroughly. If you don't understand something, ask for a simpler explanation – however foolish you may feel. You cannot hope to write well about a subject with which you do not feel comfortable.

Once you have gathered all the information you need, you are ready to start writing your article. Think carefully about the message you wish to get across. Consider the story you want to tell. Structure your article accordingly, breaking it down into a series of key points. Then look for an arresting opening to 'hook' the reader's interest. After all, there is no point in writing 2,000 words of fascinating prose if the reader turns the page before reaching the second paragraph.

Keep your text flowing and easy to read, with short sentences and active verbs. Liven up facts and figures with quotes, anecdotes and opinions. And forget what your English teacher taught you about sentences that start with conjunctions – like this one. Or having sentences with no verbs. Like this one. The English language is a flexible tool for you to use in the best and most effective way you can to communicate your thoughts and ideas.

Make sure you pay sufficient attention to the ending, too. Don't simply stop in mid flow when you reach the required number of words – ensure that your ending is a logical conclusion to what has gone before, drawing the various strands together into a satisfying whole.

Presenting Your Manuscript

Endless words have been written on the subject of presentation, yet editors still receive tidal waves of unusable manuscripts. If you wish to be seen as a serious freelance writer, you must pay careful attention to the way you lay out your articles.

Most basic of all, handwriting is out. If your manuscript is not neatly typed or printed (computer printed, that is), you will be branded immediately as a hopeless amateur. At the other end of the scale, don't try to impress by printing your document using a variety of fancy typefaces. All the editor requires is text that is clear and easy to read.

Use double-spacing on standard A4 paper, with generous margins around all edges. Number each page consecutively, adding a title page including your name, address and telephone number. Whether you staple or paper-clip the pages together is a moot point. Some editors hate staples as they have to be prised out if the document is to be photocopied or read as loose pages; others prefer documents to be stapled so that pages don't become lost in the office. The only sensible answer is to get to know your editor, and secure your manuscript accordingly.

Many magazines nowadays are happy to receive articles by fax or, if you use a word processor, on disk. Faxing documents eliminates postal delays, while sending disks save editorial staff the trouble of re-keying the text. If you are able to supply copy in either of these ways, you may find you are looked upon more favourably as a contributor.

Small points such as these can make quite a difference, as freelance writer Beverley Legge confirms. 'You must be professional in everything you do,' he says. 'It is important to project the right image to ensure that you are taken seriously. Simple things, such as using headed stationery and responding quickly to enquiries create the right impression. If you have a fax machine, for example, you can have a proposal on an editor's desk within minutes of a phone call. All these factors help to give you a head start.'

Photos Sell Features

A very useful way of increasing your success rate is to offer photographs to accompany features. They say that a picture paints a thousand words, and the expression is one that the freelance writer should bear in mind. While writers tend to think in terms of words, editors have to think in terms of both words and pictures. And a magazine that consists of nothing but slabs of text looks boring and can be a trudge to read. A few well-chosen pictures can liven up the page and can illuminate the subject of the text to great effect. Consequently, the author who can offer an editor both words and pictures is much more likely to get a commission than the writer who sells words alone.

Today's 35mm cameras are so sophisticated that even an inexperienced photographer can produce reasonable pictures with a modest compact model. And, as film technology has improved, editors have become more willing to accept 35mm transparencies, or even colour prints. Of course, many magazines still use black and white photos extensively, so it is useful to be able to offer these, too.

Before taking your photos, consider who you may wish to publish them. Some magazines use only black and white, some only colour, while many use both. Black and white photos will normally be submitted as large prints, while transparencies are preferred for colour. Choose the right film according to the markets you are aiming for.

When taking your photos, try to imagine how they will look on the printed page. Action photos will always look better than static ones – so if you are documenting an abseiling trip, for example, don't take a picture of the abseilers standing together smiling at the bottom of the cliff. Catch them in the descent, taking photos from a number of angles.

Magazines usually prefer photos in portrait format – that is, tall and thin rather than short and wide. Consequently, editors need a high percentage of photos which match this format. Fill the frame with your subject: always look for an unusual or interesting composition. To get the picture just right, it is often worth 'bracketing' the exposure, taking extra photos with slightly increased and decreased exposure.

By offering photographs, you are making the editor's job considerably easier. It is much simpler to run a 'package' feature than to spend a great deal of time and effort finding pictures for an unaccompanied piece. The costs add up much better, too. Commissioning a professional photographer to go and take some pictures of a local celebrity, for example, would be unreasonably expensive. You, on the other hand, can quite easily take a few snapshots at the end of an interview. The editor would be pleased at having to pay reproduction fees only, while you benefit from a few extra pounds in your pocket.

Payment

Writing for magazines is an unusual business. Not only do the customers decide the price and when they are prepared to pay it, but the amounts vary tremendously for very similar pieces of work. One magazine might be prepared to pay £500 for a particular article whereas its seemingly-identical competitor will offer no more than £50. Rates are to some extent related to the nature of the publication: a specialist hobby magazine with a circulation of 5,000 is clearly not going to have the same financial resources as a mass-market magazine selling over a million copies a week. But there are many modest publications that struggle valiantly to pay their contributors over the odds for their efforts. Sadly, there are also a large number of successful magazines that bolster their profits by cutting freelance rates to the bone.

Most magazines pay a set rate per thousand words. In many cases this will be for words published, not words written, which may not turn out to be the same thing at all. You are unlikely to get paid for the time you spend travelling, researching material and conducting interviews – so make sure this is not going to be out of proportion to the fee. You may be able to secure an extra payment to cover expenses, but you will almost certainly have to ask.

Whenever you receive a commission, make sure you agree a fee before starting work − preferably have it confirmed in writing. If you simply wait to see what the publisher sends, you may be disappointed. Ideally, you should receive payment on acceptance of the work; in practice, you may well be paid on publication of the relevant issue, or even months later.

Overall, the whole question of payment is a very murky area indeed. Because rates vary so much, it is difficult to assess the reasonable rate for a particular piece of writing. The National Union of Journalists (NUJ) issues extremely helpful guidelines which group magazines together according to their ability to pay − based on circulation, advertising revenue and so on. Suggested rates range from around £115 per thousand words for trade and specialist magazines, to about £250 per thousand for large-circulation titles.

Getting Down To Work

If you are used to having a regular full-time job, becoming a freelance writer can be something of a culture shock. You can start work when you want to, and stop whenever it's convenient. Instead of fighting through the commuter traffic, you can stroll in a leisurely fashion into your study with a coffee and the morning papers ... And if you decide to work in your dressing gown and slippers, who is going to stop you?

Freelancing certainly gives you more freedom than most employees have ever dreamed of. Unfortunately, this has been the downfall of many writers. As a freelance, you are paid by results − so if you don't deliver, you don't get any money. The meter is only running when you are producing creative work, so you need to use your time as efficiently as possible. And, make no mistake, you will need to earn more than you did as an employee to maintain your standard of living. You no longer have the benefit of company pension contributions, paid holidays, sick leave and a regular income − so you must make these provisions yourself and ensure that there is enough cash left over for the inevitable 'rainy days'.

Nevertheless, provided you are aware of these facts, there is no reason why you should not earn a comfortable living as a freelance writer. The most important requirements are commitment, enthusiasm and a reasonable measure of self discipline. We can assume that if you did not possess the first two qualities, you would not be considering freelancing at all. So how do you acquire enough of the third to keep you in business?

The simplest way is to ensure that you establish some kind of order and routine in your working day. If possible, you should try to maintain a clear distinction between your work and your private life. You will probably be working from home, but this does not mean that business and leisure should become an indistinguishable blur. Ideally, you should have a room to use as your study or office, so that you can shut yourself away from family life during working hours. If this is not possible, make sure that you at least have a private corner where you will not be disturbed.

It is a good idea to set yourself targets for each day. If you find that you can write 800 words comfortably in a straight morning's work, for example, you could make this your goal before breaking for lunch. On days when you reach your target, you have the afternoon free for generating new proposals, dealing with administration and telephone calls, etc. But if you find yourself lagging behind, you should complete your scheduled work before moving on. This means that you will be completing some fee-earning work every day — and the faster you finish it, the more time you will have for other business.

This 'other business' should include keeping in touch with what's happening in the world in general. As a freelance writer you cannot afford to lock yourself away in an ivory tower, as freelance Simon Jackson points out. 'As a freelance writer, you deal in information. Therefore it is important to keep abreast of current events, and read a wide variety of publications. The more informed you are, the more comprehensive and meaningful your writing will be.'

Writing Equipment

Once upon a time, a ream of paper and a fountain pen would have been enough to launch a flourishing journalistic career. With the advent of the typewriter, writers became inextricably enmeshed in the industrial age. Nowadays, even typewriters have had their day, and computers are revolutionising the writing — and publishing — process.

Freelance writing is a competitive activity and having access to the right equipment and facilities can be a vital element in determining your success. Good office equipment can help you make better use of your time, present your work more professionally and make the editor's job easier. Consequently, a modest initial investment in writing equipment can pay handsome dividends in terms of commissions and acceptances.

So what do you write with? We have already seen that handwriting is out — at least for final copy. At the barest minimum, then, you will need a typewriter and even a modest machine will generate copy of adequate quality. But if you are serious about your writing — if you want to give your work that professional edge you will almost certainly want to consider word processing on a personal computer.

Computers

Computers bring many benefits to writers. Word-processing programs help the creative process by allowing you to edit text on the screen, honing and refining your work until it is exactly right. If changes or corrections are required, these can be made quickly and easily without re-keying the whole article. With a high-quality printer, you can produce output that is virtually indistinguishable from typeset text and the ability to offer copy on disk will be welcomed by many editors. A few years ago, the question asked by editors was, 'Do you use a computer?' Nowadays it is more likely to be, 'Which system do you use?'

If you are considering buying a computer system, you will soon discover that there is a bewildering choice available. But for the typical freelance writer, these can be divided into three major groups.

1. At the lower-end of the scale in terms of cost is the Amstrad PCW series (not to be confused with Amstrad PCs). The great attraction of the PCW is that it offers a complete package of computer, printer, word-processing software and accessories for just a few hundred pounds. Even a complete novice can start creating and printing documents relatively quickly. PCWs have become extremely popular with writers, and are quite adequate for most purposes. But, as with everything in life, you only get what you pay for. If you want to enjoy the benefits that more advanced technology can offer, you will need to invest a little more.

2. The standard business computer today is the IBM-compatible PC, generally known simply as the PC. As the name suggests, these machines were originally copies of the IBM Personal Computer − this meant that they could all use the same software and peripherals, fuelling an explosion in the amount of software developed for them. In turn, this led to the production of more PCs, and the whole thing snowballed. Nowadays, there are hundreds of millions of PCs worldwide, and the number is growing rapidly. If you choose a PC you can be sure that you will be in good company. Even if a particular magazine does not use PCs, the editor will probably be able to take copy in PC format and convert it. New machines are launched virtually every week, with each range offering more power for less money than its predecessors. And with a vast range of software to choose from, you can persuade your computer to do almost anything.

3. Your third major option is an Apple Macintosh. As well as being very easy to use, the 'Mac' is a sophisticated machine which is generally considered to be at the leading-edge of technology. Apple has certainly had great success in the creative world, with Macs being used extensively by newspapers and magazines. In recent years, however, PCs have closed the gap in terms of technology − offering similar potential at competitive prices.

Printers

If you use a computer you will also need a printer to produce paper copies of your work. Again there is an enormous choice available, but there are a number of technologies to consider. Dot matrix printers are very popular, and a good model can produce high quality documents, but newer types of printer, such as ink jet and bubble jet, can offer even better quality at very keen prices. Ask your dealer to demonstrate different types and models to find one that suits your requirements and your pocket.

If you can possibly afford it, you should give serious consideration to buying a laser printer. Capable of producing extremely high quality output, laser printers have fallen in price quite considerably in recent years. A number of writers have reported that their acceptance rate has increased significantly since switching to laser printing; others have noticed that editors ask for fewer amendments. It seems that if copy *looks* good, it is presumed to *be* good.

Software

There is no point in having a state-of-the-art super-powerful computer unless you have some software − programs − to run on it. In fact, your best course of action is probably to choose your software first, and then find a suitable computer.

For writers the first major requirement is a word-processing package. There are many of these to choose from and everyone has their own personal preference. But on PCs and Macs, WordPerfect and Microsoft Word are the firm favourites − if you use one of these two, you will find it easy to submit copy on disk to a large number of magazines. However, most good word-processing software will allow you to convert files into formats used by other major packages.

Facsimile

One other piece of equipment which has become almost essential is a fax machine. Time is a valuable commodity in the publishing world, with everyone working to schedules and deadlines, and by providing a means of transmitting documents almost instantly to any part of the world, fax machines eliminate postal delays and speed up communications. When time is of the essence, having access to fax facilities can mean the difference between getting or losing a commission. Nowadays, in fact, professional writers will generally be expected to send and receive faxes as a matter of course. Fortunately, growing demand has led to a rapid fall in the cost of fax machines and a modest machine can be picked up for a very reasonable price.

Technology is becoming increasingly important throughout the publishing industry. Writers who use Information Technology (IT) to advantage will find that they not only work more quickly and efficiently, but also have a significant head start in the competitive freelance world.

Business Matters

As soon as you set out your stall as a freelance writer, you become part of the small business community. Whether you aim to write full time or merely to create some additional income, you need to take a serious approach to your work. Even if your earnings are initially modest, you can be sure that the authorities will take a considerable interest in them. So you must ensure that you are aware of your position in terms of taxation, national insurance, VAT and so on.

The first thing you need to decide is the form that your business is going to take. Are you going to be a sole trader, a partnership or a limited company? As a freelance writer, you are most likely to be a sole trader, which means that you are conducting business as an individual and you alone will be responsible for the running of the business and for profits or losses that it generates.

Although this sounds rather formal, you will be assumed to be a sole trader unless you have specifically formed a partnership or a limited company. If you become very successful, you may consider these alternatives as a way of reducing tax liabilities. However, there are as many pitfalls in such arrangements as there are advantages, and consequently you should have sound professional advice before making such a move.

Income Tax

A freelance writer is usually assessed for tax purposes as a self-employed person under Schedule D. As with any small business, you will need to keep accounts of all your business transactions for the benefit of the taxman. You will find this much easier if you keep a separate bank account for your freelance work. The administration work is annoying and time-consuming, but is essential if you want to limit your tax liabilities. If your records are not clear and complete, the Inland Revenue is likely to take an overly-optimistic view of your profits and tax you accordingly.

However, there is a plus side to the administration work. You are entitled to claim business expenses incurred in connection with your work, and these can reduce your tax liability considerably.

Business expenses are defined as payments that are made exclusively for business benefit — business lunches, for example, are not an allowable expense as you eat to live as well as to meet clients. But, in general, the rules accommodate most reasonable expenses: these include the cost of stationery and other working materials, postage, travel expenses, accountancy fees and so on. They may also cover subscriptions, photography, newspapers and theatre tickets where these are appropriate to the writer's work.

Some items may be employed for both private and business use. For example, you are likely to use your car both as a family vehicle and as a means of transport for business trips. In this case, a reasonable percentage of the running and maintenance costs can be claimed as expenses. If you work from home, you can make a similar claim for a percentage of the costs of heating, lighting, etc. But you should be wary of using one room exclusively for business use, as this has other tax implications which may not be to your advantage. In practice, most people will also use an office or study for private paperwork, so this should not present too much of a problem. Major business purchases such as computers and fax machines are also allowable, but these are classed as capital expenditure. The rules are slightly different here, with capital allowances against the cost being spread over a number of years.

In fact the whole business of preparing accounts can become extraordinarily complicated. Unless your freelance income is relatively small, you would be wise to consider investing in the services of a good accountant. You may have to fork out a few hundred pounds a year in fees, but professional advice and planning could save you considerably more in tax.

Careful planning is also needed to ensure that you are able to meet your tax liabilities when they arise. Unlike employees, freelances do not have income tax deducted from their payments. Normally you are assessed once a year, with half the payment falling due in the following January, and the rest six months later.

But just to make things more complicated than they need to be, you are usually assessed on the profits of the previous year's business. In practice, this means your tax payments will generally relate to income that you received some two years earlier. You must therefore ensure that you put enough money aside to meet these demands when they arise.

National Insurance

Income tax is not your only liability. As a self-employed person, you will also be required to pay Class 2 National Insurance contributions. And if you are modestly successful, you may also have to pay Class 4 contributions in proportion to your profits.

VAT

Another penalty of success is the obligation to register for Value Added Tax (VAT). As soon as your annual turnover exceeds the statutory threshold (£37,600 at the time of writing), you must apply for registration. Once you have your VAT number, you are required by law to add VAT to all your invoices and collect the appropriate amount from your customers. At the end of each quarter, you fill in a VAT return and forward the appropriate sum of money to HM Customs & Excise.

Dealing with VAT is undoubtedly a major inconvenience, and the source of much additional paperwork and form-filling, but there are some silver linings to this particular cloud that should not be dismissed lightly. In particular, VAT-registered persons are able to reclaim all the VAT paid on business expenses. This is a considerable advantage, especially on the purchase of major items. Publishers reclaim VAT in the same way, so adding VAT to your fees does not increase the cost of your services; in fact, editors may prefer to work with a VAT-registered writer as this is evidence of some degree of success.

Publications For Writers

Information is a very valuable commodity to a freelance writer, and a few pounds spent on relevant books and periodicals can pay handsome dividends.

Looking at magazines first of all, there are two leading publications in this sector:

Writers News, PO Box 4, Nairn, IV12 4HU. Tel: (0667) 54441.
As the title suggests, this magazine is very strong on news content, detailing a great deal of activity that is of interest to freelances. In addition, there are many useful features covering all aspects of writing. It incorporates the quarterly newstand magazine *Writing*.

Writers' Monthly, 29 Turnpike Lane, London, N8 0EP. Tel: (081-342 8879).
Well designed and presented, with the emphasis on articles rather than news. Runs features on major authors, publishers, agents and the how-to aspects of writing.

There are also a number of small-press magazines of interest to freelances. Although more modest in their ambitions, they can be very useful sources of information and advice:

Freelance Writing and Photography, Tregaraint House, Zennor, St Ives, Cornwall, TR26 3DB. Tel: (0736) 797061.
The most professionally produced of the smaller magazines, this has now progressed from quarterly to bi-monthly publication. Covers the usual range of subjects in an informative way.

Quartos, BCM Writer, 27 Old Gloucester Street, London, WC1N 3XX. Tel: (0559) 371108.
No glossy colour here, but well presented all the same. Generally a

good read with interesting articles, competitions, letters and so on. Published bi-monthly.

Freelance Market News, Cumberland House, Lissadell Street, Salford, Manchester, M5 6GG. Tel: 061-745 8850.
Very much a newsletter rather a magazine, but a useful source of information, tips and guidelines.

There are a number of very useful books for writers, too. The most popular of these are *The Writer's Handbook* (Macmillan/PEN) and *Writers' & Artists' Yearbook* (A & C Black). Both of these cover a great deal of ground and are not specifically aimed at the freelance writer for magazines. This means there is a limited amount of detail, but they are still valuable reference works.

As far as the art of writing freelance material is concerned, good advice can be found in John Hines' *The Way to Write Magazine Articles* (Elm Tree Books). Another sound text is *The Craft of Writing Articles* (Allison & Busby) by Gordon Wells, while *Journalism for Beginners* (Piatkus Books) by Joan Clayton is an excellent introduction to the subject. If you need to obtain extra information for a feature, Ann Hoffmann's *Research for Writers* (A & C Black) provides details of a wide range of sources.

A Few Final Points

Finally, some comments about the listings that follow. These are based on exhaustive interviews and in-depth questionnaires completed by editorial staff. Where appropriate, the details have been supplemented by information provided by fellow writers, or from my own past experience. Although every effort has been made to make the listings as accurate as possible, the publishing business is a fast-moving one, and editorial policies do change. Bear this in mind when approaching magazines, and be prepared to adapt your ideas where necessary.

Payment rates are rarely cast in stone. Even where a fixed rate or minimum fee is stated, there may be room to negotiate a higher payment. Please note also that, according to publishing convention, 'bi-monthly' in the context of this book means every two months, not twice a month.

Lead time is a matter which is often not taken sufficiently seriously by freelance writers. Producing a magazine is a complex, time-consuming task, and editors need to receive material well in advance of the publication date. A weekly magazine with a large staff may be able to publish a magazine within a few weeks — or even days — of the copy deadline, but a similar monthly magazine will be producing fewer issues, and so will have a smaller staff. Everyone will have more tasks to complete in the production process, and it will take longer to turn around each issue. So if it is mid-summer and you are hoping to write for a major women's monthly, don't look to the blue skies and think of sun tans and iced drinks. The magazine staff may well be working on the Christmas issue at that point in time, and articles on gift ideas and winter fires will be much better received.

For our purposes, the lead time is considered to be the time between the deadline for receipt of copy and the date of publication. Remember that, for features, you should allow extra time for busy editors to consider your proposals. Strong news stories, on the other hand, may be presented right up until the moment when the publication goes to press.

Nothing is ever black and white in the world of publishing, but this book will provide you with the information you need to develop your writing career.

Freelance writing is not always easy, but it can be extremely rewarding. If you have the determination to succeed combined with a firm sense of commitment, it is surprising what you can achieve. And with over 1,000 markets waiting for your ideas and initiatives, you have everything to work for.

So good luck – and happy writing!

Part 2

A – Z Listing
of 1000 General and
Specialist Magazines

A

AA Magazine

Greater London House
Hampstead Road
London
NW1 7QQ

Tel: 071-388 3171   **Fax:** 071-383 7570

Frequency: Quarterly

Circulation: 3,750,000

Contact: Christopher Jones, Editor

Profile: The official publication of the Automobile Association. Covers developments within the AA, and runs travel and lifestyle features.

Requirements: 2 6 7
Articles covering motoring-related subjects, especially travelling by car. Length up to 1500 words.

Comments: The magazine has a broad appeal and is not just a brochure for the AA. Well-written features of interest to the general membership are welcomed.

Approach: By telephone with ideas.

Lead time: Two months.

Payment: £200 for a 1500-word feature.

Accountancy

40 Bernard Street
London
WC1N 1LD

Tel: 071-833 3291   **Fax:** 071-833 2085

Frequency: Monthly

Circulation: 73,891

Contact: Brian Singleton-Green, Editor

Profile: A magazine for accountants in both practice and in industry. Aims to keep them abreast of current developments.

Requirements: 1 2
Articles on accounting, auditing, finance, profit improvement, taxation, legal issues and other matters of interest to accountants.

Comments: The magazine is also read by non-accountancy senior managers.

Approach: By letter with ideas.

Lead time: Two months.

Payment: £100 per page.

Accountancy Age

VNU Business Publications
VNU House
32-34 Broadwick Street
London
W1A 2HG

Tel: 071-439 4242   **Fax:** 071-437 7001

Frequency: Weekly

Circulation: 72,438

Contact: Rob Outram, Editor

Profile: Covers the world of accountancy for professionals in the business.

1/News 2/Features 3/Fiction 4/Letters 5/Fillers
6/B&W Photos 7/Colour Photos 8/Reviews

Requirements: 2 6 7
Feature articles on all aspects of
accounting, company management
and financial control. Photographs
to accompany features are always
welcome.
Comments: Freelance work is
commissioned by the magazine, so
approach with proposals initially.
Approach: In writing with ideas.
Lead time: Three weeks.
Payment: NUJ rates.

Achievement

World Trade House
49 Dartford Road
Sevenoaks
Kent
TN13 3TE

Tel: (0732) 458144   **Fax:** (0732) 456295

Frequency: Quarterly

Circulation: 10,234

Contact: Geoffrey Cuthbert, Editor
Profile: Provides news, information
and advice concerning project management on the international stage.
Requirements: 2 6 7
Bright, informative articles about
achievements by UK companies and
businessmen in the field of project
management.
Comments: Good-quality photos to
accompany features are always
welcome.
Approach: In writing.
Lead time: Three months.
Payment: By arrangement.

Action Holidays

27 Belsize Lane
London
NW3 5AS

Tel: 071-435 5472   **Fax:** 071-431 3742

Frequency: 5xYear

Circulation: 27,000

Contact: Alan Holden, Features Editor
Profile: For people who want more
from a holiday than a package deal,
with at least part of their time spent
actively engaged in sporting activity.
Requirements: 2 7
Seeks features on all kinds of
adventurous holiday activity,
ranging from walking and climbing
to deep-sea diving and white-water
rafting. Length 1000 to 1500 words.
Comments: The magazine has an
international readership, with most
readers being in the 18 to 40 age
range.
Approach: By telephone.
Lead time: Four weeks.
Payment: £175 per thousand words.

Active Life

Aspen Specialist Media
Christ Church
Cosway Street
London
NW1 5NJ

Tel: 071-262 2622   **Fax:** 071-706 4811

Frequency: Quarterly

Circulation: 300,000

Contact: Helene Hodge, Editor
Profile: A friendly, chatty magazine
aimed at those aged over 55. It
concentrates on helping readers to
make the most of an active
retirement.

Requirements: 2 3 5 7
Features on pursuits and activities of interest to the readership, plus articles about health, fitness, finance and other relevant issues.
Comments: Writers should aim to write for those in retirement, but without specifically mentioning the age group.
Approach: By letter, with ideas and examples of previous work.
Lead time: Six months.
Payment: £100 per thousand words, plus £40 per photograph.

Acumen

6 The Mount
Higher Furzeham
Brixham
South Devon
TQ5 8QY

Tel: (0803) 851098

Frequency: 2xYear

Circulation: 600

Contact: Patricia Oxley, Editor
Profile: A literary publication that covers everything from short stories to poetry.
Requirements: 2 3 8
Welcomes short fiction, articles on literary subjects and biographical features. Also runs critical pieces on individual writers.
Comments: Does not want highly-academic material, or anything too political or religious.
Approach: By letter with ideas.
Lead time: Six months.
Payment: By arrangement.

Administrator

16 Park Crescent
London
W1N 4AH

Tel: 071-580 4741   **Fax:** 071-323 1132

Frequency: Monthly

Circulation: 41,000

Contact: Jonathon Preece, Editor
Profile: Published by the Institute of Chartered Secretaries and Administrators. Covers administration in business, government and other institutions.
Requirements: 2
Informative articles on finance, development, legal issues and other matters of concern to company secretaries and other administrators. Length 750 to 1600 words.
Comments: Covers administration from an international perspective.
Approach: In writing.
Lead time: Two months.
Payment: Negotiable.

Ads International

35 Britannia Row
London
N1 8QH

Tel: 071-226 1739   **Fax:** 071-226 1540

Frequency: Quarterly

Circulation: 8000

Contact: Tim Rich, Editor
Profile: A large format magazine read by creative staff, typographers and production management in advertising agencies.
Requirements: 1 2 5 7 8
Feature-length articles analysing a certain aspect of the advertising

industry, plus shorter review pieces. International contributions are particularly welcome. Length up to 1000 words.

Comments: In the first instance, new contributors should send cuttings of previous work together with a brief CV.

Approach: By letter or fax.

Lead time: Six weeks.

Payment: Around £125 per feature.

Advantage

Enterprise House
17-21 George Street
Croydon
CR0 1LA

Tel: 081-649 7233   **Fax:** 071-538 5616

Frequency: Quarterly

Circulation: 190,000

Contact: Alan Orbell, Editor

Profile: Distributed to holders of the British Rail Annual Gold Card. Covers subjects of interest to commuters in the South East of the UK.

Requirements: 1 2 7
Features based around locations in the South East. Subjects range from railway rambling to English heritage. Length 1000 words maximum.

Comments: Features with a broad appeal but a railway perspective are most likely to achieve success.

Approach: By letter, with ideas or a complete manuscript.

Lead time: Two months.

Payment: £110 per thousand words.

Aerobics & Fitness World

207 Sherbourne Mill Studios
Morville Street
Birmingham
B16 8DG

Tel: 021-454 4454   **Fax:** 021-455 8038

Frequency: Monthly

Circulation: 60,000

Contact: Paul McMahon, Editor

Profile: A down-to-earth guide to keeping fit in the 1990s, aimed at the ordinary family.

Requirements: 2 5
Features on keeping fit and healthy living. Interviews with celebrities who keep fit are always of interest. Length 1000 to 1500 words.

Comments: Writers need not be experts. Strong writing is more important than specialised knowledge.

Approach: In writing with ideas.

Lead time: Six weeks.

Payment: By negotiation.

Aeromodeller

Argus House
Boundary Way
Hemel Hempstead
Hertfordshire
HP2 7ST

Tel: (0442) 66551   **Fax:** (0442) 66998

Frequency: Monthly

Circulation: 7017

Contact: John Stroud, Editor

Profile: Magazine containing information and advice for keen aeromodellers.

Requirements: 1 2 7
'How-to' instructional features, contest reports, hobby information and product tests. Length between 1500 and 2500 words.

1/News **2**/Features **3**/Fiction **4**/Letters **5**/Fillers
6/B&W Photos **7**/Colour Photos **8**/Reviews

Comments: Short, punchy pieces stand a much better chance of acceptance.
Approach: By letter or telephone with ideas.
Lead time: Two months.
Payment: £50 per thousand words.

Aeroplane Monthly

King's Reach Tower
Stamford Street
London
SE1 9LS
Tel: 071-261 5849   **Fax:** 071-261 7851
Frequency: Monthly
Circulation: 36,000
Contact: Richard Riding, Editor
Profile: For enthusiasts of all ages, both amateur and professional. Covers classic aeroplanes up to the 1960s, plus modern aircraft of exceptional interest.
Requirements: 1 2 6 7
Historical features detailing personal experiences with classic aircraft, up to 3000 words in length. Also news items and short articles about preserved or restored aeroplanes.
Comments: Features on personal experiences should ideally be accompanied by relevant photographs.
Approach: By letter with ideas.
Lead time: Two months.
Payment: £45 per thousand words.

Afloat!

9 Great Burrow Rise
Northam
Bideford
Devon
EX39 1TB
Tel: (0237) 475165
Frequency: Bi-monthly
Circulation: circa 5000
Contact: Dennis Davis, Editor
Profile: A magazine for small-boat enthusiasts, covering all person or wind-powered craft up to 20 feet in length.
Requirements: Boat-oriented articles of around 1000 words. Suitable subjects include reminiscences of voyages, boating with children, historical boating subjects and appropriate holiday destinations.
Comments: Details of facilities, state of water and other practical information should be incorporated where relevant.
Approach: By telephone.
Lead time: Two months.
Payment: By negotiation.

Air 2000 Inflight Magazine

82 High Street
Reigate
Surrey
RH2 9AP
Tel: (0737) 222563   **Fax:** (0737) 221290
Frequency: 2xYear
Circulation: 1 million
Contact: Sarah Palmer, Editor
Profile: Magazine for charter airline passengers, en route to or from their holiday destination.
Requirements: 2 3
Features and stories of broad interest that would appeal to holiday makers. Travel features, however, are not required.
Comments: Send ideas for contributions in May or December for consideration by the airline. Successful writers will then be commissioned.

1/News **2**/Features **3**/Fiction **4**/Letters **5**/Fillers
6/B&W Photos **7**/Colour Photos **8**/Reviews

Approach: By post only.
Lead time: Six months.
Payment: £100-£120 per thousand words.

Air Display International

Coombelands House
Coombelands Lane
Addlestone
Surrey
KT15 1HY
Tel: 081-549 4012　**Fax:** (0932) 854750
Frequency: Bi-monthly
Circulation: 15,000
Contact: Zoe Schofield, Editor
Profile: The only regular, dedicated air-show magazine. Covers the worldwide air-show scene, with a bias towards UK and European events. It is the official publication of the Air Display Association.
Requirements: 1 2 6 7
Articles which succeed in 'putting the reader in the cockpit'. Also interviews with pilots who talk about their experiences, and other background information. Length 2000-3000 words, accompanied by photos where possible.
Comments: Features do not need to be technical in content.
Approach: By telephone with ideas.
Lead time: Six weeks.
Payment: Up to £120, plus £10-£15 for photos.

Air Gunner

Romsey Publishing Co Ltd
2 The Courtyard
Denmark Street
Wokingham
Berkshire
RG11 2LW
Tel: (0734) 771677　**Fax:** (0734) 772903
Frequency: Monthly
Circulation: 20,000
Contact: Paul Dobson, Editor
Profile: Magazine for air gun enthusiasts of every age.
Requirements: 2 6
Features on field-target shooting, including club profiles and competitions. Also practical advice, reviews of equipment and historical items.
Comments: The majority of the readership is aged over 30, and articles need to be written to a high standard.
Approach: Call with an idea, or send a complete manuscript.
Lead time: Six weeks.
Payment: Around £100 per article.

Air International

PO Box 100
Stamford
Lincolnshire
PE9 1XQ
Tel: (0780) 55131　**Fax:** (0780) 57261
Frequency: Monthly
Circulation: 48,572
Contact: T. Malcolm English, Editor
Profile: Covers airforces and airlines in both military and civil sectors. Read by enthusiasts and military personnel.
Requirements: 1 2 4 5 6 7
Any article of relevance to a

knowledgeable, discerning audience. Features with a slightly unusual content are of especial interest.
Comments: Features must cover their subject in depth, and must be accurate in every detail.
Approach: By letter.
Lead time: 6 weeks.
Payment: £60 per thousand words minimum.

Aircraft Illustrated

Ian Allan Publishing
Terminal House
Shepperton
TW17 8AS

Tel: (0932) 228950   **Fax:** (0932) 247520

Frequency: Monthly

Circulation: 30,000

Contact: Allan Burney, Editor
Profile: Magazine of military and civil aviation, read by both enthusiasts and professionals worldwide.
Requirements: 2 6 7
Features on international aviation, preferably accompanied by colour or black & white photographs.
Comments: News is covered by regular writers, but other contributions are encouraged.
Approach: By letter, with ideas and examples of previous work.
Lead time: Six weeks.
Payment: By negotiation.

Airforces Monthly

PO Box 100
Stamford
Lincolnshire
PE9 1XQ

Tel: (0780) 55131   **Fax:** (0780) 57261

Frequency: Monthly
Circulation: 31,134
Contact: David Oliver, Editor
Profile: Covers all aspects of modern military aircraft. Read by enthusiasts, airforce personnel and other professionals.
Requirements: 1 2 4 5 6 7
Both news and features are welcomed, provided they are well-researched and relevant to the readership.
Comments: The magazine is only interested in material relating to modern aircraft.
Approach: By letter, with ideas or complete manuscript.
Lead time: Six weeks.
Payment: £50 per thousand words minimum.

Airgun World

10 Sheet Street
Windsor
Berks
SL4 1BG

Tel: (0753) 856061   **Fax:** (0753) 859652

Frequency: Monthly

Circulation: 19,000

Contact: Tim O'Nions, Managing Editor
Profile: Magazine covering all subjects related to the use of air guns, from rifle tests to match and fun shooting.
Requirements: 1 2 6 7
Accepts articles on expeditions, collectors' rifles and new developments. Length up to 1200 words.
Comments: Features accompanied by photographs are in short supply and are more likely to be accepted.

1/News **2**/Features **3**/Fiction **4**/Letters **5**/Fillers
6/B&W Photos **7**/Colour Photos **8**/Reviews

Approach: Send complete manuscript.
Lead time: Four weeks.
Payment: By negotiation.

Airline Business

151 Wardour Street
London
W1V 4BN

Tel: 071-411 2596   **Fax:** 071-287 2829

Frequency: Monthly

Circulation: 30,000

Contact: Richard Whitaker, Editor

Profile: A business magazine for airline management worldwide. Stylish and well-written, concentrating on strategic business issues.

Requirements: 1 2 6 7
High-quality news stories and features of interest to an international, senior-level audience. Length 500-2000 words.

Comments: Exclusive material has the best chance of acceptance. The magazine is not interested in product stories or travelogues.

Approach: By fax with ideas.
Lead time: Four weeks.
Payment: £200 per thousand words.

Airtours International Inflight Magazine

82 High Street
Reigate
Surrey
RH2 9AP

Tel: (0737) 222563   **Fax:** (0737) 221290

Frequency: 2xYear

Circulation: 1,000,000

Contact: Sarah Palmer, Editor

Profile: Magazine for charter airline passengers. Readers are all holiday-makers en route to or from their destination.

Requirements: 2 3
Features and stories of general interest to passengers. However, travel features are not required.

Comments: Send ideas in May or December only. These will be considered by the airline, and successful writers will receive commissions.

Approach: By letter only.
Lead time: Six months.
Payment: £100-£120 per thousand words.

Alpha

37 Elm Road
New Malden
Surrey
KT3 3HB

Tel: 081-942 9761   **Fax:** 081-949 2313

Frequency: Monthly

Circulation: 16,850

Contact: Dave Roberts, Editor

Profile: A magazine for 19 to 40 year old active Christians and evangelicals. It aims to be analytical yet human in its approach.

Requirements: 1 2
Articles about modern Christianity, covering topics such as youth groups, prayer and churches around the world. Length up to 2000 words. No fiction.

Comments: Will not consider unsolicited material, but is prepared to look at proposals which summarise the main points of a suggested article.

Approach: By letter only.

Lead time: Six weeks.
Payment: Up to £80 per thousand words.

Amateur Gardening

Westover House
West Quay Road
Poole
Dorset
BH15 1JG

Tel: (0202) 680586 **Fax:** (0202) 674335

Frequency: Weekly

Circulation: 86,000

Contact: Helen Warren

Profile: Covers practical aspects of gardening, with plants and people of equal interest.

Requirements: 1 2 4 7
Topical news items and features covering everything from prize-winning vegetables to environmental matters. Maximum length 800 words.

Comments: Much of the material submitted is too basic in content. This is a specialist practical magazine for keen gardeners.

Approach: By letter with ideas.

Lead time: Five weeks.

Payment: From £80 per thousand words.

Amateur Golf

PO Box 12
Wetherby
West Yorkshire
LS22 6SR

Tel: (0937) 583181 **Fax:** (0937) 583181

Frequency: Monthly

Circulation: 12,000

Contact: John Lelean, Editor

Profile: The official journal of the English Golf Union, and the only magazine devoted to club amateur golf. Circulation is by subscription only.

Requirements: 1 2 4 5 6 7 8
Welcomes features concerning the amateur game of golf and related matters. Anything connected with new golf developments is of particular interest. Length 750-1000 words.

Comments: Professional golf is not covered, except when the professional and amateur fields come together.

Approach: By telephone or letter with ideas.

Lead time: Six weeks.

Payment: By negotiation.

Amateur Photographer

King's Reach Tower
Stamford Street
London
SE1 9LS

Tel: 071-261 5000 **Fax:** 071-261 5404

Frequency: Weekly

Circulation: 50,000

Contact: Keith Wilson, Editor

Profile: Aims to cater for all photographers, from beginners through to professionals. Includes techniques, equipment, reviews and competitions.

Requirements: 1 2 4 6 7
All articles considered, but especially those on photographic technique. Anything that illustrates a good idea will be well received.

Comments: Ideas need to be backed up by photos. 'Before and after'

1/News **2**/Features **3**/Fiction **4**/Letters **5**/Fillers
6/B&W Photos **7**/Colour Photos **8**/Reviews

pictures showing improvement in photo quality are of particular interest.

Approach: By letter with ideas.

Lead time: Five weeks.

Payment: £90 per thousand words or per full page photo.

Ambit

17 Priory Gardens
Highgate
London
N6 5QY

Tel: 081-340 3566

Frequency: Quarterly

Circulation: 2000

Contact: Martin Bax, Editor

Profile: An idiosyncratic literary magazine, with content divided equally between poetry, short stories and art.

Requirements: 3 5
Modern, creative stories and poems. Suitable material is likely to be quirky and original rather than traditional in style.

Comments: New writers are encouraged, but it is essential to read the magazine first to get a feel for its unusual style.

Approach: Send complete manuscript.

Lead time: Three months.

Payment: Negotiable.

Amenity Management

38-42 Hampton Road
Teddington
Middlesex
TW11 OJE

Tel: 081-943 5000   **Fax:** 081-943 5673

Frequency: Monthly

Circulation: 6000

Contact: Jim Deen, Editor

Profile: Covers all aspects of amenity management, including council amenities, leisure management, woodland and landscaping projects.

Requirements: 1 2 5
Articles, news items and fillers relating to the management of all types of amenities. Fillers should be between 200 and 250 words, while features may run up to 2000 words.

Comments: All items should be written to interest a management-level readership.

Approach: By letter.

Lead time: Two months.

Payment: Up to £80.

Amiga Power

Future Publishing
30 Monmouth Street
Bath BA1 2BW

Tel: (0225) 442244   **Fax:** (0225) 446019

Frequency: Monthly

Circulation: 50,222

Contact: Linda Barker, Editor

Profile: A monthly magazine for owners of Amiga computer systems, covering games and entertainment.

Requirements: 2 8
Innovative and exciting features on Amiga systems and software. Also reviews of games, between 400 and 600 words in length.

Comments: A good way to break in is to send a sample review of an established game for reference.

Approach: In writing with examples of work.

Lead time: Two months.

Payment: Around £70 per thousand words.

1/News **2**/Features **3**/Fiction **4**/Letters **5**/Fillers
6/B&W Photos **7**/Colour Photos **8**/Reviews

Angler's Mail

IPC Magazines
King's Reach Tower
Stamford Street
London
SE1 9LS

Tel: 071-261 5883   **Fax:** 071-261 6016

Frequency: Weekly

Circulation: 94,000

Contact: Roy Westwood, Editor

Profile: A news-oriented publication for coarse anglers, from beginners through to those with considerable experience.

Requirements: 1 7
Strong newsy items, accompanied by colour photography.

Comments: Unsolicited material is unlikely to be used.

Approach: By fax or telephone with ideas.

Lead time: One week.

Payment: Very competitive.

Angling Times

Bretton Court
Bretton Centre
Peterborough
PE3 8DZ

Tel: (0733) 266222   **Fax:** (0733) 265515

Frequency: Weekly

Circulation: 103,303

Contact: Keith Higginbottom, Editor

Profile: A tabloid-style publication providing news from the world of angling. One third of the content is devoted to features, while the rest covers news and match reports.

Requirements: 1 2 8
Contributions are welcomed from writers who can work to tight deadlines in a succinct style. Length up to 800 words.

Comments: In addition to writing news and features, there may be opportunities for freelances to become match correspondents.

Approach: By letter.

Lead time: One week.

Payment: By negotiation.

Anglo-American Sports

Priory House
85 Priory Grove
London
SW8 2PD

Tel: 071-720 6456   **Fax:** 071-498 7982

Frequency: Monthly

Circulation: 13,000

Contact: Michael Jago, Editor

Profile: Covers all American sports where there is a proven British interest, whether played in the UK or the USA.

Requirements: Features on baseball, basketball, ice hockey, American football and other sports. Articles range from profiles of local teams to equipment reviews and details of playing techniques.

Comments: Although the subject is American sports, the material must be written from a British perspective.

Approach: By letter or fax.

Lead time: Two weeks.

Payment: £100-£150 per thousand words.

1/News **2**/Features **3**/Fiction **4**/Letters **5**/Fillers
6/B&W Photos **7**/Colour Photos **8**/Reviews

Annabel

80 Kingsway East
Dundee
DD4 8SL

Tel: (0382) 462276   **Fax:** (0382) 452491

Frequency: Monthly

Circulation: 95,000

Contact: Karen Donnelly, Features
Editor

Profile: The 'ideal' reader is a 37-year-
old woman who is married and has
two children. Consequently, the
content is quite traditional and does
not include looking-for-a-boyfriend
type material.

Requirements: 2 3 4 5 6 7
Features with a positive feel, such as
'triumph over adversity' tales and
personal success stories. Maximum
length 1500 words. Also requires
romantic and mystery fiction.

Comments: Stay away from the
downbeat, and don't try to impress
with a big vocabulary. The magazine
tends to be inundated with true
medical/illness stories.

Approach: By letter or telephone, all
ideas considered.

Lead time: Three months.

Payment: £120-£150 per thousand
words.

Antique and New Art

10-11 Lower John Street
London
W1R 3PE

Tel: 071-434 9180   **Fax:** 071-287 5488

Frequency: Quarterly

Circulation: 19,000

Contact: Alastair Hicks, Editor

Profile: An upmarket magazine,
taking a broad look at the world of
art and antiques.

Requirements: 1 2 6 7
Requires amusing or light-hearted
pieces in addition to more
heavyweight, highbrow articles.
International arts news is also of
interest.

Comments: Unsolicited manuscripts
are actively discouraged.

Approach: By telephone or letter.

Lead time: Two months.

Payment: £150-£200 per article.

The Antique Collector

Eagle House
50 Marshall Street
London
W1V 1LR

Tel: 071-439 5000   **Fax:** 071-439 5177

Frequency: 10xYear

Circulation: 15,000

Contact: David Coombs, Editor

Profile: A magazine for the antique
enthusiast, publishing authoritative
articles for specialist readers
worldwide.

Requirements: 1 2
Topical features on relevant
subjects, including both fine and
decorative arts. Articles should be
between 1500 and 2000 words.

Comments: Material should be well-
researched and well-written,
demonstrating a good understanding
of the subject.

Approach: By letter.

Lead time: Two months.

Payment: £250 per feature.

The Antique Dealer and Collectors' Guide

PO Box 805
Greenwich
London
SE10 8TD

Tel: 081-318 5868   **Fax:** 081-691 2489

Frequency: Monthly

Circulation: 14,000

Contact: J. Philip Bartlam, Editor

Profile: An upmarket publication for the antique collector. Aimed not just at the serious buyer, but also at those who only have a few pounds to spend and want to spend them well.

Requirements: 2 6 7
Features on everything from porcelain to furniture will be considered. Articles should be well-researched and of direct relevance to the readership.

Comments: Although the tone of the publication is serious, submissions do not need to be dry. Aim for a lively, informative style.

Approach: By letter, including a small 'taster' of the article.

Lead time: Three months.

Payment: £76 per thousand words.

Apollo

3 St James's Place
London
SW1A 1NP

Tel: 071-629 4331   **Fax:** 071-491 1682

Frequency: Monthly

Circulation: Not disclosed

Contact: Robin Simon, Editor

Profile: A magazine for the informed enthusiast, covering the world of arts and antiques.

Requirements: 2 6 7
Features on art, sculpture, architecture, ceramics and related topics. Length up to 2500 words.

Comments: Photographs to accompany features are always welcome.

Approach: In writing.

Lead time: Seven weeks.

Payment: By arrangement.

Applause

132 Liverpool Road
London
N1 1LA

Tel: 071-700 0248   **Fax:** 071-700 0301

Frequency: Monthly

Circulation: 5800

Contact: Fiona Harley, Editor

Profile: A business publication for the live music industry. Covers all aspects of preparing, planning and presenting shows worldwide.

Requirements: 1 2 6 7
News and features on the practical aspects of putting together a live show, covering production, technological and promotional matters. Length 800 to 1200 words.

Comments: International material is of particular interest.

Approach: By letter.

Lead time: Four weeks.

Payment: £100 per thousand words.

Aquarist & Pondkeeper

9 Tufton Street
Ashford
Kent
TN23 1QN

Tel: (0233) 621877   **Fax:** (0233) 645669

1/News 2/Features 3/Fiction 4/Letters 5/Fillers
6/B&W Photos 7/Colour Photos 8/Reviews

Frequency: Monthly
Circulation: 25,000
Contact: John Dawes, Editor
Profile: Informative magazine covering both aquarium and pondkeeping, as well as related subjects such as aquatic plant culture and the study of reptiles and amphibians.
Requirements: 1 2 6 7 8
Features on subjects such as fish health and pond-building, together with illustrations where possible. Length 1500-2500 words.
Comments: Remember the seasonal trends within the magazine − more on pond-keeping published during the summer, then more on topics such as tropical fish during the winter.
Approach: By telephone.
Lead time: Two months.
Payment: Negotiable.

Architect, Builder, Contractor and Developer

91-93 High Street
Bromsgrove
Worcestershire
B61 8AQ
Tel: (0527) 36600   **Fax:** (0527) 574388
Frequency: 10xYear
Circulation: 27,000
Contact: James Dennison
Profile: A magazine for professionals in the building industry. Includes features on architectural practice, roofing, energy efficiency and cladding.
Requirements: 2 7
Features on new innovations and developments on any of the above subjects.

Comments: This is a product-based magazine, so features based around the use of a new product will have the best chance of success.
Approach: By letter.
Lead time: Two months.
Payment: Negotiable.

Architects' Journal

33-39 Bowling Green Lane
London
EC1R 0DA
Tel: 071-837 1212   **Fax:** 071-278 4003
Frequency: Weekly
Circulation: 20,000
Contact: Stephen Greenberg
Profile: Newsy, informative magazine covering the world of architecture, from new buildings to re-fabrications.
Requirements: 2 3 7 8
Features and articles on everything from building structure to computer-aided design. 1500 words maximum.
Comments: Material that proves to be unsuitable for this publication may be passed on to other magazines in the group.
Approach: By letter or fax.
Lead time: Four weeks.
Payment: £150 per thousand words.

Architectural Design

Academy Group Ltd
42 Leinster Gardens
London
W2 3AN
Tel: 071-402 2141   **Fax:** 071-723 9540
Frequency: Bi-monthly
Circulation: 8000
Contact: Maggie Toy, Editor

Profile: Provides news and
information concerning
architectural practice and theory,
together with criticism.
Requirements: 2 6 7
Articles offering an original critical
view of achitectural history, theory
and practice.
Comments: The publication is
extensively illustrated, so
photographs are welcome.
Approach: In writing with ideas.
Lead time: Three months.
Payment: By arrangement.

Architectural Review

33-35 Bowling Green Lane
London
EC1R 0DA
Tel: 071-837 1212   **Fax:** 071-278 4003
Frequency: Monthly
Circulation: 20,000
Contact: Peter Davey, Editor
Profile: A professional journal
concerned with architecture, town
planning and interior design.
Requirements: 2 6 7
Feature articles on architectural
subjects, or on related arts.
Photographs and drawings are also
welcome.
Comments: Writers should have a
good understanding of the subject.
Approach: In writing.
Lead time: Two months.
Payment: By negotation.

Arena

3rd Floor
Block A
Exmouth House
Pine Street
London
EC1R 0JL
Tel: 071-837 7270   **Fax:** 071-837 3906
Frequency: Bi-monthly
Circulation: 81,000
Contact: Peter Brown, Deputy Editor
Profile: A fashion and style magazine
for the man about town. An
upmarket title for an intelligent and
relatively affluent readership.
Requirements: 1 2 6 7 8
Topical features and profiles on
subjects such as film, television,
design, business, art and the theatre.
Fiction is used from time to time.
Comments: Enquiries should always be
sent in writing, as the small editorial
team prefers not to be interrupted by
unnecessary telephone calls.
Approach: By letter.
Lead time: Seven weeks.
Payment: £150 per thousand words.

Army Quarterly & Defence Journal

1 West Street
Tavistock
Devon
PL19 8DS
Tel: (0822) 613577   **Fax:** (0822) 612785
Frequency: Quarterly
Circulation: 21,000
Contact: Don Bridge, Editor
Profile: Concerned with defence issues
internationally. Includes news and
reports, details of equipment, etc.

1/News **2**/Features **3**/Fiction **4**/Letters **5**/Fillers
6/B&W Photos **7**/Colour Photos **8**/Reviews

Requirements: 1 2 6 8
Historical or contemporary articles on defence matters both in the UK and worldwide. Also news of contracts and book reviews. Length up to 6000 words.
Comments: Also welcomes photos, drawings and maps to accompany submissions.
Approach: By letter with ideas.
Lead time: Three months.
Payment: By negotiation.

Art & Craft Design and Technology

Villiers House
Clarendon Avenue
Leamington Spa
Warwickshire
CV32 5PR

Tel: (0926) 887799   **Fax:** (0926) 88331

Frequency: Monthly

Circulation: 19,026

Contact: Eileen Lowcock, Editor
Profile: Concerned with art and craft in the classroom, particularly with regard to design technology.
Requirements: 2
Feature articles that will give teachers the assistance, inspiration and new ideas they need to teach the above subjects.
Comments: Writers will need a good understanding of the subject.
Approach: In writing.
Lead time: Three months.
Payment: Negotiable.

Art & Design

Academy Group Ltd
42 Leinster Gardens
London
W2 3AN

Tel: 071-402 2141   **Fax:** 071-723 9540

Frequency: Bi-monthly

Circulation: 5000

Contact: Nicola Hodges, Editor
Profile: Provides extensive coverage of the arts scene on an international scale.
Requirements: 2 6 7 8
Features on contemporary art worldwide, plus previews of exhibitions and reviews of books on art.
Comments: Particularly welcomes material on New Art.
Approach: In writing.
Lead time: Three months.
Payment: Negotiable.

Art Monthly

Suite 17
26 Charing Cross Road
London
WC2H 0DG

Tel: 071-240 0389   **Fax:** 071-240 0389

Frequency: 10xYear

Circulation: 4000

Contact: Patricia Bickers
Profile: A contemporary visual arts magazine that is concerned with current events, exhibitions and arts news.
Requirements: 1 2 8
Stories on subjects such as arts funding, art in Europe and relevant political matters. Also covers the arts on video and television.

Comments: Always looking for new writers, but unsolicited material not usually published.

Approach: By letter or fax with ideas and samples of work.

Lead time: Six weeks.

Payment: £50 per thousand words.

The Art Newspaper

Mitre House
44-46 Fleet Street
London
EC4Y 1BN

Tel: 071-936 2886   **Fax:** 071-583 6897

Frequency: 10xYear

Circulation: 15,000

Contact: Isobel Boucher

Profile: Newspaper devoted to current events in the art world.

Requirements: 1 2 4 7
Features covering museums, conservation, archaeology, books, dealers and galleries.

Comments: Tends to preview events rather than review them.

Approach: By letter with ideas initially.

Lead time: Three weeks.

Payment: £120 per thousand words.

The Artist

Caxton House
63-65 High Street
Tenterden
Kent
TN30 6BD

Tel: (0580) 763673   **Fax:** (0580) 765411

Frequency: Monthly

Circulation: 18,000

Contact: Sally Bulgin, Editor

Profile: Focuses on guiding artists who wish to develop their skills in all media. Includes reports on art products, framing, books, courses and exhibitions.

Requirements: 1 2 7
Practical, instructional features up to 1500 words in length.

Comments: Where appropriate, transparencies of the artist's work will be required.

Approach: By letter initially.

Lead time: Three months.

Payment: £60 per thousand words.

Artists Newsletter

PO Box 23
20 Villiers Street
Sunderland
SR4 6DG

Tel: 091-567 3589   **Fax:** 091-564 1600

Frequency: Monthly

Circulation: 11,800

Contact: David Butler, Editor

Profile: A magazine that identifies and highlights opportunities for visual artists, crafts people, photographers and administrators.

Requirements: 1 2 6 7
Includes features of general and practical interest to those in the artistic world, such as acquiring studio space or obtaining commissions. Maximum length 800 words.

Comments: The content does not include reviews or criticism.

Approach: By telephone or letter with ideas.

Lead time: One month.

Payment: £80 per thousand words published.

1/News **2**/Features **3**/Fiction **4**/Letters **5**/Fillers
6/B&W Photos **7**/Colour Photos **8**/Reviews

The Artist's and Illustrator's Magazine

4th Floor
4 Brandon Road
London
N7 9TP

Tel: 071-609 2177   **Fax:** 071-700 4985

Frequency: Monthly

Circulation: 40,000

Contact: Miranda Fellows, Editor

Profile: A guide for artists and illustrators, encouraging improvement of techniques in all areas of painting. Includes product information, news and reviews.

Requirements: 1 2 8
'How-to' articles by competent amateurs or professional artists. Suggestions for special features on any art-related subject linked to contemporary activities. Length 1000 to 2000 words.

Comments: The emphasis is on providing practical help for practising artists.

Approach: By letter with proposals.

Lead time: Ten weeks.

Payment: £80 per thousand words.

Artrage

28 Shacklewell Lane
London
E8 2EZ

Tel: 071-254 7275   **Fax:** 071-923 1596

Frequency: Quarterly

Circulation: 10,000

Contact: Jacob Ross, Editor

Profile: An inter-cultural arts magazine aimed specifically at the black community. Published by the Minorities Arts Advisory Service.

Requirements: 2 6 8
Articles on black literature and art, plus interviews with authors, artists and performers. Length 500 to 1800 words. Also reviews.

Comments: Photographs and line illustrations are always appreciated with features.

Approach: In writing.

Lead time: Three months.

Payment: Up to £80.

Arts Review

20 Prescott Place
Clapham
London
SW4 6BT

Tel: 071-978 1000   **Fax:** 071-978 1000

Frequency: Monthly

Circulation: 7500

Contact: David Lee, Editor

Profile: Aims to attract a new audience to visual arts, reaching people who are interested in art but who are not specialists.

Requirements: 1 2 8
Profiles of artists, general arts features and approachable critical essays. Length 1000 to 1500 words.

Comments: All material received is given careful consideration.

Approach: By telephone, followed by a letter.

Lead time: Two months.

Payment: £100 per thousand words.

Asian Times

Tower House
139-149 Fonthill Road
London
N4 3HF

Tel: 071-281 1191   **Fax:** 071-263 9656

1/News 2/Features 3/Fiction 4/Letters 5/Fillers
6/B&W Photos 7/Colour Photos 8/Reviews

Frequency: Weekly

Circulation: 19,000

Contact: Arif Ali, Editor

Profile: A newspaper for all religious and national groups in the Asian community.

Requirements: 1 2 6 8
News and features relating to developments both in Asia and throughout the UK. Particularly welcomes material on business, sport and culture.

Comments: Readers should consider material from the viewpoint of the Asian reader.

Approach: In writing.

Lead time: Two weeks.

Payment: From £10 per news item.

Astronomy Now

Intra House
193 Uxbridge Road
London
W12 9RA

Tel: 081-743 8888 **Fax:** 081-743 3062

Frequency: Monthly

Circulation: 30,000

Contact: Steven Young

Profile: Magazine carrying articles of interest to British amateur astronomers.

Requirements: 1 2 6 7
The editor would like to receive news and features on astrophotography, new products, telescopes, space missions and other relevent topics. Length 2000 to 3000 words.

Comments: As the magazine has very particular requirements, it is always advisable to discuss ideas before submitting.

Approach: By letter or fax.

Lead time: Two months.

Payment: Negotiable.

Athletics Weekly

Bretton Court
Bretton Centre
Peterborough
PE3 8DZ

Tel: (0733) 261144 **Fax:** (0733) 265515

Frequency: Weekly

Circulation: 17,000

Contact: Paul Richardson, Editor-in-Chief

Profile: Read by avid athletics followers, the magazine deals with news, views, race reports, interviews and fixtures.

Requirements: 1 2 5 6 8
Exclusive features on top-class athletes, coaching and club athletics.

Comments: All submissions and ideas are given serious consideration.

Approach: Initial telephone enquiry preferred.

Lead time: Two weeks.

Payment: By negotiation.

Audiophile

38-42 Hampton Road
Teddington
Middlesex
TW11 0JE

Tel: 081-943 5000 **Fax:** 081-943 5098

Frequency: Monthly

Circulation: 23,000

Contact: Richard Garlick, Editor

Profile: Reviews, advice and comment for enthusiastic audiophiles. Covers the more sophisticated end of the hi-fi market.

1/News 2/Features 3/Fiction 4/Letters 5/Fillers
6/B&W Photos 7/Colour Photos 8/Reviews

Requirements: 1 2 8

Some 60 per cent of the content consists of reviews, but features offer a better opening for new contributors. Subjects include new technology and practical advice.

Comments: Writers with specialised knowledge of the hi-fi scene will be very well received.

Approach: Telephone with ideas.

Lead time: Two months.

Payment: Varies.

Auto Express

Ludgate House
245 Blackfriars Road
London
SE1 9UX

Tel: 071-928 8000   **Fax:** 071-928 2847

Frequency: Weekly

Circulation: 120,000

Contact: David Williams, Features Editor

Profile: Motoring news magazine that caters for every motorist, from the family man to the company car driver.

Requirements: 1 2 7

Articles on any motoring subject, especially consumer stories, travel, adventure and news.

Comments: Topical, newsy material is more likely to be successful.

Approach: By telephone with ideas.

Lead time: Two weeks.

Payment: £200 per thousand words.

Autocar and Motor

38-42 Hampton Road
Teddington
Middlesex
TW11 0JE

Tel: 081-943 5013   **Fax:** 081-943 5653

Frequency: Weekly

Circulation: 91,000

Contact: Giles Chapman

Profile: General motoring magazine that focuses on new cars, with little coverage of used vehicles.

Requirements: 1 2 6 7

Interested in news, features and scoops on motor sport, specialised cars and similar subjects.

Comments: Please do not send material relating to classic cars, however exciting they may be.

Approach: In writing, with ideas or a complete manuscript.

Lead time: Two weeks.

Payment: £150 per thousand words.

The Automobile

Holmerise
Seven Hills Road
Cobham
Surrey
KT11 1ES

Tel: (0932) 864212   **Fax:** (0932) 862430

Frequency: Monthly

Circulation: 20,000

Contact: Brian Heath, Editor

Profile: Magazine devoted to cars and commercial vehicles from the dawn of motoring to 1950.

Requirements: 2 6 7

Lively, informative features that re-create the atmosphere of the classic age of motoring.

Comments: The editor does not wish to receive any material relating to post-1950 vehicles.
Approach: By letter.
Lead time: Three months.
Payment: Negotiable.

Autosport

60 Waldegrave Road
Teddington
Middlesex
TW11 8LG

Tel: 081-943 5000 **Fax:** 081-943 5922

Frequency: Weekly

Circulation: 53,000

Contact: Bruce Jones
Profile: Motorsport magazine dealing with all aspects of circuit racing and rallying. Also covers club activities, both nationally and internationally.
Requirements: 1 2 6 7
Profiles and interviews with prominent personalities and teams in the racing field, track tests and general features. Length up to 1500 words.
Comments: As the coverage is newsy and topical, always ring the magazine before submitting.
Approach: By telephone.
Lead time: Ten days.
Payment: Negotiable.

AutoTrade

30 Calderwood Street
London
SE18 6QH

Tel: 081-855 7777 **Fax:** 081-316 3102

Frequency: Monthly

Circulation: 35,012

Contact: Sue Gay, Editor

Profile: A full-colour, glossy magazine for the automotive market. Aimed at sales managers, bodyshop and workshop staff.
Requirements: 1 2
News and features on subjects such as equipment, components, accessories and body repairs.
Comments: Also covers forecourt petrol retailing.
Approach: By letter.
Lead time: Four weeks.
Payment: Negotiable.

Aviation News

Douglas House
Simpson Road
Bletchley
Milton Keynes
MK1 1BA

Tel: (0908) 377559 **Fax:** (0908) 366744

Frequency: Fortnightly

Circulation: 20,000

Contact: Alan Hall, Editor
Profile: A magazine for all those interested in or involved in the aircraft industry.
Requirements: 1 2 6
Articles on new types of aircraft, histories of aircraft and associated subjects. Also squadron and unit information. Length 1000 to 8000 words.
Comments: Articles should be about aircraft, rather than people in the aviation industry. Guidelines for contributors are available on request.
Approach: By letter with synopsis and suggested illustrations.
Lead time: One month.
Payment: Up to £160.

1/News **2**/Features **3**/Fiction **4**/Letters **5**/Fillers
6/B&W Photos **7**/Colour Photos **8**/Reviews

B

Baby Magazine

The Publishing House
Highbury Station Road
London
N1 1SE

Tel: 071-226 2222   **Fax:** 071-359 5225

Frequency: Quarterly

Circulation: 70,000

Contact: The Editor

Profile: For mums-to-be and mothers with children under the age of 5. A lively well-informed guide to all aspects of parenting.

Requirements: 2 4 7
Features relating to young children's education, health, food and fashion. Maximum length 1500 words.

Comments: Follow up written enquiries with a telephone call.

Approach: In writing initially, with outline synopsis.

Lead time: Two months.

Payment: £150 per thousand words.

Back Street Heroes

PO Box 28
Altrincham
Cheshire
WA15 8SH

Tel: 061-928 3480   **Fax:** 061-941 6897

Frequency: Monthly

Circulation: 41,604

Contact: Caz Carroll, Editor

Profile: Magazine for UK bikers, dealing with customised bikes and the people who ride them.

Requirements: 2 3 7
Features on bikes, customisation and the lifestyle behind the machinery.

Comments: This is a true cult publication, in which the ethos is as important as the bikes themselves.

Approach: By letter or telephone with ideas.

Lead time: Six weeks.

Payment: Varies.

Backtrack

Trevithick House
West End
Penryn
Cornwall
TR10 8HE

Tel: (0326) 373656   **Fax:** (0326) 373656

Frequency: Bi-monthly

Circulation: 25,000

Contact: David Jenkinson, Editor

Profile: Nostalgic magazine covering all aspects of railway history.

Requirements: 2 5
Articles on particular aspects of a railway's past, anecdotes and reviews.

1/News **2**/Features **3**/Fiction **4**/Letters **5**/Fillers
6/B&W Photos **7**/Colour Photos **8**/Reviews

Comments: Contributors do not need to be experts, but features should be well-researched and accurate.
Approach: By letter.
Lead time: Two months.
Payment: £25 per thousand words.

Bahrain Gateway

Mediamark Publishing International Ltd
35 Gresse Street
Rathbone Place
London
W1P 1PN

Tel: 071-580 3105   **Fax:** 071-580 1695

Frequency: Quarterly

Circulation: 40,000

Contact: Beverley Howell, Editor
Profile: In-flight magazine, containing a mix of leisure, travel and business features.
Requirements: 2 6 7
Travel features on locations served by airlines operating out of Bahrain. Also articles on business in the Gulf states.
Comments: Particularly interested in hearing from writers able to produce copy acceptable to the Arab reader.
Approach: By telephone or fax with an idea.
Lead time: Six weeks.
Payment: From £50 per thousand words.

Balance

British Diabetic Association
10 Queen Anne Street
London
W1M 0BD

Tel: 071-323 1531   **Fax:** 071-637 3644

Frequency: Bi-monthly
Circulation: 150,000
Contact: Lesley Hallett
Profile: Magazine for people with diabetes, plus their families and friends.
Requirements: 1 2 3 7
In addition to articles on diabetes, the magazine requires features covering general health, fitness and diet.
Comments: Pieces of up to 1500 words are also required for Young Balance, written by those under 18 with diabetes.
Approach: By letter with ideas.
Lead time: Two months.
Payment: £75 per thousand words.

Ballroom Dancing Times

Clerkenwell House
45-47 Clerkenwell Green
London
EC1R 0EB

Tel: 071-250 3006   **Fax:** 071-253 6679

Frequency: Monthly

Circulation: 3500

Contact: Mary Clarke, Editor
Profile: Covers all aspects of ballroom dancing, but concentrates on serious teaching, medal tests and competitions.
Requirements: 1 2
News and features on all relevant subjects for instructors, professional dancers and enthusiasts of all ages.
Comments: Where photographs are being supplied, action shots are preferred.
Approach: In writing with ideas.
Lead time: Two months.
Payment: Negotiable.

1/News **2**/Features **3**/Fiction **4**/Letters **5**/Fillers
6/B&W Photos **7**/Colour Photos **8**/Reviews

The Banker

Greystoke Place
Fetter Lane
London
EC4A 1ND

Tel: 071-405 6969   **Fax:** 071-831 9136

Frequency: Monthly

Circulation: 17,000

Contact: Stephen Timewell, Editor

Profile: International banking magazine, read by senior staff in banks worldwide.

Requirements: News and features on banking, finance, economics, banking technology and capital markets. Length 1000 to 1200 words.

Comments: Features need to be detailed and accurate.

Approach: By telephone.

Lead time: One month.

Payment: £200 plus.

Bargain Hunter

Chislehurst Business Centre
1 Bromley Lane
Chislehurst
Kent
BR7 6LH

Tel: 081-309 6576

Frequency: Monthly

Circulation: Not available

Contact: Tony Stewart, Editor

Profile: A magazine for anyone who likes to pick up a bargain or make a good deal. Covers markets throughout the Greater London area.

Requirements: 2
Strong, original features connected with any aspect of bargain hunting, market trading etc. Accuracy and reliability are very important. Length 700 to 1000 words.

Comments: Welcomes contributions from writers who may not be experienced, but who have the ability to write well.

Approach: By telephone with ideas.

Lead time: Two months.

Payment: Negotiable.

Bathrooms Magazine

Chalk Lane
Cockfosters Road
Barnet
Hertfordshire
EN4 0BU

Tel: 081-975 9759   **Fax:** 081-975 9753

Frequency: Monthly

Circulation: 7000

Contact: Debbie Smithers, Editor

Profile: A lively and informative trade magazine for the bathroom retailer, distributor and specifier.

Requirements: 2
Specialist information covering the more technical aspects of selling, planning and installing bathroom products. Length up to 1000 words.

Comments: A clear writing style and a degree of specialist knowledge will help secure commissions.

Approach: By letter.

Lead time: Two months.

Payment: On publication.

BBC Educational Computing & Technology

101 Bayham Street
London
NW1 0AG

Tel: 071-331 8111   **Fax:** 071-331 8001

Frequency: 8xYear

Circulation: 20,000

1/News **2**/Features **3**/Fiction **4**/Letters **5**/Fillers
6/B&W Photos **7**/Colour Photos **8**/Reviews

Contact: Lisa Hughes, Editor

Profile: Colour magazine for primary and secondary teachers. Covers IT and related technologies in a jargon-free style.

Requirements: 2 8

Classroom project reports and new technology features with a strong educational slant. Length 1000 to 1600 words for features, 300 words for reviews.

Comments: It's important that contributors approach topics from the educational point of view, writing for the non-specialist.

Approach: By letter.

Lead time: Two months.

Payment: £70 per thousand words.

BBC Good Health

101 Bayham Street
London
NW1 0AG

Tel: 071-331 8000   **Fax:** 071-331 8001

Frequency: Monthly

Circulation: 140,000

Contact: Janette Marshall, Editor

Profile: About healthcare for people of all ages in the family. Includes features on diet, exercise, food, cooking, drugs and complementary medicines.

Requirements: 2 5

Contributions on any of the above regular subjects, plus imaginative one-off features. Length 500 to 2000 words.

Comments: 'Be original, be accurate. Think ideas through thoroughly before making suggestions.'

Approach: By post.

Lead time: Three months.

Payment: £175 per thousand words.

BBC Holidays

101 Bayham Street
London
NW1 0AG

Tel: 071-331 8000   **Fax:** 071-831 8001

Frequency: Monthly

Circulation: 141,725

Contact: Alison Rice, Editor

Profile: A full-colour travel magazine for those aged 35 and above. Includes holiday resort features, together with suggestions for weekends and short breaks.

Requirements: 2 5

Practical features, giving information such as how to get to destinations, places to visit and things to do.

Comments: The magazine is written entirely by freelances. However, there is no room for routine travel pieces or esoteric travelogues.

Approach: Send a synopsis together with examples of previous work.

Lead time: Two months.

Payment: £175 per thousand words.

BBC Music Magazine

BBC Magazines
80 Wood Lane
London
W12 0TT

Tel: 081-576 3282   **Fax:** 081-576 3292

Frequency: Monthly

Circulation: 80,088

Contact: Fiona Maddocks, Editor

Profile: Aims to appeal to both music lovers and newcomers, striking a balance between the two extremes. The result of extensive research in conjunction with BBC Radio 3, the magazine also carries a free CD.

1/News **2**/Features **3**/Fiction **4**/Letters **5**/Fillers
6/B&W Photos **7**/Colour Photos **8**/Reviews

Requirements: 2 5
Profiles of composers and
performers, interviews and reviews.
Maximum length 1500 words.
Comments: Contributors should have
a musical background and a
reasonable knowledge of the subject.
Approach: Send a synopsis with a brief
CV.
Lead time: Two months.
Payment: Better than NUJ rates.

BBC Wildlife

Broadcasting House
Whiteladies Road
Bristol
BS8 2LR

Tel: (0272) 732211   **Fax:** (0272) 467075
Frequency: Monthly
Circulation: 142,058
Contact: Rosamund Kidman Cox,
Editor
Profile: Interesting and entertaining
magazine covering various aspects of
natural history, conservation and the
environment.
Requirements: 2 5
Contributors are expected to write
well and have a good in-depth
knowledge of their subject.
Unsolicited manuscripts are not
welcome, but ideas for original
features on wildlife subjects will be
considered.
Comments: The magazine runs a
Nature Writing Award every year,
plus other competitions of interest to
writers.
Approach: By letter.
Lead time: One month.
Payment: £250-£350 per article.

BBR

PO Box 625
Sheffield
S1 3GY

Tel: (0742) 824161   **Fax:** (0742) 796395
Frequency: 2xYear
Circulation: 4000
Contact: Chris Reed, Editor
Profile: A cult magazine for fans of
science fiction. In addition to
publishing short stories, it covers
independent and alternative
publications worldwide.
Requirements: 3
Inventive, experimental science-
fiction stories that explore the
boundaries of the genre.
Comments: Encourages newcomers as
well as publishing work by
established writers.
Approach: Submit complete
manuscript.
Lead time: In writing.
Payment: By arrangement.

The Beano

D.C. Thomson & Co Ltd
Courier Place
Dundee
DD1 9QJ

Tel: (0382) 23131   **Fax:** (0382) 22214
Frequency: Weekly
Circulation: Not available
Contact: Ewan Kerr, Editor
Profile: One of the oldest and best-
established comics for children.
Requirements: 3
Story narratives for any of the
established characters. Stories
should be suitable for adapting into
an 11-22 frame picture strip.

1/News **2**/Features **3**/Fiction **4**/Letters **5**/Fillers
6/B&W Photos **7**/Colour Photos **8**/Reviews

Comments: Narratives should be strong, simple and original.
Approach: In writing.
Lead time: Four weeks.
Payment: On acceptance.

Bedrooms Magazine

Chalk Lane
Cockfosters Road
Barnet
Hertfordshire
EN4 0BU

Tel: 081-975 9759   **Fax:** 081-975 9753

Frequency: Bi-monthly

Circulation: 6000

Contact: Lee Hibbert, Editor
Profile: Trade magazine for bedroom retailers, manufacturers, distributors and specifiers.
Requirements: 1 2 6 7
Features on design for bedrooms, furniture and furnishings. Also profiles of personalities, plus finance and general business features. Length from 700 words.
Comments: Articles should consider subjects from the trade rather than the consumer point of view.
Approach: By letter.
Lead time: Two months.
Payment: £130-£150 per thousand words.

Bella

Shirley House
25-27 Camden Road
London
NW1 9LL

Tel: 071-284 0909   **Fax:** 071-485 3774

Frequency: Weekly

Circulation: 1.3 million

Contact: Sue Reid, Features Editor
Profile: Mass-market womens' magazine with broad appeal and coverage. Dynamic, breezy style covering everything of interest to women.
Requirements: 1 2 3 4 6 7
Intriguing true tales and affairs-of-the-heart stories up to 1300 words. Modern romantic fiction and mini mysteries of 1200 to 1400 words.
Comments: Receives a great deal of similar or hackneyed material.
Approach: By letter with idea or complete manuscript.
Lead time: Three months.
Payment: £300 per thousand words.

Best

10th Floor
Portland House
Stag Place
London
SW1E 5AU

Tel: 071-245 8700   **Fax:** 071-245 8825

Frequency: Weekly

Circulation: 660,000

Contact: Jackie Hyams
Profile: Magazine for women, aimed at those in the 18 to 45 age group. Covers a wide range of topics and subjects that concern women.
Requirements: 2 3 7
Features that follow the precise format of existing sections within the magazine. Fiction of up to 1500 words for 'Five-Minute Story' and 'Romantic Fiction.'
Comments: Submissions are only read in April and October.
Approach: Send a concise, well-presented letter outlining your ideas.
Lead time: Six weeks.
Payment: £100.

1/News **2**/Features **3**/Fiction **4**/Letters **5**/Fillers
6/B&W Photos **7**/Colour Photos **8**/Reviews

Best Seller

21st Century Publishing
PO Box12
Sellarsbrooke Park
Gonerew
Monmouth
NP5 3YL

Tel: (0600) 890506   **Fax:** (0600) 890506

Frequency: Bi-monthly

Circulation: 10,000

Contact: Peter Grose

Profile: Aims to be the '*Radio Times* of books', offering a livelier and more readable approach than conventional literary criticism. Includes extensive book reviews, extracts and interviews.

Requirements: 2 8
The best opportunities are in features, especially author interviews. Articles need to have an original and clearly-defined angle. Length 1500 to 2000 words.

Comments: Although short stories are used, these are selected from published collections.

Approach: Write with ideas.

Lead time: Three months.

Payment: By negotiation.

The Big Issue

4 Albion Place
Galena Road
Hammersmith
London
W6 0LT

Tel: 081-741 8090   **Fax:** 081-741 2951

Frequency: 36xYear

Circulation: 150,000

Contact: John Bird, Editor

Profile: A magazine sold on the streets by the homeless. Revenue is shared between the seller and relevant charitable organisations. Aims to be a genuinely interesting read, covering the arts and wider issues as well as homelessness.

Requirements: 2 3
Welcomes features on social issues, music, art and theatre. Humorous pieces and suitable fiction will also be considered. Length 1500 to 2000 words.

Comments: Writers do not need extensive experience, but should be able to write well.

Approach: Send a synopsis or a complete manuscript.

Lead time: Four weeks.

Payment: Negotiable.

The Big Paper

The Design Council
28 Haymarket
London
SW1Y 4SU

Tel: 071-839 8000   **Fax:** 071-925 2130

Frequency: 3xYear

Circulation: 11,000

Contact: Laurie Johnston, Editor

Profile: A full-colour magazine for primary schools covering art, design and technology. Includes a broad range of design-related subjects, with the emphasis on an educational, practical and accessible approach.

Requirements: 2 6 7
Features on practical and accessible design-related subjects. Writers need to be able to explain complex subjects in a clear, easy-to-understand manner. Length 800 to 1000 words.

1/News **2**/Features **3**/Fiction **4**/Letters **5**/Fillers
6/B&W Photos **7**/Colour Photos **8**/Reviews

Comments: An understanding of the needs and interests of primary teachers is helpful.
Approach: By telephone or letter.
Lead time: Varies.
Payment: £110 per thousand words.

BIG!

1st Floor
Mappin House
4 Winsley Street
London
W1N 7AR

Tel: 071-436 1515   **Fax:** 071-631 0781

Frequency: Fortnightly

Circulation: 259,000

Contact: Dawn Bebe, Editor
Profile: A youth entertainment title for 11 to 17 year olds, covering all subjects of interest to teenagers.
Requirements: 1 2 6 7 8
Features on TV, pop, film, video and show business. Interviews with celebrities are of particular interest.
Comments: Writers need to have a good understanding of the magazine's style and approach.
Approach: By telephone initially.
Lead time: Five weeks.
Payment: Negotiable.

Bike

20-22 Station Road
Kettering
Northamptonshire
NN15 7HH

Tel: (0536) 416416   **Fax:** (0536) 415748

Frequency: Monthly

Circulation: 66,636

Contact: Tim Thompson, Features Editor

Profile: A magazine for motorbike enthusiasts, covering the full range of biking subjects and interests.
Requirements: 1 2 6 7
Articles on any subject of interest to bikers, ranging from touring features to lifestyle pieces and technical information. Maximum 2000 words.
Comments: The magazine is picture-led, so articles with a visual dimension will have the best chance of success.
Approach: By telephone only.
Lead time: Four weeks.
Payment: £120 per thousand words.

Bird Keeper

IPC Magazines
King's Reach Tower
Stamford Street
London
SE1 9LS

Tel: 071-261 6201   **Fax:** 071-261 6095

Frequency: Bi-monthly

Circulation: 30,000

Contact: Peter Moss, Editor
Profile: For newcomers to bird keeping and keen bird owners. Covers all aspects of bird management, especially relating to parrots and parrot-like birds.
Requirements: 2 5 6 7
Material inclined towards giving advice and tips on the care of birds, plus avian medicine. Does not want features on where birds are found in their original habitat, etc.
Comments: Keep advice and tips as simple and straightforward as possible.

1/News **2**/Features **3**/Fiction **4**/Letters **5**/Fillers
6/B&W Photos **7**/Colour Photos **8**/Reviews

Approach: Send ideas or complete manuscripts.
Lead time: Six weeks.
Payment: NUJ rates.

Bird Life

RSPB
The Lodge
Sandy
Bedfordshire
SG19 2DL

Tel: (0767) 680551   **Fax:** (0767) 692365

Frequency: Bi-monthly

Circulation: 66,000

Contact: The Editor

Profile: The biggest magazine in its sector, designed for children aged between eight and 13 years old.

Requirements: 1 2 6 7
Features on UK wildlife, habitats and conservation, geared to interest the younger reader. Maximum length 800 words.

Comments: Although most features are about birds, there is scope for features on other wildlife issues.

Approach: By telephone.
Lead time: Three months.
Payment: Varies.

Bird Watching

EMAP Pursuit Publishing Ltd
Bretton Court
Bretton Centre
Peterborough
PE3 8DZ

Tel: (0733) 264666   **Fax:** (0733) 265515

Frequency: Monthly

Circulation: 29,000

Contact: Dave Cromack, Editor

Profile: A guide to improving bird-watching skills. Includes identification, fieldcraft, equipment reviews, and competitions. Also publishes rarity photographs and provides a monthly bird-sighting service.

Requirements: 1 2 7
'How-to' articles written according to the house style – practical information presented in easy-to-understand language. Maximum 1500 words.

Comments: Avoid lyricism. Top-quality transparencies to accompany features are an asset.

Approach: By letter only.
Lead time: Two months.
Payment: £60 per thousand words.

Birds

The Lodge
Sandy
Bedfordshire
SG19 2DL

Tel: (0767) 680551   **Fax:** (0767) 692365

Frequency: Quarterly

Circulation: 510,000

Contact: Rob Hume, Editor

Profile: Wildlife magazine with bias towards wild birds and conservation. Mainly UK based, but with an increasing interest in Europe and Africa.

Requirements: 1 2 5 6 7
Well-illustrated features, and articles showing the lighter side of birdwatching. Interviews and articles on conservation.

Comments: Does not want anything on tame or hand-reared birds, or material based outside the geographic area covered.

Approach: Telephone with ideas, or send a manuscript if it is already complete.

Lead time: Six months.

Payment: £120 per thousand words plus expenses.

Birds Illustrated

EMAP Pursuit Publishing Ltd
Bretton Court
Bretton Centre
Peterborough
PE3 8DZ

Tel: (0733) 264666   **Fax:** (0733) 265515

Frequency: Quarterly

Circulation: 12,000

Contact: David Cromack, Editor

Profile: A high-quality glossy magazine that covers the whole world of bird watching. Has a very wide remit, covering Europe and North America as well as the UK.

Requirements: 2 6 7
In-depth accounts of subjects such as bird watching overseas. Also bird identification, photography and conservation. Length up to 3000 words.

Comments: Writers should try to capture the atmospherics and spirit of bird watching.

Approach: By letter only.

Lead time: Two months.

Payment: £60 per thousand words.

Birdwatch Monthly

PO Box 1786
London
E17 7JG

Tel: 081-503 7828   **Fax:** 081-503 7555

Frequency: Monthly

Circulation: 5000

Contact: Dominic Mitchell, Editor

Profile: For committed bird watchers and newcomers to the hobby. Includes articles on bird-watching sites, clubs and other subjects relevant to bird watching.

Requirements: 1 2 6 7
Features on identification, migration, international bird watching, etc. Writers should aim to inform as well as entertain.

Comments: Articles should be supported by maps, diagrams, photos or fact boxes.

Approach: By letter.

Lead time: Two months.

Payment: From £30 per thousand words.

BJC Today

22 Madrid Road
Guildford
Surrey
GU2 5NU

Tel: (0483) 577540   **Fax:** (0483) 383100

Frequency: Quarterly

Circulation: 10,000

Contact: Chris Webb

Profile: Generalist management and training publication, focusing on members of the British Junior Chamber of Commerce.

Requirements: 2 6 7 8
Feature articles on management and training initiatives, preferably with good photographs.

Comments: Read primarily by managers aged between 20 and 40.

Approach: By letter, telephone or fax.

Lead time: Three months.

Payment: Negotiable.

Blue Riband

Sea Containers House
20 Upper Ground
London
SE1 9PF

Tel: 071-928 2111 **Fax:** 071-620 1594

Frequency: 2xYear

Circulation: 700,000

Contact: Alison Booth, Editor

Profile: A magazine for passengers of Hoverspeed, distributed during channel crossings.

Requirements: 2 7
Subjects of interest to passengers en route to Europe. Much of the content is devoted to articles on duty-free products and travel in Northern France. Length 1000 to 1500 words.

Comments: The magazine does not run features about travel or locations in the UK.

Approach: By letter.

Lead time: Three months.

Payment: £350 per thousand words.

Blueprint

26 Cramer Street
London
W1M 3HE

Tel: 071-486 7419 **Fax:** 071-486 1451

Frequency: 10xYear

Circulation: 10,000

Contact: Deyan Sudjic, Editor

Profile: International design and architecture magazine. Covers everything from interior design and new products to furniture and graphics.

Requirements: 1 2 6 7
Interviews with prominent architects or designers, features on subjects such as new buildings. Maximum 1200 words.

Comments: Nothing is accepted on spec. The editor prefers to see examples of previous work before commissioning new writers.

Approach: By telephone initially.

Lead time: Two months.

Payment: £100-£120 per thousand words, depending on experience.

Blues & Soul

153 Praed Street
London
W2 1RL

Tel: 071-402 6897 **Fax:** 071-224 8227

Frequency: Fortnightly

Circulation: 37,500

Contact: Bob Killbourn, Editor

Profile: Review of black music in all its genres, from soul to house. Includes coverage of events, clubs, charts and artists.

Requirements: 1 2 5 8
Interviews with stars and personalities, reviews of concerts or records, international news. Maximum 2000 words.

Comments: Exclusive information is always well received.

Approach: By fax or letter.

Lead time: One week.

Payment: Negotiable.

Boardroom Magazine

27 Sale Place
London
W2 1YR

Tel: 071-262 5000 **Fax:** 071-224 8226

Frequency: Monthly

Circulation: 47,800

Contact: Stewart Andersen, Editor

1/News **2**/Features **3**/Fiction **4**/Letters **5**/Fillers
6/B&W Photos **7**/Colour Photos **8**/Reviews

Profile: Glossy, upmarket magazine distributed free to selected homes in the London area. Designed for an affluent readership, typically comprising senior board-level directors.

Requirements: 1 2 8
Property and lifestyle features that reflect the position and success of the readers. Length up to 1400 words.

Comments: Features do not have to be London based, but should have an angle that would interest readers in the capital.

Approach: By letter, telephone or fax.

Lead time: Two months.

Payment: NUJ rates.

Boards

196 Eastern Esplanade
Southend-on-Sea
Essex
SS1 3AB

Tel: (0702) 582245   **Fax:** (0702) 588434

Frequency: 9xYear

Circulation: 22,527

Contact: The Editor

Profile: A specialist magazine for windsurfing and boardsailing enthusiasts.

Requirements: 2 6 7
News, features and reports from around the UK, covering all aspects of the sport.

Comments: Contributors must be well-informed and up to date with recent developments.

Approach: In writing.

Lead time: Six weeks.

Payment: Negotiable.

Boat Angler

EMAP Pursuit Publishing Ltd
Bretton Court
Bretton Centre
Peterborough
PE3 8DZ

Tel: (0733) 264666   **Fax:** (0733) 265515

Frequency: Monthly

Circulation: 17,647

Contact: Cliff Brown, Editor

Profile: Everything for the angler fishing from boats at sea. Covers subjects ranging from tactics to boat tests.

Requirements: 1 2 6 7
Features on boat handling, tackle, chartering, venues, ports, species and other related issues. Length up to 1000 words.

Comments: Welcomes practical advice in the form of articles giving useful hints and tips.

Approach: By telephone.

Lead time: Six weeks.

Payment: From £60 per thousand words.

Boat Fisherman

10 Sheet Street
Windsor
Berkshire
SL4 1BG

Tel: (0753) 856061   **Fax:** (0753) 859652

Frequency: Bi-monthly

Circulation: 21,000

Contact: Christopher Pearce, Editor

Profile: A magazine for all those interested in angling off shore.

Requirements: 1 2 6 7
News and features concerned with aspects of boat owning or

chartering. Also tackle tests, plus articles on fish species and fishing equipment.

Comments: Does not wish to receive any material on shore-based fishing.
Approach: By letter.
Lead time: Six weeks.
Payment: £50 per thousand words.

Boat International

5-7 Kingston Hill
Kingston upon Thames
Surrey
KT2 7PW

Tel: 081-547 2662   **Fax:** 081-547 1201

Frequency: Monthly

Circulation: 27,000

Contact: Nick Jeffries

Profile: Covers large yachts ranging from 45-footers up to the largest super-yachts. Interested in both power and sail, with a strong element of racing coverage.
Requirements: 1 2 7
Always looking for articles on marine-related subjects. Also wants features on white-water rafting, land yachting and charter location pieces with a marine orientation.
Comments: You don't have to be an expert, provided that features are well researched.
Approach: By telephone, letter or fax.
Lead time: Five weeks.
Payment: £100 per thousand words, plus £100 per page for photos.

The Boatman

Waterside Publications
PO Box 1992
Falmouth
Cornwall
TR11 3RU

Tel: (0326) 375757   **Fax:** (0326) 378551

Frequency: Bi-monthly

Circulation: 20,000

Contact: Jenny Bennett, Editor

Profile: About the world of traditional boats and boat craftsmanship. Covers open day boats and dinghies, affordable cabin boats, work boats and derivatives. Also profiles of people, and practical building articles.
Requirements: 2 6 7
Articles from knowledgeable amateur writers on projects they have tackled or witnessed in connection with traditional boats. Maximum 3000 words.
Comments: This is a very visual magazine, so words should be accompanied by adequate illustrations.
Approach: By letter with initial ideas.
Lead time: Two months.
Payment: £60-£70 per printed page.

Bodybuilding Monthly

Tokenspire Business Park
Woodmansey
Beverley
North Humberside
HU17 0BT

Tel: (0482) 661929   **Fax:** (0482) 861891

Frequency: Monthly

Circulation: 20,000

Contact: Dean Gregory, Editor

1/News **2**/Features **3**/Fiction **4**/Letters **5**/Fillers
6/B&W Photos **7**/Colour Photos **8**/Reviews

Profile: Has recently increased its scope to cover all forms of body building. Aimed at both the beginner and those with more experience.

Requirements: 2 3 5 6 7
Training and nutritional features, plus profiles of personalities. Also general interest features relating to health, fitness and bodybuilding. Maximum 2000 words.

Comments: The writing style should be direct and to the point. The magazine is primarily British-based, although also interested in worldwide events.

Approach: By letter with initial ideas.

Lead time: Six weeks.

Payment: Up to £80.

Book and Magazine Collector

43-45 St Mary's Road
Ealing
London
W5 5RQ

Tel: 081-579 1082   **Fax:** 081-566 2024

Frequency: Monthly

Circulation: 12,500

Contact: Crispin Jackson, Editor

Profile: A collector's guide to the second-hand book market. Each issue contains seven or eight articles, mostly author profiles or round ups of the various books published about a particular subject.

Requirements: 2
Articles between 2500 and 4000 words from knowledgeable amateurs. The emphasis should be on books themselves, rather than on the lives of the authors. All relevant bibliographical and market information should be included.

Comments: An enthusiast's magazine, requiring good knowledge of the subject. Articles are not about the text of books, but rather their fabric, publication details and value.

Approach: By letter, preferably with ideas initially.

Lead time: Six weeks.

Payment: Up to £120.

Bookdealer

Suite 34
26 Charing Cross Road
London
WC2H 0DH

Tel: 071-240 5890   **Fax:** 071-379 5770

Frequency: Weekly

Circulation: 2300

Contact: Barry Shaw, Editor

Profile: Trade paper for those actively engaged in buying or selling rare and out-of-print books.

Requirements: 2 5
Articles on book auctions, exhibitions of maps, prints and manuscripts, together with library and financial news.

Comments: There is only a limited amount of space for editorial, so contributions need to be of a high standard.

Approach: By letter.

Lead time: Two weeks.

Payment: By negotiation.

Bowlers World

164 College Street
St Helens
WA10 1TT

Tel: (0744) 22285   **Fax:** (0744) 451389

Frequency: Monthly

Circulation: 13,000

Contact: Terry McGee, Editor

Profile: A monthly newspaper covering the world of crown green bowling. Circulated throughout the Midlands, North Wales and the North of England.

Requirements: 1 2
News and features about all aspects of bowling, including techniques, people and clubs.

Comments: All areas of coverage are open to freelances, and all submissions are considered.

Approach: In writing.

Lead time: Two months.

Payment: Negotiable.

Bowls International

PO Box 100
Ryhall Road Industrial Estate
Stamford
Lincolnshire
PE9 1XQ

Tel: (0780) 55131   **Fax:** (0780) 57261

Frequency: Monthly

Circulation: 13,000

Contact: Chris Mills, Editor

Profile: Read by members of bowls clubs throughout the UK. Provides news, information and advice for bowls enthusiasts.

Requirements: 1 2
Articles offering new and original information. Also features on greenkeeping, coaching, finance and playing.

Comments: Considers bowls from the perspective of the club rather than the individual player.

Approach: By telephone.

Lead time: Four weeks.

Payment: Around £25 per page.

Boxing Monthly

24 Notting Hill Gate
London
W11 3JE

Tel: 071-229 9944   **Fax:** 071-727 5442

Frequency: Monthly

Circulation: 25,000

Contact: Glyn Leach, Editor

Profile: A magazine for hard-core boxing fans, covering fights around the world.

Requirements: Details of fights, previews and interviews with personalities. There are opportunities for freelances to contribute information on smaller events.

Comments: Material on the biggest fights is not required, as these are all covered by the editorial staff.

Approach: By letter.

Lead time: One month.

Payment: £25 per thousand words.

Boys' Brigade Gazette

Selden Lodge
Hemel Hempstead
Hertfordshire
HP3 0BL

Tel: (0442) 231681   **Fax:** (0442) 235391

Frequency: Bi-monthly

Circulation: 10,000

Contact: Sydney Jones, Editor

Profile: A magazine for officers of the Boys' Brigade. Includes information on the brigade, plus details of events, special information and advice on good practice.

Requirements: 1 2 6 7 8
Information relating to running and

---

organising brigades. This could cover ideas for programmes, news of current trends or dangers to look out for.

Comments: Study the journal to get a feel for style and content.

Approach: By telephone or letter.

Lead time: Two months.

Payment: Negotiable.

Brides and Setting Up Home

Vogue House
Hanover Square
London
W1R 0AD

Tel: 071-499 9080   **Fax:** 071-493 1345

Frequency: Bi-monthly

Circulation: 72,000

Contact: Sandra Boler, Editor

Profile: A practical guide to organising your wedding. Includes fashion for brides and bridegrooms, make-up, receptions, travel and setting up a new home.

Requirements: 2 4 6 7
Particularly interested in honeymoon travel features, plus anything to do with wedding drinks and food.

Comments: The emphasis is very much on the practical aspects. Submissions should be useful rather than simply entertaining.

Approach: By letter with an idea.

Lead time: Three months.

Payment: £120 per thousand words.

The British Archer

43-45 Milford Road
Reading
Berkshire
RG1 8LG

Tel: (0734) 575444   **Fax:** (0734) 583899

Frequency: Bi-monthly

Circulation: 3000

Contact: John Histead, Editor

Profile: A magazine for archery enthusiasts in the UK, covering every aspect of the sport.

Requirements: 1 2 6 7 8
Articles on general archery, club news and equipment reviews. Also profiles of prominent archers.

Comments: Articles accompanied by photographs have a better chance of success.

Approach: Submit a complete manuscript.

Lead time: Four weeks.

Payment: Negotiable.

The British Bandsman

The Old House
64 London End
Beaconsfield
Buckinghamshire
HP9 2JD

Tel: (0494) 674411   **Fax:** (0494) 670932

Frequency: Weekly

Circulation: 8000

Contact: Peter Wilson, Editor

Profile: A weekly newspaper for brass bands, both in the UK and internationally. Mainly concerned with music, competitions and tours.

Requirements: News items, technical articles on brass playing and concert reviews. Length 1000 to 1500 words.

Comments: Items of regional interest are always welcome.
Approach: By letter.
Lead time: Two weeks.
Payment: Negotiable.

British Bike Magazine

Green Designs
PO Box 19
Cowbridge
South Glamorgan
CF7 7YD

Tel: (0446) 775033   **Fax:** (0446) 772204

Frequency: Monthly

Circulation: 15,000

Contact: Rebekka Smith, Editor
Profile: Concentrates on motorbikes manufactured in the UK between the early days of the century and the present day.
Requirements: 2 6 7
Features on touring, restoration, re-builds and racing. Road tests may also be contributed by freelances.
Comments: Keen to receive road tests on vintage, veteran or unusual bikes.
Approach: By letter.
Lead time: Two months.
Payment: Negotiable.

British Book News

The British Council
10 Spring Gardens
London
SW1A 2BN

Tel: 071-930 8466   **Fax:** 071-839 6347

Frequency: Monthly

Circulation: 7000

Contact: Jennifer Creswick, Editor

Profile: A magazine for the professional book trade. Read largely by librarians, booksellers, publishers, teachers and lecturers.
Requirements: 2 6 8
Features on trends in publishing, export, relevant technologies, etc. Length up to 2500 words.
Comments: Also runs two book surveys a month, each up to 2000 words in length.
Approach: By letter or telephone.
Lead time: Three months.
Payment: Negotiable.

British Cars

707 High Road
London
N11 0BT

Tel: 081-343 8113   **Fax:** 081-343 9616

Frequency: Monthly

Circulation: 51,000

Contact: William Kimberley, Editor
Profile: A lively, informative magazine devoted to cars produced in the UK.
Requirements: 1 2
Articles on any subject relating to British cars, including motor sport, nostalgic pieces, road tests and news of current events.
Comments: Copy should be honest and credible.
Approach: In writing.
Lead time: Two months.
Payment: Negotiable.

British Chess Magazine

9 Market Street
St Leonards-on-Sea
East Sussex
TN38 0DQ

Tel: (0424) 424009   **Fax:** (0424) 435439

Frequency: Monthly

Circulation: 4000

Contact: Murray Chandler, Editor

Profile: Provides extensive coverage of the game of chess in the UK.

Requirements: 2
Feature articles on the history of the game, books about chess, tournaments and other chess-related topics.

Comments: Also runs material on the cultural aspects of the game.

Approach: In writing.

Lead time: Two months.

Payment: By arrangement.

British Horse

British Horse Society
Stoneleigh
Kenilworth
Warwickshire
CV8 2LR

Tel: (0203) 696697   **Fax:** (0203) 692351

Frequency: 2xYear

Circulation: 55,000

Contact: Judith Draper

Profile: An official publication of the British Horse Society.

Requirements: 2
Feature articles on matters such as horse welfare, education, safety and access to the countryside.

Comments: Writers do not need to be experts but should be able to provide well-written, well-researched copy.

Approach: By letter.

Lead time: Two months.

Payment: Negotiable.

The British Journal of Photography

186-187 Temple Chambers
Temple Avenue
London
EC4Y 0DB

Tel: 071-583 3030   **Fax:** 071-583 5183

Frequency: Weekly

Circulation: 8492

Contact: The Editor

Profile: Covers the more serious side of photography for professionals and very competent amateurs.

Requirements: 2 6 7
Feature articles on commercial, professional and press photography. Also in-depth articles on the technical aspects of industrial, medical and scientific photography, etc.

Comments: Submissions should be accompanied where possible by high-quality photographs.

Approach: In writing.

Lead time: Four weeks.

Payment: Negotiable.

British Journalism Review

Cassel plc
Villiers House
41-47 Strand
London
WC2N 5JE

Tel: 071-839 4900   **Fax:** 071-839 1804

Frequency: Quarterly

Circulation: 500

Contact: Geoffrey Goodman, Editor

Profile: Concerned with the more scholarly aspects of journalism, encouraging critical discussion. Each issue includes pieces by well-known journalists.

Requirements: 2 4 6 8
Well-written articles discussing current issues in journalism. The subject matter is wide ranging, but writers should have an original voice with something to say. Average length 3000 words.
Comments: Articles on training, censorship and ethics are encouraged.
Approach: By letter with ideas.
Lead time: Three months.
Payment: Typically around £100.

British Printer

Maclean Hunter House
Chalk Farm
Cockfosters Road
Barnet
Hertfordshire
EN4 0BU

Tel: 081-975 9759   **Fax:** 081-441 1361

Frequency: Monthly

Circulation: 14,233

Contact: Sian Griffiths, Editor
Profile: One of the leading magazines for those in the printing industry. Up to 30 per cent of the content is contributed by freelance writers.
Requirements: 1 2 6 7
News and features of interest to printing and graphics arts professionals.
Comments: Writers do not need extensive experience of the industry, provided they are able to undertake meticulous research.
Approach: By letter.
Lead time: Six weeks.
Payment: Between £75 and £125 per thousand words.

British Railways Illustrated

3 Durley Avenue
Pinner
Middlesex
HA5 1JQ

Tel: (0457) 820288   **Fax:** (0457) 877225

Frequency: Bi-monthly

Circulation: 22,000

Contact: John Hooper, Editor
Profile: A magazine for railway buffs, providing a pictorial view of the classic age of rail travel in the UK.
Requirements: 2 6 7
In-depth articles on engines, branch lines, stations, etc. All should include a considerable amount of technical detail.
Comments: Writers do not need to be experts, but material must be well-researched.
Approach: In writing, with ideas or complete manuscript.
Lead time: Three months.
Payment: £25 per page.

Broadcast

EMAP Publications
33-39 Bowling Green Lane
London
EC1R 0DA

Tel: 071-837 1212   **Fax:** 071-837 8312

Frequency: Weekly

Circulation: 10,200

Contact: Quentin Smith, Assistant Editor
Profile: Professional magazine covering all aspects of broadcasting.
Requirements: 1 2
News and features on subjects of interest to those engaged in

---

1/News **2**/Features **3**/Fiction **4**/Letters **5**/Fillers
6/B&W Photos **7**/Colour Photos **8**/Reviews

producing or administering television and radio. Length 650 to 1000 words.

Comments: Considers broadcasting from a professional rather than a viewer's point of view.

Approach: By letter.

Lead time: One week.

Payment: £142 per thousand words.

Broken Clays

CTC Publishing Group
29 Victoria Street
Kettering
Northamptonshire
NN16 0BU

Tel: (0536) 416831   **Fax:** (0536) 416831

Frequency: Monthly.

Circulation: 9000

Contact: Wayne Williams

Profile: Magazine for enthusiasts of clay and skeet shooting. A large part of the editorial consists of club and competition reports.

Requirements: 1 2 6
Features on club activities, personalities in shooting and similiar subjects, together with reports on events.

Comments: Does not cover any shooting activity beyond skeet and clays.

Approach: By letter.

Lead time: Two months.

Payment: Negotiable.

Brownie

17-19 Buckingham Palace Road
London
SW1W 0PT

Tel: 071-834 6242   **Fax:** 071-828 8317

Frequency: Monthly

Circulation: 30,000

Contact: The Editor

Profile: The official Brownie magazine from the Girl Guides Association.

Requirements: 2 3
Concise features on subjects of interest to girls aged between seven and ten years old. Also serials featuring a Brownie connection in instalments of between 500 and 800 words.

Comments: Also accepts articles on things to make, etc.

Approach: In writing.

Lead time: Two months.

Payment: £40 per thousand words.

Budgerigar World

County Press Buildings
Bala
Gwynedd
LL23 7PG

Tel: (0678) 520262   **Fax:** (0678) 521262

Frequency: Monthly

Contact: Terry Tuxford, Editor

Profile: A magazine for budgerigar breeders, exhibitors and enthusiasts.

Requirements: 2 4 6 7
Articles on all aspects of caring for and exhibiting budgerigars. Also products of interest to aviary owners.

Comments: Writers should have a good understanding of the subject.

Approach: Send complete manuscript.

Lead time: Six weeks.

Payment: Negotiable.

1/News **2**/Features **3**/Fiction **4**/Letters **5**/Fillers
6/B&W Photos **7**/Colour Photos **8**/Reviews

Build It

37 High Street
Kingston
Surrey
KT1 1LQ

Tel: 081-549 2166　**Fax:** 081-398 9334

Frequency: Monthly

Circulation: 76,000

Contact: Rosalind Renshaw, Editor

Profile: A consumer guide for those who wish to build their own homes. Includes case studies, features on every aspect of home improvement, financial advice and suggestions on how to find land.

Requirements: 1 2 7
Articles on specific subjects such as plumbing, electrics, kitchens, pools and lighting. May be written either by a professional or a well-informed layman.

Comments: The magazine aims to be factual and friendly.

Approach: Letter preferred.

Lead time: Three months.

Payment: £140 per thousand words.

Bunty

D.C Thomson & Co Ltd
Albert Square
Dundee
DD1 9QJ

Tel: (0382) 23131　**Fax:** (0382) 22214

Frequency: Weekly

Contact: Jim Davie, Editor

Profile: A picture magazine for younger schoolgirls that runs picture-strip stories in serial form.

Requirements: 3
Stories for established serials in the magazine. Although the characters are owned by the publishers, freelance writers are free to contribute ideas for story lines.

Comments: Writers need to be familiar with the characters they intend to write about.

Approach: In writing with example script.

Lead time: One month.

Payment: Negotiable.

The Burlington Magazine

6 Bloomsbury Square
London
WC1A 2LP

Tel: 071-430 0481　**Fax:** 071-242 1205

Frequency: Monthly

Contact: Caroline Elam, Editor

Profile: A serious, scholarly magazine dedicated to new research in art history. Also exhibition and book reviews, and a monthly calendar of current exhibitions worldwide.

Requirements: 2
Articles between 2500 and 5000 words based on new research, on subjects such as unpublished documents or works of art.

Comments: Feature articles will not be considered, and reviews are rarely accepted.

Approach: In writing.

Lead time: Six weeks.

Payment: Up to £100.

1/News **2**/Features **3**/Fiction **4**/Letters **5**/Fillers
6/B&W Photos **7**/Colour Photos **8**/Reviews

Buses

Coombelands House
Coombelands Lane
Addlestone
Weybridge
Surrey
KT15 1HY

Tel: (0932) 855909 **Fax:** (0932) 854750

Frequency: Monthly

Circulation: 19,000

Contact: Stephen Morris, Editor

Profile: Offers news and views of the bus and coach industry throughout the British Isles. Aimed principally at laymen.

Requirements: 1 2 6 7
Interested in receiving topical items, operator profiles and similar articles of interest to the readership. Maximum length 2000 words.

Comments: Articles of tourism interest are not required.

Approach: By telephone or letter with ideas.

Lead time: Six weeks.

Payment: Up to £70 for articles, plus £5-£10 per picture.

Business Age

96-98 Baker Street
London
W1M 1LA

Tel: 071-487 5057 **Fax:** 071-487 5707

Frequency: Monthly

Circulation: 72,092

Contact: Jennifer Miles, Managing Editor

Profile: Magazine for business people in the United Kingdom. Considers itself to be the successor to *Management Week*.

Requirements: 1 2 6 7
News and features of interest to those actively involved in business in the UK. Features should be lively and informative.

Comments: Particularly interested in receiving material on fast-growing companies with a £5 million-plus turnover.

Approach: By letter.

Lead time: Four weeks.

Payment: £50-£75 per thousand words.

Business Car

Decision Publishing Ltd
77 St John Street
London
EC1M 4AN

Tel: 071-490 7444 **Fax:** 071-490 2274

Frequency: Monthly

Circulation: 31,000

Contact: Clive Frusher

Profile: A controlled-circulation magazine for those involved with business cars on a professional basis. Offers advice and guidance on everything from financial to technical matters.

Requirements: 2 7
Articles on subjects such as contract leasing, car phones and windscreen replacement. Length 750 to 1200 words.

Comments: All material will be considered and decisions are reached very quickly.

Approach: By letter only.

Lead time: Two months.

Payment: £130 per thousand words.

1/News **2**/Features **3**/Fiction **4**/Letters **5**/Fillers
6/B&W Photos **7**/Colour Photos **8**/Reviews

Business Equipment Digest

Blair House
184-186 High Street
Tonbridge
Kent
TN9 1BQ

Tel: (0732) 359990   **Fax:** (0372) 770049

Frequency: Monthly

Circulation: 41,000

Contact: Eric Fordham, Editor

Profile: Aims to help owners and managers run their businesses more efficiently with the help of new products and initiatives.

Requirements: 1 2
Case studies of companies that have found ways of saving time, money or labour.

Comments: Although on serious topics, copy should not be dull or overly technical.

Approach: In writing.

Lead time: Two months.

Payment: By arrangement.

Business Life

Premier Magazines
Berger House
36-38 Berkeley Square
London
W1X 5DA

Tel: 071-495 8788   **Fax:** 071-499 5379

Frequency: 10xYear

Circulation: 125,000

Contact: Fiona Watson

Profile: British Airways in-flight magazine for British shuttle, scheduled and Club Europe flights. Includes articles on all aspects of business, with particular emphasis on Europe.

Requirements: 2 7
Features on European countries, communications and the lighter side of business. Contributors should understand business journalism and the market of the magazine.

Comments: The magazine is aimed at senior managers and executives, providing stimulating and informative articles.

Approach: By telephone or fax with ideas.

Lead time: Three months.

Payment: £350 per article.

Business Opportunities Digest

14 Willow Street
London
EC2A 4BH

Tel: 071-417 0700   **Fax:** 071-417 0703

Frequency: Monthly

Circulation: 25,000

Contact: Colin Jones, Editor

Profile: Published by the Institute of Small Businesses. Covers matters of concern to owners and managers.

Requirements: 1 2
News and features on all aspects of running a small business, ranging from finance to marketing.

Comments: Writers should understand the issues which affect the small business community.

Approach: In writing.

Lead time: Two months.

Payment: Negotiable.

1/News **2**/Features **3**/Fiction **4**/Letters **5**/Fillers
6/B&W Photos **7**/Colour Photos **8**/Reviews

Business Scotland

Peebles Publishing Group
Bergius House
Clifton Street
Glasgow
G3 7LA

Tel: 041-331 1022 **Fax:** 041-331 1395

Frequency: Monthly

Circulation: 14,872

Contact: Graham Lironi, Editor

Profile: A controlled-circulation magazine that covers all aspects of business north of the border.

Requirements: 1 2
News items and features articles on subjects relevant to companies in Scotland. Also profiles and news of developments in the world of finance.

Comments: All material must be particularly relevant to Scotland.

Approach: In writing.

Lead time: Two months.

Payment: By arrangement.

Business Traveller

Compass House
22 Redan Place
London
W2 4SZ

Tel: 071-229 7799 **Fax:** 071-229 9441

Frequency: Monthly

Circulation: 47,000

Contact: Gillian Upton

Profile: Magazine for those who travel regularly on business. The readership is intelligent, informed and affluent.

Requirements: 2 7
City profiles, hotel and airline surveys, lighthearted travel pieces and articles on doing business overseas.

Comments: Much of the material currently received is not appropriate for the magazine.

Approach: By letter with ideas.

Lead time: Ten weeks.

Payment: £120 per thousand minimum.

Business Woman Magazine

The Martin Suite
3-5 Manchester Road
Denton
Manchester
M34 3JU

Tel: 061-337 9287 **Fax:** 061-337 9286

Frequency: 2xYear

Circulation: 50,000

Contact: Sue Lambert, Editor

Profile: Covers issues affecting women in business. These include areas such as finance, travel, fashion, education and training.

Requirements: 1 2 3
Features on any of the above subjects, plus other articles which would appeal to career-minded women.

Comments: The magazine is distributed to women in the upper echelon of the business community.

Approach: By fax.

Lead time: Three weeks.

Payment: £75 per thousand words.

Buying Cameras

EMAP Apex
Oundle Road
Peterborough
PE2 9NP

Tel: (0733) 898100 **Fax:** (0733) 894472

1/News **2**/Features **3**/Fiction **4**/Letters **5**/Fillers
6/B&W Photos **7**/Colour Photos **8**/Reviews

Frequency: Monthly

Circulation: 22,221

Contact: David Connor, Assistant Editor

Profile: A comprehensive guide to buying new, used and collectable cameras.

Requirements: 2 8
The editor is keen to hear from enthusiastic amateurs who can provide long-term tests of cameras or lenses. Requires approximately 600 words per page.

Comments: Although a lot of copy is generated in house, genuine enquiries are welcome.

Approach: Preferably by telephone initially.

Lead time: Two months.

Payment: £50 per page.

Buying Satellite

57-59 Rochester Place
London
NW1 9JU

Tel: 071-485 0011 **Fax:** 071-284 2145

Frequency: Monthly

Circulation: 60,000

Contact: Ashley Norris, Editor

Profile: For the TV viewer who wishes to buy a satellite system. Covers everything from choosing a receiver to siting the equipment.

Requirements: 2 8
Reviews of satellite equipment, features on stations or programmes, and profiles of celebrities.

Comments: Photographs are required only if they are of exceptional interest.

Approach: In writing with ideas.

Lead time: Two months.

Payment: Around £90 per thousand words.

C

Cabinet Maker

Benn House
Sovereign Way
Tonbridge
Kent
TN9 1RW

Tel: (0732) 364422   **Fax:** (0732) 361534

Frequency: Weekly

Circulation: 8193

Contact: Sandra Danby, Editor

Profile: A weekly business magazine for the UK furniture trade, read by furniture retailers and manufacturers. Covers design, new products, exhibitions and business news related to the trade.

Requirements: 1 2
General business articles and more in-depth pieces on retailers or companies. Maximum 1000 words.

Comments: All copy must have a furniture angle.

Approach: By fax with ideas.

Lead time: Four weeks.

Payment: £110 per thousand words.

Cable Guide

Communications House
5 Factory Lane
Croydon
CR9 3RA

Tel: 081-681 1133   **Fax:** 081-781 6834

Frequency: Monthly

Circulation: 280,000

Contact: Robin Jarussi, Editor

Profile: Cable and television listing magazine. Has an editorial section reflecting the programming.

Requirements: 2
Interviews with sport or entertainment figures, plus features relating to programmes on cable TV. Length up to 500 words.

Comments: Articles should be short but lively.

Approach: By fax with ideas.

Lead time: Two months.

Payment: From £200 per thousand words.

Cage & Aviary Birds

IPC Magazines
King's Reach Tower
Stamford Street
London
SE1 9LS

Tel: 071-261 6116   **Fax:** 071-261 6095

Frequency: Weekly

Circulation: 39,000

Contact: Brian Byles, Editor

Profile: For the experienced and enthusiastic aviculturist, providing information about both British and foreign bird keeping.

1/News **2**/Features **3**/Fiction **4**/Letters **5**/Fillers
6/B&W Photos **7**/Colour Photos **8**/Reviews

Requirements: 1 2

General articles on budgerigars, canaries, waterfowl, quail, birds of prey, pheasants and parrot-like birds.

Comments: Although the magazine has regular contributors, a large part of the content is written by other freelances.

Approach: By letter.

Lead time: Two months.

Payment: By negotiation.

Cambridgeshire Pride

14 Middletons Road
Yaxley
Peterborough
PE7 3LR

Tel: (0733) 242312   **Fax:** (0733) 244035

Frequency: Monthly

Circulation: 17,000

Contact: Ralph Braybrook, Editor

Profile: A regional magazine distributed free to households with high disposable incomes.

Requirements: 2

Feature articles on subjects such as gardening, motoring, jazz, pop music, literature and personal finance.

Comments: Welcomes material with a regional flavour.

Approach: In writing.

Lead time: Two months.

Payment: Negotiable.

Camcorder User

57-59 Rochester Place
London
NW1 9JU

Tel: 071-485 0011   **Fax:** 071-482 6269

Frequency: Monthly

Circulation: 35,000

Contact: Robert Uhlig, Editor

Profile: Targeted at the camcorder enthusiast, covering all aspects of video making. Predominantly technique-based, but also carries equipment reviews.

Requirements: 1 2 6 7 8

Looking for stories on camcorder or videomaking techniques, especially those that include useful hints and tips. Also articles on editing packages and other items of equipment.

Comments: Receives a lot of unsolicited material that is impossible to illustrate. A feature that has been created with a visual dimension in mind will have a much greater chance of success.

Approach: By telephone with ideas.

Lead time: Six weeks.

Payment: £85 per thousand words.

Campaign

22 Lancaster Gate
London
W2 3LY

Tel: 071-413 4036   **Fax:** 071-413 4507

Frequency: Weekly

Circulation: 23,008

Contact: Dominic Mills

Profile: Leading business magazine for the advertising and creative industries. Also covers marketing and production.

Requirements: 1 2

News and features relating to the advertising industry. The emphasis tends to be on the business rather than the creative aspects. Length up to 2000 words.

1/News **2**/Features **3**/Fiction **4**/Letters **5**/Fillers
6/B&W Photos **7**/Colour Photos **8**/Reviews

Comments: Articles need to be authoritative and well-researched.
Approach: By telephone or letter.
Lead time: Four weeks.
Payment: Up to £50 for news stories, more for features.

Camping & Caravanning

The Camping & Caravanning Club
Greenfields House
Westwood Way
Coventry
CV4 8JH

Tel: (0203) 694995 **Fax:** (0203) 694886

Frequency: Monthly

Circulation: 103,429

Contact: Peter Frost, Editor
Profile: A general family camping magazine, catering for those with tents, caravans or motor caravans. Also carries information for newcomers to camping.
Requirements: 1 2 5 7 8
Features on general camping, mainly in the UK but also including France and other European countries. Also tests on tents, caravans and equipment. Length 800 to 1000 words.
Comments: Articles on walking or exotic locations are not required. The emphasis is on family activities.
Approach: Send ideas with examples of previous work, or a complete manuscript.
Lead time: Two months.
Payment: Negotiable.

Camping Magazine

Link House
Dingwall Avenue
Croydon
CR9 2TA

Tel: 081-686 2599 **Fax:** 081-760 0973

Frequency: Monthly

Circulation: 20,000

Contact: David Roberts, Editor
Profile: Broad-ranging magazine, covering many different kinds of outdoor activity related to camping.
Requirements: 2 6 7
From hard, practical material through to anecdotal travel stories. Features that can be accompanied by panels of hints and tips are especially useful.
Comments: Considers camping just as a means to an end, so there is considerable scope for related features.
Approach: By telephone.
Lead time: Two months.
Payment: £90 per thousand words.

Canal and Riverboat

Stanley House
9 West Street
Epsom
Surrey
KT18 7RL

Tel: (0372) 741411 **Fax:** (0372) 744493

Frequency: Monthly

Circulation: 26,000

Contact: Norman Alborough, Editor
Profile: Covers all aspects of waterways, including canals, cruisers, riverboats and narrow boats.
Requirements: 1 2 3 6 7
Features offering practical advice,

1/News 2/Features 3/Fiction 4/Letters 5/Fillers
6/B&W Photos 7/Colour Photos 8/Reviews

personal experiences and cruising reports. Length up to 2000 words.

Comments: Short stories of up to 1500 words will also be considered if the subject matter is relevant.

Approach: By letter with ideas.

Lead time: Two months.

Payment: About £50.

Candis

Newhall Publications
Newhall Lane
Hoylake
Wirral
L47 4BQ

Tel: 051-632 3232   **Fax:** 051-632 5716

Frequency: Monthly

Circulation: 475,609

Contact: Eleanor Jones, Editor

Profile: A general interest magazine for all the family, having strong charity connections. Delivered door to door throughout the country, but also available on subscription.

Requirements: 2 3 7
Lively features on health, the environment, and other subjects that would appeal to a family audience.

Comments: Study the magazine carefully before suggesting features.

Approach: In writing with ideas.

Lead time: Three months.

Payment: Negotiable.

Car

EMAP National Publications
97 Earls Court Road
London
W8 6QH

Tel: 071-370 0333   **Fax:** 071-244 8692

Frequency: Monthly

Circulation: 132,000

Contact: Gavin Green

Profile: An upmarket and prestigious title, featuring high-quality writing, design and photography.

Requirements: 1 2
Some 50 per cent of the magazine's content is contributed by freelances, although much of the unsolicited material received is unsuitable. Well-written, authoritative pieces that are entertaining and informative are always welcomed. Length 800-2500 words.

Comments: The magazine has a slot called Soapbox, providing an opportunity to voice opinions on any motoring subject.

Approach: Send complete manuscript.

Lead time: Two months

Payment: £200 per thousand words.

Car Choice

38-42 Hampton Road
Teddington
Middlesex
TW11 0JE

Tel: 081-943 5000   **Fax:** 081-943 5653

Frequency: Monthly

Circulation: 45,698

Contact: Hugh Poulter, Editor

Profile: A straight-talking used-car guide. Includes articles on legal issues, what to look for when buying cars, etc. Some new models are covered, but not many.

Requirements: 2 7
Features written in a clear and simple style to reach a non-technical readership. Light-hearted and timeless pieces are also required,

---

1/News **2**/Features **3**/Fiction **4**/Letters **5**/Fillers
6/B&W Photos **7**/Colour Photos **8**/Reviews

together with articles on the best cars for businessmen, doctors or other professionals.

Comments: Women writers are always welcome. Copy on Macintosh or PC disk would be appreciated.

Approach: By telephone or letter.

Lead time: Six weeks.

Payment: Negotiable.

Car Hi-Fi

EVRO Publishing
60 Waldegrave Road
Teddington
Middlesex
TW11 8LG

Tel: 081-943 5000   **Fax:** 081-943 5871

Frequency: Bi-monthly

Circulation: 25,000

Contact: Ms Naj Marcuard

Profile: A guide to improving your in-car audio. Includes product reviews, practical advice, installation tips and advice on upgrades.

Requirements: 1 2 5 6 8
Welcomes interesting features on the above subjects. Maximum length 1800 words. Photographs or heavily-technical pieces are not usually required.

Comments: Particularly interested in material such as reader installations or pro-fits.

Approach: By fax or letter.

Lead time: Two months.

Payment: £130 per thousand words.

Car Mechanics

77 High Street
Beckenham
Kent
BR3 1AN

Tel: 081-658 3531   **Fax:** 081-650 8035

Frequency: Monthly

Circulation: 30,000

Contact: Gordon Wright, Editor

Profile: For anyone interesting in repairing and improving their cars.

Requirements: 2 6 7
Informative, detailed articles on repairing, maintaining and uprating contemporary vehicles. Length 1500 to 2000 words.

Comments: All material should be aimed at the DIY enthusiast.

Approach: By letter with ideas.

Lead time: Six weeks.

Payment: Negotiable.

Car Stereo & Security F. Fwd

Holly House
Holly Lane
Silchester
Berkshire
RG7 2NA

Tel: (0734) 701612   **Fax:** (0734) 701613

Frequency: Bi-monthly

Circulation: 20,000

Contact: Kevin O'Byrne, Editor

Profile: A magazine devoted to in-car entertainment and security systems.

Requirements: 1 2
News and features concerning any aspect of audio systems and security for cars. Information must be up-to-date and accurate.

Comments: Welcomes material on matters that might not otherwise be covered within the magazine.

Approach: In writing.
Lead time: Three months.
Payment: Negotiable.

Caravan Life

Suite 2
Northburgh House
10 Northburgh Street
Clerkenwell
London
EC1V 0AY

Tel: 071-490 8141   **Fax:** 071-336 7193

Frequency: Monthly

Circulation: 21,000

Contact: Stuart Craig, Editor
Profile: An informed title for enthusiastic caravanners. Includes product
testing, DIY and touring features,
plus the latest news and views.
Requirements: 2 7
Touring and travel articles about
caravanning. The style should be
lively without being too chatty.
Comments: Colour photography and
an understanding of caravanning are
important.
Approach: By telephone with an idea.
Lead time: Two months.
Payment: In the region of £150 per
thousand words.

Caravan Magazine

Link House
Dingwall Avenue
Croydon
CR9 2TA

Tel: 081-686 2599   **Fax:** 081-760 0973

Frequency: Monthly

Circulation: 29,017

Contact: Barry Williams, Executive
Editor

Profile: Devoted exclusively to touring
trailer caravans. Includes features on
tow cars, sites and subjects of
general interest to caravanners.
Requirements: 1 2 5 7 8
Touring articles with colour
pictures, practical and DIY-type
features, experiences of particular
caravans and tow cars. Maximum
length 1500 words.
Comments: Colour photography is
always welcome.
Approach: By telephone or letter.
Lead time: Two months.
Payment: £100-£120 for a 1500-word
feature with pictures.

Caravan, Motorcaravan & Camping Mart

89 East Hill
Colchester
Essex
CO1 2QN

Tel: (0206) 845400   **Fax:** (0206) 845400

Frequency: Monthly

Circulation: 14,000

Contact: David Bridle, Editor
Profile: A specialist publication
including a large mumber of trade
and private advertisements for
camping and caravanning
equipment, etc.
Requirements: 2 5 6 7
Interesting editorial to complement
the advertising. In particular,
practical material that includes
specific details and information. A
package of words and pictures is
preferred.
Comments: Does not want travel
material, or articles on personal
camping experiences.

1/News 2/Features 3/Fiction 4/Letters 5/Fillers
6/B&W Photos 7/Colour Photos 8/Reviews

Approach: By telephone with ideas.
Lead time: Two months.
Payment: Negotiable.

Caravan Plus

Future Publishing
30 Monmouth Street
Bath
BA1 2BW

Tel: (0225) 442244   **Fax:** (0225) 447465

Frequency: Monthly

Circulation: circa 30,000

Contact: Paul Elmer, Editor
Profile: For converted caravanners aged 45 and over, as well as younger newcomers. Designed for those who have decided on holidaying in the UK as more attractive than travelling overseas.
Requirements: 1 2 5 6 7
Looking for regional contributors who can file reports on sites and activities in their own part of the country. Length between 200 and 300 words, plus photographs.
Comments: With a 120-page magazine to fill, the editor is always open to suggestions from freelances.
Approach: Write with a synopsis and a brief CV.
Lead time: Two months.
Payment: £100 per thousand words, plus expenses.

Carers World

A.E. Morgan Publications
Stanley House
9 West Street
Epsom
Surrey
KT18 7RL

Tel: (0372) 741411   **Fax:** (0372) 744493

Frequency: Bi-monthly
Circulation: 20,000
Contact: Chris Cattrall, Editor
Profile: For those who look after the elderly and disabled on a non-professional basis. Aims to inform those who are looking after relatives in their own home.
Requirements: 1 2
Articles on short walks that would be suitable for carers, plus features on subjects such as gardening. Also welcomes regional news.
Comments: The editor may consider using fiction or poetry. Copy should ideally be on a PC disk in ASCII format.
Approach: In writing with ideas or complete manuscript.
Lead time: Three months.
Payment: £50 per thousand words.

Caribbean Times

Tower House
139-149 Fonthill Road
London
N4 3HF

Tel: 071-281 1191   **Fax:** 071-263 9656

Frequency: Weekly

Circulation: 23,500

Contact: Arif Ali, Editor
Profile: A weekly newspaper for the Afro-Caribbean community in the UK.
Requirements: 1 2 6
News items and feature articles on subjects or issues of interest to black readers nationwide.
Comments: All material must be topical and up to date.
Approach: In writing.
Lead time: Two weeks.
Payment: From £10 for news stories.

1/News **2**/Features **3**/Fiction **4**/Letters **5**/Fillers
6/B&W Photos **7**/Colour Photos **8**/Reviews

Cars and Car Conversions

Link House
Dingwall Avenue
Croydon
CR9 2TA

Tel: 081-686 2599 **Fax:** 081-760 0973

Frequency: Monthly

Circulation: 70,000

Contact: Nigel Fryatt, Editor

Profile: A lively motorsports magazine. Includes technical articles, road tests, track tests and engine conversions.

Requirements: 1 2 7 8
Features on unusual or interesting cars and conversions, technical articles on motorsport.

Comments: Features accompanied by photographs are preferred, as is copy on disk.

Approach: In writing, with ideas or complete manuscript.

Lead time: Two months.

Payment: Negotiable.

Cat World

10 Western Road
Shoreham-by-Sea
West Sussex
BN43 5WD

Tel: (0273) 462000 **Fax:** (0273) 455994

Frequency: Monthly

Circulation: 20,000

Contact: Joan Moore, Editor

Profile: An independent publication for cat lovers. Covers all aspects of cat ownership, from health to cat flaps, as well as general articles of interest to enthusiasts.

Requirements: 2 5
Short features on caring for your cat, written by those experienced in the subject. Also more original and innovative features with a feline theme. Maximum length 850 words.

Comments: A lot of unsolicited material is submitted, but unusual, interesting features are likely to be well received.

Approach: Send complete manuscript.

Lead time: Three months.

Payment: £25 per thousand words.

Catch

D.C. Thomson & Co Ltd
Albert Square
Dundee
DD1 9QT

Tel: (0382) 23131 **Fax:** (0382) 22214

Frequency: Monthly

Circulation: 126,491

Contact: Lesley Fenwick

Profile: Magazine for young women aged between 17 and 27. Includes features on fashion, beauty, true experiences, celebrities and models.

Requirements: 2 3 4 7
Emotional features and light-hearted pieces. Anything with an unusual angle. Also fiction that is not too serious in style.

Comments: Copy should not be too racy or provocative.

Approach: By letter with a synopsis.

Lead time: Three months.

Payment: On acceptance.

Caterer & Hotelkeeper

Room H415
Quadrant House
The Quadrant
Sutton
Surrey
SM2 5AS

Tel: 081-652 3500 **Fax:** 081-652 8973

1/News **2**/Features **3**/Fiction **4**/Letters **5**/Fillers
6/B&W Photos **7**/Colour Photos **8**/Reviews

Frequency: Weekly

Circulation: 45,000

Contact: Clare Walker, Editor

Profile: A business magazine for management in hotels, restaurants and the catering industry.

Requirements: 1 2
Features on management issues or trends. Regional news on issues that may affect the industry nationally. Maximum 2000 words.

Comments: Does not publish consumer-style hotel and restaurant reviews. It aims to provide business information to help managers and chefs.

Approach: By letter for features, telephone for news.

Lead time: Six weeks.

Payment: £120 per thousand words.

Catholic Gazette

114 West Heath Road
London
NW3 7TX

Tel: 081-458 3316   **Fax:** 081-905 5780

Frequency: Monthly

Circulation: 2400

Contact: Paul Billington, Editor

Profile: A wide-ranging publication covering topics of interest to the Catholic Church.

Requirements: 2 6
Features on Christianity, evangelism and the Christian way of life. Maximum 1500 words.

Comments: Writers should strive to look at familiar topics from an original viewpoint.

Approach: In writing.

Lead time: Two months.

Payment: By arrangement.

Catholic Herald

Lamb's Passage
Bunhill Row
London
EC1Y 8TQ

Tel: 071-588 3101   **Fax:** 071-256 9728

Frequency: Weekly

Circulation: 21,000

Contact: Cristina Odone

Profile: Provides news of the Catholic world, both in the UK and internationally. In addition to covering religious issues, the magazine considers secular matters from the point of view of the Church.

Requirements: 1 2 8
Articles on Catholic matters, plus more general features on social issues, humanitarian subjects, the Third World and the arts.

Comments: Writers should understand the viewpoint of the publication.

Approach: By letter.

Lead time: Two weeks.

Payment: By negotiation.

CD Classic

United Leisure Magazines
PO Box 3205
4 Selsdon Way
London
E14 9GL

Tel: 071-712 0550   **Fax:** 071-712 0557

Frequency: Bi-monthly

Circulation: 40,000

Contact: Kate Price Thomas, Editor

Profile: A magazine that aims to make classical music accessible to everyone. The target is men and women aged between 25 and 45 who do not have a specialised knowledge of music.

1/News **2**/Features **3**/Fiction **4**/Letters **5**/Fillers
6/B&W Photos **7**/Colour Photos **8**/Reviews

Requirements: Interviews with musicians, plus features on fashion for concert goers, jobs in the music industry, etc.

Comments: Although professional music journalists are used for reviews, there is plenty of scope for freelances to contribute general features.

Approach: Send a synopsis with cuttings of previous work.

Lead time: Three months.

Payment: Negotiable.

CD Review

Media House
Boxwell Road
Berkhamstead
Herts
HP4 3ET

Tel: (0442) 876191   **Fax:** (0442) 875108

Frequency: Monthly

Circulation: 45,000

Contact: Julian Haylock, Editor

Profile: A guide to classical music on CD for the serious collector. Includes latest releases, composer surveys, interviews, books etc.

Requirements: 2 8
Record reviews of approximately 300 words set out in the house style. Normally no more than three at a time. Also general features relating to classical music on CD.

Comments: Particularly interested in writers who feel comfortable with the overall tone of the magazine.

Approach: Send manuscripts with a CV.

Lead time: Two months.

Payment: £100 per thousand words.

Challenge

Revenue Buildings
Chapel Road
Worthing
West Sussex
BN11 1BQ

Tel: (0903) 214198   **Fax:** (0903) 217663

Frequency: Monthly

Circulation: 80,974

Contact: Donald Banks, Editor

Profile: Tabloid-style newspaper distributed by churches door-to-door nationwide. This Christian-based family publication aims to provide information about Christianity in a friendly way.

Requirements: 2 3 5 6 7
Articles on hobbies and interests, plus children's stories with a moral viewpoint. Also general Christian articles. Length 500 to 600 words.

Comments: Although a Christian paper, it is read by the general public. Therefore all 'churchy' articles are out.

Approach: In writing. Send an s.a.e. for a sample copy and writers' guidelines.

Lead time: Three months.

Payment: From £15 per article.

Chat

IPC Magazines
King's Reach Tower
Stamford Street
London
SE1 9LS

Tel: 071-261 6565   **Fax:** 071-261 6534

Frequency: Weekly

Circulation: 568,095

Contact: Ms Terry Tavner, Editor

1/News **2**/Features **3**/Fiction **4**/Letters **5**/Fillers
6/B&W Photos **7**/Colour Photos **8**/Reviews

Profile: A busy, chatty magazine for women, covering the usual range of subjects. Targeted at housewives in their mid-thirties, but has a much broader readership.

Requirements: 2 4 5
Features on fashion, family, finance, cookery etc. Publishes true experiences, and accepts a large number of filler items, hints, tips and readers' letters.

Comments: Also publishes short stories up to 1000 words long with a 'twist-in-the-tale' ending.

Approach: In writing.

Lead time: One month.

Payment: £100 for a 700-word feature.

Cheshire Life

Oyston Mill
Strand Road
Preston
PR1 8UR

Tel: (0772) 722022 **Fax:** (0722) 736496

Frequency: Monthly

Circulation: 12,900

Contact: Patrick O'Neil

Profile: A country magazine covering matters of interest to everyone in Cheshire.

Requirements: 2 6 7
Entertaining articles on society events, fashion, county sport, antiques and motoring.

Comments: The magazine aims to be provincial without being parochial.

Approach: By letter.

Lead time: Three months.

Payment: Around £62 per thousand words.

The Cheshire Magazine

Mansion House Chambers
24 High Street
Stockport
Cheshire
SK1 1EG

Tel: 061-474 1758 **Fax:** 061-480 2645

Frequency: Monthly

Circulation: 15,000

Contact: John Parkinson, Editor

Profile: Provides coverage of news, events and general matters concerning the county.

Requirements: 1 2
News and features on local businesses and personalities, homes, gardening, walking and motoring. Also articles on fashion and entertainment.

Comments: Welcomes material with a county flavour.

Approach: In writing.

Lead time: Two months.

Payment: By arrangement.

Child Education

Scholastic Publications
Villiers House
Clarendon Avenue
Leamington Spa
Warwickshire
CV32 5PR

Tel: (0926) 887799 **Fax:** (0926) 883331

Frequency: Monthly

Circulation: 68,945

Contact: Gill Moore, Editor

Profile: Read by teachers, nursery nurses and parents of children aged between three and eight years old.

Requirements: 1 2 6 7
News of progress in educational
methods. Also features on teaching
techniques, child development, etc.
Length 1000 to 2000 words.
Comments: Welcomes high-quality
photographs to accompany
features.
Approach: In writing with ideas.
Lead time: Two months.
Payment: Negotiable.

Choice

2 St John's Place
St John's Square
London
EC1M 4DE

Tel: 071-490 7070   **Fax:** 071-253 0393

Frequency: Monthly

Circulation: 130,000

Contact: Wendy James, Editor
Profile: A pre-retirement magazine
for the 50-plus age group.
Encourages a positive attitude to
planning and enjoying a fulfilled
retirement.
Requirements: 2 5 7 8
Original material on finance,
health, readers' rights, travel,
sporting activities and cookery.
Length 300 to 1000 words.
Comments: Copy should be written
from personal experience.
Approach: In writing, with ideas or
complete manuscripts.
Lead time: Three months.
Payment: Negotiable.

Christian Family

37 Elm Road
New Malden
Surrey
KT3 3HB

Tel: 081-942 9761   **Fax:** 081-949 2313

Frequency: Monthly

Circulation: 14,000

Contact: Clive Price, Editor
Profile: A family magazine with a
strong Biblical element. Offers
advice and information to a
readership of committed Christians.
Requirements: 2 5
Articles on relationships, parenting
issues, family matters, travel and
leisure. All seen through a religious
perspective. Length 1200 to 1400
words.
Comments: Poetry and fiction not
required. Copy on disk is preferred.
Approach: By telephone.
Lead time: Two months.
Payment: Negotiable.

Christian Herald

Herald House
96 Dominion Road
Worthing
West Sussex
BN14 8JP

Tel: (0903) 821082   **Fax:** (0903) 821081

Frequency: Weekly

Circulation: 23,000

Contact: Colin Reeves, Editorial
Director
Profile: A bright, well-established
tabloid-style paper for church
members of all denominations. Read
by ordinary Christians, typically
aged 35 and over.

1/News **2**/Features **3**/Fiction **4**/Letters **5**/Fillers
6/B&W Photos **7**/Colour Photos **8**/Reviews

Requirements: 2 6

Brief, entertaining articles, ranging from 500 to 800 words in length. There is no limit to the scope of features, provided they have a Christian basis.

Comments: Submissions should be accompanied by a word count and captions for illustrations.

Approach: In writing.

Lead time: Three weeks.

Payment: Negotiable.

Church of England Newspaper

12-13 Clerkenwell Green
London
EC1R 0DP

Tel: 071-490 0898   **Fax:** 071-490 0861

Frequency: Weekly

Circulation: 12,000

Contact: John Martin, Editor

Profile: A weekly publication that aims to keep Anglicans abreast of news from the Christian world.

Requirements: 1 2 6 7

News items and feature articles that demonstrate aspects of Christianity in everyday life. Maximum length 1000 words.

Comments: There is an emphasis on evangelical matters throughout the paper.

Approach: In writing.

Lead time: Two weeks.

Payment: £25 per thousand words.

Church Times

33 Upper Street
London
N1 6PN

Tel: 071-359 4570   **Fax:** 071-226 3073

Frequency: Weekly

Circulation: 42,158

Contact: John Whale, Editor

Profile: The leading Anglican newspaper. Covers matters relating to the Church of England and Anglican communities worldwide.

Requirements: 1 2 5 6 7

Contributions on matters relevant to the Church of England in the UK, plus other religious subjects. Length 800 to 1500 words.

Comments: Writers new to the paper are likely to be asked to contribute on spec initially.

Approach: In writing.

Lead time: Four weeks.

Payment: £80 per thousand words.

Citizen's Band

ASP Ltd
Argus House
Boundary Way
Hemel Hempstead
HP2 7ST

Tel: (0442) 66551   **Fax:** (0442) 66998

Frequency: Monthly

Circulation: 9000

Contact: Tony Hetherington, Editor

Profile: Specialist magazine for CB radio enthusiasts. Carries features, reviews and general interest articles.

Requirements: 1 2 8

Features on the use and application of CB radio, covering subjects such as equipment news, short-wave listening, and UHF CB. Length between 500 and 2000 words.

Comments: Contributors need to have a good understanding of the subject.

1/News **2**/Features **3**/Fiction **4**/Letters **5**/Fillers
6/B&W Photos **7**/Colour Photos **8**/Reviews

Approach: In writing, with ideas or complete manuscript.
Lead time: Six weeks.
Payment: From £30 per page.

Civil Aviation Training

The Lodge
High Street
Harby
Newark
Nottinghamshire
NG23 7EB

Tel: (0522) 704106   **Fax:** (0522) 704131

Frequency: Quarterly

Circulation: 13,750

Contact: Trevor Nash, Editor
Profile: Covers training topics and technology associated with commercial airlines.
Requirements: 1 2
News items on the above subjects, from 200 to 300 words in length. Also features from 1500 to 2500 words.
Comments: Study the magazine before contributing.
Approach: By telephone.
Lead time: Six weeks.
Payment: £115 per thousand words.

Classic & Motorcycle Mechanics

Suite C
Deene House
Market Square
Corby
Northamptonshire
NN17 1PB

Tel: (0536) 203003   **Fax:** (0536) 400147

Frequency: Monthly

Circulation: 20,000
Contact: Bob Berry, Publisher
Profile: Covers the mechanics of motorcycles from the 50s, 60s and 70s.
Requirements: 2
Accurate, well-presented material from writers with some knowledge of the subject.
Comments: Does not wish to receive material on more modern bikes.
Approach: Send complete manuscript.
Lead time: Two weeks.
Payment: £50 per thousand words.

Classic Bike

Bushfield House
Orton Centre
Peterborough
PE2 5UW

Tel: (0733) 237111   **Fax:** (0733) 231137

Frequency: Monthly

Circulation: 60,931

Contact: John Pearson, Editor
Profile: One of the most successful of the titles in its sector, covering mostly British bikes plus some European and Japanese machines.
Requirements: 1 2
Articles on the history or restoration of a classic bike, or profiles of people involved in motorcycle sport or production during the post-war years.
Comments: Concentrates on the period after 1945 when the British motorcycle industry was at its peak.
Approach: Send a synopsis and relevant photos.
Lead time: Two months.
Payment: Negotiable.

1/News 2/Features 3/Fiction 4/Letters 5/Fillers
6/B&W Photos 7/Colour Photos 8/Reviews

The Classic Bike Guide

PO Box 10
Whitchurch
Shropshire
SY13 1ZZ

Tel: 061-928 3480   **Fax:** 061-929 0534

Frequency: Monthly

Circulation: 24,000

Contact: Frank Westworth, Editor

Profile: A guide to buying, running and enjoying older motorbikes.

Requirements: 2 6 7
  Profiles of classic bikes, and interviews with the people who raced them or built them. Coverage of events, both past and present.

Comments: Photographs are always welcome.

Approach: Send complete manuscript.

Lead time: Two months.

Payment: £50-£250 per story.

Classic Boat

Link House
Dingwall Avenue
Croydon
CR9 2TA

Tel: 081-686 2599   **Fax:** 081-781 6535

Frequency: Monthly

Circulation: 20,000

Contact: Robin Gates, Editor

Profile: A beautifully-produced magazine with definitive articles on traditional boats and classic yachts. Has an international content and readership.

Requirements: 1 2 6 7 8
  Material on traditional boats and classic yachts, looking at design, construction and seamanship. Also historical articles and reminiscences, plus features on boat building, events and new boats. Maximum 2500 words.

Comments: Must be well-researched, preferably accompanied by photographs.

Approach: Send a synopsis initially.

Lead time: Two months.

Payment: From £75 per page.

Classic Car Weekly

Bushfield House
Orton Centre
Peterborough
PE2 5UW

Tel: (0733) 237111   **Fax:** (0733) 239527

Frequency: Weekly

Circulation: 26,000

Contact: Geoff Browne, Editor

Profile: A very broad-based magazine, covering anything to do with classic cars. Although some new cars are covered, the emphasis is on those over 25 years old.

Requirements: 1 2 6 7
  Driving features and nostalgic pieces about particular cars of which the writer has personal experience.

Comments: Receives a lot of unsolicited material from writers who do not understand the magazine's requirements. But the editor is very pleased to buy from those who can deliver.

Approach: In writing with a synopsis.

Lead time: Four weeks.

Payment: On merit, from £100 per thousand words.

1/News **2**/Features **3**/Fiction **4**/Letters **5**/Fillers
6/B&W Photos **7**/Colour Photos **8**/Reviews

Classic Cars

IPC Magazines
King's Reach Tower
Stamford Street
London
SE1 9LS

Tel: 071-261 5858   **Fax:** 071-261 6731

Frequency: Monthly

Circulation: 85,000

Contact: Tony Dron, Editor

Profile: Devoted to the restoration and
racing of post-war cars. Includes
marque histories, buyer's guides,
technical features, rally news and
driving impressions.

Requirements: 1 7
News and pictures relevant to
owners of classic cars, both at home
and abroad. News on legislation and
information about unusual cars.

Comments: Longer features should
only be written by those who are
expert in the subject.

Approach: By telephone or fax.

Lead time: Four weeks.

Payment: Negotiable.

Classic CD

Future Publishing
30 Monmouth Street
Bath
BA1 2BW

Tel: (0225) 442244   **Fax:** (0225) 460709

Frequency: Monthly

Circulation: 57,000

Contact: Rob Ainsley, Editor

Profile: A guide to the best classical
recordings of the month. Includes
explanations and descriptions of the
music, plus articles on artists and
composers.

Requirements: 1 2 8
Reviews from writers with
authority and expertise in specific
areas of classical music. Material
must be related to new releases,
and written in advance of the
release date.

Comments: A good understanding of
classical music is important.

Approach: By telephone or fax.

Lead time: Two months.

Payment: £125 per thousand words.

The Classic Motorcycle

Bushfield House
Orton Centre
Peterborough
PE2 5UW

Tel: (0733) 237111   **Fax:** (0733) 231137

Frequency: Monthly

Circulation: 36,000

Contact: Phillip Tooth, Editor

Profile: Magazine for those
interested in classic motorcycles,
concentrating on machines
produced up to the 1950s.

Requirements: 1 2
Articles on the restoration and
racing of older motorcycles, with
the emphasis on British models.

Comments: The editor does not
want to receive personal
reminiscences.

Approach: Send complete
manuscript.

Lead time: Two months.

Payment: Negotiable.

1/News **2**/Features **3**/Fiction **4**/Letters **5**/Fillers
6/B&W Photos **7**/Colour Photos **8**/Reviews

Classic Racer

Suite C
Deene House
Market Square
Corby
Northamptonshire
NN17 1PB

Tel: (0536) 203003   **Fax:** (0536) 400147

Frequency: Bi-monthly

Circulation: 20,000

Contact: Bob Berry, Publisher

Profile: Covers all aspects of bike sport from the turn of the century up to the mid-1970s.

Requirements: 2
Accurate, well-presented material from writers with a good knowledge of the subject.

Comments: Do not send material on modern racing events.

Approach: Submit complete manuscript.

Lead time: Two months.

Payment: £50 per thousand words.

Classical Guitar

Olsover House
43 Sackville Road
Newcastle-upon-Tyne
NE6 5TA

Tel: 091-276 0448   **Fax:** 091-276 1623

Frequency: Monthly

Circulation: 7,000

Contact: The Managing Editor

Profile: A magazine for classical guitarists, both amateur and professional. Also covers some lute, flamenco and jazz guitar music.

Requirements: 2 6
Articles from freelance writers are used for specialised areas. Enquire before proceeding. Length 750 to 1500 words.

Comments: No articles on other types of guitar music or playing.

Approach: By letter or fax.

Lead time: Three months.

Payment: By arrangement.

Classical Music

241 Shaftesbury Avenue
London
WC2H 8EH

Tel: 071-836 2383   **Fax:** 071-528 7991

Frequency: Fortnightly

Circulation: 8500

Contact: Keith Clarke, Editor

Profile: The trade journal for the British classical music business.

Requirements: Features on recording, broadcasting, events and other subjects of interest to those professionally involved with classical music. Maximum 1000 words.

Comments: Unsolicited manuscripts are discouraged, but all ideas will be given serious consideration.

Approach: In writing, with ideas.

Lead time: Two months.

Payment: £75 per thousand words.

Clay Shooting

4 The Courtyard
Denmark Street
Wokingham
Berks
RG11 2LW

Tel: (0372) 468758   **Fax:** (0734) 772903

Frequency: Bi-monthly

Circulation: 12,500

Contact: James Marchington, Editor
Profile: Covers all clay-shooting disciplines. Content includes reviews, shoot reports, advice and information.
Requirements: 1 2 6 7 8
Club profiles, personality interviews, shoot reports and practical tips. Length 200 to 800 words.
Comments: Keep copy lively and interesting at all times.
Approach: By letter.
Lead time: Four weeks.
Payment: Negotiable.

Climber & Hill Walker

The Plaza Tower
East Kilbride
Glasgow
G74 1LW
Tel: (0355) 246444   **Fax:** (0355) 263013
Frequency: Monthly
Circulation: 15,000
Contact: Peter Evans, Editor
Profile: Covers mountaineering, climbing and hill walking both in Britain and worldwide. Content includes articles on expeditions, equipment and reports of what is happening on the mountaineering scene.
Requirements: 2 3 7
Contributions on any of the above subjects. Humour tends to be lacking in mountaineering publications, so light-hearted pieces are always welcome. Length 1500 to 2000 words.
Comments: The more original and different an idea is, the better the chance of acceptance. Photos also help.

Approach: By letter with ideas.
Lead time: Two months.
Payment: £120-£140 per article.

The Clockmaker

Edwards Centre
Regent Street
Hinckley
Leicestershire
LE10 0BB
Tel: (0455) 616419   **Fax:** (0455) 616419
Frequency: Bi-monthly
Circulation: 3,000
Contact: Mr C. Deith, Managing Editor
Profile: Magazine for those interested in the workings and construction of mechanical and electro-mechanical clocks.
Requirements: 2
Constructional articles with plans and photographs. Also articles on tools, methods, repair and renovation of clocks.
Comments: The style is technical, so articles must be well-researched.
Approach: Write with synopsis and illustrations.
Lead time: Three months.
Payment: Up to £45 per page.

Clothes Show Magazine

101 Bayham Street
London
NW1 0AG
Tel: 071-331 8000   **Fax:** 071-331 8001
Frequency: Monthly
Circulation: 201,000
Contact: Karen McCartney, Editor

1/News **2**/Features **3**/Fiction **4**/Letters **5**/Fillers
6/B&W Photos **7**/Colour Photos **8**/Reviews

Profile: A fashion and beauty magazine covering clothes, make-up and style. The average age of the readership is 24.

Requirements: 2 5 7
Features on any subject related to fashion and beauty. Length 800-1000 words.

Comments: A lot of the magazine's content is contributed by freelances, so there is a good chance of success.

Approach: By letter.

Lead time: Three months.

Payment: Negotiable.

Club Mirror

29-31 Lower Coombe Street
Croydon
Surrey
CR9 1LX

Tel: 081-681 2099   **Fax:** 081-680 8828

Frequency: Monthly

Circulation: 15,673

Contact: Lewis Eckett, Editor

Profile: A trade publication for owners and managers of clubs throughout the UK.

Requirements: 1 2
News and features relating to products, legal issues and financial matters affecting club management. Also general advice and information on improving efficiency in clubs.

Comments: Writers should have an understanding of the particular isssues affecting the running of clubs.

Approach: In writing with ideas.

Lead time: Six weeks.

Payment: By arrangement.

Coarse Fisherman

67 Tyrrell Street
Leicester
LE3 5SB

Tel: (0533) 511277   **Fax:** (0533) 511335

Frequency: Monthly

Circulation: 27,000

Contact: Simon Roff, Editor

Profile: News, information and equipment reviews for coarse fishermen.

Requirements: 2 6 7
Informative features covering subjects such as baiting techniques, fishing trips, locations and tips on catching particular kinds of fish. Length 1000 to 2500 words.

Comments: The seasonal nature of the sport should be remembered, with topical features being submitted in good time.

Approach: Telephone with ideas.

Lead time: Two months.

Payment: Up to £150.

Coarse Fishing Today

EMAP Pursuit Publishing Ltd
Bretton Court
Bretton Centre
Peterborough
PE3 8DZ

Tel: (0733) 266222   **Fax:** (0733) 265515

Frequency: Bi-monthly

Circulation: 26,164

Contact: Peter Maskell, Editor

Profile: Aimed at the pleasure angler who specialises in larger fish. Includes technical information, tips and instruction for serious fishermen.

1/News **2**/Features **3**/Fiction **4**/Letters **5**/Fillers
6/B&W Photos **7**/Colour Photos **8**/Reviews

Requirements: 2 7
Instructional 'how-to' features with colour photographs, or examples of a good day's fishing. Length 1200 to 2500 words.
Comments: Prefers features to be at the shorter end of the scale.
Approach: Submit complete manuscript.
Lead time: Two months.
Payment: Approaching NUJ rates.

Coin News

105 High Street
Honiton
Devon
EX14 8PE

Tel: (0404) 45414   **Fax:** (0404) 45313

Frequency: Monthly

Circulation: 8000

Contact: John Mussell, Editor
Profile: A magazine for the collector, enthusiast and dealer, covering a wide range of issues relating to coins.
Requirements: 2 5
Accurate, well-researched articles on any aspect of coin collecting or dealing.
Comments: Over half of the content is contributed by freelance writers. Although a lot of material is received, the editor welcomes original submissions.
Approach: By letter or telephone.
Lead time: Two months.
Payment: Up to £40.

The Collector

Barrington Publications
54 Uxbridge Road
London
W12 8LP

Tel: 081-740 7020   **Fax:** 081-740 7020

Frequency: Monthly

Circulation: 18,500

Contact: Paul Hooper, Editor
Profile: Distributed free of charge through antique shops, salerooms, galleries and hotels.
Requirements: 2
Welcomes contributions on any aspect of collecting from writers with a good knowledge of their chosen subject. Length around 1000 words.
Comments: Study the magazine before submitting copy.
Approach: In writing with ideas.
Lead time: Six weeks.
Payment: Negotiable.

Collectors Gazette

200 Nuncargate Road
Kirkby-in-Ashfield
Nottinghamshire
NG17 9AG

Tel: (0623) 752080   **Fax:** (0623) 720443

Frequency: 10xYear

Circulation: 23,000

Contact: Martin Weiss
Profile: A tabloid-style publication that focuses on news about all aspects of collecting. The emphasis is on collecting model cars and trains.
Requirements: 2 5
News and features on auctions, shows and swapmeets, plus previews and reviews of events.

1/News **2**/Features **3**/Fiction **4**/Letters **5**/Fillers
6/B&W Photos **7**/Colour Photos **8**/Reviews

Comments: Material should be topical and accurate.
Approach: By letter.
Lead time: Two months.
Payment: Negotiable.

Command

58 Theobald's Road
London
WC1X 8SF

Tel: 071-405 4874   **Fax:** 071-831 0667

Frequency: Quarterly

Circulation: 9000

Contact: S. Catherwood, Publisher
Profile: An upmarket magazine for officers and senior NCOs in the armed forces.
Requirements: 2 6 7
Thoughtful, well-informed pieces on anything to do with warfare and life in the services. Length 750 to 3000 words. Nothing too academic. Articles should grab the attention of the browser.
Comments: Spreads often include side-bars of relevant information. Photos are often useful.
Approach: Letter preferred.
Lead time: Six weeks.
Payment: £100 per thousand words.

Commercial Motor

Quadrant House
The Quadrant
Sutton
Surrey
SM2 5AS

Tel: 081-652 3302   **Fax:** 081-652 8969

Frequency: Weekly

Circulation: 28,500

Contact: Brian Weatherley, Editor

Profile: A trade publication for those concerned with road transport on a professional basis.
Requirements: 2 6 7
Feature articles on technical subjects and other matters relating to commercial road transport.
Comments: Photos to accompany features are always welcome.
Approach: In writing with ideas.
Lead time: Weekly.
Payment: Negotiable.

Commodore Format

Future Publishing
30 Monmouth Street
Bath
BA1 2BW

Tel: (0225) 442244   **Fax:** (0225) 446019

Frequency: Monthly

Circulation: 44,442

Contact: Trenton Webb, Editor
Profile: A specialist title for users and enthusiasts of Commodore computers.
Requirements: 2
Articles relating to Commodore software, products and accessories. Also reviews of games and new releases.
Comments: Contributors should be familiar with the style of the magazine.
Approach: In writing.
Lead time: Two months.
Payment: Negotiable.

1/News **2**/Features **3**/Fiction **4**/Letters **5**/Fillers
6/B&W Photos **7**/Colour Photos **8**/Reviews

Communications International

EMAP Publications
33-39 Bowling Green Lane
London
EC1R 0DA

Tel: 071-837 1212   **Fax:** 071-278 6125

Frequency: Monthly

Circulation: 26,205

Contact: Ian Scales

Profile: For those professionally involved in the field of electronic communications. Covers telecommunications, plus data and satellite links. The largest magazine of its type outside the US.

Requirements: 1 2 7 8
Contributions which identify changes in technology and applications. Also company profiles, strategic issues and overseas reports. Length 600 to 2500 words.

Comments: Has a fairly technical content, but also includes marketing and political matters.

Approach: By telephone or letter.

Lead time: Four weeks.

Payment: £180 per thousand words.

Communications News

127a Oatlands Drive
Weybridge
Surrey
KT13 9LB

Tel: (0932) 820100   **Fax:** (0932) 821665

Frequency: Monthly

Circulation: 23,000

Contact: Steve Hannington, Editor

Profile: A tabloid-style, news-driven magazine, read by voice and data communications managers in medium to large companies.

Requirements: 1 2 6 7
Case studies, application stories, news of technical developments and any other topical material.

Comments: The editor is always willing to listen to ideas.

Approach: By telephone.

Lead time: Six weeks.

Payment: £150 per thousand words.

Community Care

14th Floor
Quadrant House
The Quadrant
Sutton
Surrey
SM2 5AS

Tel: 081-652 4886   **Fax:** 081-652 4739

Frequency: Weekly

Circulation: 33,000

Contact: Jane King, Deputy Editor

Profile: Read by social workers and policy makers. Provides up-to-date news, views and features.

Requirements: 1 2 6 7
Articles on legislation, training, practice, child protection and social policies. Length 900 to 1400 words.

Comments: Guidelines for contributors are available on request.

Approach: By telephone.

Lead time: Ten days.

Payment: Up to £125 per thousand words.

Community Outlook

4 Little Essex Street
London
WC2R 3LF

Tel: 071-379 0970   **Fax:** 071-497 2664

1/News 2/Features 3/Fiction 4/Letters 5/Fillers
6/B&W Photos 7/Colour Photos 8/Reviews

Frequency: 11xYear

Circulation: 17,500

Contact: Sue Smith, Editor

Profile: Promotes discussion between district nurses, health visitors and community nursing specialists. Includes news, letters, skills updates and reviews.

Requirements: 1 2

Articles from writers with knowledge of nursing, medicine, social work etc. All material should be based on hard facts. Length up to 1500 words.

Comments: As specific guidelines need to be given, always contact the editor first.

Approach: By letter or telephone.

Lead time: Two months.

Payment: According to the experience of the writer.

Company

National Magazine House
72 Broadwick Street
London
W1V 2BP

Tel: 071-439 5000   **Fax:** 071-439 5117

Frequency: Monthly

Circulation: 220,972

Contact: Tara Barker, Deputy Editor

Profile: An upmarket glossy magazine for career women in their 20s. A typical reader would be a graduate, single, with her own flat.

Requirements: 2 4

Emotional features, together with news and stories on topical issues. Length 1500 to 2000 words.

Comments: Features on health and beauty are not required.

Approach: By telephone initially.

Lead time: Two months.

Payment: £150 per thousand words.

Company Car

Queensway House
Queensway
Redhill
Surrey
RH1 1QS

Tel: (0737) 768611   **Fax:** (0737) 760564

Frequency: Monthly

Circulation: 20,759

Contact: Curtis Hutchinson, Editor

Profile: Trade magazine aimed at car fleet operators. Covers latest developments in the industry and reviews cars aimed at this sector.

Requirements: 2

Feature ideas on anything relating to the acquisition, running and disposal of car fleets. Length 1000 words.

Comments: Interested in original ideas which are not necessarily related to the magazine's features list.

Approach: By telephone, followed by faxed synopsis.

Lead time: Six weeks.

Payment: £120 per thousand words.

Company Clothing

578 Kingston Road
Raynes Park
London
SW20 8DR

Tel: 081-540 8381   **Fax:** 081-540 8388

Frequency: Monthly

Circulation: 11,000

Contact: The Editor

1/News **2**/Features **3**/Fiction **4**/Letters **5**/Fillers
6/B&W Photos **7**/Colour Photos **8**/Reviews

Profile: Britain's only magazine for the corporate clothing trade, covering business uniforms and other items of company clothing.
Requirements: 1 2
News and features relating to issues and developments within the industry.
Comments: Always contact the magazine before submitting articles.
Approach: By letter.
Lead time: Two months.
Payment: Negotiable.

Company Secretary's Review

Tolley House
2 Addiscombe Road
Croydon
Surrey
CR9 5AF

Tel: 081-686 9141   **Fax:** 081-686 3155

Frequency: Fortnightly

Circulation: 6000

Contact: Alexandra Evans, Editor
Profile: A technical, legal and accounting newsletter. Updates company secretaries on all aspects of their responsibilities.
Requirements: 2
Will consider relevant precisely-directed articles on business or legal issues. Length 1500 to 1700 words.
Comments: Only topical material from knowledgeable contributors will be considered.
Approach: By telephone.
Lead time: Four weeks.
Payment: £85 per thousand words published. For commissioned articles only.

Compass Sport

37 Sandycombe Road
Twickenham
TW1 2LR

Tel: 081-892 9429   **Fax:** 081-892 9429

Frequency: Bi-monthly

Circulation: 5500

Contact: Ned Paul
Profile: An orienteering magazine, read by people in outdoor centres, schools, youth groups and service personnel. For those who enjoy active outdoor pursuits.
Requirements: 1 2
Feature articles on orienteering, mapping and related outdoor activities. Length 800 to 1000 words. Also news of fixtures and results, etc.
Comments: Much of the unsolicited material received is poorly written, so contributions from competent freelances are welcome.
Approach: In writing with ideas.
Lead time: Three months.
Payment: Negotiable.

Computer & Video Games

Priory Court
30-32 Farringdon Lane
London
EC1R 3AU

Tel: 071-972 6700   **Fax:** 071-972 6703

Frequency: Monthly

Circulation: 106,000

Contact: Garth Sumpter, Editor
Profile: A computer games review magazine which looks at new releases and developments in the market.

1/News **2**/Features **3**/Fiction **4**/Letters **5**/Fillers
6/B&W Photos **7**/Colour Photos **8**/Reviews

Requirements: 1 2 5 7
Reviews of games in the magazine's house style, including screen-grabs. Also games-related features, news and off-beat humorous articles. Length 600 words and above.

Comments: Good photography is an asset, as is knowledge of the games market.

Approach: By letter with ideas.

Lead time: Four weeks.

Payment: From £60 per thousand words.

Computer Shopper

19 Bolsover Street
London
W1P 7HJ

Tel: 071-323 9113   **Fax:** 071-436 2594

Frequency: Monthly

Circulation: 127,339

Contact: Diane Charlton, Editor

Profile: A magazine for those who buy computers and computing accessories direct. A multi-format publication with broad coverage of computing products.

Requirements: 2 7
Articles on choosing, buying and using computers. Length varies, but is usually above 1000 words.

Comments: More likely to take articles from writers who can demonstrate a good understanding of specialist areas.

Approach: By letter.

Lead time: Two months.

Payment: £120-£140 per thousand words.

Computer Weekly

Quadrant House
The Quadrant
Sutton
Surrey
SM2 5AS

Tel: 081-652 3122   **Fax:** 081-652 8979

Frequency: Weekly

Circulation: 113,000

Contact: Lindsay Nicolle, Features Editor

Profile: Read by IT managers, programmers and computing sales and marketing staff. Aimed at management-level professionals who are competent in their own field.

Requirements: 1 2 7 8
News and features on subjects of interest to computer users, rather than manufacturers. Angle copy towards the ideal reader, who is an IT manager in Croydon. Also book reviews of up to 500 words.

Comments: The emphasis is on the business significance, rather than the technical detail. Product reviews are not required.

Approach: By telephone.

Lead time: Six weeks.

Payment: £150 to £250 for a 1400-word article.

Computing

32-34 Broadwick Street
London
W1A 2HG

Tel: 071-439 4242   **Fax:** 071-437 3516

Frequency: Weekly

Circulation: 116,000

Contact: Helen Beckett, Features Editor

1/News **2**/Features **3**/Fiction **4**/Letters **5**/Fillers
6/B&W Photos **7**/Colour Photos **8**/Reviews

Profile: Read by managers and professionals in the computer industry. A glossy newspaper that concentrates on business issues in computing.

Requirements: 2 7

Articles on subjects relating to corporate computing. Covers everything from PCs to mainframes, but the emphasis is on larger installations.

Comments: Features must have business significance. Opinion pieces are not welcome.

Approach: By letter.

Lead time: Four weeks.

Payment: £150 per thousand words.

Construction Weekly

30 Calderwood Street
London
SE18 6QH

Tel: 081-855 7777   **Fax:** 081-854 8058

Frequency: Weekly

Circulation: 30,281

Contact: Richard Northcote, Editor

Profile: A controlled circulation publication for civil engineers, contractors and manufacturers of plant and equipment. Length 1000 to 2000 words.

Requirements: 2 7

Detailed technical articles and analysis of issues of concern to those in the construction industry. Length 1000 to 2000 words.

Comments: Charts, diagrams and illustrations to accompany features are appreciated where appropriate.

Approach: By letter with ideas.

Lead time: Two months.

Payment: By arrangement.

Continental Modeller

Underleys
Beer
Seaton
Devon
EX12 3NA

Tel: (0297) 20580   **Fax:** (0297) 20229

Frequency: Monthly

Circulation: 15,000

Contact: Andrew Taylor, Editor

Profile: Enthusiasts' magazine covering the construction and operation of continental railway models.

Requirements: 2 5

Articles on subjects related to modelling continental railways. These include planning and historical features, scale drawings and trade reports.

Comments: The emphasis is on the practical aspects of modelling.

Approach: By letter.

Lead time: Six weeks.

Payment: Negotiable.

Convenience Store

William Reed
Broadfield Park
Crawley
West Sussex
RH11 9RT

Tel: (0293) 613400   **Fax:** (0293) 613206

Frequency: Fortnightly

Circulation: 50,000

Contact: Tony Hurren, Editor

Profile: A trade magazine for owners and managers of convenience stores. Covers grocery, confectionery, news-agency, tobacco and off-licensed trade.

1/News **2**/Features **3**/Fiction **4**/Letters **5**/Fillers
6/B&W Photos **7**/Colour Photos **8**/Reviews

Requirements: 1 2

News and features on developments within the retail sector. Profiles of stores and interviews with prominent personalities in the trade.

Comments: Aimed at the independent sector of the trade, rather than the national grocery chains.

Approach: By letter

Lead time: Three weeks.

Payment: Approximately NUJ rates.

Convivium

The Neuadd
Rhayader
Radnorshire
LD6 5HH

Tel: (0597) 810227   **Fax:** (0597) 811386

Frequency: Quarterly

Circulation: 5000

Contact: David Wheeler, Editor

Profile: The Journal of Good Eating, covering everything from growing of vegetables to finished meals.

Requirements: 1 2 8

Original ideas relating to the food industry or the preparation of food and drink. The magazine is not vegetarian, but there should be no emphasis on red meat. Length usually 1500 to 5000 words. Also book reviews.

Comments: Manuscripts should be complete with references and acknowledgements where necessary.

Approach: In writing, with synopsis or complete manuscript.

Lead time: Three months.

Payment: By arrangement.

Cornish Life

45 Queen Street
Exeter
Devon
EX4 3SR

Tel: (0392) 216766   **Fax:** (0392) 71050

Frequency: Monthly

Circulation: 4500

Contact: Neville Hutchinson, Editor

Profile: A county magazine covering matters relating to life in Cornwall. Subjects range from flora and fauna to business and the environment.

Requirements: 1 2 5 6 7

News and features on antiques, finance, fashion, food, travel, property, etc. Length up to 1500 words.

Comments: Features accompanied by photographs stand a better chance of acceptance.

Approach: By letter or telephone.

Lead time: Two months.

Payment: £20 per thousand words.

Corporate Image

3 Percy Street
London
W1P 9FA

Tel: 071-436 1673   **Fax:** 071-436 1675

Frequency: 10xYear

Circulation: 10,000

Contact: Paul Bond, Editor

Profile: A stylish magazine for communications and marketing professionals in UK corporations.

Requirements: 1 2 6 7 8

News and features on subjects such as corporate publishing, video and presentations. Also reviews of new products relevant to the readership.

1/News **2**/Features **3**/Fiction **4**/Letters **5**/Fillers
6/B&W Photos **7**/Colour Photos **8**/Reviews

Comments: Runs combined issues for July/August and December/January.
Approach: By letter or fax.
Lead time: Two months.
Payment: Negotiable.

Cosmopolitan

National Magazine House
72 Broadwick Street
London
W1V 2BP

Tel: 071-439 5000   **Fax:** 071-439 5016

Frequency: Monthly

Circulation: 472,480

Contact: Vanessa Raphaely, Features Editor
Profile: A women's magazine that couples emotional issues with hard-hitting news reports, fashion and beauty.
Requirements: 1 2 3 5
Particularly interested in relationship features, which are 'the heartland of Cosmo'. Length 1500 to 2000 words. Also high-quality short stories for today's modern woman.
Comments: Receives a lot of submissions, but wants to attract very good writers.
Approach: By letter with ideas.
Lead time: Three months.
Payment: £250 per thousand words.

Cotswold Life

West One House
23 St George's Road
Cheltenham
Gloucestershire
GL50 3DT
Tel: (0242) 226367   **Fax:** (0242) 222665

Frequency: Monthly
Circulation: 10,000
Contact: John Drinkwater, Editor
Profile: For the top end of the market, aiming to reflect the essence of life in the Cotswolds. Seeks to entertain and inform with well-written articles.
Requirements: 1 2 6 7 8
Interesting material on the heritage, culture and distinction of the Cotswolds. Also articles on local personalities and villages. Length 500 to 1000 words.
Comments: Relies on receiving interesting stories from freelances, so has an open cheque book for good writers.
Approach: Send complete manuscript.
Lead time: Four weeks.
Payment: Up to £50.

Country

Hill Crest Mews
London Road
Baldock
Hertfordshire
SG7 6MD

Tel: (0462) 490206   **Fax:** (0462) 893565

Frequency: Monthly

Circulation: 25,000

Contact: Tony Bush
Profile: A glossy magazine produced for the Country Gentleman's Association. The readership is both male and female, affluent and usually lives in the country.
Requirements: 2 6 7
Accurate features on rural subjects such as historic houses and gardens, use of land and profiles with country personalities. Length up to 1000 words. Also shorter articles on matters of unusual interest.

1/News **2**/Features **3**/Fiction **4**/Letters **5**/Fillers
6/B&W Photos **7**/Colour Photos **8**/Reviews

Comments: Material must be thoroughly researched and correct in every detail.
Approach: Submit complete manuscript.
Lead time: Two months.
Payment: Negotiable but good.

Country Homes & Interiors

IPC Magazines
King's Reach Tower
Stamford Street
London
SE1 9LS

Tel: 071-261 6433   **Fax:** 071-261 6895

Frequency: Monthly

Circulation: 88,100

Contact: Victoria Hinton, Features Editor
Profile: An upmarket magazine about homes in the country and the merchandise associated with them.
Requirements: 2 7 8
Features on the homes of celebrities or on country lifestyle. Length up to 1500 words.
Comments: Likes writers who can supply photographs, or who can team up with a photographer to offer a 'package deal'.
Approach: By letter with ideas.
Lead time: Three months.
Payment: £150 per thousand words.

Country Life

IPC Magazines
King's Reach Tower
Stamford Street
London
SE1 9LS

Tel: 071-261 7058   **Fax:** 071-261 5139

Frequency: Weekly
Circulation: 42,500
Contact: Clive Aslet, Editor
Profile: A magazine for affluent country dwellers, concerned with British country life, social history, fine art, agriculture and gardening.
Requirements: 1 2 5 7
News and topical features on architecture, the environment, rural issues, art and gardening. Length 1200 to 2500 words.
Comments: Contributors know their subject and write with authority.
Approach: Send ideas and cuttings of previous work.
Lead time: Two weeks.
Payment: £200 to £250.

Country Living

National Magazine House
72 Broadwick Street
London
W1V 2BP

Tel: 071-439 5000   **Fax:** 071-439 5093

Frequency: Monthly

Circulation: 180,000

Contact: Francine Lawrence, Editor
Profile: A large, glossy magazine covering not just life in the country, but also other subjects of interest to the readership.
Requirements: 2 5
Articles on famous country homes, traditional crafts, country food, holiday breaks, etc.
Comments: Uses a good percentage of freelance material.
Approach: By letter.
Lead time: Three months.
Payment: £250 per thousand words.

1/News **2**/Features **3**/Fiction **4**/Letters **5**/Fillers
6/B&W Photos **7**/Colour Photos **8**/Reviews

Country Music People

225a Lewisham Way
London
SE4 1UY

Tel: 081-692 1106   **Fax:** 081-469 3091

Frequency: Monthly

Circulation: 30,000

Contact: Craig Baguley

Profile: Magazine devoted to American country music in all its forms.

Requirements: 2 6 7
Interviews with artists or composers, plus general articles about the music itself.

Comments: Concert reviews are not required.

Approach: By letter.

Lead time: Two months.

Payment: Negotiable.

Country Quest

PO Box 658
Mold
Clwyd
CH7 1FB

Tel: (0352) 700022   **Fax:** (0352) 752180

Frequency: Monthly

Circulation: 7490

Contact: Joe Kelly, Editor

Profile: For people living in Wales and the border counties. Covers matters of historical interest, natural history and general regional matters.

Requirements: 1 2
Features on subjects relating to the region, such as customs, traditions, towns and villages. Length 750 to 1,400 words.

Comments: Many of the readers are those who now live away from the area but wish to keep in touch.

Approach: In writing.

Lead time: Three months.

Payment: Negotiable.

Country Walking

EMAP Pursuit Publishing Ltd
Bretton Court
Bretton Centre
Peterborough
PE3 8DZ

Tel: (0733) 264666   **Fax:** (0733) 265515

Frequency: Monthly

Circulation: 36,884

Contact: Samantha Williams

Profile: A guide to walks around Britain and, to a lesser extent, Europe. Also countryside news and product reviews.

Requirements: 2 7
Articles on interesting walks and walking experiences. All material should be written with genuine feeling from personal experience. Length up to 1000 words.

Comments: High-quality photographs of landscapes, wildlife, walking scenes and places of historical interest are also wanted.

Approach: By telephone with initial idea.

Lead time: Two months.

Payment: Up to £100 per article.

The Countryman

Sheep Street
Burford
Oxon
OX18 4LH

Tel: (0993) 822258   **Fax:** (0993) 822703

1/News **2**/Features **3**/Fiction **4**/Letters **5**/Fillers
6/B&W Photos **7**/Colour Photos **8**/Reviews

Frequency: Bi-monthly

Circulation: 60,000

Contact: Christopher Hall

Profile: A magazine for older readers who either live in the country, or wish that they did.

Requirements: 2 5

Informed articles on country issues, wildlife, craft and rural customs. The magazine does not run material on blood sports or political issues.

Comments: About a third of the content of the material is contributed by freelances, but the bulk of unsolicited submissions are unsuitable.

Approach: In writing, with synopsis or complete manuscript.

Lead time: Three months.

Payment: £40 per thousand words.

Countryside

Countryside Commission
John Dower House
Crescent Place
Cheltenham
Gloucestershire
GL8 8UN

Tel: (0242) 521381   **Fax:** (0242) 584270

Frequency: Bi-monthly

Circulation: 15,000

Contact: Marcia Nash, Editor

Profile: Lively, easy-to-read magazine for a well-informed but general readership.

Requirements: 1 2 7

News and features about the English countryside, covering areas such as landscape, conservation, public access and agriculture.

Comments: All articles are commissioned, so send ideas only in the first instance.

Approach: By letter or fax.

Lead time: Six weeks.

Payment: £100 per thousand words, up to £300 maximum.

Countryweek Hunting

PO Box 4041
London
W9 12H

Tel: 071-266 4558   **Fax:** 071-289 4850

Frequency: Monthly

Circulation: 10,000

Contact: Julie Spencer, Editor

Profile: A specialist magazine covering all subjects relating to the hunting scene.

Requirements: 1 2 5

News, reports of events and features of general interest. Good black & white photographs are also welcome.

Comments: Open to non-specialists who have a good knowledge of the countryside.

Approach: By letter.

Lead time: Two months.

Payment: Variable but good.

The County Forum

18 Nursery Road
Blandford
Dorset
DT11 7EZ

Tel: (0258) 459369   **Fax:** (0258) 459360

Frequency: Fortnightly

Circulation: 16,900

Contact: Ieke van Stokum

Profile: A general news magazine for the area of North Dorset.

1/News **2**/Features **3**/Fiction **4**/Letters **5**/Fillers
6/B&W Photos **7**/Colour Photos **8**/Reviews

Requirements: 1 2
News stories and feature items on topical themes relating to the region. Usually in the range of 50 to 250 words.

Comments: The shorter the piece, the more likely it is to be used.

Approach: By letter.

Lead time: One week.

Payment: Varies.

County Warwickshire & Worcestershire

Post & Mail House
28 Colmore Circus
Queensway
Birmingham
B4 6AX

Tel: 021-212 4141   **Fax:** 021-212 2468

Frequency: Monthly

Circulation: 10,000

Contact: Howard Reynolds, Editor

Profile: A high-quality magazine about country life in the region.

Requirements: 1 2 6 7
Relevant articles on historical buildings, places of interest, local villages and special events.

Comments: Material needs to be based firmly within the counties of Warwickshire and Worcestershire.

Approach: By letter.

Lead time: Three weeks.

Payment: Negotiable.

Crack

Ride Publications
Poundbury Farmhouse
Dorchester
Dorset
DT1 2RT

Tel: (0305) 263662   **Fax:** (0305) 251263

Frequency: Monthly

Circulation: 19,500

Contact: Mark Noble, Editor

Profile: Magazine for skateboard enthusiasts, reflecting the news and activity on the skateboarding scene.

Requirements: 1 2
Articles from experienced writers who are familiar with the subject. Tests, interviews, tips and practical advice.

Comments: A large percentage of the content is contributed by freelances, but writers must know what readers want.

Approach: In writing with ideas or complete manuscript.

Lead time: Six weeks.

Payment: Up to £100 per thousand words.

Crafts

44a Pentonville Road
Islington
London
N1 9BY

Tel: 071-278 7700   **Fax:** 071-837 6891

Frequency: Bi-monthly

Circulation: 14,000

Contact: The Editor

Profile: Concerned with the entire spectrum of applied arts. Publishes work by experts in every craft.

Requirements: 2
Features on art and craft, emphasising high-quality work from skilled craftsmen and women.

Comments: Copy must be detailed, accurate and informative.

Approach: In writing.

Lead time: Three months.

Payment: By arrangement.

1/News **2**/Features **3**/Fiction **4**/Letters **5**/Fillers
6/B&W Photos **7**/Colour Photos **8**/Reviews

Cricket World

Mews House
2A Chelverton Road
Putney
London
SW15 1RH

Tel: 081-788 3230   **Fax:** 081-788 2641

Frequency: Monthly

Circulation: 20,000

Contact: Michael Blumberg, Editor

Profile: Covers cricket from the village green to the test stadium, for a readership that ranges from under 11 to over 50.

Requirements: 1 2 3 5
Features on the culture of cricket, club histories, profiles, humorous pieces, fiction, etc. No more than 1000 words, except by arrangement.

Comments: Overwhelmed with cricket editorial, but always looking for new, analytical and irreverent features.

Approach: By telephone with ideas.

Lead time: Six weeks.

Payment: From £40 for 800 words, £10 minimum for fillers.

The Cricketer International

Third Street
Langton Green
Tunbridge Wells
Kent
TN3 0EN

Tel: (0892) 862551   **Fax:** (0892) 863755

Frequency: Monthly

Circulation: 40,000

Contact: Peter Perchard, Editor

Profile: Covers cricket both nationally and internationally. Includes all aspects of the game from grass-roots level through to test matches.

Requirements: 1 2 3 4 6 7
Anniversary and topical features, statistical articles and profiles of lesser-known players. Also accepts humorous pieces, fiction and information on age-group cricket. Maximum 1000 words.

Comments: Articles are selected on merit, not through personal contacts.

Approach: Send synopsis or complete manuscript.

Lead time: Two months.

Payment: £50 per thousand words.

Crimesearch

Blacker, Ives & Philips
58-62 Holywell Hill
St Albans
Hertfordshire
AL1 1BX

Tel: (0727) 868633   **Fax:** (0727) 862779

Frequency: Monthly

Circulation: Not available

Contact: Andrew Gravette, Editor

Profile: A magazine for anyone interested in detecting and preventing crime.

Requirements: 2 5
Articles about crime prevention in areas such as antiques, property, computers and cars. Length between 600 and 750 words.

Comments: This is not a 'true detective' magazine.

Approach: Send a synopsis with examples of previous work.

Lead time: Two months.

Payment: £100-£150 per page.

1/News **2**/Features **3**/Fiction **4**/Letters **5**/Fillers
6/B&W Photos **7**/Colour Photos **8**/Reviews

CTN

Maclaren House
19 Scarbrook Road
Croydon
CR9 1QH

Tel: 081-688 7788   **Fax:** 081-688 9657

Frequency: Weekly

Circulation: 25,832

Contact: Anne Baxter, Editor

Profile: A trade publication for confectioners, newsagents and tobacconists.

Requirements: 1 2
News items on topics of concern to the owners and managers of independent retail outlets. Also concise articles and case studies. Length 600 to 800 words.

Comments: All material must be directly relevant to the retailer.

Approach: In writing with ideas.

Lead time: Two weeks.

Payment: £65 per thousand words.

Custom Bike

Bushfield House
Orton Centre
Peterborough
PE2 5UW

Tel: (0733) 237111

Frequency: Quarterly

Contact: Mark Graham

Profile: For people of all ages interested in custom motorcycles. Provides advice and information in a practical manner.

Requirements: 2 5
'How-to' articles, reviews of events, technical advice and tips. Writers should aim to capture the whole biking ethos in their work. Length 1200 to 2000 words.

Comments: The magazine also caters for those who aspire to owning a custom motorbike.

Approach: Send a synopsis or a complete manuscript.

Lead time: Three months.

Payment: £100 per thousand words.

Custom Car

Link House
Dingwall Avenue
Croydon
CR9 2TA

Tel: 081-686 2599   **Fax:** 081-781 6042

Frequency: Monthly

Circulation: 33,000

Contact: Keith Seume, Editor

Profile: For people working on their own custom cars.

Requirements: 1 2
Features about designing, building and running custom cars. Profiles of designers in places such as the USA and news of drag racing events. Length up to 1000 words.

Comments: Study the magazine before submitting ideas.

Approach: By telephone or letter.

Lead time: Two months.

Payment: Negotiable.

Cycle Touring and Campaigning

69 Meadrow
Godalming
Surrey
GU7 3HS

Tel: (0483) 417217   **Fax:** (0483) 426994

Frequency: Bi-monthly

Circulation: 33,500

Contact: Tim Hughes, Editor

Profile: The official journal of the Cyclists' Touring Club. Promotes cycling for both leisure and other purposes, and campaigns on issues that concern the cycling community.

Requirements: 1 2 6 7 8
Touring features and technical articles, together with reviews and information about campaigns for the rights and safety of cyclists.

Comments: Guidelines for contributors are available on request.

Approach: By letter with ideas.

Lead time: Six weeks.

Payment: £60 per page.

Cycling Plus

Future Publishing
30 Monmouth Street
Bath
BA1 2BW

Tel: (0225) 442244   **Fax:** (0225) 484896

Frequency: Monthly

Circulation: 33,089

Contact: Andy Ide

Profile: For cyclists aged between 25 and 45 who are keen but not fanatical.

Requirements: 1 2 5
Articles on all kinds of bikes, from racers to BMX. Contributors must be able to write with authority about the subject.

Comments: Although a lot of material is written in house, strong original ideas are likely to be taken up.

Approach: By letter.

Lead time: Six weeks.

Payment: Around £100 per thousand words.

Cycling Weekly

IPC Magazines
King's Reach Tower
Stamford Street
London
SE1 9LS

Tel: 071-261 5588   **Fax:** 071-261 5758

Frequency: Weekly

Circulation: 39,000

Contact: Andrew Sutcliffe, Editor

Profile: The oldest and best-established cycling magazine in the UK. Covers the whole spectrum of cycling, but focuses on sport.

Requirements: 1 2 5 7 8
Anything interesting or unusual, especially news or features connected with cycle racing. Length 1000 to 2000 words.

Comments: Since being re-launched, the magazine has become more dynamic in style and content.

Approach: By letter or fax with ideas.

Lead time: Ten days.

Payment: £55-£75 per thousand words.

Cycling World

Andrew House
2a Granville Road
Sidcup
Kent
DA14 4BN

Tel: 081-302 6150   **Fax:** 081-300 2315

Frequency: Monthly

Circulation: 17,000

Contact: Robert Griffiths, Editor

1/News 2/Features 3/Fiction 4/Letters 5/Fillers
6/B&W Photos 7/Colour Photos 8/Reviews

Profile: A specialist title for cycling
   enthusiasts, providing news,
   information and advice.
Requirements: 1 2
   News and features relating to all
   aspects of cycling. Material should
   be lively, interesting and
   entertaining.
Comments: Study the style of the
   magazine before contributing.
Approach: In writing.
Lead time: Two months.
Payment: Negotiable.

D

Dalesman

Stable Courtyard
Broughton Hall
Skipton
N. Yorks
BD23 3AE

Tel: (0756) 701381 **Fax:** (0756) 701326
Frequency: Monthly
Circulation: 57,034
Contact: David Joy, Editor
Profile: Regional magazine covering matters of interest to everyone in Yorkshire. The emphasis is on people rather than places.
Requirements: 2 7 8
Pieces on subjects such as local events, regional humour, personalities and history. Length around 1000 words.
Comments: Despite the title, the magazine covers the whole of Yorkshire rather than just the Dales.
Approach: By letter with ideas.
Lead time: Two months.
Payment: Negotiable.

Dance & Dancers

214 Panther House
38 Mount Pleasant
London
WC1X 0AP

Tel: 071-837 2711 **Fax:** 071-837 2711
Frequency: Monthly
Circulation: 5000
Contact: John Percival, Editor
Profile: A specialist title covering both classical and modern dancing.
Requirements: 2 6 7 8
Articles on all aspects of dance, profiles of dancers, etc. Also reviews of interest to the readership.
Comments: Colour photography is used for the cover only.
Approach: In writing with ideas.
Lead time: Two months.
Payment: Negotiable.

Dance Gazette

36 Battersea Square
London
SW11 3RA

Tel: 071-223 0091 **Fax:** 071-924 3129
Frequency: 3xYear
Circulation: 16,000
Contact: Janet Gill, Editor
Profile: A general dance magazine distributed internationally. Read by members of the Royal Academy of Dancing.
Requirements: 2 6 7
Profiles of dance companies, technical articles and features on historical dance. Length 1500 to 1800 words.

1/News 2/Features 3/Fiction 4/Letters 5/Fillers
6/B&W Photos 7/Colour Photos 8/Reviews

Comments: News items are not accepted.
Approach: By telephone.
Lead time: Two months.
Payment: £125 per thousand words.

Dancing Times

Clerkenwell House
45-47 Clerkenwell Green
London
EC1R 0BE

Tel: 071-250 3006   **Fax:** 071-253 6679

Frequency: Monthly

Circulation: 12,000

Contact: Mary Clarke, Editor
Profile: Covers all aspects of ballet and stage dancing.
Requirements: 2 6 7
Articles on the technicalities of dance, plus historical and critical pieces. Also general articles on dance-related subjects.
Comments: If photographs are submitted, these should ideally be action shots.
Approach: In writing with ideas.
Lead time: Two months.
Payment: By arrangement.

Darts Player

241 High Street
Beckenham
Kent
BR3 1BN

Tel: 081-650 6580   **Fax:** 081-650 2534

Frequency: Annual

Circulation: 26,000

Contact: Tony Wood, Editor
Profile: For darts players of all levels, covering various aspects of the game.

Requirements: 2 7
Articles about any subject connected with darts, from player profiles to developments within the game.
Comments: Study the publication before contributing.
Approach: By telephone or fax.
Lead time: Two weeks.
Payment: £55 per thousand words.

Darts World

241 High Street
Beckenham
Kent
BR3 1BN

Tel: 081-650 6580   **Fax:** 081-650 2534

Frequency: Monthly

Circulation: 31,500

Contact: Tony Wood, Editor
Profile: Newsy, informative magazine for darts players both in the UK and worldwide.
Requirements: 1 2 6 7
News and features of interest to players, officials and manufacturers.
Comments: Articles must impart some knowledge of the subject. Always looking for new ideas and suggestions.
Approach: Initially by telephone or fax.
Lead time: Three weeks.
Payment: £55 per thousand words.

Data Broadcasting News

M2 Communications Ltd
184 Brookside Avenue
Coventry
CV5 8AD

Tel: (0203) 717417   **Fax:** (0203) 717418

Frequency: Fortnightly

1/News **2**/Features **3**/Fiction **4**/Letters **5**/Fillers
6/B&W Photos **7**/Colour Photos **8**/Reviews

Circulation: Not available

Contact: Darren Ingram, Editor

Profile: Provides a worldwide perspective on satellite and terrestrial data broadcasting.

Requirements: 1 2 5
News and features covering the whole world of broadcast data. Length varies.

Comments: Expects to accept a growing number of freelance contributions.

Approach: By fax or letter.

Lead time: Fortnightly.

Payment: According to the quality of the idea.

Datacom

EMAP Publications
33-39 Bowling Green Lane
London
EC1R 0DA

Tel: 071-837 1212   **Fax:** 071-278 4003

Frequency: Monthly

Circulation: 17,970

Contact: Jim Hayes, Editor

Profile: A professional magazine covering local area networking and distributed computing.

Requirements: 1 2 7 8
Case studies, technical articles and general features covering subjects relating to data communications. Maximum 3000 words.

Comments: Writers should have an understanding of the subject.

Approach: In writing.

Lead time: Six weeks.

Payment: £130 per thousand words minimum.

Dateline Magazine

23 Abingdon Road
Kensington
London
W8 6AL

Tel: 071-938 1011   **Fax:** 071-937 3146

Frequency: Monthly

Circulation: 23,000

Contact: Mr N. Spreckley, Editor

Profile: A contacts magazine for single people. Includes editorial relevant to those who want to find friendship or a partner.

Requirements: 2 5 6
Informative and helpful features for single people, covering dating, single life, the opposite sex and so on. Length around 1000 words.

Comments: Interested in main features which deal with relevant serious topics.

Approach: By telephone with initial ideas.

Lead time: Six weeks.

Payment: From £50 per thousand words.

David Hall's Coarse Fishing Magazine

Stationer's House
17 Bank Street
Rugby
Warwickshire

Tel: (0788) 535218   **Fax:** (0788) 541845

Frequency: Monthly

Circulation: 50,000

Contact: David Hall, Editor

Profile: Aimed at the keen angler. Covers every element of coarse fishing.

1/News 2/Features 3/Fiction 4/Letters 5/Fillers
6/B&W Photos 7/Colour Photos 8/Reviews

Requirements: 2 3 7 8
Features on any element of inland
fishing, from matches and
competitions to big-fish hunting.
Comments: Writers need to be able to
write authoritatively on the subject.
Approach: By telephone in the first
instance.
Lead time: Two months.
Payment: £50.

David Hall's Match Fishing Magazine

Stationer's House
17 Bank Street
Rugby
Warwickshire

Tel: (0788) 535218   **Fax:** (0788) 541845

Frequency: Monthly

Circulation: 20,000

Contact: Roger Mortimer, Editor
Profile: A magazine for the freshwater
competition angler.
Requirements: 2 7 8
Features and reviews covering the
world of match angling on inland
waters.
Comments: Articles must be informed
and well-researched.
Approach: By telephone initially.
Lead time: Two months.
Payment: £50.

Decanter

Priory House
8 Battersea Park Road
London
SW8 4BG

Tel: 071-627 8181   **Fax:** 071-738 8688

Frequency: Monthly

Circulation: 35,000

Contact: David Rowe, Editor
Profile: Deals with fine wines and the
world of wine, from inexpensive
well-produced products to top-class
claret.
Requirements: 2 7 8
Articles which deal with wine on a
serious basis. May include producer
profiles, details of wine-producing
areas, individual wines and tastings.
Length 1500 to 2000 words.
Comments: All ideas are given serious
consideration.
Approach: By telephone with ideas.
Lead time: Three months.
Payment: £150 per thousand words.

Dental Laboratory

Chapel House
Noel Street
Nottingham
NG7 6AS

Tel: (0602) 704321   **Fax:** (0602) 422675

Frequency: Monthly

Circulation: 2000

Contact: William Courtney, Editor
Profile: Magazine for those who run or
work in dental laboratories.
Requirements: 2 5
Articles about products, finance,
employment and management issues
of relevance to those in dental
laboratories.
Comments: Open to original ideas for
articles from knowledgeable writers.
Approach: In writing.
Lead time: Two months.
Payment: Around £50 per thousand
words.

1/News **2**/Features **3**/Fiction **4**/Letters **5**/Fillers
6/B&W Photos **7**/Colour Photos **8**/Reviews

Dental Update

20 Leas Road
Guildford
Surrey
GU1 4QT

Tel: (0483) 304944 **Fax:** (0483) 303191

Frequency: 10xYear

Circulation: 7000

Contact: Ted Porter, Editor

Profile: News and features of general interest to those in the dental profession throughout the UK.

Requirements: 2 7
Articles on subjects relating to clinical matters and practice management, etc.

Comments: Colour photos are only required for cover pictures.

Approach: In writing.

Lead time: Two months.

Payment: £50 per thousand words.

Derbyshire Life & Countryside

Lodge Lane
Derby
DE1 3HE

Tel: (0332) 47087 **Fax:** (0332) 290688

Frequency: Monthly

Circulation: 12,045

Contact: Vivienne Irish, Editor

Profile: A county magazine dealing with social and country matters. Aimed at an AB readership.

Requirements: 1 2 6 7 8
News and features about the country, rural people, interesting places and wildlife. Length 800 to 1000 words.

Comments: All material must relate to Derbyshire and its people.

Approach: Send complete manuscript.

Lead time: Six weeks.

Payment: Negotiable.

Derbyshire Now

Abbots Hill Chambers
Gower Street
Derby
DE1 1SD

Tel: (0332) 204058 **Fax:** (0332) 204008

Frequency: Monthly

Circulation: 13,000

Contact: Jim Fearn, Editor

Profile: A county news magazine with a bright and breezy style.

Requirements: 1 2 7 8
News and features about Derbyshire people who do interesting things. Length around 1500 words.

Comments: Unusual or original ideas have the best chance of success.

Approach: Write with ideas.

Lead time: Four weeks.

Payment: Negotiable.

Descent

Suite 1
Fullers Court
40 Lower Quay Street
Gloucester
GL1 2LW

Tel: (0452) 417554 **Fax:** (0452) 423430

Frequency: Bi-monthly

Circulation: 3450

Contact: Chris Howes, Editor

Profile: Devoted to cavers and caving. Biased towards Britain, but has an international circulation.

Requirements: 1 2 3 4 5 6 8
Informed articles about caving and
historical associations with mining.
Where possible, these should be
accompanied by maps, photos and
surveys. Length 1000 to 1500 words.

Comments: Much of the unsolicited
material received is unsuitable as the
contributors are not familiar with
the magazine and its style.

Approach: By telephone.

Lead time: Four weeks.

Payment: Negotiable.

Design and Technology Teaching

16 Wellesbourne Close
Walton Road
Wellesbourne
CV35 9JB

Tel: (0789) 470007   **Fax:** (0789) 841955

Frequency: 3xYear

Circulation: 3500

Contact: Jane Howden, Editor

Profile: Focuses attention on
developments in design and
technology teaching.

Requirements: 2
Articles on the development of
teaching skills in the areas of art and
design, business studies and
information technology.

Comments: Encourages the
development of technology as a new
subject.

Approach: In writing.

Lead time: Four months.

Payment: Negotiable.

Design Magazine

28 Haymarket
London
SW1Y 4SU

Tel: 071-839 8000   **Fax:** 071-925 2130

Frequency: Monthly

Circulation: 10,500

Contact: Gaynor Williams, Editor

Profile: Aims to help business and
industry to a better understanding of
design and the design process.

Requirements: 1 2 8
Always looking for practical case
studies illustrating the successful use
of design.

Comments: Unsolicited manuscripts
are not accepted.

Approach: By letter with ideas.

Lead time: Two months.

Payment: £180 per thousand words.

Designing

The Design Council
28 Haymarket
London
SW1Y 4SU

Tel: 071-839 8000   **Fax:** 071-925 2130

Frequency: 3xYear

Circulation: 8,500

Contact: Debra Staplehurst, Editor

Profile: A magazine for teachers and
students of art, design and
technology in secondary schools.
Includes features on design-related
topics, school project work, reviews
and news.

Requirements: 1 2 6 7 8
Features on design-related topics of
interest to schools, including design
history, new design developments,
'how-to' articles and reviews.
Maximum 1200 words.

Comments: An understanding of the needs and interests of teachers and students is helpful.
Approach: By telephone with ideas.
Lead time: Three months.
Payment: £110 per thousand words.

Devon Life

34 Burlington Court
Redcliff Mead Lane
Bristol
BS1 6FB

Tel: (0272) 252052   **Fax:** (0272) 252052

Frequency: Monthly

Circulation: 5500

Contact: Neil Pickford, Editor
Profile: A lifestyle magazine for Devon, covering everything from local history to current events.
Requirements: 2 6 7
Articles on property, antiques, boating, fishing, wining, dining and other subjects relevant to Devonians. Length 800 to 1800 words.
Comments: Illustrations or suggestions for illustrations are always useful.
Approach: By telephone.
Lead time: Six weeks.
Payment: £20 per thousand words, plus £5 per photograph.

Diesel Car

4 Wessex Building
Bancombe Road Trading Estate
Somerton
Somerset
TA11 6BS

Tel: (0458) 744447   **Fax:** (0458) 74059

Frequency: Monthly

Circulation: 29,000

Contact: John Kerswill, Editor
Profile: All about owning and driving diesel cars. Also covers other diesel-engined vehicles such as motorcycles.
Requirements: 2 6 7 8
Travel features, car tests, DIY articles and so on. Also material on vintage diesel cars.
Comments: Particularly interested in material which cannot be obtained by staff writers, such as news of diesel events in the USA.
Approach: Telephone in the first instance.
Lead time: Three months.
Payment: Negotiable.

Director

Mountbarrow House
Elizabeth Street
London
SW1W 9RB

Tel: 071-730 6060   **Fax:** 071-235 5627

Frequency: Monthly

Circulation: 40,000

Contact: Stuart Rock, Editor
Profile: A business and management magazine published by the Institute of Directors for its members.
Requirements: 1 2
Company profiles, political discussion, country insights and practical business advice. Maximum 2500 words.
Comments: Looking for contributions that are more interesting than the press material it receives.
Approach: In writing with ideas.
Lead time: Six weeks.
Payment: Negotiable.

1/News **2**/Features **3**/Fiction **4**/Letters **5**/Fillers
6/B&W Photos **7**/Colour Photos **8**/Reviews

Dirt Bike Rider

PO Box 100
Stamford
Lincolnshire
PE9 1XQ

Tel: (0780) 55131   **Fax:** (0780) 57261

Frequency: Monthly

Circulation: 21,000

Contact: Mike Greenough, Editor

Profile: Magazine for those interested in off-road dirt bikes. Covers motorcross, trial, trail and enduro.

Requirements: 1 2 7
Personality features, event coverage, bike tests and fashion features. Length up to 2500 words.

Comments: Does not run any features on pedal-powered mountain biking.

Approach: By letter.

Lead time: Three weeks.

Payment: £100 for 1200 words, maximum £250.

Disability Arts Magazine

10 Woad Lane
Great Coates
Grimsby
DN37 9NH

Tel: (0472) 280031   **Fax:** (0472) 280031

Frequency: Quarterly

Circulation: 1500

Contact: Roland Humphrey

Profile: Covers everything connected with disabled people and the arts. Also aims to provide an outlet for the work of the disabled.

Requirements: 2 3 6 7
Short stories, poetry, articles, mini-epics, and reviews. Maximum length 3000 words.

Comments: Only disabled contributors will be paid.

Approach: By letter.

Lead time: Three months.

Payment: By arrangement, but very competitive.

Disability Now

12 Park Crescent
London
W1N 4EQ

Tel: 071-636 5020   **Fax:** 071-436 4582

Frequency: Monthly

Circulation: 28,000

Contact: Mary Wilkinson, Editor

Profile: A campaigning newspaper for disabled people and their families, carers and other relevant professionals.

Requirements: 2 5 6 7 8
News and features on subjects ranging from fashion, home and gardening to more serious issues concerning the disabled.

Comments: Particularly welcomes contributions from disabled writers.

Approach: By letter to the editor.

Lead time: Six weeks.

Payment: £75 per thousand words.

Diver Magazine

55 High Street
Teddington
Middlesex
TW11 8HA

Tel: 081-943 4288   **Fax:** 081-943 4312

Frequency: Monthly

Circulation: 55,000

Contact: Bernard Eaton, Editor

Profile: Covers all forms of sport and sub-aqua diving. Read mainly by amateur divers.

1/News **2**/Features **3**/Fiction **4**/Letters **5**/Fillers
6/B&W Photos **7**/Colour Photos **8**/Reviews

Requirements: 1 2
 News and features on wrecks,
 salvage archeology, underwater
 photography, marine biology, diving
 holidays and conservation. Length
 2000 words on average.
Comments: Welcomes submissions
 from professionals or good
 amateurs.
Approach: In writing, with a synopsis.
Lead time: Six weeks.
Payment: From £50 per page.

DIY Week

Benn Publications
Sovereign Way
Tonbridge
Kent
TN9 1RW

Tel: (0732) 364422   **Fax:** (0732) 361534

Frequency: Weekly

Circulation: 17,000

Contact: Colin Petty, Editor
Profile: Hard news weekly for the
 retail DIY, hardware, garden and
 housewares trade.
Requirements: 1 5 6 7
 Newsy material that will help
 managers and owners of stores to
 run their businesses more efficiently
 and profitably. Hard news only is
 required, and copy must be written
 tightly. Length 50 to 400 words.
Comments: The editor invites
 freelances to 'flood us with copy'.
 The magazine has been running as a
 fortnightly temporarily during the
 recession.
Approach: By letter, telephone or fax.
Lead time: One week.
Payment: £100 per thousand words
 published.

Doctor

Quadrant House
The Quadrant
Sutton
Surrey
SM2 5AS

Tel: 081-652 8740   **Fax:** 081-652 8701

Frequency: Weekly

Circulation: 38,000

Contact: Helena Sturridge, Editor
Profile: A newspaper for general
 practitioners, which claims to be
 'working for all GPs'.
Requirements: News and features on
 both clinical and political subjects.
 Humorous or light-hearted pieces
 are also welcome.
Comments: Good photographs to
 accompany features are always
 appreciated.
Approach: In writing.
Lead time: Three weeks.
Payment: NUJ rates.

Dogs Monthly

RTC Associates
The Abbey
Skillington
Nr Grantham
Lincolnshire
NG33 5HH

Tel: (0476) 860456   **Fax:** (0476) 861326

Frequency: Monthly

Circulation: Not available

Contact: Di Johnson, Editor
Profile: A specialised magazine aimed
 at owners and breeders of pedigree
 dogs.
Requirements: 2 5
 Articles on the breeding and showing

of pedigree dogs, profiles of breeders and information about specific breeds.
Comments: Study the magazine carefully before submitting material.
Approach: In writing.
Lead time: Two months.
Payment: From £25.

Dogs Today

Pet Subjects
6 Station Parade
Sunningdale
Berks
SL5 0EP

Tel: (0344) 875442   **Fax:** (0344) 875443

Frequency: Bi-monthly

Circulation: 55,000

Contact: Beverley Cuddy
Profile: For anyone who loves dogs. A lighthearted magazine taking a broad look at the world of dog ownership.
Requirements: 1 2 5 6 7
Most likely to accept features of a factual nature, especially if accompanied by good photographs. Also interested in anything unusual. Length up to 800 words, although short pieces up to 400 words are very useful.
Comments: No material on dog shows, or anything which demonstrates dogs being used as objects rather than man's best friend.
Approach: Send complete manuscript.
Lead time: Six weeks.
Payment: Budget limited following a management buy-out, but increasing as the magazine becomes established.

Dolls House & Miniature Scene

EMF Publishing
5 Cissbury Road
Ferring
West Sussex
BN12 6QJ

Tel: (0903) 506626

Frequency: Bi-monthly

Circulation: Not available

Contact: Edward Fancey, Editor
Profile: Covers dolls, dolls' houses and miniatures, with the emphasis on modern products and models.
Requirements: 2 5 8
Articles about designing and making dolls houses, their contents and settings. Also features about collectors, book reviews and reports of events.
Comments: The style of the magazine is friendly and approachable, appealing to newcomers to the hobby as well as enthusiasts.
Approach: By letter.
Lead time: Three months.
Payment: £100 for an 800-word piece.

Dorset County Magazine

Trinity Lane
Wareham
Dorset
BH20 4LN

Tel: (0929) 551264

Frequency: Monthly

Circulation: 8000

Contact: John Newth, Editor
Profile: A magazine covering anything and everything connected with the county of Dorset. Includes both historic material and news of current activities.

Requirements: 1 2 7

Features on the people, the history and the natural history of the county. Also news of events and social occasions. Maximum 1200 words.

Comments: All material must be related in some way to the county of Dorset.

Approach: In writing.

Lead time: Two months.

Payment: Negotiable.

Drapers Record

Maclaren House
19 Scarbrook Road
Croydon
CR9 1QH

Tel: 081-688 7788   **Fax:** 081-686 7224

Frequency: Weekly

Circulation: 14,906

Contact: Sally Bain

Profile: The established trade publication for professionals in the fashion business.

Requirements: 1 2

News of developments within the industry, plus features on issues affecting both large and small fashion retailers.

Comments: Concerned with fashion from the trade and professional point of view only.

Approach: In writing with ideas.

Lead time: Two weeks.

Payment: By arrangement.

Dressage

55-63 Goswell Road
London
EC1V 7EN

Tel: 071-490 3398   **Fax:** 071-490 3394

Frequency: Monthly

Circulation: 12,500

Contact: Jane Kidd

Profile: Covers dressage both in the UK and internationally. Also includes general articles on horse welfare, feeding and breeds.

Requirements: 1 2 5 6 7

Show reports, original articles on dressage and practical information about horse care.

Comments: All material is produced by freelance contributors.

Approach: In writing.

Lead time: One month.

Payment: £125 per thousand words.

Driving Magazine

Safety House
Beddington Farm Road
Croydon
CR0 4XZ

Tel: 081-665 5151   **Fax:** 081-665 5565

Frequency: Bi-monthly

Circulation: 33,000

Contact: Jeni Bergin

Profile: About advanced driving and road safety for the discerning motorist.

Requirements: 2 5 6

Road safety articles, plus humorous photographs of traffic scenes and signs. Maximum length for features is 2000 words.

Comments: Copy about driving or the teaching of driving must be of a technical nature.

Approach: Send complete manuscript.

Lead time: Six weeks.

Payment: £65 per thousand words, plus £10 per photograph.

1/News **2**/Features **3**/Fiction **4**/Letters **5**/Fillers
6/B&W Photos **7**/Colour Photos **8**/Reviews

Durham County

Powdene House
26 Pudding Chare
Newcastle-upon-Tyne
NE1 1UE

Tel: 091-230 3454 **Fax:** 091-232 1710

Frequency: Quarterly

Circulation: 7000

Contact: Stewart Bonney, Editor
Profile: A countryside magazine which carries local news, details of walks, profiles of people and information about places of interest.
Requirements: 2 7
Articles on the history of the county or about its countryside. No news or poetry. Length up to 1000 words maximum.
Comments: Writers should adopt a factual rather than a literary style.
Approach: By letter with ideas.
Lead time: Two months.
Payment: Negotiable.

E

Early Music

3 Park Road
London
NW1 6XN

Tel: 071-724 1707 **Fax:** 071-723 5033

Frequency: Quarterly

Circulation: Not available

Contact: Dr Tess Knighton, Editor

Profile: An academic publication
which covers renaissance, mediaeval
and baroque music. Particular
emphasis on performance practice.

Requirements: 2 8
Articles on the above subjects, music
and book reviews, etc.

Comments: Does not require news
items or concert reviews.

Approach: By letter.

Lead time: Three months.

Payment: Negotiable.

Early Times

2-4 Leigham Court Road
Streatham
London
SW16 2PD

Tel: 081-546 2261 **Fax:** 081-769 6052

Frequency: Weekly

Circulation: 27,000

Contact: Dolly Clew, Editor

Profile: An informative, non-political
newspaper for 8 to 16 year olds,
which aims to be an enjoyable read
as well as a source of news.

Requirements: 1 2 6 7 8
Newsworthy material on subjects
such as the environment, celebrities
and education. Maximum 800
words.

Comments: Copy should be wacky,
fun and informative, never
predictable or dull.

Approach: Send complete manuscript.

Lead time: One week.

Payment: £60 per thousand words.

East Lothian Life

2 Beveridge Row
Belhaven
Dunbar
East Lothian
EH42 1TP

Tel: (0368) 63593 **Fax:** (0368) 63593

Frequency: Quarterly

Circulation: 3000

Contact: Pauline Jaffray, Editor

Profile: A regional publication
covering subjects of interest to
everyone living in East Lothian.

Requirements: 2
Feature articles on life in East
Lothian, local history and places of
interest. Length up to 1000 words.

1/News 2/Features 3/Fiction 4/Letters 5/Fillers
6/B&W Photos 7/Colour Photos 8/Reviews

Comments: All material submitted must have a regional angle.
Approach: In writing.
Lead time: Three months.
Payment: By arrangement.

Echoes

15-16 Newman Street
London
W1P 3HD

Tel: 071-436 4540   **Fax:** 071-436 4573

Frequency: Weekly

Circulation: 26,000

Contact: C. Wells, Editor
Profile: Black music paper covering soul, reggae, jazz, hip-hop and dance music. Includes features, interviews, reviews and competitions.
Requirements: 1 2 6 7 8
Welcomes suggestions for copy, especially interviews and feature articles.
Comments: Always contact the editor before submitting material.
Approach: By telephone or fax.
Lead time: Two weeks.
Payment: £50 per thousand words.

Edinburgh Review

22 George Square
Edinburgh
EH8 9LF

Tel: 031-650 4215   **Fax:** 031-662 0053

Frequency: 2xYear

Circulation: 1500

Contact: Murdo Macdonald, Editor
Profile: Devoted to cultural, literary and philosophical subjects. Covers matters relating both to Scotland and the wider international arena.

Requirements: 2 3
Submissions on philosophy and literature, serious fiction, plus short items on issues of political or cultural significance.
Comments: Unsolicited contributions are welcome.
Approach: Send complete manuscript.
Lead time: Six months.
Payment: Negotiable.

Education

21-27 Lamb's Conduit Street
London
WC1N 3NJ

Tel: 071-242 2548   **Fax:** 071-831 2855

Frequency: Weekly

Circulation: 31,000

Contact: George Low, Editor
Profile: The magazine of education management and policy. Provides a topical view of the world of education.
Requirements: 2 6
Articles of up to 1100 words on educational matters, ranging from the implementation of the National Curriculum to education politics.
Comments: 'News led but features based.'
Approach: By telephone or letter.
Lead time: Two weeks.
Payment: Up to £100 per thousand words.

Education Matters

1 Oaten Hill Place
Canterbury
Kent
CT1 3HJ

Tel: (0227) 452609   **Fax:** (0227) 768587

1/News **2**/Features **3**/Fiction **4**/Letters **5**/Fillers
6/B&W Photos **7**/Colour Photos **8**/Reviews

Frequency: 3xYear

Circulation: 10,000

Contact: Jane Murrell, Editor

Profile: A newsy magazine for heads, deputy heads and heads of department in South-East schools. Keeps them abreast of new ideas and local authority policy decisions.

Requirements: 1 2 6
Welcomes specialist subject features, particularly the sciences and music. More general features on 'out and about' in the South-East, plus places of interest. Maximum 1500 words.

Comments: Please ensure that articles are relevant to the South-East.

Approach: By telephone or fax with ideas.

Lead time: Six weeks.

Payment: From £40 per thousand words.

Electrical Review

Quadrant House
The Quadrant
Sutton
Surrey
SM2 5AS

Tel: 081-652 3113   **Fax:** 081-652 8951

Frequency: Fortnightly

Circulation: 15,000

Contact: Tim Tunbridge, Editor

Profile: Provides comprehensive coverage of the world of electrical and control engineering for professionals in the industry.

Requirements: 1 2 6 7
News of developments and announcements within the industry. Also technical articles and general business features on all aspects of electrical engineering.

Comments: Contributors should study the publication before submitting material.

Approach: In writing.

Lead time: Four weeks.

Payment: According to merit.

Electrical Times

Quadrant House
The Quadrant
Sutton
Surrey
SM2 5AS

Tel: 081-652 3115   **Fax:** 081-652 8972

Frequency: Monthly

Circulation: 16,000

Contact: Bill Evett, Editor

Profile: For managers and engineers within the electrical installation industry. Covers ordinary installations, the electrical supply industry and manufacturers.

Requirements: 2 5
Technical and business information about the industry, with the emphasis on installations. Length 850 words maximum.

Comments: All material should be of interest to an electrical engineer or a manager in the industry.

Approach: By telephone, followed by a synopsis.

Lead time: Six weeks.

Payment: £100 for 850 words.

1/News 2/Features 3/Fiction 4/Letters 5/Fillers
6/B&W Photos 7/Colour Photos 8/Reviews

Electronics Today International

Argus Specialist Publications
Argus House
Boundary Way
Hemel Hempstead
Hertfordshire
HP2 7ST

Tel: (0442) 66551   **Fax:** (0442) 66998

Frequency: Monthly

Circulation: 26,000

Contact: Paul Freeman, Editor
Profile: A magazine covering
electronics for both the amateur and
the professional. Includes
constructional articles, together with
general features on science and
technology.
Requirements: 1 2 6 8
Features on any subject with an
electronic application, in fields such
as biology, physics and astronomy.
Length 2500 to 3000 words.
Comments: Most readers are aged
under 25.
Approach: By letter.
Lead time: Two months.
Payment: Negotiable.

Elle

20 Orange Street
London
WC2H 7ED

Tel: 071-957 8383   **Fax:** 071-957 8400

Frequency: Monthly

Circulation: 250,000

Contact: Features Editor
Profile: A high-profile fashion
monthly for the professional woman
who knows what she wants. Very
topical and up to date.

Requirements: 1 2 3
Features angled towards the
modern woman. Especially ideas
for unusual subjects such as
women boxers or female gamblers.
Comments: Looking for a new
perspective with a hard-news basis.
Approach: By letter followed by a
telephone call.
Lead time: Three months.
Payment: £150 per thousand words.

Elle Decoration

EMAP Elan PLC
Victory House
14 Leicester Square
London WC2

Tel: 071-437 9011   **Fax:** 071-434 0656

Frequency: Two months

Circulation: 50,000

Contact: Ilse Crawford, Editor
Profile: An ideas magazine for
outward-looking home enthusiasts.
Glamorous but accessible,
featuring merchandise across the
price range.
Requirements: 2 7
Ideas for interior decoration
features, both escapist and
practical. Also suggestions for
house profiles. Maximum length
1000 words.
Comments: Writers should have a
strong idea of the visual direction
of their features.
Approach: By telephone with ideas.
Lead time: Four months.
Payment: £250 per thousand words.

1/News **2**/Features **3**/Fiction **4**/Letters **5**/Fillers
6/B&W Photos **7**/Colour Photos **8**/Reviews

Embroidery

PO Box 42B
East Molesley
Surrey
KT8 9BB

Tel: 081-943 1229   **Fax:** 081-977 9882

Frequency: Quarterly

Circulation: 14,500

Contact: Valerie Campbell-Harding, Editor

Profile: Published by the Embroiderers' Guild. Covers the art and craft of embroidery in all its forms.

Requirements: 2 5
Practical 'how-to' articles on embroidery techniques, features on historical embroidery or work from overseas, and profiles of artists and their work. Maximum length 1000 words.

Comments: Unsolicited manuscripts are encouraged.

Approach: In writing with complete manuscript.

Lead time: Four months.

Payment: Negotiable.

Empire

Mappin House
4 Winsley Street
London
W1N 7AR

Tel: 071-436 1515   **Fax:** 071-637 7031

Frequency: Monthly

Circulation: 108,000

Contact: Line Rudberg

Profile: Movie-related and cinema entertainment. For people aged 15 to 25 who go to the movies, plus anyone interested in the film industry.

Requirements: 2 5
Topical articles related to movie releases and other activity in the industry. Also profiles and interviews of movie people. Length 500 to 1500 words.

Comments: No film reviews, as contributors are unlikely to have the same access as editorial staff.

Approach: By letter with ideas.

Lead time: Four weeks.

Payment: £125 per thousand words.

The Engineer

30 Calderwood Street
London
SE18 6QH

Tel: 081-855 7777   **Fax:** 081-316 3040

Frequency: Weekly

Circulation: 40,000

Contact: Chris Barrie, Editor

Profile: Read by managers and professionals in the manufacturing industry. Based on news rather than technology.

Requirements: 1 2 6 7
Articles on all branches of engineering, from mining to the steel industry. Length 750 to 1500 words.

Comments: Study the magazine's features list to identify relevant opportunities.

Approach: By telephone with ideas.

Lead time: Two weeks.

Payment: NUJ rates.

Engineering

The Design Council
28 Haymarket
London
SW1Y 4SU

Tel: 071-839 8000   **Fax:** 071-925 2130

1/News 2/Features 3/Fiction 4/Letters 5/Fillers
6/B&W Photos 7/Colour Photos 8/Reviews

Frequency: Monthly
Circulation: 22,000
Contact: Lucia Constanzo, Feature Editor
Profile: A magazine for senior managers in manufacturing industries. Covers management, business and technology.
Requirements: 2
Always looking for writers with expertise in environmental, automotive and electrical engineering. Average length 600 words.
Comments: Also interested in material on plastic-composite material applications.
Approach: By telephone.
Lead time: Eight weeks.
Payment: £200.

Engineering in Miniature

Edwards Centre
Regent Street
Hinckley
Leicestershire
LE10 0BB

Tel: (0455) 616419   **Fax:** (0455) 616419
Frequency: Monthly
Circulation: 20,000
Contact: Mr C.L. Deith, Managing Editor
Profile: A magazine for both amateur and professional model engineers. Includes constructional articles and news of current affairs relating to the hobby.
Requirements: 2
Constructional articles on all aspects of model engineering, plus features on topical events.
Comments: Articles must be well-researched and accurate.

Approach: Write with synopsis and suggested illustrations.
Lead time: Two months.
Payment: £45 per page.

English Heritage

Film House
142 Wardour Street
London
W1V 3AU

Tel: 071-734 6030   **Fax:** 071-437 6085
Frequency: Quarterly
Circulation: 130,000
Contact: Jackie Lindsay, Editor
Profile: Published on behalf of the English Heritage Organisation. Covers conservation and heritage issues in general.
Requirements: 1 2 7
News and features on conservation in the UK, plus articles about English Heritage properties. Length 600 to 1200 words.
Comments: External contributions are welcome.
Approach: In writing.
Lead time: Three months.
Payment: £150 per thousand words.

Environment Risk

Nestor House
Playhouse Yard
London
EC4V 5EX

Tel: 071-779 8699   **Fax:** 071-779 8667
Frequency: 10xYear
Contact: Katherine Morton, Editor
Profile: An environmental strategy magazine. Read by executives in large corporations.

Requirements: 1 2 6 7
Articles about the relationship between business and the environment. Covers areas such as legislation and environmental projects. Maximum 3000 words.
Comments: Has an international readership and perspective.
Approach: By telephone.
Lead time: Four weeks.
Payment: £150 per thousand words.

Escape

Tregeraint House
Zennor
St Ives
Cornwall
TR26 3DB

Tel: (0736) 797061   **Fax:** (0736) 797061

Frequency: Bi-monthly

Circulation: 3500

Contact: John Wilson, Editor
Profile: Aimed at teachers and other professionals looking for a new career. Carries news, views, information and features.
Requirements: 1 2
Success stories about setting up in business, plus articles on jobsearch, freelancing, alternative lifestyles and any other practical information.
Comments: Guidelines for contributors are available on request. Send an s.a.e. to the above address.
Approach: In writing.
Lead time: Three months.
Payment: £20 per thousand words.

Esquire

National Magazine House
72 Broadwick Street
London
W1V 2BP

Tel: 071-439 5000   **Fax:** 071-439 5067

Frequency: Monthly

Circulation: 64,500

Contact: Rosie Boycott, Editor
Profile: An upmarket style magazine for affluent and successful men.
Requirements: 2 5
Confident authoritative features on contemporary issues of interest to men in the UK.
Comments: Most rejected manuscripts fail because of an inappropriate writing style. Contributors should study the 'new journalism' editorial approach.
Approach: By letter, with examples of previous work.
Lead time: Two months.
Payment: £250 per thousand words.

Essentials

Elme House
133 Long Acre
London
WC2E 9AD

Tel: 071-836 0519   **Fax:** 071-836 3644

Frequency: Monthly

Circulation: 519,000

Contact: Gilly Cubitt, Editor
Profile: A practical magazine for women aged between 28 and 35. Now carries more general interest features, as well as 'how-to' articles and advice.
Requirements: 2 3 5 7 8
Features on homes, gardens and other subjects of interest to the

modern woman. Also fiction that reflects the style of the magazine. Length 2000 words maximum.

Comments: Short stories should cover areas beyond the traditional vein of romantic fiction.

Approach: Unsolicited manuscripts accepted, but written enquiry preferred.

Lead time: Four months.

Payment: £100 per thousand words.

Essex Countryside

Market Link House
Tye Green
Elsenham
Bishop's Stortford
Hertfordshire
CM22 6DY

Tel: (0279) 647555   **Fax:** (0279) 815300

Frequency: Monthly

Circulation: 15,132

Contact: Meg Davis-Berry

Profile: A regional title devoted to the heritage and countryside of Essex.

Requirements: 2 6 7
Feature articles on antiques, farming, property and eating out in Essex. Length up to 1000 words.

Comments: All material should have a regional and rural angle.

Approach: In writing.

Lead time: Two months.

Payment: Negotiable.

The Estate Agent

Arbon House
21 Jury Street
Warwick
CV34 4EH

Tel: (0926) 496800   **Fax:** (0926) 403958

Frequency: 8xYear

Circulation: 10,000

Contact: Peter Cliff, Editor

Profile: A news magazine for estate agents and property professionals.

Requirements: 2
Business features and other articles relating to estate agency. All material should be factual and objective.

Comments: Quote sources and statistics where appropriate.

Approach: By telephone with an idea, or send complete manuscript.

Lead time: Six weeks.

Payment: From £100 per thousand words.

Estate Car & MPV

The Studios
Masters House
Main Road
Westcott
Surrey
RH4 3NG

Tel: (0306) 743744   **Fax:** (0306) 742525

Frequency: Bi-monthly

Circulation: 25,000

Contact: Tony Robinson, Editor

Profile: Devoted to estate cars, four-wheel drive and multi-purpose vehicles.

Requirements: 2 7
Driving experiences, road tests and other motoring features in line with the content of the magazine. Length 1500 to 2000 words.

Comments: Copy on disk preferred.

Approach: Write with ideas, or send complete manuscript.

Lead time: Four weeks.

Payment: £100-£150 per thousand words.

1/News **2**/Features **3**/Fiction **4**/Letters **5**/Fillers
6/B&W Photos **7**/Colour Photos **8**/Reviews

European Drinks Buyer

Crier Publications Ltd
Arctic House
Rye Lane
Dunton Green
Sevenoaks
Kent
TN14 5HB

Tel: (0732) 451515   **Fax:** (0732) 451383

Frequency: Bi-monthly

Circulation: 10,275

Contact: Heather Buckle, Editor

Profile: A trade magazine for professional drinks buyers throughout Europe.

Requirements: 1 2
News and features relating to wines, beers and spirits internationally. Length up to 1000 words. News from European countries is of particular interest.

Comments: Contributors do not need to be experts. Writers visiting a relevant country may be able to contribute something of value.

Approach: In writing.

Lead time: Three months.

Payment: From £80 per thousand words.

European Frozen Food Buyer

Crier Publications Ltd
Arctic House
Rye Lane
Dunton Green
Sevenoaks
Kent
TN14 5HB

Tel: (0732) 451515   **Fax:** (0732) 451383

Frequency: Bi-monthly

Circulation: 10,820

Contact: Heather Buckle, Editor

Profile: For those involved in buying frozen foods in European countries.

Requirements: 1 2
Articles about the production and purchasing of frozen foods. News items are of particular interest.

Comments: Freelances going to Eastern Europe and surrounding countries on holiday or on business may be able to contribute.

Approach: In writing.

Lead time: Three months.

Payment: From £80 per thousand words.

Evergreen

PO Box 52
Cheltenham
Gloucestershire
GL50 1YQ

Tel: (0242) 577775   **Fax:** (0242) 222034

Frequency: Quarterly

Circulation: 75,000

Contact: Stephen Garnett, Editor

Profile: For anyone who treasures the country's character and traditions. Covers historical subjects, reminiscences and the English way of life.

Requirements: 2 5
Interesting articles that capture the spirit of the customs and traditions of Britain. Some poetry is also published.

Comments: The overall tone of the publication is nostalgic. Guidelines for contributors are available on request.

Approach: In writing.

Lead time: Four months.

Payment: Negotiable.

1/News **2**/Features **3**/Fiction **4**/Letters **5**/Fillers
6/B&W Photos **7**/Colour Photos **8**/Reviews

Eventing

IPC Magazines
King's Reach Tower
Stamford Street
London
SE1 9LS

Tel: 071-261 5000   **Fax:** 071-261 5429

Frequency: Monthly

Circulation: 10,000

Contact: Kate Green, Editor

Profile: An international magazine devoted to the sport of equestrian trials.

Requirements: 1 2
Profiles, practical 'how-to' features, opinion pieces, trials reports and news items.

Comments: Contributors do not need to be riders, but should have a good understanding of the field.

Approach: Send ideas or finished manuscripts.

Lead time: Two months.

Payment: From £75 per thousand words.

Everyday with Practical Electronics

6 Church Street
Wimbourne
Dorset
BH21 1JH

Tel: (0202) 881749   **Fax:** (0202) 841692

Frequency: Monthly

Circulation: 24,000

Contact: Mike Kennard, Editor

Profile: Projects and instruction for trainers and hobbyists involved in electronics.

Requirements: 2 7
Construction articles for unusual electronics projects. Information about new technology from the electronics industry. Length 1000 to 3000 words.

Comments: Guidelines for contributors are available on request.

Approach: By letter with synopsis.

Lead time: Up to ten months.

Payment: £55 per thousand words.

Everywoman

34 Islington Green
London
N1 8DU

Tel: 071-359 5496   **Fax:** 071-226 9448

Frequency: Monthly

Circulation: 15,000

Contact: Barbara Rogers, Editor

Profile: A current affairs magazine for women. Has a feminist slant, with an emphasis on practical matters.

Requirements: 1 2 6 8
Articles for intelligent women covering finance, relationships, work etc. No fiction.

Comments: Contributors should make it clear which section of the magazine submissions are aimed at.

Approach: By letter with synopsis.

Lead time: Six weeks.

Payment: £40 per thousand words.

Exchange Contracts

HHL Publishing
Greater London House
Hampstead Road
London
NW1 7QQ

Tel: 071-822 2307   **Fax:** 071-387 9518

Frequency: 2xYear

Circulation: 280,000

1/News 2/Features 3/Fiction 4/Letters 5/Fillers
6/B&W Photos 7/Colour Photos 8/Reviews

Contact: Sarah Hawkes, Editor

Profile: Ideas for all rooms of the home. Covers styling, products and creative DIY.

Requirements: 2 5
Articles suggesting different ways of covering major rooms of the house. Must have general appeal — not too upmarket or London-based.

Comments: No features on buying a home or the property market.

Approach: Write or telephone with ideas.

Lead time: Three months.

Payment: Negotiable.

Executive Living

Commerce House
Wakefield Road
Aspley
Huddersfield
HD5 9AA

Tel: (0484) 435455   **Fax:** (0484) 514199

Frequency: Bi-monthly

Circulation: 8000

Contact: Edward Johnstone, Editor

Profile: A magazine for people living in executive homes in the West Yorkshire area.

Requirements: 1 2 6 7 8
Features on gardening, homes, holidays, travel and fashion. Length 1100 to 1500 words.

Comments: Welcomes suggestions for features on children's fashion.

Approach: By letter.

Lead time: Three months.

Payment: Near to NUJ rates.

Executive PA

Astley House
33 Notting Hill Gate
London
W11 3JQ

Tel: 071-490 1166   **Fax:** 071-727 4222

Frequency: Quarterly

Circulation: 25,000

Contact: Claire Gillman, Editor

Profile: A complimentary publication for senior secretaries and personal assistants in industry, business and other organisations.

Requirements: 2 7
Features on travel, office technology, employment legislation and other matters relevant to office life. Length 1500 to 2250 words.

Comments: All material should aim to entertain as well as inform.

Approach: In writing with ideas.

Lead time: Three months.

Payment: £110 per thousand words.

Executive Secretary

Marriots
Castle Street
Buckingham
MK18 1BP

Tel: (0280) 824110   **Fax:** (0280) 823768

Frequency: Quarterly

Circulation: 500

Contact: Jo Denby

Profile: For international PAs or executive secretaries operating within a senior management team. Provides entertaining, easy-to-read concrete stories about companies, people, activities or events.

Requirements: 2 5
Articles on topics of concern to the profession, such as career management, training, technology,

legislation, research and key management disciplines. Length 1500 to 3000 words.

Comments: All material should be appropriate to an international market.

Approach: By telephone.

Lead time: Two months.

Payment: Negotiable for commissioned writers.

Executive Travel

6 Chesterfield Gardens
London
W1Y 8DN

Tel: 071-355 1600   **Fax:** 071-355 9630

Frequency: Monthly

Circulation: 40,000

Contact: Colin Ellson, Features Editor

Profile: For the frequent, corporate traveller. Aims to be informative, interesting, entertaining and educational.

Requirements: 1 2 7
News and features on any subject of interest to the readership, from frequent-fly programmes to survival guides. Length up to 1000 words.

Comments: Copy should always be entertaining.

Approach: By telephone or letter.

Lead time: Two months.

Payment: £150 per thousand words.

Executive Woman

2 Chantry Place
Harrow
Middlesex
HA3 6NY

Tel: 081-420 1210   **Fax:** 081-420 1693

Frequency: Quarterly

Circulation: 15,500

Contact: The Editor

Profile: For women in business, especially professionals, account managers and personnel officers.

Requirements: 1 2
News and features on business matters affecting women, plus articles on subjects such as stress, training and career opportunities.

Comments: Also runs some general material on leisure and the arts.

Approach: In writing.

Lead time: Three weeks.

Payment: By arrangement.

Expat Investor

Tolley House
2 Addiscombe Road
Croydon
CR9 5AF

Tel: 081-686 9141   **Fax:** 081-760 0588

Frequency: Bi-monthly

Circulation: 35,000

Contact: Peter Jolly, Editor

Profile: Authorative magazine for Britons living overseas. Covers investment, lifestyle and property.

Requirements: 1 2 6 7
News and features relating to investment, assurance, pensions, property and leisure. Length 800 words plus.

Comments: Incorporates Expatextra.

Approach: By telephone with ideas.

Lead time: Six weeks.

Payment: NUJ or better.

1/News **2**/Features **3**/Fiction **4**/Letters **5**/Fillers
6/B&W Photos **7**/Colour Photos **8**/Reviews

Expat Newsline

Barclays Bank Building
High Street
Chepstow
Gwent
NP6 5QX

Tel: (0291) 627016   **Fax:** (0291) 627285

Frequency: 10xYear

Circulation: 17,500

Contact: Peter Sharkey, Editor
Profile: News magazine for British
expatriates around the world.
Requirements: 2 6 7
Features on finance, investment and
other subjects of interest to Britons
abroad.
Comments: Study the magazine before
submitting material.
Approach: In writing.
Lead time: Three weeks.
Payment: Negotiable.

Expatriate Today

148 Upper Richmond Road West
London
SW14 8DP

Tel: 081-392 2838   **Fax:** 081-392 2817

Frequency: Bi-monthly

Circulation: 12,000

Contact: Jonathon Hill
Profile: Aimed at affluent expatriates.
A typical reader would be male aged
between 25 and 54 – married, a
frequent traveller and a second
property owner.
Requirements: 2 5
Features on education, property,
finance, savings, tax and pensions.
Comments: Do not send unsolicited
manuscripts.

Approach: By letter.
Lead time: Six weeks.
Payment: By arrangement.

Expression

101 Bayham Street
London
NW1 0AG

Tel: 071-331 8000   **Fax:** 071-331 8030

Frequency: Bi-monthly

Circulation: 600,000

Contact: Sue Thomas, Editor
Profile: An upmarket lifestyle
magazine sent to holders of
American Express cards.
Requirements: 2 5 7
Travel pieces and general features.
Length up to 2000 words.
Comments: Travel articles should
relate to places where American
Express cards are accepted.
Approach: In writing with ideas or
finished manuscript.
Lead time: Three months.
Payment: £250 per thousand words.

Eye Magazine

Wordsearch
26 Cramer Street
London
W1M 3HE

Tel: 071-486 7419   **Fax:** 071-486 1451

Frequency: Quarterly

Circulation: 8000

Contact: Rick Poyner, Editor
Profile: A magazine for graphic
designers, which aims to publish the
best graphics around the world.

1/News **2**/Features **3**/Fiction **4**/Letters **5**/Fillers
6/B&W Photos **7**/Colour Photos **8**/Reviews

Requirements: 2 6 7
Articles on the graphic aspects of
design, covering high-quality work,
both historical and modern. Length
up to 1500 words.

Comments: The magazine aims to give
graphic designs greater attention
than they have had in the past.

Approach: By telephone or letter with
ideas.

Lead time: Three months.

Payment: Negotiable.

F

The Face

Third Floor Block A
Exmouth House
Pine Street
London
EC1R 0JL

Tel: 071-837 7270   **Fax:** 071-837 3906

Frequency: Monthly

Circulation: 89,615

Contact: Amy Raphael, Features
 Editor

Profile: A fresh, lively style magazine
 read by both men and women aged
 16 to 30. Covers music, fashion,
 film, clubs, youth culture and
 leadership.

Requirements: 1 2
 Original material that the editorial
 staff may not be able to cover.
 Regional events, plus fresh faces in
 music, film, fashion and clubs.

Comments: Think visually. Untested
 writers are more likely to be used if
 they have special access to
 information, perhaps through
 geographical location.

Approach: By fax or letter with ideas
 and examples of previous work.

Lead time: Two months.

Payment: From £100 per thousand
 words.

Family Circle

IPC Magazines
King's Reach Tower
Stamford Street
London
SE1 9LS

Tel: 071-261 5000   **Fax:** 071-261 5929

Frequency: Monthly

Circulation: 406,190

Contact: The Editor

Profile: Women's magazine centred
 around the home and family.

Requirements: 2 4 5
 Features on subjects relating to
 home-making and the family. Also
 stories of 300 words plus on
 'moments of truth' − experiences
 which have changed the writer's life.

Comments: Unsolicited manuscripts
 are rarely used.

Approach: In writing with ideas.

Lead time: Three months.

Payment: From £100 per thousand
 words.

The Family Magazine

The Family Assurance Society
19 New Road
Brighton
BN1 1WF

Tel: (0273) 725272   **Fax:** (0273) 206026

Frequency: 2xYear

Circulation: 400,000

Contact: Sharon Slaughter, Editor

Profile: A magazine for customers of the Family Assurance Society.

Requirements: 2
Feature articles on subjects relating to the home and personal finance. All copy must be accurate and well researched.

Comments: Writers should have a good understanding of their subject.

Approach: In writing with ideas.

Lead time: Six months.

Payment: By arrangement.

Family Tree

15-16 Highlode
Ramsey
Huntingdon
Cambridgeshire
PE17 1RB

Tel: 081 652 4911   **Fax:** (0487) 814050

Frequency: Monthly

Circulation: 24,500

Contact: Avril Cross, Editor

Profile: Publication devoted to the subject of genealogy.

Requirements: 1 2
News and features about genealogy, especially less-well-known sources of information and research techniques. Length up to 3000 words.

Comments: Does not want to receive any personal family histories.

Approach: In writing.

Lead time: Two months.

Payment: Up to £54.

Farmers Weekly

13th Floor
Quadrant House
The Quadrant
Sutton
Surrey
SM2 5AS

Tel: 081-652 4911   **Fax:** 081-652 8901

Frequency: Weekly

Circulation: 96,000

Contact: Stephen Howe, Editor

Profile: Serves the whole UK agricultural industry. A complete window on the changing scene of modern farming.

Requirements: 1 2 7
News and features of general interest to the farming community. Also items on farm life of interest to farmers' families. Length 1000 to 1500 words.

Comments: Read not just by farmers, but also by those working in ancillary businesses.

Approach: Submit complete manuscript.

Lead time: Three weeks.

Payment: £80 per thousand words.

Farming Life

c/o News Letter
46-56 Boucher Crescent
Belfast
BT12 6QY

Tel: (0232) 680033   **Fax:** (0232) 664432

Frequency: 104xYear

Circulation: 485,000

Contact: David McCoy, Editor

Profile: A general agri-food business publication, with the emphasis towards pure farming.

1/News **2**/Features **3**/Fiction **4**/Letters **5**/Fillers
6/B&W Photos **7**/Colour Photos **8**/Reviews

Requirements: 1 2 5 6 7
  News features on subjects ranging
  from machinery to animal health.
  Length up to 500 words.
Comments: Articles tied into the
  features list have the best chance of
  success.
Approach: By telephone, letter or fax.
Lead time: Four days.
Payment: NUJ rates.

Farming News

30 Calderwood Street
Woolwich
London
SE18 6QH

Tel: 081-855 7777   **Fax:** 081-854 6795

Frequency: Weekly

Circulation: 74,000

Contact: Donald Taylor, Editor
Profile: Controlled-circulation
  magazine offering all-embracing
  coverage of the week's agricultural
  news. Read by farmers and those in
  the agricultural supply industry.
Requirements: 1 2 6 7
  Welcomes short regional news items
  up to 200 words. Also technical
  features with illustrations up to 3000
  words, and captioned news or
  technical photos.
Comments: Particularly interested in
  freestanding illustrated features of
  direct relevance to farmers.
Approach: By telephone with initial
  ideas.
Lead time: Two weeks minimum.
Payment: £107.45 per thousand words.

Fashion Weekly

19 Scarbrook Road
Croydon
Surrey
CR9 1QH

Tel: 081-688 7788   **Fax:** 081-688 0306

Frequency: Weekly

Circulation: 8134

Contact: Martin Raymond, Editor
Profile: For decision-makers in the
  retail, wholesale and manufacturing
  areas of the fashion trade.
Requirements: 1 2 7
  Information on trends in fashion
  retailing and business. Also features
  on marketing.
Comments: Very open to good ideas.
Approach: By letter or fax.
Lead time: Four weeks.
Payment: £130 per thousand words.

Fast Bikes

Sports Report Ltd
84 Vale Farm Road
Woking
Surrey
TW21 1DP

Tel: (0483) 770765   **Fax:** (0483) 750427

Frequency: Monthly

Circulation: 45,000

Contact: Colin Shiller, Editor
Profile: For experienced and novice
  bikers and newcomers aged between
  17 and 50. Read by both men and
  women.
Requirements: 1 2 6 7
  Touring features, road tests, racing
  news and information on unusual
  motorbikes.
Comments: Unsolicited manuscripts
  are unlikely to be accepted.

1/News **2**/Features **3**/Fiction **4**/Letters **5**/Fillers
6/B&W Photos **7**/Colour Photos **8**/Reviews

Approach: Write with ideas and synopsis.
Lead time: Two months.
Payment: Negotiable.

Fast Car Magazine

Argosy House
161a-163a High Street
Orpington
Kent
BR6 0LW

Tel: (0689) 874025   **Fax:** (0689) 896847

Frequency: Monthly

Circulation: 48,000

Contact: Danny Morris, Editor
Profile: Aimed at performance-oriented motoring enthusiasts, primarily 17 to 30 year olds. Covers every aspect of enhancement, including styling, engines, chassis.
Requirements: 1 2
Material on the above subjects, plus motor sports, clubs and industry. The magazine style is very important, and writers should aim to get the right angle. Length 1000 to 1500 words.
Comments: Heavy emphasis on practical 'hands-on' work and testing.
Approach: By telephone with ideas.
Lead time: Two months.
Payment: Negotiable.

Fast Forward

Room A1118
Woodlands
80 Wood Lane
W12 0TT

Tel: 081-576 3254   **Fax:** 081-576 3267

Frequency: Weekly

Circulation: 129,000

Contact: Roderick Jones, Editor
Profile: A magazine for 7-14 year olds, covering the latest bands, gossip, etc.
Requirements: 2 3 7 8
Always looking for features with an original angle. Also short stories of interest to children in the relevant age group.
Comments: Has a strong emphasis on music.
Approach: By telephone or letter.
Lead time: Three weeks.
Payment: £300 per thousand words.

Fast Lane

Perry Motor Press
Compass House
22 Redan Place
London
W2 4SZ

Tel: 071-229 7799   **Fax:** 071-221 7846

Frequency: Monthly

Circulation: 55,000

Contact: David Raeside, Executive Editor
Profile: Goes behind the wheels of performance cars. Covers both affordable ones and those to dream about.
Requirements: 1 2 7
New ideas for features, or original slants on old ones. Length 600 to 2500 words.
Comments: Don't let lack of specialised knowledge put you off.
Approach: Short synopsis by fax or letter.
Lead time: Two months.
Payment: £175 per thousand words.

1/News **2**/Features **3**/Fiction **4**/Letters **5**/Fillers
6/B&W Photos **7**/Colour Photos **8**/Reviews

The Field

10 Sheet Street
Windsor
Berkshire
SL4 1BG

Tel: (0753) 856061   **Fax:** (0753) 831086

Frequency: Monthly

Circulation: 30,675

Contact: Jonathon Young, Editor

Profile: Established magazine for those interested in country sports and activities.

Requirements: 1 2 5
Articles on countryside sports, farming, travel and similar topics. Length 1500 to 2000 words. Now also runs shorter items of around 200 words.

Comments: Most work is commissioned, so contact the editor first.

Approach: In writing.

Lead time: Two months.

Payment: Negotiable but good.

050

Thames House
18 Park Street
London
SE1 9ER

Tel: 071-378 7131   **Fax:** 071-403 4682

Frequency: Quarterly

Circulation: 112,000

Contact: Niall Sweeney, Editor

Profile: Published by the Association of Retired Persons and 050 Club.

Requirements: 2 7 8
Features covering the magazine's five main areas - gardening, books, cookery, DIY and the arts. Also travel articles.

Comments: Mainly read by younger, more active retired persons.

Approach: By letter with ideas.

Lead time: Two months.

Payment: Negotiable.

50-Forward

1-2 Ravey Street
London
EC2A 4QP

Tel: 071-739 7883   **Fax:** 071-739 1060

Frequency: Quarterly

Circulation: 50,000

Contact: Kevin Ellard, Editor

Profile: A magazine for those who have retired, or who are about to do so.

Requirements: 2 5 6 7
Majors on health, finance, travel, leisure, gardening and motoring. Length 1000 to 1500 words.

Comments: The readership is split equally between men and women.

Approach: By telephone.

Lead time: Two months.

Payment: £125 per thousand words.

Fifty Plus

25 Catherine Street
London
WC2B 5JW

Tel: 071-379 3036   **Fax:** 071-240 6840

Frequency: Quarterly

Circulation: 20,000

Contact: Rosemary Aynsley, Editor

Profile: Aimed at those aged over 50 earning in excess of £30,000 per household.

Requirements: 2 6 7 8
Articles on finance, health, leisure, holidays and leisure breaks. Length up to 1000 words.

Comments: Good photographs are always welcome.
Approach: By telephone.
Lead time: One month.
Payment: NUJ rates.

Fighters

Peterson House
Northbank
Berryhill Industrial Estate
Droitwich
Worcestershire
WR9 9BL

Tel: (0905) 795564　**Fax:** (0905) 795905

Frequency: Monthly

Circulation: 23,000

Contact: Tim Ayling, Editor
Profile: A magazine devoted to all aspects of the martial arts.
Requirements: 1 2 6 7
Interviews with martial-arts personalities, reports, profiles, training advice and medical information.
Comments: Study the magazine before contributing.
Approach: By letter or fax.
Lead time: Six weeks.
Payment: Negotiable.

Film Review

PO Box 371
London
SW14 8JL

Tel: 081-878 5486　**Fax:** 081-876 9455

Frequency: Monthly

Circulation: 37,000

Contact: Nick Briggs, Editor
Profile: A comprehensive review of the film scene. Concentrates on blockbuster releases.

Requirements: 1 2 6 7 8
Interviews with stars or directors. Also reviews, features and profiles. Length up to 1500 words.
Comments: Copy on PC-compatible disk preferred.
Approach: By letter with a concrete idea.
Lead time: Four weeks.
Payment: Negotiable.

Financial Adviser

Boundary House
91-93 Charterhouse Street
London
EC1M 6HR

Tel: 071-608 3471　**Fax:** 071-250 0004

Frequency: Weekly

Circulation: 45,000

Contact: Ceri Jones, Editor
Profile: A professional publication for financial intermediaries.
Requirements: 1 2
News of developments in the personal finance sector, plus feature articles on subjects of interest to financial consultants.
Comments: Contributors should have a good understanding of their subject.
Approach: In writing.
Lead time: Three weeks.
Payment: By arrangement.

Financial Director

VNU Business Publications
32-34 Broadwick Street
London
W1A 2HG

Tel: 071-439 4242　**Fax:** 071-437 7001

Frequency: Monthly

Circulation: 24,970

Contact: Jane Simms, Editor

Profile: A controlled-circulation magazine that provides broad coverage of finance and the business world for financial directors.

Requirements: 2 6 7

Feature articles on financial matters, management and business strategy. Length 1500 to 2000 words.

Comments: Submissions should be designed to interest senior-level board members with considerable experience.

Approach: In writing with ideas.

Lead time: Two months.

Payment: £120-£150 per thousand words.

Finesse

Mega House
Crest View Drive
Petts Wood
Orpington
BR5 1BT

Tel: (0689) 836211   Fax: (0689) 875367

Frequency: Monthly

Circulation: 40,000

Contact: Sandra Graffham, Editor

Profile: A free magazine distributed to homes throughout South-East London.

Requirements: 2 3 6 7 8

Articles on the theatre, arts, fashion, finance, gardening and motoring. Length up to 1000 words. Also book reviews.

Comments: Unsolicited manuscripts welcome.

Approach: In writing.

Lead time: Six weeks.

Payment: Negotiable.

First

77 Oxford Street
London
W1R 1RB

Tel: 071-439 1188   Fax: 071-287 1437

Frequency: Quarterly

Circulation: 20,295

Contact: Rupert Goodman

Profile: A prestigious magazine for leaders in industry and government. Focuses on long-term business and political strategy.

Requirements: 2

Features covering business issues at board level. Material should have a broad, international perspective, and must be authoritative.

Comments: Articles are usually serious in-depth approaches to. key issues.

Approach: By letter.

Lead time: Four weeks.

Payment: Negotiable.

First Down

The Spendlove Centre
Enstone Road
Charlbury
Chipping Norton
Oxon
OX7 3PQ

Tel: (0608) 811266   Fax: (0608) 811380

Frequency: Weekly

Circulation: 21,000

Contact: Lee Berry, UK Editor

Profile: A tabloid-style publication devoted to American football. Includes the British amateur game, Canadian football, statistics and gossip.

1/News 2/Features 3/Fiction 4/Letters 5/Fillers
6/B&W Photos 7/Colour Photos 8/Reviews

Requirements: 1 2 5 6 7 8

Profiles of up-and-coming players, light-hearted features and news. Length up to 1400 words.

Comments: Writers travelling to the USA may be able to make useful contributions.

Approach: By telephone or letter.

Lead time: Three weeks.

Payment: NUJ rates.

First Voice

Mediamark Publishing
35 Gresse Street
Rathbone Place
London
W1P 1PN

Tel: 071-580 3105   **Fax:** 071-580 1695

Frequency: Bi-monthly

Circulation: 58,000

Contact: Isobel Kesby, Editor

Profile: The official journal of the Federation of Small Businesses.

Requirements: 1 2

News and feature material relating to the self-employed and those running small companies. Length up to 1000 words.

Comments: The emphasis is on topical issues throughout the year.

Approach: By telephone.

Lead time: Six weeks.

Payment: £180 per thousand words.

Fishkeeping Answers

EMAP Pursuit Publishing Ltd
Bretton Court
Bretton Centre
Peterborough
PE3 8DZ

Tel: (0733) 264666   **Fax:** (0733) 265515

Frequency: Monthly

Circulation: 23,940

Contact: Sue Parslow, Editor

Profile: Designed to reach less-experienced fishkeepers who have a thirst for knowledge in a form they can understand.

Requirements: 1 2 7 8

Informative articles on keeping particular breeds, special problems, fish health and breeding.

Comments: Material should be informed and well-researched.

Approach: By letter with examples of previous work.

Lead time: Four weeks.

Payment: Up to £100 per thousand words.

Flicks

PO Box 137
London
SW6 5BA

Tel: 071-384 1818   **Fax:** 071-371 7573

Frequency: Monthly

Circulation: 350,000

Contact: Quentin Falk, Editor

Profile: A free film magazine for consumers, covering new releases from the industry.

Requirements: 2

Previews of forthcoming releases written in a punchy and informative style. The magazine does not run reviews.

Comments: No unsolicited manuscripts. All work is commissioned.

Approach: In writing.

Lead time: Two months.

Payment: Negotiable.

1/News **2**/Features **3**/Fiction **4**/Letters **5**/Fillers
6/B&W Photos **7**/Colour Photos **8**/Reviews

Flight International

Quadrant House
The Quadrant
Sutton
Surrey
SM2 5AS

Tel: 081-652 3882   **Fax:** 081-652 3840

Frequency: Weekly

Circulation: 59,000

Contact: David Learmount, Features Editor

Profile: A technical publication aimed at all sectors of the aerospace industry. Covers aircraft of every size and description, both military and civil.

Requirements: 1 2 5 7
Up-to-date news and features that would not otherwise be covered by the magazine. Particularly interested in articles on specific geographic areas. Length up to 2000 words.

Comments: Articles should cover subjects in detail, with quotes from relevant people in the industry.

Approach: By telephone.

Lead time: Three weeks.

Payment: NUJ rates.

Flightpath

Furlongs House
Peasemore
Newbury
Berkshire
RG16 0JE

Tel: (0635) 247770   **Fax:** (0635) 247272

Frequency: Quarterly

Circulation: 10,000

Contact: Diana Breadmore, Editor

Profile: An in-flight magazine for passengers of Loganair.

Requirements: 2
Features on subjects related to Loganair destinations, covering both business and leisure matters. Articles should take an original view of their subject.

Comments: Features that attract advertising revenue are likely to be well received.

Approach: In writing with ideas.

Lead time: Three months.

Payment: £100 per thousand words.

Flora International

46 Merlin Grove
Eden Park
Beckenham
Kent
BR3 3HU

Tel: 081-658 1080

Frequency: Bi-monthly

Circulation: 15,000

Contact: Russell Bennett, Editor

Profile: Devoted to all aspects of flowers, flower arranging and floristry. Includes practical information, history and crafts related to flowers.

Requirements: 2 6 7
Features on any floral subject, between 500 and 1500 words in length. Writers should have a good understanding of the subject.

Comments: Practical floristry items are particularly welcome. Photographs or drawings are essential.

Approach: Submit complete manuscript.

Lead time: Twelve months.

Payment: Up to £40 per thousand words.

1/News **2**/Features **3**/Fiction **4**/Letters **5**/Fillers
6/B&W Photos **7**/Colour Photos **8**/Reviews

Flutter

Country Barn Publications
Clymshurst Barn
Burwash Common
East Sussex
TN19 7NB

Tel: (0435) 883568 **Fax:** (0435) 883354

Frequency: Monthly

Circulation: 10,000

Contact: Mike Raxworthy, Editor

Profile: Aimed at the sensible gambler and the person who enjoys the occasional flutter. The emphasis is on smaller-scale gambling.

Requirements: 2 5
Features on techniques, strategies and systems, plus hints and tips for success. Particularly interested in hearing from contributors who can write about greyhounds and bingo.

Comments: Colour photographs to accompany features are always welcome.

Approach: In writing.

Lead time: Six weeks.

Payment: About £120 per article, plus reproduction fees for photos.

Fly-Fishing & Fly-Tying

The Lodge
Meridian House
Bakewell Road
Orton
Southgate
Peterborough
PE2 0XU

Tel: (0733) 371937 **Fax:** (0733) 361056

Frequency: Bi-monthly

Circulation: 20,239

Contact: Mark Bowler, Editor

Profile: Aimed at the fly-tying fly fisherman, with an emphasis on stillwater trout angling.

Requirements: 2 5 6 7
Articles on fly-tying, fisheries, tactics and techniques. Humorous and atmospheric pieces are also used occasionally. Length 800 to 1500 words.

Comments: It helps if the writer is experienced in this area.

Approach: Submit finished manuscript.

Lead time: Two months.

Payment: £48 per thousand words.

Flyer

Insider Publications
43 Queensferry Street Lane
Edinburgh
EH2 4PF

Tel: 031-459 4646 **Fax:** 031-220 1203

Frequency: Monthly

Circulation: 30,000

Contact: David Mason, Editor

Profile: Aims to capture the excitement of personal flying. Covers everything from aircraft to finding finance.

Requirements: 2 5
Features on destinations, flying techniques, technical matters and similar subjects of interest to the readership.

Comments: Read by individual pilots and business people.

Approach: In writing.

Lead time: Two months.

Payment: Negotiable.

1/News **2**/Features **3**/Fiction **4**/Letters **5**/Fillers
6/B&W Photos **7**/Colour Photos **8**/Reviews

Flypast

PO Box 100
Stamford
Lincolnshire
PE9 1XQ

Tel: (0780) 55131 **Fax:** (0780) 57261

Frequency: Monthly

Circulation: 42,070

Contact: Ken Ellis

Profile: A magazine covering historical aircraft for enthusiasts.

Requirements: 1 2 7 8
News and features about particular types of classic aircraft. All material should be well-researched and authoritative.

Comments: The editor does not wish to receive any material on modern aircraft.

Approach: By letter.

Lead time: Six weeks.

Payment: £50 per thousand words.

Focus

Portland House
Stag Place
London
SW1E 5AU

Tel: 071-222 1011 **Fax:** 071-233 0009

Frequency: Monthly

Circulation: circa 100,000

Contact: Mick Hurrell, Editor

Profile: A consumer science and technology publication, covering subjects ranging from history to astrophysics. Aimed primarily at men aged between 18 and 35.

Requirements: 1 2 5
Accessible, informative pieces on medicine, the environment, scientific developments, and so on. Writers should aim to adopt the technical style of the magazine.

Comments: The magazine has a very distinctive approach to constructing articles. Consequently, writers should work closely with editorial staff, rather than submitting manuscripts on spec.

Approach: By telephone, letter or fax.

Lead time: Two months.

Payment: £250-£300 per thousand words.

Folk Roots

PO Box 337
London
N4 1TW

Tel: 081-340 9651 **Fax:** 081-348 5626

Frequency: Monthly

Circulation: 13,000

Contact: Ian Anderson, Editor

Profile: A magazine covering the world of folk music.

Requirements: 2 5
Feature articles on folk and roots music, together with profiles of musicians and interviews. Length up to 3000 words.

Comments: Most unsolicited manuscripts received are not suitable. Always contact the editor before submitting.

Approach: By telephone.

Lead time: Three months.

Payment: Around £40 per thousand words.

1/News **2**/Features **3**/Fiction **4**/Letters **5**/Fillers
6/B&W Photos **7**/Colour Photos **8**/Reviews

Football Management

16 Long Acre Court
Hampshire Street
Portsmouth
PO1 5LJ

Tel: (0705) 822122   **Fax:** (0705) 822122

Frequency: 8xYear

Circulation: 3,000

Contact: Michael Lenihan

Profile: The business-to-business journal for the football industry. Read only by football administrators.

Requirements: 1 2 5 6 7
Non-playing related articles relevant to the day-to-day running of football clubs. Minimum 500 words.

Comments: The editorial policy is not to get involved in tabloid-style journalism. Readers should always be allowed to draw their own conclusions at the end of an article.

Approach: By letter, telephone or fax.

Lead time: Six weeks.

Payment: £40 per thousand words.

Football Monthly

21 Caldbeck Avenue
Worcester Park
Surrey
KT4 8BQ

Tel: 081-546 0048   **Fax:** 081-868 5801

Frequency: Monthly

Circulation: 25,000

Contact: Tony Flood, Editor

Profile: A hard-hitting, news magazine for football fans aged between 18 and 45.

Requirements: 2 7
Features that look ahead and won't date. All material should be informative, authoritative and topical.

Comments: Articles based on personalities are particularly welcome if backed up with quotes.

Approach: By telephone or letter with initial ideas.

Lead time: Six weeks.

Payment: From £38 per thousand words.

Footballers World

Newton Wells
57 High Street
Hampton
Middlesex
TW12 2SX

Tel: 081-979 9791   **Fax:** 081-979 8407

Frequency: Bi-monthly

Circulation: 100,000

Contact: John Taylor, Editor

Profile: Provides coverage of all aspects of the game of football.

Requirements: 1 2
News and features about players, fans, management, etc. Copy should be factual and hard hitting.

Comments: Contributors should be enthusiastic about the game of football.

Approach: In writing.

Lead time: Six weeks.

Payment: Negotiable.

For Him

9/11 Curtain Road
London
EC2A 3LT

Tel: 071-247 5447   **Fax:** 071-247 5892

Frequency: 10xYear

Circulation: 62,632

Contact: Andrew Anthony, Deputy Editor

1/News **2**/Features **3**/Fiction **4**/Letters **5**/Fillers
6/B&W Photos **7**/Colour Photos **8**/Reviews

Profile: A fashion-led, general interest title for men aged between 20 and 35.

Requirements: 2 6 7
Feature articles on fashion, sport, travel, relationships and popular culture. Length 1200 to 4000 words.

Comments: The editorial team is not able to accept telephone calls.

Approach: In writing, with a synopsis.

Lead time: Ten weeks.

Payment: £150 per thousand words.

Foresight

BLA Group Limited
2 Duncan Terrace
London
N1 8BZ

Tel: 071-278 7603   **Fax:** 071-278 6246

Frequency: Quarterly

Circulation: 250,000

Contact: Anne Caborn, Editor

Profile: For customers of the Sun Alliance insurance company. A newsy, informal but informative magazine concerning personal finance.

Requirements: 1 2
Good original pieces about broad themes and issues where there is an insurance angle. Examples include buildings, contents, motoring, illness and investment.

Comments: Originality and accuracy are the mainstays of this magazine. An ability to research general as well as financial material is a must.

Approach: In writing with synopsis.

Lead time: Three months.

Payment: From £100 per thousand words.

Formula 1 News

116-118 Liscombe
Birch Hill
Bracknell
Berkshire
RG12 7DE

Tel: (0344) 427846   **Fax:** (0344) 484918

Frequency: Fortnightly

Circulation: 40,000

Contact: Derek Wright, Editor

Profile: News-led publication covering the world of Formula 1 racing for the enthusiast.

Requirements: 1 2
News and features about cars, events and people. Also historical pieces about former champions, etc.

Comments: Does not cover any kind of racing or cars beyond Formula 1.

Approach: In writing with ideas.

Lead time: Two months.

Payment: £100 per thousand words.

Forte

3rd Floor
Regent Palace Hotel
Piccadilly Circus
London
W1A 4BZ

Tel: 071-437 7777   **Fax:** 071-734 8489

Frequency: Quarterly

Circulation: 65,000

Contact: Delia Cooke, Editor

Profile: The guest magazine of Forte Hotels, distributed via the hotels in the company's chain.

Requirements: 2 6 7
Features on antiques, summer sports and similar subjects of general interest.

1/News **2**/Features **3**/Fiction **4**/Letters **5**/Fillers
6/B&W Photos **7**/Colour Photos **8**/Reviews

Comments: Also interested in features on famous people who have stayed in Forte hotels.
Approach: In writing.
Lead time: Two months.
Payment: NUJ rates.

Fortean Times

PO Box 2409
London
NW5 4NP

Tel: 071-485 5002 **Fax:** 071-485 5002

Frequency: Bi-monthly

Circulation: 15,000

Contact: Paul Sieveking, Editor
Profile: The magazine of strange phenomena. Covers mysteries, experiences, curiosities, prodigies and portents.
Requirements: 1 2 6 8
Well-researched material on current or historical mysteries, or first-hand accounts of oddities. Length up to 2000 words.
Comments: Does not require poetry, fiction or re-workings of existing material.
Approach: By letter with proposal.
Lead time: Four weeks.
Payment: Negotiable.

Foul

Leisure Max
30-38 Dock Street
Leeds
LS10 1JF

Tel: (0532) 429744 **Fax:** (0532) 42991

Frequency: Bi-monthly

Circulation: 15,000

Contact: Neil Howson

Profile: A lively, informative magazine for the intelligent football fan. Aimed principally at males between the age of 16 and 35.
Requirements: 1 2 6 7
Incisive material on football in the upper divisions. In particular, articles which go beyond the usual star profiles to add to the fans' knowledge of the game.
Comments: Looking for writers with a modern, dynamic approach to football.
Approach: By telephone with ideas.
Lead time: Three months.
Payment: £50 per thousand words.

4x4 Magazine

Greenlight Publishing
Hatfield Peverel
Essex
CM3 2HF

Tel: (0245) 381011 **Fax:** (0245) 381960

Frequency: Monthly

Circulation: 20,000

Contact: Iain MacKenzie, Editor
Profile: Four-wheel drive recreation and adventure, plus news of topical current events. Readers are mostly well-informed enthusiasts and owners.
Requirements: 1 2 5 6 7
Copy on unusual 4x4 travel, military, products, DIY tips, restoration etc. Length 800 to 2500 words. Must be factual, well-presented, easy to read, portraying the enthusiasm and fun associated with the off-roading fraternity.
Comments: The editor is keen to hear from freelances with proven technical, DIY off-roading experience.

1/News 2/Features 3/Fiction 4/Letters 5/Fillers
6/B&W Photos 7/Colour Photos 8/Reviews

Approach: By telephone.
Lead time: Four weeks.
Payment: £75 per thousand words.

Franchise World

James House
37 Nottingham Road
London
SW17 7EA

Tel: 081-767 1371   **Fax:** 081-767 2211

Frequency: Bi-monthly

Circulation: 9000

Contact: Robert Riding, Editor
Profile: Gives advice and information to prospective franchisees. Also read by existing franchisees as a source of business information.
Requirements: 1 2 6 8
Business features relevant to the franchise community, covering subjects such as accountancy, finance and legal issues.
Comments: Does not require general small-business articles. Material must be geared towards franchising.
Approach: Submit complete manuscript.
Lead time: Three weeks.
Payment: Negotiable.

Freedom Today

35 Westminster Bridge Road
London
SE1 7JB

Tel: 071-928 9925   **Fax:** 071-928 9524

Frequency: Bi-monthly

Circulation: 10,000

Contact: Philip Vander Elst, Editor
Profile: The journal of the Freedom Assocation, covering political issues worldwide.

Requirements: 1 2 8
Articles on political matters both at home, in Europe and internationally. Maximum 700 words.
Comments: Keep material short, relevant and interesting.
Approach: By letter, with ideas or complete manuscript.
Lead time: Two months.
Payment: Up to £60.

Freelance Writing & Photography

Weavers Press Publishing
Tregeraint House
Zennor
St Ives
Cornwall
TR26 3DB

Tel: (0736) 797061   **Fax:** (0736) 797061

Frequency: Bi-monthly

Circulation: 1000

Contact: John Wilson, Editor
Profile: A magazine for both beginning and experienced freelances. Concentrates mainly on writing, but also covers photography.
Requirements: 1 2 5
News and articles on how to improve your success as a freelance, plus anecdotes and relevant experiences. Also news of new markets, opportunities, etc.
Comments: Most of the magazine is contributed by external writers. Guidelines for contributors are available on request.
Approach: In writing with complete manuscript.
Lead time: Three months.
Payment: £20 per thousand words.

1/News **2**/Features **3**/Fiction **4**/Letters **5**/Fillers
6/B&W Photos **7**/Colour Photos **8**/Reviews

Furniture Components & Production International

4 Red Barn Mews
High Street
Battle
East Sussex
TN33 0AG

Tel: (0424) 774982   **Fax:** (0424) 774321

Frequency: Monthly

Circulation: 8500

Contact: John Legg, Editor

Profile: Trade newspaper containing news, views, product launches and other relevant information. Read by production managers and directors of furniture and component manufacturers.

Requirements: 1 2 4 5 6 7 8 Interested in articles about furniture components and production machinery, from drawer slides to lacquers.

Comments: Material must be relevant to the market, accurate, sympathetic and technically correct.

Approach: By letter or fax.

Lead time: Four weeks.

Payment: From £50 per thousand words.

Future Music

Future Publishing
30 Monmouth Street
Bath
BA1 2BW

Tel: (0225) 442244   **Fax:** (0225) 446019

Frequency: Monthly

Circulation: circa 23,500

Contact: Karl Foster, Editor

Profile: A feature-based magazine for both amateur musicians working at home and studio professionals.

Requirements: 1 2 8 Reviews of equipment, interviews with musicians and other creative individuals, tutorials and news items. Length up to 4000 words.

Comments: Concentrates on affordable equipment, both hardware and software.

Approach: Write with synopsis and examples of previous work.

Lead time: Two months.

Payment: £80 per thousand words.

G

Game Zone

19 Bolsover Street
London
W1P 7HJ

Tel: 071-631 1433   **Fax:** 071-323 9343

Frequency: Monthly

Circulation: 50,000

Contact: Jackie Ryan, Editor

Profile: A reviews-based magazine for young console players.

Requirements: 1 2 8
News and reviews of new games and products for the video console user. Also occasional lifestyle features relevant to the typical user. Length up to 1000 words.

Comments: The magazine aims for a lighthearted, humorous style.

Approach: By telephone.

Lead time: Six weeks.

Payment: £100 per thousand words.

Gamesmaster

Future Publishing
30 Monmouth Street
Bath
BA1 2BW

Tel: (0225) 442244   **Fax:** (0225) 446019

Frequency: Monthly

Circulation: 190,000

Contact: Jim Douglas, Editor

Profile: Video games magazine covering news and releases from around the world. Based on the TV show of the same name.

Requirements: 1 2 8
Features on new technology and developments, plus news of international events and exhibitions. Maximum 800 words.

Comments: The magazine is very visual in style, and contributors should bear this in mind when suggesting ideas.

Approach: In writing.

Lead time: Two months.

Payment: £100 per thousand words.

Garage News

60 Waldegrave Road
Teddington
Middlesex
TW11 8LG

Tel: 081-943 5906   **Fax:** 081-943 5927

Frequency: Monthly

Circulation: 20,000

Contact: Richard Longworth, Editor

Profile: A trade publication for the car service and repair business.

Requirements: 1 2
News and features on cars, equipment, accessories and motor components, etc. Length up to 1500 words.

1/News **2**/Features **3**/Fiction **4**/Letters **5**/Fillers
6/B&W Photos **7**/Colour Photos **8**/Reviews

Comments: All material must reflect the trade rather than the consumer point of view.
Approach: By telephone with ideas.
Lead time: Six weeks.
Payment: £120 per thousand words.

Garden Answers

Apex House
Oundle Road
Peterborough
PE2 9NP

Tel: (0733) 898100   **Fax:** (0733) 898433

Frequency: Monthly

Circulation: 141,727

Contact: Adrienne Wild, Managing Editor
Profile: A practical magazine for gardeners, produced by gardeners. Shows how to grow a better garden and the best products needed to do the job.
Requirements: 1 2 7
'How-to' articles from experienced gardeners, plus plant profiles and good garden features. Length up to 1,000 words, including bullet points and captions.
Comments: Particularly interested in practical features with a new angle.
Approach: By letter with ideas.
Lead time: Four months.
Payment: From £60 per thousand words.

Garden News

Apex House
Oundle Road
Peterborough
PE2 9NP

Tel: (0733) 898100   **Fax:** (0733) 898433

Frequency: Weekly

Circulation: 114,000

Contact: Andrew Blackford, Editor
Profile: For the very keen amateur gardener. Contains mostly cultural information, written in a fairly serious style.
Requirements: 1 2 5 6 7 8
Any material on species, plants and their culture. Also stories on individual gardens that would interest the average reader. Length about 500 words.
Comments: Receives a lot of information with a narrative, story-like style. Articles should be more detailed and practical.
Approach: Submit complete manuscript.
Lead time: Four weeks.
Payment: NUJ rates.

The Gardener

HHL Publications Ltd
Greater London House
Hampstead Road
London
NW1 7QQ

Tel: 071-388 3171   **Fax:** 071-387 9518

Frequency: Monthly

Circulation: 45,000

Contact: Cathy Buchanan, Editor
Profile: A magazine for gardeners aged between 35 and 50. Design-oriented with a strong practical emphasis.
Requirements: 1 2 5
Features on garden design and products. Also profiles of plants, especially in groups or families. Length up to 1500 words.
Comments: Contributors should remember that the magazine has more female than male readers.

1/News **2**/Features **3**/Fiction **4**/Letters **5**/Fillers
6/B&W Photos **7**/Colour Photos **8**/Reviews

Approach: By letter only.
Lead time: Three months.
Payment: £75-£100 per thousand words.

Gardeners' World

Redwood Publishing
20-26 Brunswick Place
London
N1 6DJ

Tel: 071-331 8000   **Fax:** 071-331 8030

Frequency: Monthly

Circulation: 260,000

Contact: Kathryn Bradley-Hole, Editor
Profile: A popular approach to gardening, featuring well-known TV personalities and expert contributors.
Requirements: 2 5
News and features covering all aspects of gardening, with an emphasis on practical and instructional pieces.
Comments: Contributors need a good horticultural background and strong original ideas.
Approach: In writing, with synopsis and examples of previous work.
Lead time: Two months.
Payment: Negotiable.

Geographical

BBC Enterprises
80 Wood Lane
London
W12 0TT

Tel: 081-576 2000   **Fax:** 081-576 2931

Frequency: Monthly

Circulation: 30,000

Contact: Alexander Goldsmith, Editor

Profile: A general-interest geographical magazine for a highly-educated readership, covering subjects such as the environment.
Requirements: 1 2 6 7 8
Well-researched articles on contemporary geographical issues. Expedition or exploration stories are also considered. Maximum length 2000 words.
Comments: In thinking of concepts, don't just follow the headlines. Look for ideas which take a broader, long-term perspective.
Approach: By telephone.
Lead time: Six weeks.
Payment: £100 per thousand words.

Generator

Gillies Publications
102-108 Clerkenwell Road
London
EC1M 5SA

Tel: 071-608 3025   **Fax:** 071-454 7855

Frequency: Monthly

Circulation: 80,000

Contact: Ian Jenkinson, Editor
Profile: A cult magazine for people aged between 14 and 30 who enjoy rave parties, etc.
Requirements: 1 2 8
News of forthcoming music events, interviews with personalities and features on rave subjects or cult music.
Comments: Articles should be aimed at a readership that is very aware and has money to spend.
Approach: By telephone with ideas.
Lead time: Six weeks.
Payment: Negotiable.

1/News **2**/Features **3**/Fiction **4**/Letters **5**/Fillers
6/B&W Photos **7**/Colour Photos **8**/Reviews

Get in Touch

185 Eastney Road
Southsea
Hampshire
PO4 8EA

Tel: (0705) 812749   **Fax:** (0705) 827819

Frequency: Monthly

Circulation: 24,000

Contact: Helen Shaw, Editor

Profile: An independent magazine for single people in the UK. Aimed at three groups – the unmarried, the divorced and those who have been widowed.

Requirements: 2 5
Articles on subjects such as travel, single-parenting etc. Copy should be light-hearted and interesting.

Comments: Try to avoid straightforward romantic material.

Approach: In writing.

Lead time: Two months.

Payment: By arrangement.

Getting About Britain

21 Church Way
Thames Ditton
Surrey
KT7 0NP

Tel: 081-398 8332   **Fax:** 081-398 8332

Frequency: 3xYear

Circulation: 43,000

Contact: Clive Lewis, Editor

Profile: A colour features and listings guide to UK destinations produced by the British Tourist Authority. Read by overseas visitors using the train, plane, coach and ferry.

Requirements: 2
Features on destinations, including

personalities that add character and interest to the subject. Length 600 to 700 words.

Comments: Writing must be tight, robust and imaginative, conveying a keen sense of observation which will attract visitors from abroad.

Approach: By letter with synopsis.

Lead time: Six weeks.

Payment: From £75 per thousand words.

Girl About Town

9 Rathbone Street
London
W1P 1AF

Tel: 071-872 0033   **Fax:** 071-255 2352

Frequency: 104xYear

Circulation: 95,000

Contact: The Editor

Profile: Distributed free to women working in the Greater London area. Targets career women in the 16 to 35 year age range.

Requirements: 2 6 7
Features on subjects of interest to busy women working in the metropolis. Usual subjects include everything from beauty and fashion to theatre and travel. Length around 1000 words.

Comments: Features should aim to grab the attention of a reader with a few moments to spare on the tube or train.

Approach: In writing with ideas.

Lead time: Two weeks.

Payment: Negotiable.

1/News **2**/Features **3**/Fiction **4**/Letters **5**/Fillers
6/B&W Photos **7**/Colour Photos **8**/Reviews

Giroscope

Downside House
Shepton Mallet
Somerset
BA4 4JL

Tel: (0749) 342516 **Fax:** (0749) 344956

Frequency: Bi-monthly

Circulation: 1.3 million

Contact: Ned Halley, Editor

Profile: The magazine for Girobank customers. Covers subjects ranging from travel and leisure to antiques and small businesses.

Requirements: 2 5 7
Articles on any subject that has a banking angle. Most features relate to personal finance in some way. Length up to 800 words.

Comments: Although bank-related, the magazine strives to be of broad interest to readers.

Approach: Submit complete manuscript.

Lead time: Three months.

Payment: £100 per thousand words.

Gladiators

19 Bolsover Street
London
W1P 7HJ

Tel: 071-631 1433 **Fax:** 071-436 1321

Frequency: Monthly

Circulation: 100,000

Contact: Christina Neal, Editor

Profile: A magazine for eight to 15 year olds, based around the Gladiators TV shows.

Requirements: 2 5
Ideas for feature articles relating to Gladiators programmes, covering personalities, the contests and related material.

Comments: Much of the material is produced in house, but the editor welcomes suggestions from freelances.

Approach: In writing with ideas.

Lead time: Six weeks.

Payment: Negotiable.

The Gleaner

Ventura House
176-188 Acre Lane
London
SW2 5UL

Tel: 071-733 7014 **Fax:** 071-326 0794

Frequency: Weekly

Circulation: 18,000

Contact: George Ruddock, Editor

Profile: A newspaper for Afro-Caribbeans, covering news both from the Caribbean and from the UK. Distributed throughout Britain.

Requirements: 1 2 5 6 7
Information on issues affecting the Afro-Caribbean community in the UK, from housing and jobs to racism. Length 400 to 500 words.

Comments: Overseas news is of particular interest.

Approach: By telephone.

Lead time: One week.

Payment: £2 per single column inch.

Gloucestershire & Avon Life

34 Burlington Court
Redcliff Mead Lane
Bristol
BS1 6FB

Tel: (0272) 252052 **Fax:** (0272) 252052

Frequency: Monthly

Circulation: 4000

Contact: Neil Pickford, Editor

1/News **2**/Features **3**/Fiction **4**/Letters **5**/Fillers
6/B&W Photos **7**/Colour Photos **8**/Reviews

Profile: A county lifestyle magazine. Covers both modern and historical matters relating to the area.

Requirements: 2 6 7

Articles on any subject relating to Gloucestershire and Avon. Length 800 to 1800 words.

Comments: Illustrations or ideas for illustrations are always welcome.

Approach: By telephone.

Lead time: Six weeks.

Payment: £20 per thousand words.

Golf Club Management

Harling House
47-51 Great Suffolk Street
London
SE1 0BS

Tel: 071-261 1604   **Fax:** 071-633 0281

Frequency: 10xYear

Circulation: 3400

Contact: Steve Rankin, Editor

Profile: Read by those responsible for the day-to-day running of golf clubs throughout the UK.

Requirements: 2 5

Articles on all aspects of management relating to golf clubs, plus related issues such as technology and security.

Comments: The official journal of the Association of Golf Club Secretaries.

Approach: In writing.

Lead time: Three months.

Payment: Negotiable.

Golf Link

328 Antrim Road
Belfast
BT15 5AB

Tel: (0232) 740471   **Fax:** (0232) 774392

Frequency: 3xYear

Circulation: 4000

Contact: Ray Bingham, Editor

Profile: Concentrates on the Irish golf scene, especially in clubs. Covers competitions, personalities and big events, plus health and fitness.

Requirements: 1 2

International items, articles on instruction and general features.

Comments: Features which stimulate advertising are more likely to be accepted.

Approach: By letter or telephone.

Lead time: Four weeks.

Payment: £50 per article.

Golf Monthly

IPC Magazines
King's Reach Tower
Stamford Street
London
SE1 9LS

Tel: 071-261 7237   **Fax:** 071-261 7240

Frequency: Monthly

Circulation: 95,800

Contact: Colin Callander, Editor

Profile: A mix of instructional articles, interviews with top golfers, course reviews and articles on golf equipment.

Requirements: 1 2 5 7 8

Features on players or courses, plus articles on topical features in golf.

Comments: Material should have national rather than local or regional appeal.

Approach: By telephone, followed up with a letter.

Lead time: Three months.

Payment: NUJ rates.

1/News **2**/Features **3**/Fiction **4**/Letters **5**/Fillers
6/B&W Photos **7**/Colour Photos **8**/Reviews

Golf Weekly

Advance House
37 Millharbour
Isle of Dogs
London
E14 9TX

Tel: 071-538 1031   **Fax:** 071-537 2053

Frequency: Weekly

Circulation: 20,000

Contact: The Editor

Profile: One of Europe's leading golf news magazines. Predominantly focusing on developments and activities on the golf scene.

Requirements: 1 2 5 7
News and features relating to all aspects of golf, especially tours and events.

Comments: Material must be current and topical.

Approach: By letter or fax.

Lead time: One week.

Payment: Broadly NUJ rates.

Golf World

Advance House
37 Millharbour
London
E14 9TX

Tel: 071-538 1031   **Fax:** 071-538 4106

Frequency: Monthly

Circulation: 108,000

Contact: Peter Masters, Features Editor

Profile: Runs feature-led articles on the golf world generally. The emphasis is on instruction and tour players.

Requirements: 1 2 7
General interest golf features, covering subjects such as course architecture, players etc. Length

between 500 and 4000 words, although a typical feature will be about 2000 words.

Comments: The editor does not wish to receive unsolicited manuscripts.

Approach: In writing, with ideas or complete manuscript.

Lead time: Three months.

Payment: £200 per thousand words.

The Golfer

Village Publishing Ltd
24a Brook Mews North
Paddington
W2 3BW

Tel: 071-224 9242   **Fax:** 071-402 2994

Frequency: Monthly

Circulation: 100,000

Contact: Paul Barden

Profile: A high-quality magazine for consumer golfers.

Requirements: 1 2 7
Features on golf, equipment, clothing and travel worldwide. Maximum length 1500 words.

Comments: A re-launch of *Golfers News*.

Approach: By telephone.

Lead time: Four weeks.

Payment: NUJ rates or better.

Good Food Retailing

Stanstead Publications
177 Stanstead Road
Caterham
Surrey
CR3 6AJ

Tel: (0883) 345481   **Fax:** (0883) 344838

Frequency: 10xYear

Circulation: 8500

Contact: Jenni Muir, Editor

1/News 2/Features 3/Fiction 4/Letters 5/Fillers
6/B&W Photos 7/Colour Photos 8/Reviews

Profile: Food and beverage magazine targeted directly at buyers of better quality products. Read by purchasers in supermarkets, food halls, cash and carries, symbol groups and upmarket independent retailers.

Requirements: 1 2 7
News and features from freelances who can write intelligently on food for the retail trade. Length 300 to 1800 words.

Comments: Writers should be prepared to research and interview, as the magazine does not work from press releases.

Approach: In writing, with ideas and examples of previous work.

Lead time: Two months.

Payment: £120 per thousand words.

Good Health

Redwood Publishing
101 Bayham Street
London
NW1 0AG

Tel: 071-331 8000   **Fax:** 071-331 8168

Frequency: Monthly

Circulation: 120,000

Contact: Janette Marshall, Editor

Profile: A mass-market health magazine for mothers with children at home and women aged over 55.

Requirements: 2 5
Features covering general health care, exercise, medicine, diet and hospitals. Length up to 1500 words.

Comments: Most of the magazine content is contributed by freelance writers.

Approach: Send ideas with a brief CV.

Lead time: Two months.

Payment: Negotiable.

Good Holiday Magazine

91 High Street
Esher
Surrey
KT10 9QD

Tel: (0372) 468140   **Fax:** (0372) 470765

Frequency: Quarterly

Circulation: 100,000

Contact: John Hill, Editor

Profile: An upmarket, glossy magazine for consumers, covering interesting holidays and destinations.

Requirements: 2 7
Well-written features on unusual or original destinations around the world. Length from 1000 words.

Comments: Material should match the quality of editorial in the Sunday Times travel section.

Approach: By letter only.

Lead time: Three months.

Payment: From £150 .

Good Housekeeping

National Magazine House
72 Broadwick Street
London
W1V 2BP

Tel: 071-439 5000   **Fax:** 071-439 5591

Frequency: Monthly

Circulation: 446,219

Contact: Hilary Robinson, Features Editor

Profile: A lifestyle magazine read by women aged between 24 and 54.

Requirements: 2 4 5 8
Humorous pieces, together with human-interest and personal-growth features. Length up to 2000 words.

Comments: The magazine is not currently accepting fiction.

1/News **2**/Features **3**/Fiction **4**/Letters **5**/Fillers
6/B&W Photos **7**/Colour Photos **8**/Reviews

Approach: By letter only.
Lead time: Four months.
Payment: £200 per thousand words.

Good Idea

Redwood Publishing
101 Bayham Street
London
NW1 0AG

Tel: 071-331 8000   **Fax:** 071-331 8001

Frequency: Quarterly

Circulation: 1.2 million

Contact: Richard Barber, Editor
Profile: A publication in the style of
Best and Bella, produced on behalf
of Woolworths.
Requirements: Features on
entertainment, celebrities, the home,
cookery, etc. Length up to 1500
words.
Comments: All articles must relate in
some way to products sold in
Woolworths.
Approach: By telephone or letter.
Lead time: Three months.
Payment: £250 per thousand words.

Good Motoring

Station Road
Forest Row
East Sussex
RH18 5EN

Tel: (0342) 825676   **Fax:** (0342) 824847

Frequency: Quarterly

Circulation: 59,000

Contact: D. Hainge, Editor
Profile: General-interest motoring
title, covering all aspects of driving.

Requirements: 2 6 7
Travel or touring features, plus
leisure articles related to motoring.
Length about 1000 words.
Comments: Copies of the magazine are
available for guidance.
Approach: Telephone or write with
ideas.
Lead time: Two months.
Payment: From £65 per thousand
words.

Good Ski Guide

91 High Street
Esher
Surrey
KT10 9QD

Tel: (0372) 468140   **Fax:** (0372) 470765

Frequency: Bi-monthly

Circulation: 150,000

Contact: John Hill, Editor
Profile: An upmarket consumer title
for enthusiastic skiers.
Requirements: 2 7
Well-written features about possible
destinations for skiing holidays.
Length from 700 words.
Comments: Sample copies of the
magazine are available on request.
Approach: By letter only.
Lead time: Three months.
Payment: From £150.

Good Stories

23 Mill Crescent
Kingsbury
Warwickshire
B78 2LX

Tel: (0827) 873435

Frequency: Quarterly

Circulation: 5000

Contact: Andrew Jenns, Editor

Profile: An A5-format publication devoted to short fiction.

Requirements: 3 4 5

Short stories of up to 2500 words on any subject. Also short filler items based on true experiences and humorous letters of interest to readers of short fiction.

Comments: Stories of up to 1000 words are always in demand.

Approach: In writing.

Lead time: Two months.

Payment: About £20 per thousand words.

The Good Van Guide

60 Waldegrave Road
Teddington
Middlesex
TW11 8LG

Tel: 081-943 5881   **Fax:** 081-943 5871

Frequency: Bi-monthly

Circulation: 40,000

Contact: Alan Anderson, Editor

Profile: All you need to know about vans for people who want to get more out of their businesses.

Requirements: 1 2 6 7 8

News stories, plus information about any specialist vans. Articles on subjects such as accessories, sign-writing etc. Length up to 1500 words.

Comments: Contact the editor before submitting any material.

Approach: By telephone or letter.

Lead time: Three weeks.

Payment: £130 per thousand words.

Good Woodworking

Future Publishing
30 Monmouth Street
Bath
BA1 2BW

Tel: (0225) 442244   **Fax:** (0225) 462986

Frequency: Monthly

Circulation: Not available

Contact: Nick Gibbs, Editor

Profile: A magazine for the woodworker who is not an expert, but who is not a raw beginner, either.

Requirements: 2 5

Articles about projects that can be completed within a few days by a competent amateur. These should be neither too complex for the ordinary woodworker, not too simple for the enthusiast.

Comments: The editor will commission features on suitable projects.

Approach: In writing with ideas.

Lead time: Two months.

Payment: Negotiable.

Goodnews Magazine

Editorial
34 Duite Road
Chiswick
London
W4 2DD

Tel: 081-994 3239   **Fax:** 081-994 8088

Frequency: Quarterly

Circulation: 382,000

Contact: Brian Charig, Editor

Profile: A publication for the home and family, distributed throughout the UK.

Requirements: 1 2 4 6 7 8

News, features and fillers relating to all aspects of home life.

1/News **2**/Features **3**/Fiction **4**/Letters **5**/Fillers
6/B&W Photos **7**/Colour Photos **8**/Reviews

Comments: Contact the editor before submitting material.
Approach: By letter.
Lead time: Three months.
Payment: £50 to £150.

GQ

Vogue House
Hanover Square
London
W1R 0AD

Tel: 071-499 9080   **Fax:** 071-495 1679

Frequency: Monthly

Circulation: 92,000

Contact: Angus MacKinnon, Features Editor
Profile: A style magazine for men aged 25 to 40, mostly earning in excess of £25,000 a year.
Requirements: 1 2 6 7 8
Features of interest to affluent, intelligent men. Length 3000 to 4000 words.
Comments: Material must be original, accurate and well-researched.
Approach: Letter followed by a telephone call.
Lead time: Three months.
Payment: £110 per thousand words.

Gramophone

177-179 Kenton Road
Harrow
HA3 0HA

Tel: 081-907 4476   **Fax:** 081-907 0073

Frequency: Monthly

Circulation: 72,000

Contact: James Jolly, Editor
Profile: Devoted entirely to classical music. Deals mainly with new recordings of classical works.

Requirements: 1 2 8
Reviews of musical releases across the whole field of classical music. Also occasional features or interviews on related subjects.
Comments: Although features are used, the majority of the magazine is given over to reviews, which provide the best opportunity for unknown writers.
Approach: By letter with examples of work.
Lead time: Four weeks.
Payment: Negotiable.

Granta

2-3 Hanover Yard
Noel Road
London
N1 8BE

Tel: 071-704 9776   **Fax:** 071-704 0474

Frequency: Quarterly

Circulation: 100,000

Contact: Bill Buford, Editor
Profile: A literary publication produced in conjunction with Penguin. Features a distinctive blend of cultural and political material, both fiction and non-fiction.
Requirements: 2 3 6
Short fiction, extended cultural journalism and journalistic travel writing. Length 1000 to 10,000 words.
Comments: Readers should be familiar with the publication's narrative style.
Approach: In writing, with ideas or complete manuscript.
Lead time: Three months.
Payment: £175 per thousand words.

Graphics International

35 Britannia Row
London
N1 8QH

Tel: 071-226 1739   **Fax:** 071-226 1540

Frequency: Bi-monthly

Circulation: 8500

Contact: Tim Rich, Editor

Profile: Large format magazine
   covering the creative and business
   aspects of graphic design.

Requirements: 1 2 7 8
   Articles relating to the design of
   annual reports, brochures,
   packaging, corporate identities,
   books and record sleeves. Typical
   length 1000 words.

Comments: The editor will commission
   writers to produce both features and
   shorter reviews.

Approach: By letter or fax.

Lead time: Six weeks.

Payment: Circa £125 per thousand
   words.

The Great Outdoors

The Plaza Tower
The Plaza
East Kilbride
Glasgow
G74 1LW

Tel: (0355) 246444   **Fax:** (0355) 263013

Frequency: Monthly

Circulation: 25,500

Contact: Cameron McNeish, Editor

Profile: For walkers, backpackers and
   climbers throughout the UK. Read
   mainly by men aged between 25 and
   54 who enjoy hill walking, lowland
   walking, conservation, photography
   and backpacking.

Requirements: 2 5
   General features on interesting
   walking and climbing locations.
   Focuses mainly on the UK, but does
   include some material on accessible
   locations overseas. Length 1500 to
   2000 words.

Comments: Would like to receive more
   material from lady walkers.
   Specialist topics such as equipment
   tests are mainly handled in house.

Approach: In writing.

Lead time: Two months.

Payment: Around £120 per feature.

Great Western Railway Journal

1-3 Hagbourne Road
Didcot
Oxon
OX11 8DP

Tel: (0235) 816478

Frequency: Quarterly

Contact: John Copsey

Profile: Devoted to the history of the
   Great Western Railway.

Requirements: 2 5
   News and features about the trains,
   stations, people and history of the
   railway. Subjects are often covered
   in considerable depth.

Comments: Does not run material on
   other railways.

Approach: In writing.

Lead time: Three months.

Payment: Negotiable.

1/News **2**/Features **3**/Fiction **4**/Letters **5**/Fillers
6/B&W Photos **7**/Colour Photos **8**/Reviews

Green Magazine

PO Box 3205
4 Selsdon Way
London
E14 9GL

Tel: 071-712 0550   **Fax:** 071-712 0557

Frequency: Monthly

Circulation: 55,000

Contact: Alistair Townley, Editor

Profile: An independent publication devoted to all aspects of the environment.

Requirements: 2 6 7
Features on environmental issues, ranging from local development to international and global problems. Length up to 2500 words.

Comments: Ideas for new, original features are always welcome.

Approach: By telephone.

Lead time: Seven weeks.

Payment: £120 per thousand words.

Greyhound Star

Spirella Building
Bridge Road
Letchworth
Hertfordshire
SG6 4ET

Tel: (0462) 679439   **Fax:** (0462) 483709

Frequency: Monthly

Circulation: 10,000

Contact: Floyd Amphlett, Editor

Profile: A specialist magazine for greyhound owners, breeders, trainers and track operators.

Requirements: 1 2 5 6 7
Off-beat, off-diary news and features covering the world of greyhound racing throughout the UK. Length up to 1000 words.

Comments: Writers are advised not to attempt profiles, as these are handled in house.

Approach: By telephone.

Lead time: Six weeks.

Payment: Negotiable.

The Grocer

Broadfield Park
Crawley
West Sussex
RH11 9RT

Tel: (0293) 613400   **Fax:** (0293) 515174

Frequency: Weekly

Circulation: 57,386

Contact: Clive Beddall, Editor

Profile: News magazine for the grocery trade, covering retailing and business issues across the board.

Requirements: 1 2 5
Articles about developments within the trade, trends, new products etc. Also case studies of highly-successful grocery retailers.

Comments: The principal magazine for the grocery trade, providing authoritative information.

Approach: By telephone.

Lead time: One week.

Payment: Broadly NUJ rates.

The Grower

50 Doughty Street
London
WC1N 2LS

Tel: 071-405 0364   **Fax:** 071-831 2230

Frequency: Weekly

Circulation: 11,194

Contact: Peter Rogers, Editor

Profile: A trade journal for everyone involved in commercial horticulture.

1/News **2**/Features **3**/Fiction **4**/Letters **5**/Fillers
6/B&W Photos **7**/Colour Photos **8**/Reviews

Requirements: 1 2 6 7
News and features on horticultural topics, covering anything from fruit and vegetables to flowers and ornamentals.
Comments: Does not require any material on amateur horticulture.
Approach: By letter.
Lead time: Three weeks.
Payment: Negotiable.

The Grown Ups Magazine

45 Station Road
Redhill
Surrey
RH1 1QH
Tel: (0737) 767213   **Fax:** (0737) 771662
Frequency: Quarterly
Circulation: 65,000
Contact: David Hoppit, Editor
Profile: For active middle-aged men and women with money to spare. Advises them on how to spend it, which charities to support, and recommends investments.
Requirements: 2 5 7
Features on travel, investment, wines, sport holidays etc. Length 800 to 900 words.
Comments: Always glad to receive ideas for filler items. Features which attract advertising revenue are likely to be well received.
Approach: By letter with ideas.
Lead time: Four weeks.
Payment: From £200 per thousand words.

Guide Patrol

The Girl Guides Association
17-19 Buckingham Palace Road
London
SW1W 0PT
Tel: 071-834 6242   **Fax:** 071-828 8317
Frequency: Monthly
Circulation: 25,000
Contact: Mary Richards, Editor
Profile: A 'how-to' publication for Girl Guides. Full of ideas for crafts and sports that they can try.
Requirements: 2 3
Practical step-by-step instructions for possible activities. Also short stories, although these must have a Guiding angle. Length about 800 words.
Comments: Purely factual articles are not required.
Approach: In writing with ideas.
Lead time: Three months.
Payment: £40 per thousand words.

Guiding

The Girl Guides Association
17-19 Buckingham Palace Road
London
SW1W 0PT
Tel: 071-834 6242   **Fax:** 071-828 8317
Frequency: Monthly
Circulation: 30,000
Contact: Nora Warner, Editor
Profile: Read by Rangers, young leaders and adult leaders within the Guide movement. Concerned with their interests, activities and programme help.
Requirements: 1 2 7
Features on newsworthy members or accounts of local special events.

Comments: The readers know their subject very well, so make sure that facts and terminology are correct.
Approach: By telephone or fax.
Lead time: Three months.
Payment: £70 per thousand words.

Guitar

United Leisure Magazines
PO Box 3205
4 Selsdon Way
London
E14 9ZR

Tel: 071-712 0550   **Fax:** 071-712 0557

Frequency: Monthly

Circulation: 34,000

Contact: Michael Leonard, Editor
Profile: Covers guitars, guitarists and modern guitar-based music. Aims to include up-and-coming bands as well as established ones.
Requirements: 1 2 5 6 7
News and features on guitars, equipment, guitarists and bands. Also retrospective features on well-known musicians. Length up to 4000 words.
Comments: The editor is looking for people who can come up with good ideas, especially on heavy metal music.
Approach: By telephone or letter.
Lead time: Five weeks.
Payment: Around £100 per thousand words.

Gymnast

Main Street
Bruntingthorpe
Leicestershire
LE17 5QF

Tel: (0533) 478766   **Fax:** (0533) 478766

Frequency: Bi-monthly

Circulation: 12,000

Contact: Trevor Low, Editor
Profile: A magazine of broad interest to gymnasts, covering everything from the sport itself to fitness, education and fund raising.
Requirements: 1 2 5
Informative, entertaining articles about the sport of gymnastics. Length 300 to 500 words.
Comments: Contact the editor before submitting manuscripts.
Approach: By telephone or fax.
Lead time: Three months.
Payment: £50 per thousand words.

H

Hair

IPC Magazines
King's Reach Tower
Stamford Street
London
SE1 9LS

Tel: 071-261 5000   **Fax:** 071-261 7382

Frequency: Bi-monthly

Circulation: 174,443

Contact: Annette Davies, Editor

Profile: A hair, beauty and fashion magazine for women in the 15 to 35 age group.

Requirements: 2 6 7
Features not just on hair, but also on other fashion and lifestyle subjects for women. Length up to 1000 words.

Comments: This is not a trade magazine, so all material should be of direct relevance to the consumer.

Approach: Submit complete manuscript.

Lead time: Two months.

Payment: £200-£250 per piece.

Hairflair

178-182 Pentonville Road
London
N1 9LB

Tel: 071-278 4393   **Fax:** 071-837 8219

Frequency: Monthly

Circulation: 56,397

Contact: Hellena Barnes, Editor

Profile: A practical hair-care magazine that shows ways of making the most of your hair. Primarily hair-based, but also covers make up.

Requirements: 1 2 6 7
Features on styling techniques, perms, seasonal styles and so on. Length up to 1000 words.

Comments: Features that tie into the magazine's features list will have a good chance of success.

Approach: By letter with examples of previous work.

Lead time: Three months.

Payment: £100.

Hampshire County Magazine

74 Bedford Place
Southampton
SO1 2DF

Tel: (0703) 333457   **Fax:** (0703) 227190

Frequency: Monthly

Circulation: 9350

Contact: Dennis Stevens, Editor

Profile: County magazine covering all subjects of interest to the residents of Hampshire.

Requirements: 1 2 6 7
Historical and topical news items, plus features on people and places in the county.

1/News **2**/Features **3**/Fiction **4**/Letters **5**/Fillers
6/B&W Photos **7**/Colour Photos **8**/Reviews

Comments: Features accompanied by photographs are always welcome.
Approach: By letter.
Lead time: Two months.
Payment: Negotiable.

Harpers & Queen

National Magazine House
72 Broadwick Street
London
W1V 2BP

Tel: 071-439 5000   **Fax:** 071-439 5506

Frequency: Monthly

Circulation: 82,767

Contact: Richard Preston, Senior Editor
Profile: A stylish, upmarket magazine for women aged between 30 and 50.
Requirements: 2 5 6 7 8
Features on travel, food, drink, fashion and other subjects that would interest the readership. Length up to 2000 words.
Comments: Do not send fiction of any kind.
Approach: By letter with ideas.
Lead time: Three months.
Payment: Negotiable.

Headlight

PO Box 96
Coulsden
Surrey
CR5 2TE

Tel: 081-660 2811   **Fax:** 081-660 2824

Frequency: Monthly

Circulation: 18,797

Contact: Bob Scott, Editor
Profile: A monthly title aimed at lorry drivers and owners, plus those operating small fleets of trucks.

Requirements: 1 2
News and features on subjects of interest to those involved with truck driving. Copy should be informative, but approachable and easy to read.
Comments: Articles with an original or unusual angle will be more likely to succeed.
Approach: In writing.
Lead time: Two months.
Payment: Negotiable.

Health & Efficiency

28 Charles Square
Pitfield Street
London
N1 6HP

Tel: 071-253 4037   **Fax:** 071-253 0539

Frequency: Monthly

Circulation: 120,000

Contact: Kate Sturdy, Editor
Profile: Magazines covering health and naturist subjects.
Requirements: 2
Articles about relationships, nudity and naturism. Also features on health, food, fitness and naturist travel. Length up to 2000 words.
Comments: Short features of up to 1000 words are always welcome.
Approach: By letter or fax.
Lead time: Two months.
Payment: £40 per thousand words.

Health & Fitness

Greater London House
Hampstead
London
NW1 7QQ

Tel: 071-388 3171   **Fax:** 071-377 4890

1/News **2**/Features **3**/Fiction **4**/Letters **5**/Fillers
6/B&W Photos **7**/Colour Photos **8**/Reviews

Frequency: Monthly

Circulation: 35,000

Contact: Sharon Walker, Editor

Profile: Magazine for all those interested in healthy living and healthy lifestyles.

Requirements: 2 5
Articles on all aspects of health and fitness, plus related subjects.

Comments: Contact the magazine before submitting manuscripts.

Approach: In writing.

Lead time: Two months.

Payment: Negotiable.

Health Guardian

Premier House
Madeira Road
West Byfleet
Surrey
KT14 6NF

Tel: (0932) 336325   **Fax:** (0932) 353670

Frequency: Bi-monthly

Circulation: 150,000

Contact: Brian McLoughlin, Editor

Profile: A full-colour magazine dealing with all aspects of natural health and nutritious food.

Requirements: 1 2 5 7
Unusual recipe features that use all natural ingredients, reader's own stories of how natural treatments cured them, and articles on healthy hobbies. Length 1000 words maximum.

Comments: The publication is sold through health food shops. Therefore a good knowledge of products sold in such outlets is an advantage.

Approach: By telephone with initial ideas.

Lead time: Six weeks.

Payment: From £50 per thousand words.

Health Now

79-81 High Street
Godalming
Surrey
GU7 1AW

Tel: (0483) 426064   **Fax:** (0483) 426005

Frequency: Bi-monthly

Circulation: 350,000

Contact: Alice Peet, Editor

Profile: A magazine distributed to customers of health-food shops around the country.

Requirements: 1 2 5 6 7
Articles on the natural healing process, remedies and recipes. Length 500 to 1000 words.

Comments: The magazine does not cover conventional drugs or medicine.

Approach: In writing, with ideas or finished manuscript.

Lead time: Four weeks.

Payment: £100 per item.

Healthy Eating

9 Vermont Place
Tongwell
Milton Keynes
MK15 8JA

Tel: (0908) 613323   **Fax:** (0908) 210656

Frequency: Bi-monthly

Circulation: 60,000

Contact: Pamela Brook

1/News **2**/Features **3**/Fiction **4**/Letters **5**/Fillers
6/B&W Photos **7**/Colour Photos **8**/Reviews

Profile: The magazine for people who care about what they eat. A food-based magazine concerned with creating and enjoying a balanced diet.
Requirements: 2 5
Features on foods and meals that contribute to the formation of a healthy diet. Length up to 1000 words.
Comments: Does not cover alternative medicine.
Approach: By telephone.
Lead time: Two months.
Payment: Negotiable.

Heavy Duty

PO Box 44
Bexley
Kent
Tel: (0322) 555959   **Fax:** (0322) 527290
Frequency: Bi-monthly
Circulation: 20,000
Contact: Stu Garland, Editor
Profile: A motorcycle title for bikers aged between 25 and 45. As well as conventional biking material, the magazine also covers relevant music, etc.
Requirements: 1 2
News and features covering biking events, dealer information, legal matters and other relevant subjects. Length 2000 to 3000 words.
Comments: Colour transparencies or black & white photos to accompany features are always welcome.
Approach: By letter with ideas.
Lead time: Six weeks.
Payment: Negotiable.

Helicopter International

75 Elm Tree Road
Locking
Weston-super-Mare
Avon
BS24 8EL
Tel: (0934) 822524   **Fax:** (0934) 822400
Frequency: Bi-monthly
Circulation: 23,000
Contact: Elfan ap Rees, Editor
Profile: News of international military and civil helicopter operations for consumption by helicopter executives, pilots, military government departments, etc.
Requirements: 1 2 6
Informed and accurate news items or features on helicopter subjects, preferably accompanied by photos. Length 1000 to 3000 words.
Comments: Particularly interested in first-hand stories from outside the UK.
Approach: By letter, telephone or fax.
Lead time: Six weeks.
Payment: From £30 per thousand words.

Hello!

Wellington House
69-71 Upper Ground
London
SE1 9PQ
Tel: 071-334 7404   **Fax:** 071-334 7411
Frequency: Weekly
Circulation: 444,257
Contact: Maggie Goodman, Editor
Profile: Glitzy magazine devoted to the lives and activities of the rich and famous.

Requirements: 2

Interviews with well-known personalities, and other personality-based features.

Comments: Features tend to be uncritical of their subjects.

Approach: In writing with suggestions.

Lead time: One month.

Payment: Negotiable.

Here's Health

Victory House
14 Leicester Square
London WC2H 7BP

Tel: 071-437 9011   **Fax:** 071-434 0656

Frequency: Monthly

Circulation: 38,000

Contact: Mandy Francis, Editor

Profile: A natural health magazine that covers everything from diet and healthy eating to complementary therapies.

Requirements: 1 2 7

Articles on natural treatments, new developments, complementary medicines, etc. Length 1500 to 2000 words.

Comments: Although unsolicited manuscripts are accepted, most work is commissioned.

Approach: By letter.

Lead time: Two months.

Payment: £125 per thousand words.

Here's How

R.A.P. Publishing
120 Wilton Road
London
SW1V 1JZ

Tel: 071-834 8534   **Fax:** 071-873 8557

Frequency: Monthly

Circulation: 50,000

Contact: Barbara Reine Allen

Profile: A home improvements magazine for both men and women. Includes both technical instructional features and simpler craft-type topics.

Requirements: 2 5

Articles on DIY projects and suitable products, plus advice and tips. Also features on the homes of DIY enthusiasts.

Comments: Project features should be accompanied by lists of tools and materials required.

Approach: In writing with ideas.

Lead time: Two months.

Payment: £100 per thousand words.

Heritage Magazine

4 The Courtyard
Denmark Street
Wokingham
Berkshire
RG11 2AZ

Tel: (0734) 771677   **Fax:** (0734) 772903

Frequency: Bi-monthly

Circulation: 27,000

Contact: Sian Ellis, Assistant Editor

Profile: A celebration of British life, homes and countryside for all those interested in the country's heritage.

Requirements: 2 7

Features on villages and towns, people and crafts, houses and gardens. Length around 1200 words.

Comments: Particularly interested in material on places that are less well known, but which are historic and photogenic.

Approach: Telephone or send synopsis.
Lead time: Two months.
Payment: Around £100 per thousand words.

Hertfordshire Magazine

4 Mill Bridge
Hertford
Hertfordshire
SG14 1PY

Tel: (0992) 553571   **Fax:** (0992) 587713

Frequency: Monthly

Circulation: 14,000

Contact: The Editor
Profile: A county magazine concerned with both topical news and the historical aspects of Hertfordshire.
Requirements: 1 2 6
News and features on fashion, the arts, gardening, property, antiques and home-interest subjects. Length around 1000 words.
Comments: Welcomes line drawings and photographs to accompany features.
Approach: In writing with ideas.
Lead time: Two months.
Payment: From £25 per thousand words.

Hi-Fi Choice

19 Bolsover Street
London
W1V 2BP

Tel: 071-631 1433   **Fax:** 071-323 3547

Frequency: Monthly

Circulation: 30,000

Contact: The Editor
Profile: A specialist magazine for hi-fi enthusiasts.

Requirements: 1 2 7
News and features about new hi-fi products and developments.
Comments: Contact the magazine before submitting reviews or features.
Approach: In writing.
Lead time: One month.
Payment: £120-£150 per thousand words.

Hi-Fi News

Link House
Dingwall Avenue
Croydon
CR9 2TA

Tel: 081-686 2599   **Fax:** 081-781 6046

Frequency: Monthly

Circulation: 30,013

Contact: Steve Harris, Editor
Profile: Reviews hi-fi and audio equipment, plus new music releases.
Requirements: 1 2 6 7 8
Hi-fi DIY articles, equipment tests and reviews of new releases in classical music, jazz and rock. Length 1500 to 4000 words.
Comments: Don't waste your time sending unsolicited manuscripts.
Approach: By letter with ideas.
Lead time: Five weeks.
Payment: Negotiable.

Hi-Fi World

64 Castellain Road
Maida Vale
London
W9 1EX

Tel: 071-289 3533   **Fax:** 071-289 5620

Frequency: Monthly

Circulation: 20,000

1/News **2**/Features **3**/Fiction **4**/Letters **5**/Fillers
6/B&W Photos **7**/Colour Photos **8**/Reviews

Contact: Noel Keywood, Editor
Profile: Caters for both the hi-fi enthusiast and the music lover. Most readers are aged between 25 and 35, and spend between £500 and £1000 a year on hi-fi equipment.
Requirements: 2 8
Reviews of musical releases, covering jazz, rock, classical and pop. Also articles about component products, etc. Length up to 2500 words.
Comments: Reviews offer the best opportunities for unknown writers.
Approach: By letter or fax.
Lead time: Ten weeks.
Payment: Broadly in line with NUJ rates.

Hi-Time

Centurion Press
52 George Street
London
W1H 5RF

Tel: 071-487 4284   **Fax:** 071-487 5398

Frequency: 5xYear

Circulation: 1.2 million

Contact: Jane Harris, Editor
Profile: Asda's in-store consumer publication, aimed at women readers. The main focus is food and cookery, but subjects such as fashion, beauty and the home are also covered.
Requirements: 2
Occasional cookery articles and features on babies, home interest, etc. Length up to 750 words.
Comments: The magazine is primarily a marketing tool, so features having some connection to Asda products will have the best chance of success.

Approach: By telephone, letter or fax with ideas.
Lead time: Three months.
Payment: £250 per 750-word feature.

High Magazine

336 Abbey Lane
Sheffield
S8 0BY

Tel: (0742) 369296   **Fax:** (0742) 366647

Frequency: Monthly

Circulation: 18,000

Contact: Geoff Birtles, Editor
Profile: Covers mountaineering, rock climbing and serious hill walking, both in the UK and worldwide.
Requirements: 1 2 6 7
News and features on the above subjects, plus articles on other mountain-related sports such as cross-country skiing. Length 1500 to 2000 words.
Comments: Material must be written from first-hand experience.
Approach: Submit finished manuscript.
Lead time: Five weeks.
Payment: £30 per thousand words.

HIM

Worldwide House
116-134 Bayham House
London
NW1 0BA

Tel: 071-482 2576   **Fax:** 071-284 0329

Frequency: Monthly

Circulation: 28,000

Contact: Pas Paschali, Editor
Profile: Covers all subjects of interest to the gay community.

1/News 2/Features 3/Fiction 4/Letters 5/Fillers
6/B&W Photos 7/Colour Photos 8/Reviews

Requirements: 1 2 3 8
  News and features on relevant topics, plus reviews and some fiction.
Comments: Contact the editor before submitting manuscripts.
Approach: By telephone.
Lead time: One month.
Payment: Up to £100.

Historic Race & Rally

178 Old Christchurch Road
Bournemouth
Dorset
BH1 1NU

Tel: (0202) 317007   **Fax:** (0202) 319422

Frequency: Bi-monthly

Circulation: 45,000

Contact: Clive Richardson, Editor
Profile: Provides extensive coverage of historic racing and rallying.
Requirements: 1 2 6 7
  In-depth features on all aspects of current historic racing, rallying and events. Also reports of meetings and information about interesting cars.
Comments: The magazine is read in every country around the world.
Approach: By letter or fax.
Lead time: Six weeks.
Payment: Negotiable.

History Today

20 Old Compton Street
London
W1V 5PE

Tel: 071-439 8315

Frequency: Monthly

Circulation: 30,000

Contact: Gordon Marsden, Editor

Profile: A historical magazine, covering all aspects of history both in the UK and worldwide.
Requirements: 1 2 6 7 8
  News and features on any historical topic. News pieces are generally between 800 and 1000 words, while features run from 3000 to 4000 words.
Comments: Editorial is very broad in range and scope.
Approach: Write with brief synopsis.
Lead time: Six months.
Payment: Negotiable.

Hockey Digest

Unit E6
Aladdin Workspace
426 Long Drive
Greenford
Middlesex
UB6 8UH

Tel: 081-575 3121   **Fax:** 081-575 1320

Frequency: 10xYear

Circulation: 5000

Contact: Peter Luck, Editor
Profile: Covers men and women's hockey in the UK, from school to international level. Includes playing, coaching and umpiring techniques, etc.
Requirements: 1 2 5 6 7
  Profiles of players and clubs, news of tournaments and events, articles on rules and coaching.
Comments: Contact the magazine before submitting any material.
Approach: By telephone.
Lead time: Three weeks.
Payment: Negotiable.

1/News **2**/Features **3**/Fiction **4**/Letters **5**/Fillers
6/B&W Photos **7**/Colour Photos **8**/Reviews

Holiday UK

26 High Street
Billericay
Essex
CM12 9BQ

Tel: (0277) 63311   **Fax:** (0277) 65400

Frequency: Quarterly

Circulation: 35,000

Contact: David Ward, Editor

Profile: A guide to holidays for all the
family throughout the UK. Includes
local tourist information, what's on
and where to stay.

Requirements: 1 2 4 7
Regional or resort articles from local
people who write in an easy-to-read
style, providing all the necessary
information.

Comments: Copy must be original, not
simply re-writes of handouts from
tourist board offices.

Approach: By telephone with ideas.

Lead time: Six weeks.

Payment: By negotiation.

Home & Away

Expats House
29 Lacon Road
East Dulwich
SE22 9HE

Tel: 081-299 4986   **Fax:** 081-299 2484

Frequency: Monthly

Circulation: 7600

Contact: Pauline O'Brien, Editor

Profile: Covers all matters of interest
to British expatriates around the
world.

Requirements: 2 3 6 7
Serious and light-hearted pieces on
subjects such as international job
finding, tax and investment. Always
looking for technical writers who

can write about industries such as
construction and petro-chemicals on
an international basis.

Comments: Humorous articles are
always welcome.

Approach: By telephone.

Lead time: Two weeks.

Payment: £100 per page.

Home and Country

104 New Kings Road
London
SW6 4LY

Tel: 071-731 5777   **Fax:** 071-736 4061

Frequency: Monthly

Circulation: 95,000

Contact: Penny Kitchen, Editor

Profile: Read by subscribing members
of the Women's Institute. A typical
reader will be a housewife in her 50s.

Requirements: 2 5 6 7
Articles on any subject of interest to
the readership, especially those with
an environmental or country angle.
Length up to 1000 words.

Comments: Articles should be slanted
to interest the typical reader as
above.

Approach: By telephone.

Lead time: Two months.

Payment: Negotiable but good.

Home & Family

The Mother's Union
Mary Sumner House
24 Tufton Street
London
SW1P 3RB

Tel: 071-222 5533   **Fax:** 071-222 5533
ext.200

Frequency: Quarterly

1/News 2/Features 3/Fiction 4/Letters 5/Fillers
6/B&W Photos 7/Colour Photos 8/Reviews

Circulation: 140,000

Contact: Margaret Duggan, Editor

Profile: Devoted to advancing Christianity in the sphere of marriage and family life.

Requirements: 2 5
Features on social issues, life in the home, marriage and Christianity. Length up to 1000 words.

Comments: Features do not need to be blatantly religious.

Approach: In writing.

Lead time: Four months.

Payment: £30 for a 300-word article.

Home & Studio Recording

Alexander House
Forehill
Ely
Cambridgeshire
CB7 4AF

Tel: (0353) 665577   **Fax:** (0353) 662489

Frequency: Monthly

Circulation: 18,000

Contact: Dan Goldstein, Editor

Profile: A product and advice magazine for studio users and owners. Covers home, semi-pro and professional studios.

Requirements: 2 5 7 8
Short appraisals of new studio products, technique features, interviews with producers and studio profiles. Length 700 to 2700 words.

Comments: Copy on disk is preferred.

Approach: Send complete manuscript.

Lead time: Three weeks.

Payment: £75 per thousand words.

Home Business

Merlin Publications
95 Ditchling Road
Brighton
BN1 4SE

Tel: (0273) 621186   **Fax:** (0273) 621189

Frequency: Monthly

Circulation: 40,000

Contact: Mike Beardall, Editor

Profile: About starting and running a small business based in the home. The editorial emphasises potentially profitable businesses that can be started on a modest budget.

Requirements: 1 2
Articles giving ideas for new businesses that can be run from home, covering anything from basket weaving to computer programming. Length 600 to 1200 words.

Comments: Features should concentrate on starting a business, rather than general information for the self employed.

Approach: By letter with ideas.

Lead time: Six weeks.

Payment: £66 per thousand words.

Home Entertainment

14 Rathbone Place
London
W1P 1DE

Tel: 071-631 1433   **Fax:** 071-636 1640

Frequency: Quarterly

Circulation: 35,000

Contact: John Baldie, Editor

Profile: A home cinema magazine, covering the world of wide-screen television, video recorders and complete media systems.

1/News **2**/Features **3**/Fiction **4**/Letters **5**/Fillers
6/B&W Photos **7**/Colour Photos **8**/Reviews

Requirements: 1 2 8
Reviews covering releases on video tape and laser disk. Also features on personalities, interviews with directors, etc. Length up to 2500 words.
Comments: Aimed at those who want to go beyond ordinary video rental, creating a virtual cinema at home.
Approach: In writing with synopsis and examples of previous work.
Lead time: Four months.
Payment: £120 per thousand words.

Home Farm

Buriton House
Station Road
Newport
Saffron Walden
Essex
CB11 3PL

Tel: (0709) 40922   **Fax:** (0709) 41367

Frequency: Bi-monthly

Circulation: 11,000

Contact: Katie Thear, Editor
Profile: A practical magazine for smallholders and farmers. Covers organic gardening and growing, keeping livestock, etc.
Requirements: 1 2 5 6 7
Practical features on the above subjects. All material must be practical in nature, well-researched and authoritative. Length up to 2000 words.
Comments: Articles on country crafts are also welcome.
Approach: Submit complete manuscript.
Lead time: Four weeks.
Payment: £20 per thousand words.

Home Run

Active Information
PO Box 2841
London
W6 9ZQ

Tel: 081-741 2440   **Fax:** 081-846 9244

Frequency: 10xYear

Circulation: 3500

Contact: Sophie Chalmers, Editor
Profile: A guide to running a successful business from home. Includes everything from cottage industries to modern technology-based businesses.
Requirements: 1 2
News and features on topics such as finance, marketing, taxation, etc. Also case studies of successful enterprises, and articles giving sound, practical advice.
Comments: The editor welcomes good, original ideas for features.
Approach: In writing.
Lead time: Two months.
Payment: Around £100 per thousand words.

Home Words

PO Box 44
Guildford
Surrey
GU1 1XL

Tel: (0483) 33944

Frequency: Monthly

Contact: The Editor
Profile: An illustrated magazine published by the Church of England.
Requirements: 2 6 7
General articles on subjects of

1/News 2/Features 3/Fiction 4/Letters 5/Fillers
6/B&W Photos 7/Colour Photos 8/Reviews

interest to Christians. All material should have an Anglican angle. Length 400 to 800 words.
Comments: Photographs are welcomed.
Approach: By letter.
Lead time: Two months.
Payment: Negotiable.

Homebrew Supplier

304 Northridge Way
Hemel Hempstead
Hertfordshire
HP1 2AB

Tel: (0442) 67228   **Fax:** (0442) 67228

Frequency: Quarterly

Circulation: 2100

Contact: Evelyn Barrett
Profile: A trade magazine for businesses supplying home brewers.
Requirements: 1 2
News and features on products and developments relating to the making of wine and beer at home.
Comments: Material is considered from the trade rather than the brewer's point of view.
Approach: In writing.
Lead time: Four weeks.
Payment: £40 per thousand words.

Homebrew Today

304 Northridge Way
Hemel Hempstead
Hertfordshire
HP1 2AB

Tel: (0442) 67228   **Fax:** (0442) 67228

Frequency: Quarterly

Circulation: 150,000

Contact: Evelyn Barrett, Editor
Profile: For the home wine and beer maker. Covers both kits and production from natural ingredients.
Requirements: 2 5 6 7
'How-to' articles accompanied by recipes, plus features about interesting personalities. All copy must be factual. Length 1000 to 1500 words.
Comments: Definitely no stories about beer bottles exploding in the attic, etc.
Approach: In writing, with ideas or complete manuscript.
Lead time: Four weeks.
Payment: £40 per thousand words.

Homeflair Magazine

Regal House
Regal Way
Watford
Hertfordshire
WD2 4YJ

Tel: (0923) 237799   **Fax:** (0923) 246901

Frequency: 10xYear

Circulation: 80,000

Contact: Dawn Leahey, Editor
Profile: An interior design publication, showing how to make the most of your home on an average budget.
Requirements: 1 2 7 8
Anything on interior design for typical homes, using flair and skill rather than great expense. Length up to 1200 words.
Comments: Cookery-type home features are not required.
Approach: By letter.
Lead time: Three months.
Payment: Comparable with NUJ rates.

1/News **2**/Features **3**/Fiction **4**/Letters **5**/Fillers
6/B&W Photos **7**/Colour Photos **8**/Reviews

Homes and Antiques

Redwood Publishing
101 Bayham Street
London
NW1 0AG

Tel: 071-331 8000   **Fax:** 071-331 8001

Frequency: Monthly

Circulation: 120,000

Contact: Jill Churchill, Editor

Profile: A BBC magazine about houses that use antiques tastefully and imaginatively.

Requirements: 2 5
Features on interesting homes, celebrity homes and design using antiques. Features should be aimed at middle-aged readers with a little money to spend.

Comments: No features on antiques, as these are covered by experts.

Approach: In writing with ideas.

Lead time: Two months.

Payment: Negotiable.

Homes and Gardens

IPC Magazines
King's Reach Tower
Stamford Street
London
SE1 9LS

Tel: 071-261 5678   **Fax:** 071-261 6247

Frequency: Monthly

Circulation: 179,000

Contact: Emma Warlow, Features Editor

Profile: An interior design magazine that also covers gardening, crafts and practical features.

Requirements: 2 5
Features about all aspects of interior design of interest to the average home owner. Length up to 1000 words.

Comments: No crosswords, puzzles or poems.

Approach: By letter with ideas.

Lead time: Four months.

Payment: From £200 per thousand words.

Homes & Savings

HHL Publications Ltd
Greater London House
Hampstead Road
London
NW1 7QQ

Tel: 071-377 4633   **Fax:** 071-383 7570

Frequency: Quarterly

Circulation: 500,000

Contact: Steven Day, Editor

Profile: The magazine of the Halifax Building Society.

Requirements: 2
Features about people, lifestyles, homes and savings. Anything between 600 and 2000 words.

Comments: Welcomes bright, imaginative writers.

Approach: In writing with examples of previous work.

Lead time: Five months.

Payment: Negotiable but good.

Horse and Hound

IPC Magazines
King's Reach Tower
Stamford Street
London
SE1 9LS

Tel: 071-261 6315   **Fax:** 071-261 5429

Frequency: Weekly

1/News **2**/Features **3**/Fiction **4**/Letters **5**/Fillers
6/B&W Photos **7**/Colour Photos **8**/Reviews

Circulation: 82,000

Contact: Michael Clayton, Editor

Profile: The longest-established title in the equestrian sector, now revamped with a modern design and full colour throughout.

Requirements: 1 2

News and features on showjumping, dressage, horse trials and cross-country. Also instructional articles, breeding reports and book reviews.

Comments: Also includes a section for younger readers.

Approach: In writing, with ideas or complete manuscript.

Lead time: Three weeks.

Payment: £100 per thousand words.

Horse & Pony

EMAP Pursuit Publishing Ltd
Bretton Court
Bretton Centre
Peterborough
PE3 8DZ

Tel: (0733) 264666   **Fax:** (0733) 265515

Frequency: Fortnightly

Circulation: 54,112

Contact: Sarah Haw, Editor

Profile: Aimed at teenage riders, about half of whom have a horse or pony of their own. Almost all the readers are girls.

Requirements: 2 5

Concise, light-hearted features on pony care and riding. Also features on celebrity riders.

Comments: Keep articles and paragraphs short and punchy to retain the interest of the young readership.

Approach: In writing.

Lead time: One month.

Payment: Negotiable.

Horse and Rider

296 Ewell Road
Surbiton
Surrey
KT6 7AQ

Tel: 081-390 8547   **Fax:** 081-390 8696

Frequency: Monthly

Circulation: 39,000

Contact: Alison Bridge, Editor

Profile: For horse owners and riding enthusiasts throughout the UK.

Requirements: 1 2 5 6 7

Practical instructional features on riding, stable management and horse health. Length up to 2000 words.

Comments: Illustrated features are more likely to be accepted.

Approach: By letter with ideas.

Lead time: Two months.

Payment: £65 per thousand words.

Horse Chatter

9 Ladywood Road
Spalding
Lincolnshire
PE11 2DA

Tel: (0775) 711856   **Fax:** (0775) 712446

Frequency: Monthly

Circulation: 12,000

Contact: Daphne Witcombe, Editor

Profile: For members of riding clubs and the British Horse Society. For the once-a-week rider rather than the competitor.

Requirements: 1 2 7

Features on dressage, cross-country or other riding disciplines. Also articles on other matters that riders should be aware of, plus personal 'horsey' stories.

1/News **2**/Features **3**/Fiction **4**/Letters **5**/Fillers
6/B&W Photos **7**/Colour Photos **8**/Reviews

Comments: Welcomes reports from shows that the editorial team may not be able to cover.
Approach: By telephone.
Lead time: Four weeks.
Payment: £40 per thousand words.

Horticulture Week

38-42 Hampton Road
Teddington
Middlesex
TW11 0JE

Tel: 081-943 5719   **Fax:** 081-943 5673

Frequency: Weekly

Circulation: 10,000

Contact: Stovin Hayter, Editor
Profile: The trade magazine for the horticultural industry. Covers commercial nurseries, landscape companies, garden centres and park departments.
Requirements: 1 2 6 7
News and features of developments within the industry affecting the above groups of readers. Length up to 1500 words.
Comments: Always contact the editor in the first instance.
Approach: By telephone.
Lead time: Four weeks.
Payment: £85 per thousand words.

Hortus

The Neuadd
Rhayader
Radnorshire
Wales
LD6 5HH

Tel: (0597) 810227   **Fax:** (0597) 811386

Frequency: Quarterly

Circulation: 3000

Contact: David Wheeler, Editor
Profile: A literary journal for the intelligent gardener.
Requirements: 2 8
Features on the history of horticulture and botany, plus articles on present-day gardens, plants, people, design and literature. Length usually between 1500 and 5000 words.
Comments: Manuscripts should be complete with references and acknowledgements where necessary.
Approach: By letter with synopsis, or complete manuscript.
Lead time: Three months.
Payment: By arrangement.

Hot Air

John Brown Publishing Ltd
The Boathouse
Crabtree Lane
London
SW6 8NJ

Tel: 071-381 6007   **Fax:** 071-381 3930

Frequency: Quarterly

Circulation: 165,000

Contact: Alex Finer, Editor
Profile: An in-flight magazine for passengers of Virgin Atlantic. Aims to inform as well as entertain.
Requirements: 2
Travel features, personality profiles and general articles with an original theme.
Comments: Welcomes contributions from experienced freelances able to produce high-quality work.
Approach: In writing with ideas.
Lead time: Four months.
Payment: By arrangement.

1/News 2/Features 3/Fiction 4/Letters 5/Fillers
6/B&W Photos 7/Colour Photos 8/Reviews

Hotel & Catering Business

Dewberry Boyes Ltd
64 Woodrow
London
SE18 5DH

Tel: 081-317 8800   **Fax:** 081-317 3636

Frequency: Monthly

Circulation: 31,000

Contact: Robert Redman, Editor

Profile: Business magazine for caterers in all sectors of the hospitality industry.

Requirements: 1 2
News and features on all catering subjects, ranging from de luxe hotels to prison food.

Comments: Most work is commissioned, but the editor is always keen to hear from freelance contributors.

Approach: By telephone.

Lead time: Five weeks.

Payment: £100 per thousand words.

Hotline

HHL Publications Ltd
Greater London House
Hampstead Road
London
NW1 7QQ

Tel: 071-388 3171   **Fax:** 071-387 9518

Frequency: 3xYear

Circulation: 1 million

Contact: Steven Day, Editor

Profile: A glossy magazine posted to BT's top one million residential customers. Target readers are homeworkers, dispersed families, teenagers in love and those with an active social life.

Requirements: 1 2
Articles aimed at one or more of the above target groups. Features may be linked to BT or telecommunications, but do not have to be.

Comments: Much of the content is contributed by freelance writers. New writers are encouraged.

Approach: In writing.

Lead time: Four months.

Payment: From £120 per thousand words.

Hotshoe International

35 Britannia Row
London
N1 8QH

Tel: 071-226 1739   **Fax:** 071-226 1540

Frequency: Quarterly

Circulation: 6,500

Contact: Tim Rich, Editor

Profile: For the corporate, design and advertising photographer. Covers the creative and business aspects of professional photography.

Requirements: 1 2 7 8
Reviews of new equipment, plus coverage of the photographic industry in general.

Comments: Welcomes contact from journalists able to interview top photographers.

Approach: In writing, unless it's urgent news.

Lead time: Six weeks.

Payment: Around £125 per feature.

1/News **2**/Features **3**/Fiction **4**/Letters **5**/Fillers
6/B&W Photos **7**/Colour Photos **8**/Reviews

House Beautiful

National Magazine House
72 Broadwick Street
London
W1V 2BP

Tel: 071-439 5000   **Fax:** 071-439 5595

Frequency: Monthly

Circulation: 306,377

Contact: Caroline Atkins

Profile: Information and ideas for those who want to improve their home environment. Read largely by women.

Requirements: 1 2 5 7 8
News and features about decoration, home improvements, furnishings and related finance.

Comments: Articles should be practical in nature and easy to read. All submissions are given serious consideration.

Approach: Send complete manuscript.

Lead time: Three months.

Payment: Negotiable.

House Builder

82 New Cavendish Street
London
W1M 8AD

Tel: 071-580 5588   **Fax:** 071-323 0890

Frequency: Monthly

Circulation: 22,867

Contact: Phillip Cooke, Editor

Profile: The official publication of the National House-Building Council and the House-Builders' Federation.

Requirements: 2 6 7
Features with a technical bias, covering the design and construction of flats, houses and estates. Minimum length 500 words.

Comments: Plans, charts and illustrations should be submitted with articles where appropriate.

Approach: In writing.

Lead time: Six weeks.

Payment: Negotiable.

House Buyer

137 George Lane
South Woodford
London
E18 1AJ

Tel: 081-530 7555   **Fax:** 081-530 7609

Frequency: Monthly

Circulation: 18,000

Contact: Con Crowley, Editor

Profile: Aimed at all those purchasing houses, from first-time buyers to those moving into retirement homes.

Requirements: 1 2
News items and feature articles on all aspects of home buying, including mortgage advice, legal issues etc.

Comments: Do not send unsolicited manuscripts, as these will not be read.

Approach: By letter or fax with ideas.

Lead time: Two months.

Payment: Negotiable.

House & Garden

Vogue House
Hanover Square
London
W1R 0AD

Tel: 071-499 9080   **Fax:** 071-493 1345

Frequency: Monthly

Circulation: 146,000

Contact: Robert Harling, Editor

1/News 2/Features 3/Fiction 4/Letters 5/Fillers
6/B&W Photos 7/Colour Photos 8/Reviews

Profile: Covers all aspects of property, home leisure and horticulture.

Requirements: 2 7
Features relating to homes and gardens. The best opportunities for freelance writers are in the wine and food sections.

Comments: Features are commissioned following discussion with the editorial staff.

Approach: In writing with synopsis.

Lead time: Two months.

Payment: £100 per thousand words.

Ice Hockey World

9 Victoria Road
Mundesley-on-Sea
Norfolk
NR11 8JG

Tel: (0263) 720038

Frequency: Monthly during the season.

Circulation: 5000

Contact: Phil Drackett, Editor

Profile: A magazine for everyone interested in ice hockey and skating. Provides international coverage, but with the emphasis on the UK.

Requirements: 2 3 5 6 7 8
Always interested in human interest stories on players or even spectators. Also welcomes fiction and controversial material on the rules of the game, etc.

Comments: The magazine is feature rather than news led. Does not include match reports.

Approach: By letter with ideas.

Lead time: Two weeks.

Payment: £30 per thousand words.

ID Magazine

5th Floor
Seven Dials Warehouse
44 Earlham Street
London
WC2H 9LA

Tel: 071-240 3282   **Fax:** 071-240 3250

Frequency: Monthly

Circulation: 60,000

Contact: Matthew Colin, Editor

Profile: A style and fashion magazine for men and women aged under 24. Covers ideas, clubs, music, etc.

Requirements: 2 5 6 7 8
Always looking for writers with a fresh voice and something original to say. Features may be on any subject of interest to a style-conscious readership. Length up to 2500 words.

Comments: Each issue has a particular theme, and writers are advised to plan features to suit a forthcoming issue.

Approach: By fax or letter.

Lead time: Six weeks.

Payment: £80 per thousand words.

Ideal Home

IPC Magazines
King's Reach Tower
Stamford Street
London
SE1 9LS

Tel: 071-261 6474   **Fax:** 071-261 6697

Frequency: Monthly

Circulation: 253,000

Contact: Terence Whelan, Editor

1/News **2**/Features **3**/Fiction **4**/Letters **5**/Fillers
6/B&W Photos **7**/Colour Photos **8**/Reviews

Profile: Suggests ideas for making the most of your home, covering a broad range of subjects. Aimed at those in the middle of the market who have ambitions for their home.

Requirements: 2 7
Aspirational and practical features related to the home, together with articles on mortgages, etc.

Comments: There must be a practical element to contributions. Decorating features are written in house.

Approach: By letter with ideas.

Lead time: Three months.

Payment: Broadly in line with NUJ rates.

Illustrated London News

20 Upper Ground
London
SE1 9PF

Tel: 071-928 2111   **Fax:** 071-620 1594

Frequency: Bi-monthly

Circulation: 53,970

Contact: James Bishop, Editor

Profile: Although London-based, this magazine covers the whole of the UK. Includes articles on fashion, wine, food and current events.

Requirements: 1 2 6 7 8
Features on travel, or on topical developments in the capital.

Comments: Ideas for picture opportunities are always appreciated.

Approach: By letter or fax, with ideas or complete manuscripts.

Lead time: Two months.

Payment: Negotiable but good.

Improve Your Sea Fishing

10 Sheet Street
Windsor
Berkshire
SL4 1BG

Tel: (0753) 856061   **Fax:** (0753) 859652

Frequency: Monthly

Circulation: Not available

Contact: Chris Pearce, Editor

Profile: A publication for sea anglers who take their hobby seriously. Aims to be more informative than competing titles.

Requirements: 1 2
News of events, matches and catches. Also articles that answer commonly-asked fishing questions, concentrating on places to go, equipment to buy and the best way to use it.

Comments: Particularly interested in obtaining regional news from around the UK.

Approach: Submit complete manuscript.

Lead time: Two months.

Payment: From £50 per thousand words.

In Britain

HHL Publications Ltd
Greater London House
Hampstead Road
London
NW1 7QQ

Tel: 071-388 3171   **Fax:** 071-383 7570

Frequency: Monthly

Circulation: 86,000

Contact: Sue Rose, Editor

Profile: For people planning a trip to Britain from overseas. A large

---

1/News 2/Features 3/Fiction 4/Letters 5/Fillers
6/B&W Photos 7/Colour Photos 8/Reviews

percentage of subscribers are Americans, but the magazine is read worldwide.

Requirements: 1 2 7 8
Features on interesting areas in the UK. Material should ideally be linked to local history, myths, culture or something peculiarly British. Include as much information as possible.

Comments: The readership is largely over 50 and affluent.

Approach: By letter, with ideas or complete manuscript.

Lead time: Three months.

Payment: £250 per thousand words, plus photos.

Incentive Today

Blenheim House
630 Chiswick High Road
London
W4 5BG

Tel: 081-742 2828   **Fax:** 081-747 4012

Frequency: Monthly

Circulation: 22,000

Contact: Charles Ford, Editor

Profile: The leading magazine covering promotional marketing, incentives, motivation, business gifts, travel, hotels and conferences.

Requirements: 1 2 6 7
Brilliant crisp and crackling copy on the above subjects with correctly-spelled brand names, immaculate punctuation and no split infinitives. Length up to 2000 words.

Comments: Study the magazine before contributing.

Approach: In writing.

Lead time: Two weeks.

Payment: Negotiable.

Independent Business

26 Addison Place
London
W11 4RJ

Tel: 071-371 1299   **Fax:** 071-602 1922

Frequency: Quarterly

Circulation: 18,500

Contact: Toby Aykroyd, Editor

Profile: Provides a means for the small business community to air its views.

Requirements: 1 2
News and features on issues of concern to those running independent companies and small businesses.

Comments: Particularly interested in material on topical affairs.

Approach: In writing.

Lead time: Three months.

Payment: By arrangement.

Independent Grocer

Quadrant House
The Quadrant
Sutton
Surrey
SM2 5AS

Tel: 081-652 8754   **Fax:** 081-652 8936

Frequency: 35xYear

Circulation: 40,425

Contact: Jim Muttram, Editor

Profile: Trade title for owners and managers of independent groceries and convenience stores.

Requirements: 1 2 7
News and features relating to developments within the grocery trade, plus business features relevant to independent retailers. Also case studies of grocers who have made a success of their businesses.

Comments: Published weekly in April, May, September and October. Fortnightly at all other times.
Approach: By letter or telephone.
Lead time: Three weeks.
Payment: In line with NUJ rates.

Index on Censorship

32 Queen Victoria Street
London
EC4N 4SS

Tel: 071-329 6434   **Fax:** 071-329 6461

Frequency: 10xYear

Circulation: 6000

Contact: Andrew Graham-Yooll, Editor
Profile: Concerned with political censorship internationally.
Requirements: 2 8
  Articles discussing issues relating to censorship motivated by politics. Length up to 5000 words. Also reviews of relevant books, 750 to 1500 words.
Comments: All material must be well-researched and accurate.
Approach: In writing.
Lead time: Three months.
Payment: £50 per thousand words.

Individual Homes

91-93 High Street
Bromsgrove
Worcestershire
B61 8AQ

Tel: (0527) 36600   **Fax:** (0527) 574388

Frequency: 10xYear

Circulation: 40,000

Contact: Peter Harris, Editor
Profile: A publication devoted to those who wish to build their own houses.

Requirements: 2 7
  Articles on products and energy efficiency, plus features about people who have built or renovated their own houses. Length up to 1500 words.
Comments: Study the magazine before contributing.
Approach: By letter.
Lead time: Two months.
Payment: Negotiable.

Infusion

16 Trinity Churchyard
Guildford
Surrey
GU1 3RR

Tel: (0483) 62888   **Fax:** (0483) 302732

Frequency: 3xYear

Circulation: 800,000

Contact: Lorna Swainson
Profile: A publication sponsored by the Tea Council.
Requirements: 2 5
  General features of interest to women, plus articles on leisure, health and tea-related subjects.
Comments: Do not send unsolicited manuscripts as all work is commissioned.
Approach: In writing.
Lead time: Four months.
Payment: By arrangement.

Inside Soap

4 Tottenham Mews
London
W1P 9PJ

Tel: 071-436 5220   **Fax:** 071-436 5277

Frequency: Monthly

Circulation: 70,000

1/News **2**/Features **3**/Fiction **4**/Letters **5**/Fillers
6/B&W Photos **7**/Colour Photos **8**/Reviews

Contact: Vicky Mayer, Editor
Profile: All about TV soaps and their stars. Includes news, gossip, features and interviews.
Requirements: 2 5
Inspired features on soap subjects or exclusive interviews with stars. Writers with in-depth knowledge of soaps are encouraged to submit ideas.
Comments: Unsolicited manuscripts are not read.
Approach: In writing with ideas.
Lead time: Six weeks.
Payment: £100 per thousand words.

Insurance Age

EMAP Publications
33-39 Bowling Green Lane
London
EC1R 0DA

Tel: 071-837 1212   **Fax:** 071-833 2128

Frequency: Monthly

Circulation: 20,500

Contact: John Jackson, Editor
Profile: Professional title for general insurance brokers.
Requirements: 1 2 6
News and features on motor, health and home insurance, together with mortgages, investment and commercial insurance.
Comments: Copy must be well-researched, as the magazine is read by an informed and knowledgeable business audience.
Approach: By fax or letter.
Lead time: Two months.
Payment: £180 to £220 per thousand words.

Insurance Brokers' Monthly

7 Stourbridge Road
Lye
Stourbridge
West Midlands
DY9 7DG

Tel: (0384) 895228   **Fax:** (0384) 893666

Frequency: Monthly

Circulation: 9000

Contact: Brian Susman, Editor
Profile: Read by insurance brokers and others who are professionally involved in the insurance industry.
Requirements: 2 6
Technical and non-technical articles on motor insurance, computer systems and other business matters which affect brokers. Length 1000 to 1500 words.
Comments: Sometimes runs features on general financial or City matters.
Approach: In writing with ideas.
Lead time: Six weeks.
Payment: Up to £30.

Insurance Times

MSM International
Thames House
18 Park Street
London
SE1 9ER

Tel: 071-378 7131   **Fax:** 071-403 4682

Frequency: Monthly

Circulation: 17,000

Contact: Niall Sweeney, Editor
Profile: The professional journal of the Insurance Brokers' Registration Council.
Requirements: 1 2
News and features about new

1/News **2**/Features **3**/Fiction **4**/Letters **5**/Fillers
6/B&W Photos **7**/Colour Photos **8**/Reviews

products, industry developments and statistics. Length up to 1500 words.

Comments: Does not require material on pensions or investment.

Approach: In writing with ideas or complete manuscript.

Lead time: Two months.

Payment: Negotiable.

InterCity

Redwood Publishing
101 Bayham Street
London
NW1 0AG

Tel: 071-331 8000   **Fax:** 071-331 8168

Frequency: 10xYear

Circulation: 150,000

Contact: Paul Keers, Editor

Profile: Business magazine distributed free to British Rail passengers travelling first class on major routes.

Requirements: 2 5
General business articles likely to be of interest to those who travel by rail. Material should be targeted at successful, informed businessmen.

Comments: Contact the magazine before submitting manuscripts.

Approach: In writing with ideas.

Lead time: Three months.

Payment: Negotiable.

Intermedia

International Institute of
   Communications
Tavistock House South
Tavistock Square
London
WC1H 9LF

Tel: 071-388 0671   **Fax:** 071-380 0623

Frequency: Bi-monthly

Circulation: 2500

Contact: Karen Anderson, Assistant Editor

Profile: A journal that focuses on broadcasting, telecommunications and media issues. Provides international coverage.

Requirements: 2 6 8
Articles of approximately 2000 words on the above subjects. Material from Latin America, Africa and Asia are always welcome. Length 1500 to 2000 words.

Comments: Often acts as a forum for discussion on topics internationally.

Approach: By letter with initial ideas.

Lead time: Six weeks.

Payment: Approx. £150.

The International

Greystoke Place
Fetter Lane
London
EC4A 1ND

Tel: 071-405 6969   **Fax:** 071-831 2181

Frequency: Monthly

Circulation: 52,107

Contact: David Turner, Editor

Profile: For expatriates interested in international investment.

Requirements: 1 2 8
Articles on any aspect of personal finance for expatriates, from savings to equity. Length up to 1500 words.

Comments: Do not send unsolicited manuscripts.

Approach: By telephone, letter or fax.

Lead time: Two months.

Payment: Negotiable.

1/News **2**/Features **3**/Fiction **4**/Letters **5**/Fillers
6/B&W Photos **7**/Colour Photos **8**/Reviews

International News

United Distillers Group
Landmark House
Hammersmith Bridge Road
London
W6 9DG

Tel: 081-846 8040   **Fax:** 081-748 5397

Frequency: Monthly

Circulation: 11,000

Contact: Frank Page, Editor
Profile: A newspaper produced by
United Distillers for its staff. Read
by employees around the world.
Requirements: 2 5
Features on subjects of interest to
those working in the spirits industry.
These may include legal matters,
packaging, health and safety, etc.
Length 250 to 750 words.
Comments: Material should be
relevant to United Distillers
employees internationally.
Approach: In writing with ideas.
Lead time: Two months.
Payment: Negotiable but good.

International Off-Roader

PO Box 237
Crawley
West Sussex
RH10 5YH

Tel: (0293) 525152   **Fax:** (0293) 538253

Frequency: Monthly

Circulation: 19,000

Contact: Colin Dawson, Editor
Profile: For owners and drivers of
sports utility, 4x4 and off-road
vehicles.
Requirements: 1 2 6 7 8
Original pieces about off-road

driving, events and adventure travel,
plus technical articles, sport and
travel.
Comments: Study the magazine before
contributing.
Approach: By telephone.
Lead time: Three weeks.
Payment: Comparable with NUJ rates.

Interzone

217 Preston Drive
Brighton
BN1 6FL

Tel: (0273) 504710

Frequency: Monthly

Circulation: 10,000

Contact: David Pringle, Editor
Profile: Britain's leading science
fiction and fantasy magazine.
Requirements: 3
Innovative, entertaining, well-
written and up-to-date science
fiction and fantasy. No hackneyed
space opera, sword-and-sorcery tales
or traditional ghost stories. Length
2000 to 6000 words.
Comments: The magazine has a very
distinctive style and sets high
standards. You must be familiar
with the magazine before
contributing.
Approach: Send complete manuscript.
Lead time: Two months.
Payment: £30 per thousand words.

Intro

4 Red Barn Mews
High Street
Battle
East Sussex
TN33 0AG

Tel: (0424) 775304   **Fax:** (0424) 774321

1/News **2**/Features **3**/Fiction **4**/Letters **5**/Fillers
6/B&W Photos **7**/Colour Photos **8**/Reviews

Frequency: Weekly

Circulation: 12,000

Contact: Keith Johnson, Editor

Profile: A weekly newspaper for single, separated, divorced and widowed people. Distributed in the South-East of the UK.

Requirements: 1 2 4 6
Welcomes articles and features which relate to the singles scene. Length up to 1500 words.

Comments: Any constructive or valid articles will be considered.

Approach: By fax or letter.

Lead time: Two weeks.

Payment: From £50 per thousand words.

Investors Chronicle

Greystoke Place
Fetter Lane
London
EC4A 1ND

Tel: 071-405 6969   **Fax:** 071-405 5276

Frequency: Weekly

Circulation: 25,015

Contact: Gillian O'Connor, Editor

Profile: A news-led publication which provides information on possible investments. Includes company accounts, new share issues, details of savings schemes, etc.

Requirements: 1 2
News and information on regional financial developments. Surveys of promising but less-well-known companies.

Comments: Contact the magazine to obtain copies of surveys lists and details of individual surveys.

Approach: In writing.

Lead time: Three weeks.

Payment: By negotiation.

Involvement & Participation

42 Colebrooke Row
London
N1 8AF

Tel: 071-354 8040   **Fax:** 071-354 8041

Frequency: Quarterly

Circulation: 1400

Contact: Anthony Barry, Editor

Profile: The official journal of the Involvement & Participation Association.

Requirements: 2
Articles concerning the encouragement of workers' involvement in business, industrial relations, employee shareholding, etc. Length up to 3000 words.

Comments: All material should be written from the practical point of view, concentrating on facts and figures.

Approach: In writing.

Lead time: Two months.

Payment: Negotiable.

Issue

22-24 Worple Road
London
SW19 4DD

Tel: 081-947 3131   **Fax:** 081-944 6139

Frequency: 2xYear

Circulation: 70,000

Contact: Sharon Watson, Editor

Profile: A hard-hitting, glossy lifestyle magazine with a conscience. Aimed at a readership aged under 27 years.

Requirements: 1 2 5 7 8
News and features on union activities, music, politics, youth and social issues.

1/News **2**/Features **3**/Fiction **4**/Letters **5**/Fillers
6/B&W Photos **7**/Colour Photos **8**/Reviews

Comments: Strive for a 'young' style
of writing. Features and ideas on a
wide range of subjects are always
welcome, as are colour photos.
Approach: By letter or telephone.
Lead time: Four weeks.
Payment: NUJ rates.

J

Jane's Defence Weekly

Sentinel House
163 Brighton Road
Coulsdon
Surrey
CR5 2NH

Tel: 081-763 1030 **Fax:** 081-763 1007

Frequency: Weekly

Circulation: 29,000

Contact: Peter Howard, Editor

Profile: An international defence news title, covering military and political issues.

Requirements: 1 2 4 5 6 7
News and features on major military developments and equipment worldwide. Length 200 to 1500 words.

Comments: No historical material is used within the publication.

Approach: By telephone initially.

Lead time: One week.

Payment: £125 per thousand words.

Jazz Express

29 Romilly Street
London
W1V 6HP

Tel: 071-437 6437 **Fax:** 071-434 1214

Frequency: 10xYear

Circulation: 10,000

Contact: Catherine Bassindale, Editor

Profile: Covers both the present and the classic jazz scene in the UK. The emphasis is on modern jazz.

Requirements: 1 2 6 7 8
Interviews with musicians, general articles about jazz and record reviews. Length 1000 to 2000 words.

Comments: Anything humorous is always appreciated.

Approach: By letter.

Lead time: Three weeks.

Payment: £50 per thousand words.

Jazz Journal International

1-5 Clerkenwell Road
London
EC1M 5PA

Tel: 071-608 1348 **Fax:** 071-608 1292

Frequency: Monthly

Circulation: 12,000

Contact: Eddie Cook, Editor

Profile: For the jazz enthusiast, covering everything from musicians to cinema and video. Has an international readership.

Requirements: 2 5
Interviews with jazz musicians, unusual features on jazz history, etc.

Comments: Readers must have a good understanding of the subject.

Approach: In writing.

Lead time: Four weeks.

Payment: Negotiable.

1/News **2**/Features **3**/Fiction **4**/Letters **5**/Fillers
6/B&W Photos **7**/Colour Photos **8**/Reviews

Jazz: The Magazine

Observer Publications
Chelsea Bridge House
Queenstown Road
London
SW8 4NN

Tel: 071-340 3450   **Fax:** 071-627 8154

Frequency: Bi-monthly

Circulation: 15,000

Contact: Tony Russell, Editor

Profile: Informed, accessible, stylish coverage of jazz past and present worldwide. Aimed at jazz enthusiasts, both committed and casual.

Requirements: 2 6 7 8
Features concerning local or visiting musicians, plus record and book reviews.

Comments: Always interested in hearing from writers with jazz background knowledge and a fresh but literate view of the jazz scene.

Approach: Unsolicited material is rarely used. Always discuss ideas with the editor first.

Lead time: Two months.

Payment: £100 per thousand words for features.

Jet Ski & Personal Water Craft News

Cambridge Style Ltd
45 Grafton Court
Cambridge
CB1 1DS

Tel: (0223) 460490   **Fax:** (0223) 68052

Frequency: Monthly

Circulation: 9500

Contact: Chris Boiling, Editor

Profile: A magazine for water sports enthusiasts, focusing on personal craft.

Requirements: 1 2
News and features about fun and sports boats or personal watercraft. Also articles on subjects such as water safety.

Comments: Study the magazine before contributing.

Approach: In writing.

Lead time: Two months.

Payment: Negotiable.

Journal of Alternative and Complementary Medicine

Mariner House
53a High Street
Bagshot
Surrey
GU19 5AH

Tel: (0276) 451522   **Fax:** (0276) 451557

Frequency: Monthly

Circulation: 5500

Contact: Leon Chaitow, Editor

Profile: For practitioners of alternative medicine and associated healthcare professionals.

Requirements: 1 2 6 7
News and features covering new therapies and developments, research information and reports from conferences. Length 250 to 2000 words.

Comments: The editor welcomes unsolicited manuscripts from freelance writers.

Approach: In writing.

Lead time: Two months.

Payment: £100 per thousand words.

Junior Education

Scholastic Publications Ltd
Villiers House
Clarendon Avenue
Leamington Spa
Warwickshire
CV32 5PR

Tel: (0926) 887799   **Fax:** (0926) 883331

Frequency: Monthly

Circulation: 39,134

Contact: The Editor

Profile: A magazine for teachers, students and other professionals concerned with children aged between seven and twelve.

Requirements: 2 6
Practical material on teaching methods, together with discussions of current educational matters, reviews of products and curriculum articles. Length 800 to 1200 words.

Comments: Contributors must be able to write authoritatively about their subject.

Approach: In writing.

Lead time: Two months.

Payment: By arrangement.

Just Seventeen

20 Orange Street
London
WC2H 7ED

Tel: 071-957 8383   **Fax:** 071-957 8400

Frequency: Weekly

Circulation: 244,000

Contact: Ekow Eshun

Profile: A fashion and beauty magazine for girls in their teens. Covers everything from boyfriends to pop.

Requirements: 1 2 3 6 7
Features on more serious subjects such as racism or school issues. Length 1000 to 1500 words. Also short stories relevant to the readership, preferably brief and concise.

Comments: Unsolicited manuscripts are rarely accepted, but commissions for new writers are encouraged.

Approach: Send ideas with examples of previous work.

Lead time: Three weeks.

Payment: £150.

K

Kart Racing Monthly

32 Higher Market Street
Farnworth
Bolton
BL4 9AJ

Tel: (0204) 795594   **Fax:** (0204) 795633

Frequency: Monthly

Circulation: 5000

Contact: Mike Smith, Editor

Profile: Covers all aspects of karting, from club level to international competition.

Requirements: 1 2 6 7 8
News and views, race reports and technical articles, plus any other features of interest to karting enthusiasts.

Comments: Includes a section for cadet classes.

Approach: By telephone.

Lead time: Six weeks.

Payment: £25-£30.

Karting

Bank House
Summerhill
Chislehurst
Kent
BR7 5RD

Tel: 081-467 6533   **Fax:** 081-468 7999

Frequency: Monthly

Circulation: 12,800

Contact: M.C. Burgess, Editor

Profile: General karting magazine, covering the world of kart racing.

Requirements: 2 6 7
Features articles about racing, plus race reports and technical articles.

Comments: Study the magazine before contributing material.

Approach: Send complete manuscript.

Lead time: Two months.

Payment: Negotiable.

Kennel Gazette

Kennel Club
1-5 Clarges Street
Piccadilly
London
W1Y 8AB

Tel: 071-493 6651   **Fax:** 071-495 6162

Frequency: Monthly

Circulation: 13,000

Contact: Charles Colborn, Editor

Profile: A magazine for dog breeders, breed clubs and people starting to show dogs.

Requirements: 1 2 3 6 7 8
News and features about veterinary matters or issues related to showing dogs. Length up to 2500 words. Also concise short stories with a dog angle.

Comments: A special souvenir bumper issue is also produced for sale at Crufts.

1/News **2**/Features **3**/Fiction **4**/Letters **5**/Fillers
6/B&W Photos **7**/Colour Photos **8**/Reviews

Approach: By letter, with ideas or complete manuscripts.
Lead time: Two months.
Payment: £70 per thousand words.

Kerrang!

52-55 Carnaby Street
London
W1V 1PF

Tel: 071-437 8050   **Fax:** 071-734 2287

Frequency: Weekly

Circulation: 52,958

Contact: John Hotten, Commissioning Editor
Profile: A heavy metal magazine. Covers rock, metal, thrash, etc.
Requirements: 2
Interviews with musicians and bands, plus live music and record reviews. Length around 1500 words.
Comments: Contact the magazine before submitting manuscripts.
Approach: Send ideas and examples of previous work. Follow up with a phone call.
Lead time: Two weeks.
Payment: Negotiable.

Keyboard Player

27 Russell Road
Enfield
Middlesex
EN1 4TN

Tel: 081-367 2938   **Fax:** 081-367 2359

Frequency: Monthly

Circulation: 16,000

Contact: Steve Miller, Editor
Profile: Reviews, information and tuition features connected with home music-making on keyboards.

Requirements: 1 2 6 7 8
Interviews with keyboard personalities, plus practical, informative features. Length 1000 to 1500 words.
Comments: Reviews are normally handled in house.
Approach: By telephone, letter or fax.
Lead time: Six weeks.
Payment: Approaching NUJ rates.

Keyboard Review

Alexander House
Forehill
Ely
Cambridgeshire
CB7 4AF

Tel: (0353) 665577   **Fax:** (0353) 662489

Frequency: Monthly

Circulation: 18,000

Contact: Sandra Stafford, Deputy Editor
Profile: News, views, interviews and instrument profiles of modern keyboards.
Requirements: 2 8
Would consider technique articles, keyboard player interviews and reviews of instruments. Length up to 2000 words.
Comments: Writers should be knowledgeable and literate.
Approach: By letter with initial ideas.
Lead time: Six weeks.
Payment: From £45 per thousand words.

Kindred Spirit

Foxhole
Dartington
Totnes
Devon
TQ9 6EB

Tel: (0803) 866686   **Fax:** (0803) 866591

Frequency: Quarterly

Circulation: 30,000

Contact: Richard Beaumont, Editor
Profile: The UK's leading holistic
guide to body, mind and spirit
issues. Covers new science, spiritual
teachings, earth mysteries,
complementary medicines and the
environment.
Requirements: 2 6 7
Original perspective on personal and
planetary healing. Maximum 2000
words.
Comments: A lot of unsolicited
material is received, but most of it
is not of a sufficiently high
standard.
Approach: In writing.
Lead time: Two months.
Payment: Approaching NUJ rates.

Kit Car

Mailergraphic Ltd
Old Run Road
Leeds
LS10 2AA

Tel: (0532) 718666   **Fax:** (0532) 774009

Frequency: Monthly

Circulation: 30,000

Contact: Ewan Scott, Editor
Profile: The leading and longest-
established magazine in the kit car
sector.

Requirements: 1 2 6 7
Build features, travelogues featuring
kit-car products and technical
features. Length 1000 to 2500 words.
Comments: Looking for unusual
material and features which show
the products at their best.
Approach: By telephone.
Lead time: Four weeks.
Payment: £75 per thousand words.

Kitchens

Maclean Hunter House
Chalk Farm
Cockfosters Road
Barnet
Hertfordshire
EN4 0BU

Tel: 081-975 9759   **Fax:** 081-975 9753

Frequency: Monthly

Circulation: 12,000

Contact: Amanda Waggott, Editor
Profile: Read by specialist kitchen
retailers, designers, manufacturers
and specifiers.
Requirements: 2 5
Features on kitchen design, plus
profiles of companies in this market.
Also general articles on business and
finance.
Comments: Concerned with the trade
rather than the consumer point of
view.
Approach: In writing.
Lead time: Two months.
Payment: Negotiable.

1/News 2/Features 3/Fiction 4/Letters 5/Fillers
6/B&W Photos 7/Colour Photos 8/Reviews

Knitting International

Benjamin Dent Publications
Eastern Boulevard
Leicester
LE2 7BN

Tel: (0533) 548271   **Fax:** (0533) 470194

Frequency: Monthly

Circulation: Not available

Contact: John Gibbon, Editor

Profile: Technical textile magazine for management, marketing, production and design staff. Coverage includes fibres, yarns, fabrics, garments and machinery in all textile sectors.

Requirements: 1 2 6 7
Informed management and technical articles, together with relevant pictures, tables and charts. Length 750 to 3000 words.

Comments: Particularly interested in technical textile articles for an informed readership.

Approach: By letter or fax with ideas.

Lead time: Six weeks.

Payment: £90-£150 per thousand words.

L

Ladies First

33 Wellfield Road
Cardiff
CF2 3PA

Tel: (0222) 461007   **Fax:** (0222) 493605

Frequency: Quarterly

Circulation: 50,000

Contact: Hilary Hughes, Editor

Profile: A women's magazine aimed at the upper end of the market.

Requirements: 2 3 6 7
Features on homes and interiors, fashion, beauty, cookery and gardening. Length 800 to 1200 words.

Comments: It may take a long time to get a reply, but unsolicited contributions are often used.

Approach: Send complete manuscript.

Lead time: Three months.

Payment: Negotiable.

The Lady

39-40 Bedford Street
Strand
London
WC2E 9ER

Tel: 071-379 4717   **Fax:** 071-497 2137

Frequency: Weekly

Circulation: 66,000

Contact: Arline Usden, Editor

Profile: A general-interest title for an older, affluent readership.

Requirements: 2 5 6
Articles on travel both in the UK and overseas. Length up to 1000 words. Also filler items up to 700 words in length.

Comments: No politics, religion or health articles.

Approach: In writing.

Lead time: Three weeks.

Payment: £55 per thousand words.

Lancashire Life

Oyston Mill
Strand Road
Preston
PR1 8UR

Tel: (0772) 722022   **Fax:** (0722) 736496

Frequency: Monthly

Circulation: 8500

Contact: Brian Hargreaves, Editor

Profile: A county magazine covering events and activities throughout Lancashire.

Requirements: 2 6 7
Feature articles on county shows, fashion, county sport, motoring and antiques.

Comments: Aims to be provincial but not parochial.

1/News **2**/Features **3**/Fiction **4**/Letters **5**/Fillers
6/B&W Photos **7**/Colour Photos **8**/Reviews

Approach: In writing.
Lead time: Three months.
Payment: Negotiable.

The Leisure Manager

Queensway House
2 Queensway
Redhill
Surrey
RH1 1QS

Tel: (0737) 768611   **Fax:** (0737) 760564

Frequency: Monthly

Circulation: 7500

Contact: Mathew Moggridge, Editor
Profile: The journal of the Institute of
Leisure and Amenity Management.
Requirements: 1 6 7
News relating to the leisure industry,
seen from the perspective of local
authority departments.
Comments: Do not send unsolicited
manuscripts. All work is
commissioned.
Approach: By telephone, letter or fax.
Lead time: Two months.
Payment: Negotiable.

Leisure Painter

63-65 High Street
Tenterden
Kent
TN30 6BD

Tel: (0580) 763315   **Fax:** (0580) 765411

Frequency: Monthly

Circulation: 23,500

Contact: Irene Briers, Editor
Profile: For amateur artists who
wish to improve their painting
skills.

Requirements: 2 6 7
Practical 'how-to' articles on
painting and fine arts subjects. Also
other information of interest to the
amateur painter.
Comments: Welcomes original
artwork, line drawings and
photographs to accompany features.
Approach: In writing.
Lead time: Two months.
Payment: £60 per thousand words.

Leisure Times

Baltimore House
21 Macklin Street
Derby
DE1 1LE

Tel: (0332) 295516   **Fax:** (0332) 293649

Frequency: Monthly

Circulation: 10,000

Contact: John Harrison, Managing
Editor
Profile: A leisure-oriented publication
distributed throughout the East
Midlands.
Requirements: 2 3
Features on pubs, clubs, music,
gardening, holidays and books. Also
light-hearted fiction. Length up to
2000 words.
Comments: A splash of humour is
always welcome.
Approach: By letter with ideas.
Lead time: Two weeks.
Payment: Up to £50 per thousand
words.

1/News **2**/Features **3**/Fiction **4**/Letters **5**/Fillers
6/B&W Photos **7**/Colour Photos **8**/Reviews

Let's Make It

New Lane
Havant
Hampshire
PO9 2ND

Tel: (0705) 486221 **Fax:** (0705) 492769

Frequency: Quarterly

Circulation: 30,000

Contact: Gail Goldie
Profile: A specialist craft title, encompassing everything from needlework to woodcraft.
Requirements: 1 2 6 7
News items and practical, instructional articles aimed at the beginner.
Comments: Writers should be familiar with the magazine's style and approach.
Approach: By letter.
Lead time: Three months.
Payment: Negotiable.

Life and Work

121 George Street
Edinburgh
EH2 4YN

Tel: 031-225 5722 **Fax:** 031-220 3113

Frequency: Monthly

Circulation: 81,183

Contact: Peter Macdonald, Editor
Profile: The largest religious publication north of the border, produced by the Church of Scotland.
Requirements: 2 5
Convincing articles on religious topics aimed at the general reader. These should not be too evangelical but must be sincere. Length around 1000 words.

Comments: Receives a lot of unsuitable material from people who have clearly never read the magazine.
Approach: In writing.
Lead time: Six weeks.
Payment: £35 per thousand words.

Lime Lizard

Unit 2b
22 Highbury Grove
London
N5 3EA

Tel: 071-704 9767 **Fax:** 071-359 1692

Frequency: Monthly

Circulation: 70,000

Contact: Patrick Fraser, Editor
Profile: An independent, alternative music magazine in full colour. Includes rock, indie and dance music.
Requirements: 1 2
News items and articles on subjects that complement the music coverage − film, video, comedians, etc. Length up to 3000 words.
Comments: Encourages intelligent, inspired writers.
Approach: By letter or fax.
Lead time: Four weeks.
Payment: £50 per thousand words.

Lincolnshire Life

PO Box 8
Newark
NG23 7AJ

Tel: (0522) 778567 **Fax:** (0522) 778463

Frequency: Monthly

Circulation: 10,000

Contact: Jenny Walton, Executive Editor

1/News **2**/Features **3**/Fiction **4**/Letters **5**/Fillers
6/B&W Photos **7**/Colour Photos **8**/Reviews

Profile: Devoted to county topics relating to Lincolnshire.
Requirements: 1 2 3 5 6 7
Features on the county and its history, plus contemporary pieces. Length between 350 and 2000 words.
Comments: Most of the content is contributed by freelance writers.
Approach: By letter or telephone.
Lead time: Two months.
Payment: £25 per page.

Living

IPC Magazines
King's Reach Tower
Stamford Street
London
SE1 9LS

Tel: 071-261 5000   **Fax:** 071-261 6892

Frequency: Monthly

Circulation: 214,000

Contact: Olwen Rice, Editor
Profile: Sold at supermarket checkouts. Readers are likely to be women who are married, working and with children of school age.
Requirements: 2 5
Controversial, investigative features on issues relating to family life. Also articles on cookery and the home. Length up to 2000 words.
Comments: Does not cover health, beauty or fashion.
Approach: By letter with ideas.
Lead time: Five months.
Payment: Negotiable.

Local Government Chronicle

33-39 Bowling Green Lane
London
EC1R 0DA

Tel: 071-837 1212   **Fax:** 071-278 9509

Frequency: Weekly
Circulation: 9407

Contact: Paul Keenan, Editor
Profile: A professional publication for all those involved in local government.
Requirements: 2 6
Contributions concerning the work of local government officers, covering subjects such as finance, politics and administration.
Comments: Writers should have some knowledge of matters affecting local government.
Approach: In writing.
Lead time: Three weeks.
Payment: Negotiable.

London Portrait Magazine

21st Floor
IPC Magazines
King's Reach Tower
Stamford Street
London
SE1 9LS

Tel: 071-261 7215   **Fax:** 071-261 7229

Frequency: Monthly

Circulation: 87,652

Contact: Emma Burn, Assistant Editor
Profile: A general lifestyle magazine for the central London area.
Requirements: 2 6 7 8
Features on people and places in London, but with the emphasis on people and personalities. Length 850 to 1000 words.
Comments: Does not require articles on familiar places such as the Albert Hall.
Approach: By telephone or letter.
Lead time: Two months.
Payment: From £250 per thousand words.

1/News **2**/Features **3**/Fiction **4**/Letters **5**/Fillers
6/B&W Photos **7**/Colour Photos **8**/Reviews

The London Magazine

30 Thurloe Place
London
SW7 2HQ

Tel: 071-589 0618

Frequency: Monthly

Circulation: 4500

Contact: Alan Ross, Editor

Profile: An upmarket general-interest magazine. The readership is largely aged over 30.

Requirements: 1 2 6 7 8
News and features on fashion, restaurants and lifestyle. Also literature, travel and the arts. Length up to 2000 words.

Comments: A well-respected literary publication.

Approach: By letter with synopsis.

Lead time: Three months.

Payment: Negotiable.

London Review of Books

Tavistock House South
Tavistock Square
London
WC1H 9JZ

Tel: 071-388 6751   **Fax:** 071-383 4792

Frequency: Bi-monthly

Circulation: 18,000

Contact: Mary-Kay Wilmers, Editor

Profile: Offers discussion and review of the latest releases and publications.

Requirements: 2 3 6 8
Feature articles, comment, essays and analysis on literary subjects. Also short fiction and poetry.

Comments: Only high-quality work will be considered for publication.

Approach: Submit complete manuscript.

Lead time: Three months.

Payment: By negotiation.

Look-in

Floor 27
IPC Magazines
King's Reach Tower
Stamford Street
London
SE1 9LS

Tel: 071-261 6385   **Fax:** 071-261 6032

Frequency: Weekly

Circulation: 85,000

Contact: Frank Hopkinson, Editor

Profile: A TV-based magazine for boys and girls aged between 8 and 12. Covers pop, TV, film, computers and sport.

Requirements: 1 2 5 7
Anything on celebrities or personalities of interest to the age group reading the magazine. Also sports features and any weird or wacky material.

Comments: Writing for children is very different from writing for adults, requiring much more explanation.

Approach: By telephone with ideas.

Lead time: Four weeks.

Payment: From £80 per thousand words.

Looks

20 Orange Street
London
WC2H 7ED

Tel: 071-957 8383   **Fax:** 071-957 8400

Frequency: Monthly

Circulation: 231,000

1/News **2**/Features **3**/Fiction **4**/Letters **5**/Fillers
6/B&W Photos **7**/Colour Photos **8**/Reviews

Contact: Sue Wheeler, Deputy Editor

Profile: A fashion and beauty bible for young women.

Requirements: 1 2 7

Features loosely based around fashion and beauty. These could include models, fashion news, celebrities and gossip.

Comments: Do not send material on spec.

Approach: By letter or fax.

Lead time: Six weeks.

Payment: £200 per thousand words.

Loving

IPC Magazines
King's Reach Tower
Stamford Street
London
SE1 9LS

Tel: 071-261 6376   **Fax:** 071-261 6032

Frequency: Monthly

Circulation: 45,000

Contact: Lorna Read, Editor

Profile: Romantic fiction for women aged between 18 and 30. Also includes general and emotional features.

Requirements: 2 3 4 5

Romantic, sometimes passionate, stories usually told from the point of view of a young female narrator. Length between 1000 and 4500 words. Interesting features that complement the stories.

Comments: All material must be modern and relevant. The editor will commission stories from outlines.

Approach: By letter, with ideas or complete manuscripts.

Lead time: Three months.

Payment: Up to £50 per thousand words.

Ludus

Galaxy Publications
PO Box 312
Witham
Essex
CM8 3SZ

Tel: (0376) 510555   **Fax:** (0376) 510680

Frequency: Monthly

Circulation: 75,000

Contact: Pauline Brown, Editor

Profile: A raunchy magazine for women which aims to inform about sex.

Requirements: 2 3

Features on all aspects of sexuality. Also accepts fiction contributions from women writers, which may be written from the male or female point of view.

Comments: Aim for a lively, distinctive style of writing.

Approach: In writing with synopsis.

Lead time: Two months.

Payment: £100 per thousand words.

1/News 2/Features 3/Fiction 4/Letters 5/Fillers
6/B&W Photos 7/Colour Photos 8/Reviews

M

M & S Magazine

101 Bayham Street
London
NW1 0AG

Tel: 071-331 8000   **Fax:** 071-331 8001

Frequency: Quarterly

Circulation: 1 million

Contact: Felicity Green, Editor

Profile: An upmarket glossy magazine published by Marks & Spencer. Contains a wide range of features that would appeal to customers.

Requirements: 2

Feature articles on subjects such as fashion, the home, beauty etc. All copy must be well-written and authoritative.

Comments: This is not a catalogue of M&S products, but a high-quality consumer magazine.

Approach: In writing with ideas.

Lead time: Four months.

Payment: Negotiable.

Making Music

20 Bowling Green Lane
London
EC1R 0BD

Tel: 071-251 1900   **Fax:** 071-251 2619

Frequency: Monthly

Circulation: 56,675

Contact: John Levin, Editor

Profile: Aimed at rock and pop musicians aged between 18 and 30. Covers music-making for both amateurs and professionals.

Requirements: 1 2 8

Any new material on creating music and making it in the music business. How to get a record deal, music technology, etc.

Comments: Features must be concise and tightly focused.

Approach: By telephone.

Lead time: Four weeks.

Payment: £80 per thousand words.

Management Decision

62 Toller Lane
Bradford
West Yorkshire
BD8 9BY

Tel: (0274) 499821   **Fax:** (0274) 547143

Frequency: 8xYear

Circulation: 1000

Contact: Dr John Peters, Editor

Profile: Concerned with management, corporate planning and industrial issues. Distributed to companies, libraries and research institutions.

Requirements: 1 2 6 8

Articles on management techniques, strategy and training of interest to a general manager. Length up to 5000 words.

1/News **2**/Features **3**/Fiction **4**/Letters **5**/Fillers
6/B&W Photos **7**/Colour Photos **8**/Reviews

Comments: Guidelines for contributors are available on request.
Approach: By letter.
Lead time: Three months.
Payment: Negotiable.

Management Retirement Guide

Newhall Publications
Newhall Lane
Hoylake
Wirral
L47 4BQ

Tel: 051-632 3232   **Fax:** 051-632 5716

Frequency: 2xYear

Circulation: 50,000

Contact: Vanessa Greatorex, Editor
Profile: An upmarket guide to making the most of your retirement. Aimed at the recently retired and those approaching retirement.
Requirements: 2 5 6 7
Informative, entertaining articles on health, finance, home and garden, hobbies and retiring abroad. Also features on adjusting to retirement, new careers, unusual holidays and hobbies. Length 600 to 1500 words.
Comments: Upbeat, positive, crisp, lively style essential.
Approach: Send ideas or finished manuscript.
Lead time: Two months.
Payment: £100 per thousand words.

Management Services

1 Cecil Court
London Road
Enfield
Middlesex
EN2 6DD

Tel: 081-363 7452   **Fax:** 081-367 8149

Frequency: Monthly
Circulation: 10500
Contact: D.M. Charlton, Editor
Profile: The official publication of the Institute of Management Services.
Requirements: 1 2 6 7 8
Any features on management-related topics, such as information technology, productivity and efficiency. Length 2000 to 5000 words.
Comments: Study the magazine before contributing material.
Approach: By telephone, letter or fax.
Lead time: Four weeks.
Payment: £60 per article.

Management Today

22 Lancaster Gate
London
W2 3LY

Tel: 071-413 4566   **Fax:** 071-413 4138

Frequency: Monthly

Circulation: 98,000

Contact: Mick Hasell
Profile: A general business magazine, providing a blend of company profiles and themed issues on management.
Requirements: 1 2
Profiles of interesting companies, plus articles on new management techniques. Length up to 3000 words.
Comments: Quirky business stories are always welcome.
Approach: By letter.
Lead time: Two months.
Payment: £250 per thousand words.

1/News **2**/Features **3**/Fiction **4**/Letters **5**/Fillers
6/B&W Photos **7**/Colour Photos **8**/Reviews

The Manager

1st Floor
6 Trinity
161 Old Christchurch Road
Bournemouth
BH1 1JW

Tel: (0202) 666626   **Fax:** (0202) 666309

Frequency: Quarterly

Circulation: 6000

Contact: Peter Hodgkins, Editor
Profile: The official publication of the Institute of Commercial Management. Addresses issues of self-improvement, business and economics.
Requirements: 1 2 6
News and features on business issues, success, training tips, books and videos. Length up to 1000 words.
Comments: All submissions are given serious consideration.
Approach: By telephone.
Lead time: Four weeks.
Payment: NUJ rates.

Mandy & Judy

D.C. Thomson & Co Ltd
Albert Square
Dundee
DD1 9QJ

Tel: (0382) 23131   **Fax:** (0382) 22214

Frequency: Weekly

Contact: Ken Peters, Editor
Profile: For girls aged between 10 and 14 years old. Mostly devoted to picture stories.
Requirements: 3
Storylines for picture scripts based on the characters in the established series within the magazine.

Comments: Existing characters are the property of the publisher, but writers may contribute stories that use them.
Approach: In writing.
Lead time: Six weeks.
Payment: Negotiable.

Manufacturing Clothier

Benjamin Dent Publications
Eastern Boulevard
Leicester
LE2 7BN

Tel: (0533) 548271   **Fax:** (0533) 470194

Frequency: 10xYear

Circulation: 5804

Contact: John Gibbon, Editor
Profile: A technical magazine for management, marketing staff and production personnel. Covers fabrics, garments and machinery, etc.
Requirements: 1 2 6 7
Informed technical and management articles, accompanied by pictures, tables and charts. Length 750 to 3000 words.
Comments: Welcomes technical articles of interest to an informed readership.
Approach: By letter or fax with ideas.
Lead time: Six weeks.
Payment: £90-£150 per thousand words.

Manx Tails

1 The Raggett
19 Sartfell Road
Douglas
Isle of Man

Tel: (0624) 661566   **Fax:** (0624) 661659

1/News **2**/Features **3**/Fiction **4**/Letters **5**/Fillers
6/B&W Photos **7**/Colour Photos **8**/Reviews

Frequency: Monthly
Circulation: 14,000
Contact: Eunice Salmond, Editor
Profile: The in-flight magazine of Manx Airlines, read by passengers flying to and from the Isle of Man.
Requirements: 2 5 6 7
Articles on people and places, covering destinations throughout Britain. Length up to 2000 words.
Comments: Contact the magazine before submitting manuscripts.
Approach: By letter.
Lead time: Two months.
Payment: Up to £80.

Map Collector

48 High Street
Tring
Hertfordshire
HP23 5BH

Tel: (0442) 891004   **Fax:** (0296) 623398

Frequency: Quarterly

Circulation: 3000

Contact: V.G. Scott, Editor
Profile: A glossy quarterly for lovers of antique maps. Includes articles by well-known researchers, book reviews, news and auction price guides.
Requirements: 1 2 6 7 8
Short articles on collecting maps and looking after them. Length between 1000 and 2000 words.
Comments: Particularly interested in short articles as most longer pieces are contributed by experts.
Approach: Send ideas or complete manuscripts.
Lead time: Two months.
Payment: From £50 per thousand words.

Marie Claire

195 Knightsbridge
London
SW7 1RE

Tel: 071-261 5240   **Fax:** 071-261 5277

Frequency: Monthly

Circulation: 310,059

Contact: Michele Lavery, Features Editor
Profile: An upmarket monthly for the intelligent woman. Lead on fashion and features.
Requirements: 1 2 5 6 7 8
Strong material on fashion, social issues, health, etc. Length up to 3000 words.
Comments: No subject is out, but the approach must be right.
Approach: By letter with ideas.
Lead time: Three months.
Payment: Negotiable.

Marine Modelling

Traplet House
Severn Drive
Upton-on-Severn
Worcestershire
WR8 0JL

Tel: (0684) 594505   **Fax:** (0684) 594586

Frequency: Monthly

Circulation: 20,000

Contact: C. Jackson, Editor
Profile: Coverage of the world of model boat building, including both static and radio-controlled models.
Requirements: 2 7
'How I did it' articles are always popular. Also unusual subjects not covered by regular writers. Length 1500 to 2000 words.

1/News **2**/Features **3**/Fiction **4**/Letters **5**/Fillers
6/B&W Photos **7**/Colour Photos **8**/Reviews

Comments: Good quality photos are important.
Approach: By telephone with ideas.
Lead time: Eight weeks.
Payment: Up to £50.

Market Trader

Daltry Street
Oldham
OL1 4BB

Tel: 061-624 3687   **Fax:** 061-628 6921

Frequency: Weekly

Circulation: 28,000

Contact: Philip Clegg, Editor
Profile: Aimed at market traders, small retailers and wholesalers.
Requirements: 1 2 6 7
Articles on issues such as Sunday trading, legal issues and financial matters.
Comments: Look out for good products and unusual news items.
Approach: By letter.
Lead time: One week.
Payment: Negotiable.

Marketing

30 Lancaster Gate
London
W2 3LP

Tel: 071-413 4150   **Fax:** 071-413 4504

Frequency: Weekly

Circulation: 45,000

Contact: Susanne Bidlake, News Editor
Profile: Trade magazine for those involved in marketing and associated disciplines.

Requirements: 1 2 6 7
News and features on marketing and related subjects, aimed at a professional business audience. Maximum 1500 words.
Comments: Writers should have a good understanding of the subject.
Approach: By letter.
Lead time: One week.
Payment: Negotiable.

Marketing Business

Greater London House
Hampstead Road
London
NW1 7QQ

Tel: 071-388 3171   **Fax:** 071-387 9518

Frequency: Monthly

Circulation: 35,000

Contact: Stuart Derrick
Profile: The official journal of the Chartered Institute of Marketing. Features led, with coverage that reflects the broad readership.
Requirements: 1 2 7
Case studies, nitty-gritty business articles, features on technology, etc. Length up to 2500 words.
Comments: Has a much wider remit than other marketing magazines.
Approach: By letter.
Lead time: Three months.
Payment: Negotiable.

Marketing Week

St Giles House
50 Poland Street
London
W1V 4AX

Tel: 071-439 4222   **Fax:** 071-439 9669

Frequency: Weekly

1/News **2**/Features **3**/Fiction **4**/Letters **5**/Fillers
6/B&W Photos **7**/Colour Photos **8**/Reviews

Circulation: 37,000

Contact: Stuart Smith, Editor

Profile: Covers marketing, advertising and media. Read by marketing managers at all levels.

Requirements: 1 2 5 7
News and features on any of the above subjects. Original and imaginative ideas will have the best chance of success.

Comments: Copy should be written in a bright and newsy style.

Approach: By telephone.

Lead time: Two weeks.

Payment: £120 per thousand words.

Martial Arts Today

HHL Publications Ltd
Greater London House
Hampstead Road
London
NW1 7QQ

Tel: 071-377 4633   Fax: 071-387 9518

Frequency: Bi-monthly

Circulation: 40,000

Contact: Steven Day, Editor

Profile: Offers a broad perspective on the world of martial arts. Includes all disciplines from judo and karate to Akido and kick-boxing.

Requirements: 2 5
General features on martial arts subjects. Also more specialist articles on training, diet and fitness.

Comments: Contributors do not need to be experts, but they must be able to research their subject thoroughly.

Approach: By telephone with ideas.

Lead time: Three months.

Payment: From £120 per thousand words.

Match

EMAP Pursuit Publishing Ltd
Bretton Court
Bretton Centre
Peterborough
PE3 8DZ

Tel: (0733) 260333   Fax: (0733) 265515

Frequency: Weekly

Circulation: 146,000

Contact: Adrian Curtis, Editor

Profile: A bright, colourful football title with plenty of illustrations. Targeted at boys aged between 9 and 16.

Requirements: 1 2 5
Newsy items based around matches and statistics, covering football from around the country. Exclusives are always welcome.

Comments: Copy must be lively and upbeat.

Approach: In writing.

Lead time: Two weeks.

Payment: £100 per thousand words.

Matchday

PO Box 49
Bordon
Hampshire
GU35 0AF

Tel: (0420) 489474   Fax: (0420) 488797

Frequency: Monthly

Circulation: Not available

Contact: Michael Heatley

Profile: A football monthly covering first-division teams, matches and players. Distributed in towns with first-division teams.

Requirements: 2 5
Interviews and profiles of players, plus articles on the history of first-division clubs.

Comments: Aims to cover the teams neglected by the national press.
Approach: In writing with ideas or complete manuscript.
Lead time: Six weeks.
Payment: £100 per thousand words.

Maternity & Mothercraft

HHL Publications Ltd
Greater London House
Hampstead Road
London
NW1 7QQ
Tel: 071-388 3171   **Fax:** 071-822 2391
Frequency: Bi-monthly
Circulation: 140,000
Contact: Jackie Marsh, Editor
Profile: For expectant women and new Mums and Dads.
Requirements: 2 5 7
Helpful articles on pregnancy and newborn babies. Material based on personal experiences is always welcome. Length up to 1500 words.
Comments: Interested in unusual personal experiences of pregnancy and birth.
Approach: Send complete manuscript, on disk if possible.
Lead time: Two months.
Payment: £100 per thousand words.

Max Power

EMAP Nationals
Lincoln Court
Lincoln Road
Peterborough
Cambridgeshire
PE1 2RF
Tel: (0733) 237111   **Fax:** (0733) 371273
Frequency: Monthly

Circulation: 100,000
Contact: Grahame Steed, Editor
Profile: For younger drivers who wish to improve the performance and appearance of their cars.
Requirements: 2 6 7
Technical pieces on modifying vehicles, especially older cars. These may cover engines, tuning, styling, wheels etc.
Comments: Copy should be light-hearted, sharp and free of jargon.
Approach: By telephone or letter.
Lead time: Two months.
Payment: Negotiable.

Me

Elme House
133 Long Acre
London
WC2E 9AD
Tel: 071-836 0519   **Fax:** 071-497 2364
Frequency: Weekly
Circulation: 500,000
Contact: Kay Goddard, Editor
Profile: For women aged 18 to 35, typically working mothers or housewives with younger children.
Requirements: 1 2 3 4 5
Informative features, advice pieces and other articles of interest to the readership. Length up to 1000 words. Also short fiction, either romance or with a twist in the tail.
Comments: Always interested in hearing new ideas.
Approach: By letter with ideas.
Lead time: Three months.
Payment: Negotiable.

Medal News

105 High Street
Honiton
Devon
EX14 8JW

Tel: (0404) 45414   **Fax:** (0404) 45313

Frequency: 10xYear

Circulation: 2500

Contact: The Editor

Profile: A magazine for collectors and dealers, reviewing the market for medals.

Requirements: 2 6
Detailed, informative and accurate articles on all aspects of military history, with the emphasis on medals.

Comments: Writers should study the magazine before submitting material.

Approach: In writing.

Lead time: Two months.

Payment: Negotiable.

Media Week

EMAP Publications
33-39 Bowling Green Lane
London
EC1R 0DA

Tel: 071-837 1212   **Fax:** 071-837 3285

Frequency: Weekly

Circulation: 17,000

Contact: Richard Gold, Editor

Profile: For people involved in buying and selling media, plus top management in media companies and advertising agencies.

Requirements: 1 2
News and features on all aspects of the world of media sales. Length 800 to 2500 words.

Comments: Does not cover production in any form.

Approach: By telephone.

Lead time: Ten days.

Payment: £150 per thousand words.

Medieval History

PO Box 41
Bangor
Gwynedd
LL57 1SB

Tel: (0248) 351816   **Fax:** (0248) 362115

Frequency: 3xYear

Circulation: 1000

Contact: Judith Loades, Editor

Profile: A periodical aimed at both history students and the general public. Contains both academic articles and accounts of local history for an international readership.

Requirements: 2 3
Articles on the medieval history of a writer's local area, covering anything from factual records to legends and ghost stories. Also fiction on historical subjects. Length up to 3000 words.

Comments: The magazine's readership ranges from professors of history to taxi drivers.

Approach: Submit complete manuscript.

Lead time: Four months.

Payment: £50-£75 per article.

Megatech

Priory Court
30-32 Farringdon Lane
London
EC1R 3AU

Tel: 071-972 6700   **Fax:** 071-972 6703

1/News 2/Features 3/Fiction 4/Letters 5/Fillers
6/B&W Photos 7/Colour Photos 8/Reviews

Frequency: Monthly

Circulation: 40,030

Contact: Paul Glancey, Editor

Profile: A specialist title for users and buyers of Megadrive games.

Requirements: 2 8
Articles about all aspects of Megadrive entertainment. Also reviews of new games and releases.

Comments: Contributors should be familiar with the style of the magazine.

Approach: In writing.

Lead time: Six weeks.

Payment: Negotiable.

Melody Maker

IPC Magazines
King's Reach Tower
Stamford Street
London
SE1 9LS

Tel: 071-261 5000   **Fax:** 071-261 6706

Frequency: Weekly

Circulation: 70,000

Contact: Allan Jones, Editor

Profile: Tabloid-style music paper covering current news and events in rock and pop music.

Requirements: 1 2 8
Interviews with major bands and musicians, plus reviews of concerts and recordings.

Comments: Reviews offer the best chance of publication for new writers.

Approach: In writing with examples of previous work.

Lead time: Two weeks.

Payment: NUJ rates.

Mensa Magazine

Mensa House
St John's Square
Wolverhampton
WV2 4AH

Tel: (0902) 772771   **Fax:** (0902) 22327

Frequency: Monthly

Circulation: 36,500

Contact: Simon Clark, Editor

Profile: The official publication of British Mensa Ltd. Covers subjects of intellectual interest.

Requirements: 2
Informative features for an intelligent readership, covering issues such as the environment, education, science and technology. Length 1500 to 2000 words.

Comments: Guidelines for contributors are available on request.

Approach: In writing.

Lead time: Two months.

Payment: Negotiable.

The Mentor Management Digest

33 Kingsley Place
Newcastle-upon-Tyne
NE6 5AN

Tel: 091-265 0838   **Fax:** 091-265 0838

Frequency: 10xYear

Circulation: 1000

Contact: Chris Ashton, Editor

Profile: Concerned with management development, human resources, training and business development. Focuses on case reports, techniques and best practice.

Requirements: 1 2 4 5
Welcomes case studies and actuality articles from knowledgeable writers.

1/News **2**/Features **3**/Fiction **4**/Letters **5**/Fillers
6/B&W Photos **7**/Colour Photos **8**/Reviews

Must be newsy. Digests and snapshots also sought as regional reports. Length 300 to 1000 words for articles. Up to 100 words for digests.
Comments: Because of the range of material published, it is always advisable to contact the editor with ideas.
Approach: By letter or fax.
Lead time: Three weeks.
Payment: By negotiation.

Meridian

16 Vanbrugh Court
Wincott Street
London
SE11 4NS

Tel: 071-582 2421   **Fax:** 071-587 5147

Frequency: Quarterly

Circulation: 100,000

Contact: Carol Howland, Editor
Profile: A controlled circulation magazine, distributed to a selection of Midland Bank customers.
Requirements: 2
Contributions that educate and inform readers about matters of personal finance. Length 1000 to 1500 words.
Comments: All material must be consumer or money-oriented.
Approach: By letter with ideas and examples of previous work.
Lead time: Four months.
Payment: £250 per thousand words.

Metal Bulletin

16 Lower Marsh
London
SE1 7RJ
Tel: 071-827 9977   **Fax:** 071-928 6539

Frequency: 104xYear
Circulation: 9000
Contact: Reginald Massey
Profile: Trade magazine providing business and market news for the international steel and metal industry.
Requirements: 1 2
Concise, topical items on developments and activities within the metal industry. Copy must be succinct and newsworthy. Length 200 to 500 words.
Comments: Looking for writers who can become regular contributors.
Approach: In writing.
Lead time: One week.
Payment: About £100 per thousand words.

Metal Bulletin Monthly

16 Lower Marsh
London
SE1 7RJ

Tel: 071-827 9977   **Fax:** 071-928 6539

Frequency: Monthly

Circulation: 10,000

Contact: Reginald Massey
Profile: Concerned with the production of both ferrous and non-ferrous metals.
Requirements: 1 2
Articles on steel and the international metal industry. Material should be well-researched, current and aimed at engineering executives. Length 1000 to 3000 words.
Comments: Considers metal production from the management point of view.

Approach: In writing.
Lead time: Six weeks.
Payment: About £100 per thousand words.

Micromouse

Broad Leys Publishing
Buriton House
Station Road
Newport
Saffron Walden
Essex
CB11 3PL

Tel: (0799) 40922   **Fax:** (0799) 41367

Frequency: Bi-monthly

Circulation: 2000

Contact: Katie Thear, Editor
Profile: For people using PCs at home or in small businesses. The emphasis is on the user, not the products.
Requirements: 1 2 6 7
Features that will help users to make the most of their computer technology. Topics might include lesser-known software packages, innovative ways of using technology, etc. Length up to 2000 words.
Comments: Copy must be practical, clear and free of jargon.
Approach: By telephone or letter.
Lead time: Four weeks.
Payment: £20 per thousand words.

Middle East Expatriate

Crescent Court
102 Victor Road
Teddington
Middlesex
TW11 8SS

Tel: 081-943 3630   **Fax:** 081-943 3701

Frequency: 9xYear

Circulation: 16,200
Contact: Nick Horne, Publishing Editor
Profile: A lifestyle publication for working expatriates in the Middle East. Features wide-ranging editorial content.
Requirements: 1 2
Articles on travel, water sports, etc. Also amusing local stories or anything with a zany sense of humour. Length 500 to 1000 words.
Comments: Less concentration on finance than other expat magazines.
Approach: By fax or letter.
Lead time: Four weeks.
Payment: Negotiable.

Milestones

359 Chiswick High Road
London
W4 4HS

Tel: 081-994 4403   **Fax:** 081-994 9249

Frequency: 3xYear

Circulation: 102,000

Contact: Ian Webb, Editor
Profile: For members of the Institute of Advanced Motorists. Emphasises driving, traffic and road safety.
Requirements: 2
Features on any aspect of road safety or better driving. Length 1000 to 2500 words.
Comments: Study the magazine before submitting material.
Approach: By letter.
Lead time: Four weeks.
Payment: From £100 per thousand words.

1/News **2**/Features **3**/Fiction **4**/Letters **5**/Fillers
6/B&W Photos **7**/Colour Photos **8**/Reviews

Military Hobbies

34 Chatsworth Road
Bournemouth
BH8 8SW

Tel: (0202) 512355   **Fax:** (0202) 512355

Frequency: Bi-monthly

Circulation: 8000

Contact: Iain Dickie, Editor
Profile: Covers everything related to
  military miniatures.
Requirements: 1 2
  Articles on re-enactments, collecting
  toy soldiers, figure painting and so
  on. Length 1700 to 3000 words.
Comments: Illustrations are always an
  asset.
Approach: By telephone.
Lead time: Two months.
Payment: £34 per feature.

Military Illustrated Past & Present

43 Museum Street
London
WC1A 1LY

Tel: 071-404 0304   **Fax:** 071-242 1865

Frequency: Monthly

Circulation: 15,000

Contact: Bruce Quarrie, Editor
Profile: Devoted to military uniforms,
  armour, personal weapons and
  soldier's equipment. Covers all
  nationalities and historical periods.
Requirements: 2 5 6 7
  Articles on any of the above
  subjects, up to 2000 words in length.
  Where the subject warrants it, longer
  features can be split into more than
  one instalment.
Comments: The magazine sells to a

highly literate audience and the
approach should be scholarly rather
than popular.
Approach: Send ideas first.
Lead time: Three months.
Payment: £50 per published page.

Military in Scale

Traplet House
Severn Drive
Upton-on-Severn
Worcestershire
WR8 0JL

Tel: (0684) 594505   **Fax:** (0684) 594586

Frequency: Monthly

Circulation: 15,000

Contact: Ian Young, Editor
Profile: Devoted to the construction of
  miniature military models.
Requirements: 2 5 6 7
  Features on fine-scale modelling,
  perhaps covering the history of the
  original item and the construction of
  the model.
Comments: Submissions should be
  accompanied by photos.
Approach: In writing with ideas.
Lead time: Two months.
Payment: £30 per printed page.

Military Simulation & Training

The Lodge
High Street
Harby
Newark
Nottinghamshire
NG23 7EB

Tel: (0522) 704106   **Fax:** (0522) 704131

Frequency: Bi-monthly

Circulation: 21,500

Contact: Trevor Nash, Editor

1/News **2**/Features **3**/Fiction **4**/Letters **5**/Fillers
6/B&W Photos **7**/Colour Photos **8**/Reviews

Profile: Concerned with training topics and technology associated with the world's land, sea and air forces.

Requirements: 1 2
News items of between 200 and 300 words, plus features of 1500 to 2500 words, covering any of the above subjects.

Comments: Study the magazine before contributing.

Approach: By telephone.

Lead time: Six weeks.

Payment: £115 per thousand words.

Mind Your Own Business

106 Church Road
London
SE19 2UB

Tel: 081-771 3614   **Fax:** 081-771 4592

Frequency: Monthly

Circulation: 45,000

Contact: Bill Gledhill, Editor

Profile: Covers issues connected with running and owning a small business.

Requirements: 2 3
Articles on management issues and related topics. Also light-hearted fiction with a business angle.

Comments: Receives a lot of unsolicited material, but welcomes strong contributions.

Approach: In writing, with ideas or complete manuscript.

Lead time: Two months.

Payment: £80-£120 per thousand words.

Miniature War Games

34 Chatsworth Road
Bournemouth
BH8 8SW

Tel: (0202) 512355   **Fax:** (0202) 512355

Frequency: Bi-monthly

Circulation: 8000

Contact: Iain Dickie, Editor

Profile: Covers every aspect of wargaming, throughout all periods of history and war theatres.

Requirements: 1 2
Light and informative articles on the above subjects. Length 1700 to 3000 words.

Comments: Guidelines for contributors are available on request.

Approach: In writing.

Lead time: Two months.

Payment: From £34 per feature.

Mixmag

PO Box 89
London
W14 8ZW

Tel: 071-602 3977   **Fax:** 071-602 8707

Frequency: Monthly

Circulation: 36,000

Contact: David Davies, Editor

Profile: Bright, informative magazine covering dance music and clubbing.

Requirements: 1 2 6 7
Information, features and photos relating to the sphere of dance music and clubbing.

Comments: Study the magazine before contributing.

Approach: Write with synopsis.

Lead time: Two weeks.

Payment: £75 per thousand.

Mizz

27th Floor
IPC Magazines
King's Reach Tower
Stamford Street
London
SE1 9LS

Tel: 071-261 6319 **Fax:** 071-261 6032

Frequency: Fortnightly

Circulation: 161,000

Contact: Simon Geller, Editor

Profile: A lively magazine for teenage girls. Tells them what they need to know, concentrating on real-life people and events.

Requirements: 2
Human interest 'it happened to me' stories about life-changing events. Also general human interest stories concerning teenagers. Length up to 1800 words.

Comments: Human interests stories may occasionally be seen from the male point of view.

Approach: By telephone.

Lead time: Four weeks.

Payment: £150-£200 per thousand words.

Mobile & Holiday Homes

Link House
Dingwall Avenue
Croydon
CR9 2TA

Tel: 081-686 2599 **Fax:** 081-781 6044

Frequency: Monthly

Circulation: 25,000

Contact: Ann Webb, Editor

Profile: A guide to residential park homes, mostly for those of – or approaching – retirement age. Also covers caravan holiday homes for leisure users.

Requirements: 1 2 5 6 7
Site stories and items on unusual uses of park homes and holiday caravans. Also articles on hobbies of interest to the elderly and retired.

Comments: Also includes profiles of new models, parks and sites.

Approach: By telephone with ideas.

Lead time: Two months.

Payment: From £40 per thousand words.

Model & Collectors Mart

Castle House
97 High Street
Colchester
Essex
CO1 1TH

Tel: (0206) 571322 **Fax:** (0206) 564214

Frequency: Monthly

Circulation: 35,000

Contact: Meredith Pfeffer, Editor

Profile: A specialist title for all those interested in collecting and exchanging models.

Requirements: 1 2 6 7
News and features on every aspect of model making and collecting. Subjects may include cars, aeroplanes, railways, boats, engineering and science fiction models.

Comments: Also covers related areas such as the collecting of cards, etc.

Approach: Send complete manuscript, together with photographs and illustrations.

Lead time: Two months.

Payment: Negotiable.

1/News 2/Features 3/Fiction 4/Letters 5/Fillers
6/B&W Photos 7/Colour Photos 8/Reviews

Model Boats

Argus Specialist Publications
Argus House
Boundary Way
Hemel Hempstead
Hertfordshire
HP2 7ST

Tel: (0442) 66551   **Fax:** (0442) 66998

Frequency: Monthly

Circulation: 12,000

Contact: John Cundell, Editor

Profile: Provides comprehensive
coverage of the world of watercraft
modelling. Aimed at readers of all
ages.

Requirements: 2 6
Advice and instructional features
concerning model boats. All
material submitted must be practical
and informative.

Comments: Welcomes plans, sketches
and drawings to accompany
features.

Approach: In writing.

Lead time: Six weeks.

Payment: £25 per page, plus £80 for
plans.

Model Collector

Link House
Dingwall Avenue
Croydon
CR9 2TA

Tel: 081-686 2599   **Fax:** 081-781 6044

Frequency: Monthly

Circulation: 28,000

Contact: Richard West, Editor

Profile: Devoted to die cast, white
metal and plastic models.

Requirements: 2 6 7 8
In-depth studies of specific areas of
model collecting, or features about
lesser-known manufacturers.

Comments: Copy must be accurate and
detailed.

Approach: By letter.

Lead time: Two months.

Payment: Negotiable.

Model Engineer

Argus Specialist Publications
Argus House
Boundary Way
Hemel Hempstead
Hertfordshire
HP2 7ST

Tel: (0442) 66551   **Fax:** (0442) 66998

Frequency: Fortnightly

Circulation: 29,000

Contact: E.J. Jolliffe, Editor

Profile: About all forms of engineering
which can be carried out in a home
workshop.

Requirements: 2 6 7 8
Articles on a wide range of model
engineering subjects, covering
trains, ships, clocks, and models of
armaments.

Comments: Looking for something
different from the vague, woolly
material about trains usually
received. Copy on disk preferred.

Approach: By letter.

Lead time: Two months.

Payment: Up to £35.

Model Engineers' Workshop

Argus Specialist Publications
Argus House
Boundary Way
Hemel Hempstead
Hertfordshire
HP2 7ST

1/News **2**/Features **3**/Fiction **4**/Letters **5**/Fillers
6/B&W Photos **7**/Colour Photos **8**/Reviews

Tel: (0442) 66551   Fax: (0442) 66998

Frequency: Bi-monthly

Circulation: 20,000

Contact: Harold Hall, Editor

Profile: For anyone with a home metal workshop. Also read by people who restore bikes, vehicles, etc.

Requirements: 1 2 6 7 8
Articles pertaining to the usage or construction of workshop equipment.

Comments: Concerned with the use of machines, rather than actual modelling.

Approach: By telephone or letter.

Lead time: Six months.

Payment: Up to £200.

Model Railways

Argus Specialist Publications
Argus House
Boundary Way
Hemel Hempstead
Hertfordshire
HP2 7ST

Tel: (0442) 66551   Fax: (0442) 66998

Frequency: Monthly

Circulation: 9000

Contact: Roy Johnston, Editor

Profile: A specialist title for modelling enthusiasts. Includes society news and building tips.

Requirements: 2 6 7
Features on the planning, wiring and construction of railways, plus descriptive articles and engineering information.

Comments: Interested in original material on experimental railways.

Approach: In writing.

Lead time: Six weeks.

Payment: By arrangement.

The Modern Review

6 Hopgood Street
London
W12 7JU

Tel: 081-749 0593   Fax: 081-749 0593

Frequency: Bi-monthly

Circulation: 30,000

Contact: Toby Young, Editor

Profile: A publication that offers 'low culture for highbrows'.

Requirements: 2 8
Analytical criticism of contemporary mass culture. Length 500 to 2500 words.

Comments: Copy must be intelligent and intellectual.

Approach: By telephone.

Lead time: Two weeks.

Payment: £50 per thousand words.

Modus

Hamilton House
Mabledon Place
London
WC1H 9BJ

Tel: 071-387 1441   Fax: 071-383 7230

Frequency: 8xYear

Circulation: 6200

Contact: The Editor

Profile: Provides information on all aspects of home economics for teachers and professionals in industry.

Requirements: 2 6
Informative material concerning tuition in home economics and technology, together with associated material. Length 1500 words.

Comments: Contributions should be topical and well informed.

Approach: In writing.

Lead time: Three months.

Payment: Negotiable.

1/News 2/Features 3/Fiction 4/Letters 5/Fillers
6/B&W Photos 7/Colour Photos 8/Reviews

Money Week

EMAP Publications
33-39 Bowling Green Lane
London
EC1R 0DA

Tel: 071-837 1212   **Fax:** 071-278 6550

Frequency: Weekly

Circulation: 30,000

Contact: Tony McMahon, News
Editor

Profile: Circulated to independent
financial advisers, pension providers
and building societies.

Requirements: 2 6 7
Analytical pieces looking behind
recent developments in the field of
life insurance, mortgages and
pensions. Length up to 1000 words.

Comments: Send graphs and photos
where appropriate.

Approach: By telephone.

Lead time: Four weeks.

Payment: £150 per thousand words.

MoneyMarketing

50 Poland Street
London
W1V 4AX

Tel: 071-287 5678   **Fax:** 071-734 9379

Frequency: Weekly

Circulation: 30,000

Contact: Tim Potter, Editor

Profile: A professional publication for
financial intermediaries. Includes
information on life assurance and
other matters relating to investment.

Requirements: 1 2 6 7
News from the finance and
insurance industries, plus surveys,
opinion and features. Length from
900 words.

Comments: Also welcomes cartoons
on relevant subjects.

Approach: By letter with ideas.

Lead time: Three weeks.

Payment: £100 per thousand words.

Moneywise

Berkeley Square House
Berkeley Square
London
W1X 6AB

Tel: 071-629 8144   **Fax:** 071-409 5261

Frequency: Monthly

Circulation: 100,734

Contact: Christine Whelan, Editor

Profile: A financial advice magazine
aimed at the ordinary consumer as
well as the serious investor. Readers
tend to be older people with
relatively high incomes.

Requirements: 2 5
Features suggesting new and
promising investment opportunities.
These should be fairly serious in
tone, and of interest to financially
aware readers. Length 800 to 900
words.

Comments: Submissions are
encouraged, but much of the
material currently received is too
basic in content.

Approach: In writing.

Lead time: Six weeks.

Payment: From £150 per thousand
words.

Monocle

10 Queen Street
Godalming
Surrey
GU7 1BD

Tel: (0483) 425454   **Fax:** (0483) 420031

1/News **2**/Features **3**/Fiction **4**/Letters **5**/Fillers
6/B&W Photos **7**/Colour Photos **8**/Reviews

Frequency: Monthly

Circulation: 12,134

Contact: Peter Tribe, Editor

Profile: Distributed throughout Surrey via hotels, golf courses, etc. Concentrates on the fun side of life for affluent readers.

Requirements: 2 6 7 8
Interviews with people who live in Surrey and make a positive contribution to the county. Also articles on local history, fashion, polo etc. Length 800 to 1500 words.

Comments: Geared towards the social and leisure aspects of life in Surrey.

Approach: By telephone or letter.

Lead time: Two months.

Payment: £65 per thousand words.

More!

20 Orange Street
London
WC2H 7ED

Tel: 071-957 8383   **Fax:** 071-957 8400

Frequency: Fortnightly

Circulation: 262,000

Contact: Marie O'Riorden, Deputy Editor

Profile: Aimed at working women aged between 16 and 25. Majors on men, sex, humour and careers.

Requirements: 2 3 4 7
Emotional features, articles about interesting people, and quirky, experimental pieces. Length up to 1600 words.

Comments: Fiction relevant to the readership is also used sporadically.

Approach: By letter followed up with a telephone call.

Lead time: Four weeks.

Payment: £250 per spread.

Mortgage Finance Gazette

South Quay Plaza
183 Marsh Wall
London
E14 9FS

Tel: 071-538 5386   **Fax:** 071-538 8624

Frequency: Monthly

Circulation: 6800

Contact: Neil Madden, Editor

Profile: An independent publication which provides information concerning building societies and housing finance.

Requirements: 2 6
Feature articles on mortgages, financial services and the management of building societies. Maximum length 2000 words.

Comments: Considers mortgages from the professional rather than the consumer point of view.

Approach: By letter with ideas.

Lead time: Two months.

Payment: Around £135 per thousand words.

Mother and Baby

Victory House
14 Leicester Square
London
WC2H 7BP

Tel: 071-437 9011   **Fax:** 071-434 0656

Frequency: Monthly

Circulation: 109,061

Contact: Sharon Parsons, Deputy Editor

Profile: For pregnant women and mothers of children under the age of three.

1/News 2/Features 3/Fiction 4/Letters 5/Fillers
6/B&W Photos 7/Colour Photos 8/Reviews

Requirements: 1 2 7 8
Practical features on babycare, plus readers' personal experiences. Length up to 1800 words.

Comments: Unsolicted manuscripts are welcome, although it may take a while to get a response.

Approach: Send complete manuscript.

Lead time: Three months.

Payment: From £100 per thousand words.

Motor Boat and Yachting

IPC Magazines
King's Reach Tower
Stamford Street
London
SE1 9LS

Tel: 071-261 5333   **Fax:** 071-261 5419

Frequency: Monthly

Circulation: 28,000

Contact: Alan Harper, Editor

Profile: The leading motor cruising magazine, sold throughout the UK, Europe and worldwide. Includes cruising guides, boat and engine tests, equipment reviews and practical advice on navigation and seamanship.

Requirements: 1 2 7
First-person motor cruising accounts, technical motor boating information and features on interesting or unusual motor boats. Length 1500 to 2500 words.

Comments: A wide range of boat types and sizes are covered to suit a wide range of waters.

Approach: By letter, telephone or fax.

Lead time: Two months.

Payment: £80-£100 per thousand words.

Motor Caravan Magazine

Link House
Dingwall Avenue
Croydon
CR9 2TA

Tel: 081-686 2599   **Fax:** 081-781 6044

Frequency: Monthly

Circulation: 14,000

Contact: Paul Carter, Editor

Profile: Provides coverage of all matters relating to motor caravanning.

Requirements: 2 6 7 8
Touring features, owner reports on motor caravans, site reports and practical features. Length up to 2000 words.

Comments: Uses a considerable amount of material from freelance writers, and is prepared to consider unsolicited manuscripts.

Approach: By telephone with ideas.

Lead time: Six weeks.

Payment: Up to £150.

Motor Cycle News

20-22 Station Road
Kettering
NN15 7HH

Tel: (0536) 411111   **Fax:** (0536) 411750

Frequency: Weekly

Circulation: 139,385

Contact: Adam Smallman, Features Editor

Profile: The world's number one motorcycle newspaper.

Requirements: 1 2 6 7 8
News of new products, launches of bikes and other matters of interest to bikers.

Comments: All ideas will be given serious consideration.

Approach: By letter.
Lead time: Two weeks.
Payment: Negotiable.

Motorboats Monthly

Link House
Dingwall Avenue
Croydon
CR9 2TA

Tel: 081-686 2599 **Fax:** 081-781 6065

Frequency: Monthly

Circulation: 15,000

Contact: Kim Hollamby, Editor
Profile: Covers all powered craft from 15ft to 65 ft. Provides a broad balance of practical articles, tests and entertaining features.
Requirements: 1 2 7
All subjects except boat and equipment tests, which are covered by the in-house team. Maximum length 3500 words.
Comments: Material must relate to the style of boats covered by the magazine.
Approach: In writing with ideas.
Lead time: Six weeks.
Payment: Around £110 per page.

Motorcaravan Motorhome Monthly

8 Swan Meadow
Pewsey
Wiltshire
SN9 5HW

Tel: (0672) 62574 **Fax:** (0264) 324794

Frequency: Monthly

Circulation: 21,000

Contact: Penny Smith, Editor
Profile: Covers the whole world of motor caravanning.

Requirements: 2 3 5 6 7
Owner reports, DIY features, travel reports, fiction and cookery articles related to motor caravanning. Length up to 2500 words, although longer articles may be run in up to three instalments.
Comments: Photographs with captions or maps and diagrams are essential.
Approach: By letter with ideas.
Lead time: Ten weeks.
Payment: Negotiable.

Motorcycle International

3 Acton Hill Mews
310-328 Uxbridge Road
London
W3 9QU

Tel: 081-993 4136 **Fax:** 081-993 8702

Frequency: Monthly

Circulation: 38,577

Contact: Tom Isitt, Editor
Profile: About motorcycling in general, including sports touring and road tests.
Requirements: 1 2 5 7
Touring articles, opinion pieces and features about bikes which are unusual or not available in the UK. Length from 1000 words.
Comments: A good story is the key requirement.
Approach: By telephone.
Lead time: Three months.
Payment: Negotiable.

Motorcycle Sport

Standard House
Bonhill Street
London
EC2A 4DA

Tel: 071-628 4741 **Fax:** 071-638 8497

1/News 2/Features 3/Fiction 4/Letters 5/Fillers
6/B&W Photos 7/Colour Photos 8/Reviews

Frequency: Monthly

Circulation: 15,000

Contact: Cyril Ayton, Editor

Profile: Takes a serious approach to the world of motorcycle sport.

Requirements: 2 6 7
Looking for technical articles about re-building bikes, etc. Also touring features and articles on biking personalities.

Comments: Copy on disk preferred, most formats accepted.

Approach: By letter.

Lead time: Four weeks.

Payment: £100 per thousand words.

Motorhome Magazine

2a Granville Road
Sidcup
Kent
DA14 4BN

Tel: 081-302 6150   **Fax:** 081-300 2315

Frequency: Quarterly

Circulation: 18,000

Contact: Dave Randall, Editor

Profile: Aimed specifically at owners and users of the larger, more expensive A Class motorcaravans.

Requirements: 2
Travel features, exhibition reviews, interviews with celebrities who use motorhomes, etc.

Comments: Contributors should have extensive knowledge of the subject.

Approach: In writing.

Lead time: Three months.

Payment: Up to £50.

Motoring News

PO Box 35
Standard House
Bonhill Street
London
EC2A 4DA

Tel: 071-628 4741   **Fax:** 071-638 8497

Frequency: Weekly

Circulation: 68,000

Contact: Mark Skewis, Editor

Profile: A motoring weekly specialising in racing and rallying.

Requirements: 1 2 6 7
News and features relating to all aspects of motorsport, from hill climbing to hot rods.

Comments: Does not include general motoring news.

Approach: By fax or letter.

Lead time: One week.

Payment: £1.40 per column inch.

The Motorist

34 Duke Road
Chiswick
London
W4 2DD

Tel: 081-994 3239   **Fax:** 081-994 8088

Frequency: Weekly

Circulation: 500,000

Contact: Brian Charig, Editor

Profile: Distributed via petrol stations, garages and supermarkets in Greater London. Covers motoring news and general interest articles.

Requirements: 1 2 6 7
Features on classic cars, new cars and auctions, plus general articles on subjects as diverse as furniture, health and places to visit. Length up to 2000 words.

1/News 2/Features 3/Fiction 4/Letters 5/Fillers
6/B&W Photos 7/Colour Photos 8/Reviews

Comments: General interest articles do not need to be related to motoring.
Approach: By letter.
Lead time: Two weeks.
Payment: NUJ rates.

Mountain Biker International

United Leisure Magazines
PO Box 3205
4 Selsdon Way
London
E14 9GL

Tel: 071-712 0565   **Fax:** 071-712 0557

Frequency: Monthly

Circulation: 40,000

Contact: Nicky Crowther, Editor
Profile: A fashionable, technical magazine for mountain biking enthusiasts.
Requirements: 1 2 8
Particularly seeking knowledgeable bike writers who can provide informative and entertaining features for a young cycling readership.
Comments: Study the magazine before submitting material.
Approach: By telephone.
Lead time: Two weeks.
Payment: £100 per thousand words.

Moving Pictures UK

Moving Pictures International
1 Richmond Mews
London
W1B 5AG

Tel: 071-287 0070   **Fax:** 071-287 9637

Frequency: Weekly

Circulation: 8000

Contact: Sophie Hanscombe, Editor

Profile: A trade magazine relating specifically to the distribution and exhibition of films in Britain.
Requirements: 1 2
News and features of interest to managers of cinemas throughout the UK. Possible subjects include advertising, legal requirements, etc. Length 800 to 1000 words.
Comments: All submissions should be well informed and authoritative.
Approach: In writing.
Lead time: Four weeks.
Payment: By negotiation.

Mrs Beeton Traditional Housekeeping Today

EMP House
Pembroke Road
London
N10 2HR

Tel: 081-444 3401   **Fax:** 081-883 9504

Frequency: Quarterly

Circulation: 50,000

Contact: Susan Wolk, Editor
Profile: Everything about cookery and housekeeping for today's modern woman.
Requirements: 2 5 7 8
Articles on modern housekeeping with traditional values, recipe features and general interest items.
Comments: Aimed at the contemporary Mrs Beeton.
Approach: By letter.
Lead time: Four months.
Payment: NUJ rates.

Ms London

7-9 Rathbone Street
London
W1V 1AF

1/News 2/Features 3/Fiction 4/Letters 5/Fillers
6/B&W Photos 7/Colour Photos 8/Reviews

Tel: 071-636 6651   **Fax:** 071-872 0806

Frequency: Weekly

Circulation: 127,000

Contact: Bill Williamson,
Editor-in-Chief

Profile: Distributed to working women
in the London area, aimed at those
aged between 18 and 35.

Requirements: 2 5
Features on fashion, careers, homes
and relationships. All material
should have a London angle, and
should not run to more than 1500
words.

Comments: Particularly welcomes
writers who are in touch with life
and events in the capital.

Approach: In writing with ideas.

Lead time: Three weeks.

Payment: Around £125 per thousand
words.

Musclemag International

53 Lichfield Road
Aston
Birmingham
B6 5RW

Tel: 021-328 7525   **Fax:** 021-327 7525

Frequency: Monthly

Circulation: 55,000

Contact: David McInerney, Editor

Profile: A body building and physique
development title. Includes training,
diet, supplementation and lifestyles
for both body builders and general
weight trainers.

Requirements: 2 6 7
Articles on body building, power
lifting or general weight training for
beginners and intermediate
enthusiasts. Length up to 1000
words.

Comments: Welcomes training
routines and dietary regimes that are
easy to understand. Multi-part
features are encouraged.

Approach: By fax or letter.

Lead time: Four weeks.

Payment: £50 per thousand words.

Museums Journal

The Museums Association
42 Clerkenwell Close
London
EC1R 0PA

Tel: 071-608 2933   **Fax:** 071-250 1929

Frequency: Monthly

Circulation: 5000

Contact: Maurice Davies, Editor

Profile: Provides news, information
and advice for everyone concerned
with museum management and
administration.

Requirements: 1 2 6 7 8
Articles on the running of museums
and art galleries, plus news of
developments and features on
display and architecture. Length up
to 2500 words.

Comments: Will also consider reviews
of books relevant to the readership.

Approach: In writing.

Lead time: Two months.

Payment: Negotiable.

Music Technology

Alexander House
Forehill
Ely
Cambridgeshire
CB7 4AF

Tel: (0353) 665577   **Fax:** (0353) 662489

Frequency: Monthly

1/News **2**/Features **3**/Fiction **4**/Letters **5**/Fillers
6/B&W Photos **7**/Colour Photos **8**/Reviews

Circulation: 25,000

Contact: Nigel Lord, Editor

Profile: Covers the world of hi-tech music for both amateur and professional musicians.

Requirements: 2 6 7 8
Interviews with prominent musicians, product reviews, documentary pieces and general features. Length between 800 and 2500 words.

Comments: Writers should be familiar with the style and content of the magazine.

Approach: By letter or fax with complete manuscript.

Lead time: Two weeks.

Payment: £70-£90 per thousand words.

Music Week

Spotlight Publications
8th Floor
Ludgate House
245 Blackfriars Road
London
SE1 9UR

Tel: 071-620 3636   **Fax:** 071-401 8035

Frequency: Weekly

Circulation: 13,280

Contact: Steve Redmond, Editor

Profile: A trade weekly for all those involved in the music business.

Requirements: 1 2
News stories up to 350 words in length about developments within the music industry. Also features analysing current trends or events. Length up to 2000 words.

Comments: Concerned only with trade and industry matters.

Approach: In writing.

Lead time: Three weeks.

Payment: Negotiable.

Musical Opinion

2 Princes Road
St Leonards on Sea
East Sussex
TN37 6EL

Tel: (0424) 715167   **Fax:** (0424) 712214

Frequency: Monthly

Circulation: 5000

Contact: Denby Richards, Editor

Profile: Covers the world of classical music in the broadest sense of the term.

Requirements: 2 8
Topical articles on musicians, festivals, and music generally, plus reviews of concerts, ballet, opera, CDs, jazz and books.

Comments: Articles relating to specific events should be submitted six months previously.

Approach: In writing.

Lead time: Six months.

Payment: Negotiable.

Musical Times

4th Floor
Centro House
Mandela Street
London
NW1 0DU

Tel: 071-387 3848   **Fax:** 071-388 8532

Frequency: Monthly

Circulation: 4000

Contact: Anthony Bye, Editor

Profile: An authoritative publication that covers music and musicians.

Requirements: 2 8
Serious and thought-provoking features about music, plus reviews of books, records and concerts.

Comments: Material should have a practical style.

1/News 2/Features 3/Fiction 4/Letters 5/Fillers
6/B&W Photos 7/Colour Photos 8/Reviews

Approach: In writing.
Lead time: Six weeks.
Payment: £45-£50 per thousand words.

My Weekly

80 Kingsway East
Dundee
DD4 8SL

Tel: (0382) 23131   **Fax:** (0382) 452491

Frequency: Weekly

Circulation: 500,000

Contact: Sandra Monks, Editor
Profile: A women's-interest title that
    focuses on fiction, cookery, knitting
    and similar subjects.
Requirements: 2 3
    Human-interest and light-hearted
    pieces ranging from 1000 to 1500
    words in length. Also fiction which
    may be romantic or quirky in style.
Comments: Guidelines for
    contributors are available on
    request.
Approach: Send complete manuscript.
Lead time: Two months.
Payment: £60-£150 per thousand
    words.

1/News **2**/Features **3**/Fiction **4**/Letters **5**/Fillers
6/B&W Photos **7**/Colour Photos **8**/Reviews

N

The National Trust Magazine

36 Queen Anne's Gate
London
SW1H 9AS

Tel: 071-222 9251   **Fax:** 071-222 5097

Frequency: 3xYear

Circulation: 1.3 million

Contact: Sarah-Jane Forder, Editor

Profile: For the members of the National Trust, dealing with the conservation of historic houses, vernacular architecture, coast, countryside and the environment.

Requirements: 2
Feature articles on the above topics, by writers with a good knowledge of the subject. Length up to 1000 words.

Comments: Material must be linked to the National Trust.

Approach: By letter with ideas.

Lead time: Six months.

Payment: £300 per thousand words.

Natural World

20 Upper Ground
London
SE1 9PF

Tel: 071-928 2111   **Fax:** 071-620 1594

Frequency: 3xYear

Circulation: 165,000

Contact: Linda Bennett, Editor

Profile: The journal of the RSNC Wildlife Trusts Partnership. Covers wildlife and countryside conservation related to the associated charities.

Requirements: 1 2 7
Successful local action stories related to the Wildlife Trusts. Length 300 to 1200 words.

Comments: Lively first-hand involvement makes for a more interesting read.

Approach: By letter with ideas.

Lead time: Three months.

Payment: £100 per thousand words.

Navy International

Hunters Moon
Hogspudding Lane
Newdigate
Surrey
RH5 5DS

Tel: (0306) 631442   **Fax:** (0306) 631226

Frequency: Bi-monthly

Circulation: 2200

Contact: A.J. Watts, Editor

Profile: Concerned with navy strategy, tactics and organisation. Read by navy professionals worldwide.

Requirements: 2 6 7
Good descriptive material that is well-researched and includes plenty of detail. No historical articles.

1/News **2**/Features **3**/Fiction **4**/Letters **5**/Fillers
6/B&W Photos **7**/Colour Photos **8**/Reviews

Comments: Some subscribers read English as a second language. Therefore, style should be basic without talking down to readers.
Approach: By telephone with ideas.
Lead time: Two months.
Payment: £75 per thousand words.

Needlecraft

Future Publishing
30 Monmouth Street
Bath
BA1 2BW

Tel: (0225) 442244   **Fax:** (0225) 462986

Frequency: Bi-monthly

Circulation: 105,057

Contact: Martin Penny or Susan Penny
Profile: Covers all kinds of needlework, except home sewing and dressmaking.
Requirements: 2 5
'How-to' features and projects about cross-stitch, needlepoint, bobbin lace, patchwork and freestyle embroidery. Also profiles of needlecraft personalities.
Comments: Writers should emphasise the practical element, and include plenty of hints and tips.
Approach: In writing.
Lead time: Two months.
Payment: Negotiable.

Needlework

PO Box 379
Wolverhampton
WV8 1BU

Tel: (0902) 845575   **Fax:** (0902) 845575

Frequency: Monthly

Circulation: 70,000

Contact: Anna Davenport
Profile: A practical guide to the craft and techniques of needlework.
Requirements: 1 2
News of events or exhibitions around the country, plus interviews with designers and other personalities in the world of needlework.
Comments: Most project work is covered by the editorial staff.
Approach: In writing with ideas.
Lead time: Six weeks.
Payment: £75-£100 per feature.

Network

32-34 Broadwick Street
London
W1A 2HG

Tel: 071-439 4242   **Fax:** 071-437 8985

Frequency: Monthly

Circulation: 20,000

Contact: Ken Young, Editor
Profile: Overall coverage of network computing for end users. Aimed at the professional data processing manager.
Requirements: 1 2
General features and analysis of the networking and communications world. Length 1000 to 2000 words.
Comments: Writers should have a good understanding of network computing.
Approach: In writing with ideas.
Lead time: Six weeks.
Payment: £130 per thousand words.

New Cyclist

Stonehart Leisure Magazines
67-71 Goswell Road
London
EC1V 7EN

Tel: 071-250 1881   **Fax:** 071-410 9440

Frequency: Monthly

Circulation: 24,473

Contact: Jim McGurn, Editor

Profile: A magazine for keen cyclists, providing up-to-date information on a range of relevant subjects.

Requirements: 1 2
News and features on topics of interest to the cycling enthusiast. All copy must be well-researched and accurate.

Comments: Study the style of the magazine before submitting manuscripts.

Approach: In writing.

Lead time: Six weeks.

Payment: By arrangement.

New DIY Magazine

Link House
Dingwall Avenue
Croydon
CR9 2TA

Tel: 081-686 2599   **Fax:** 081-760 0973

Frequency: Monthly

Circulation: 42,000

Contact: John McGowan, Editor

Profile: Home improvements for the handy person around the house. Covers both internal and external work.

Requirements: 1 2 5 6 7
Step-by-step projects for the keen amateur, practical features and garden ideas. Length up to 1000 words.

Comments: A re-launched version of *Do-It-Yourself* magazine.

Approach: By letter.

Lead time: Two months.

Payment: Negotiable.

New Electronics

Franks Hall
Franks Lane
Horton Kirby
Dartford
Kent
DA4 9LL

Tel: (0322) 222222   **Fax:** (0322) 289577

Frequency: Monthly

Circulation: 27,500

Contact: Louise Joselyn, Editor

Profile: A technical journal for electronics designers and engineering managers. Mainly technology and applications.

Requirements: 2 8
Case studies on electronics applications or general technology articles. Length from 1200 to 2000 words.

Comments: Copy should be informative and useful to the reader, offering more than press release information.

Approach: By fax, followed up with a telephone call.

Lead time: Three months.

Payment: From £150 per thousand words.

New Internationalist

55 Rectory Road
Oxford
OX4 1BW

Tel: (0865) 728181   **Fax:** (0865) 793152

1/News **2**/Features **3**/Fiction **4**/Letters **5**/Fillers
6/B&W Photos **7**/Colour Photos **8**/Reviews

Frequency: Monthly

Circulation: 65,000

Contact: Vanessa Baird

Profile: A radical magazine concerned with international issues with an emphasis on developing and undeveloped countries.

Requirements: 2 5
Feature articles on subjects such as peace, poverty and politics on the global stage.

Comments: Each issue has its own theme, and writers should target material around forthcoming themes.

Approach: In writing.

Lead time: Two months.

Payment: £100 per thousand words.

New Musical Express

25th Floor
IPC Magazines
King's Reach Tower
Stamford Street
London
SE1 9LS

Tel: 071-261 6472   **Fax:** 071-261 5185

Frequency: Weekly

Circulation: 118,000

Contact: Steve Sutherland, Editor

Profile: The world's biggest-selling rock/pop weekly. Includes news, reviews, interviews, features and competitions.

Requirements: 1 2 6 7 8
News and features relating to contemporary music and musicians. Reviews of gigs, concerts and recordings.

Comments: Looking for enthusiasts and experts alike, but writers must have 'attitude'.

Approach: By letter, fax or telephone.

Lead time: One week.

Payment: NUJ rates.

New Scientist

King's Reach Tower
Stamford Street
London
SE1 9LS

Tel: 071-261 7301   **Fax:** 071-261 6464

Frequency: Weekly

Circulation: 101,540

Contact: Alun Anderson, Editor

Profile: An informative consumer publication concerned with developments in science and technology.

Requirements: 2 5 6 7
Well-informed features on matters of current interest in the world of science. Length 1000 to 3000 words.

Comments: Filler items from contributors who are experts in the relevant subject.

Approach: By telephone or letter with ideas.

Lead time: Three weeks.

Payment: Around £160 per thousand words.

New Statesman & Society

Foundation House
Perseverance Works
38 Kingsland Road
London
E2 8DQ

Tel: 071-739 3211   **Fax:** 071-739 9307

Frequency: Weekly

Circulation: 22,271

Contact: Alida Campbell

1/News **2**/Features **3**/Fiction **4**/Letters **5**/Fillers
6/B&W Photos **7**/Colour Photos **8**/Reviews

Profile: Britain's leading radical weekly, covering the whole breadth of political and cultural affairs.

Requirements: 1 2

Various short and feature-length pieces, plus diary items. Material with a topical edge is always welcome. Length 50 to 3000 words.

Comments: A lively, accessible and colourful style is essential whatever the subject. The content should aim to bring new information to informed readers.

Approach: Send complete manuscript.

Lead time: Three weeks.

Payment: By arrangement.

New Woman

20 Orange Street
London
WC2H 7ED

Tel: 071-957 8383   **Fax:** 071-957 8400

Frequency: Monthly

Circulation: 261,706

Contact: Gill Hudson, Editor

Profile: Glossy monthly that focuses on working women aged 25 to 35, with particular emphasis on personal lives.

Requirements: 2 3 4

Feature ideas on relationships, sex, emotions and self-development. Also articles on social trends, work and health.

Comments: Welcomes material from experienced writers.

Approach: By letter or fax with ideas and examples of previous work.

Lead time: Ten weeks.

Payment: From £100 per thousand words.

News in Action

31 Penylan Road
Roath
Cardiff
CF2 3PG

Tel: (0222) 493362   **Fax:** (0222) 485711

Frequency: Monthly

Circulation: 50,000

Contact: Malcolm Lee, Editor

Profile: An A3-format glossy distributed nationally.

Requirements: 1 2 5 6 7

Feature articles on a wide range of subjects, including education, entertainment, sport and business. Length 500 to 1000 words.

Comments: Illustrations will be appreciated.

Approach: By letter.

Lead time: Six weeks.

Payment: Negotiable.

Nexus

International House
500 Purley Way
Croydon
CR0 4NZ

Tel: 081-760 5100   **Fax:** 081-760 0469

Frequency: Monthly

Circulation: 8500

Contact: Sheila Hare, Editor

Profile: Magazine for expatriates, ranging from contract workers to medical staff.

Requirements: 1 2 6 7

News and features about recruitment, financial matters, health and other subjects of interest to expatriates.

Comments: Good financial writers are always in demand.

1/News 2/Features 3/Fiction 4/Letters 5/Fillers
6/B&W Photos 7/Colour Photos 8/Reviews

Approach: By letter with ideas.
Lead time: Two weeks.
Payment: £80 per page.

19

IPC Magazines
King's Reach Tower
Stamford Street
London
SE1 9LS

Tel: 071-261 6410   **Fax:** 071-261 6032

Frequency: Monthly

Circulation: 200,000

Contact: Verity Watkins, Features
Editor
Profile: A trendy, fashionable glossy
for women aged between 16 and 22.
Requirements: 1 2 4
First-person stories, interviews with
well-known personalities and articles
on issues that concern young
women. Length up to 1500 words.
Comments: For young women who are
interested in current events.
Approach: By telephone.
Lead time: Three months.
Payment: Better than NUJ rates.

90 Minutes

IPC Magazines
King's Reach Tower
Stamford Street
London
SE1 9LS

Tel: 071-261 7454   **Fax:** 071-261 7474

Frequency: Weekly

Circulation: 75,000

Contact: Paul Hawksbee, Editor
Profile: Youth football title aimed

primarily at 16 to 24 year olds.
Features news, interviews and
statistics from Britain and overseas.
Requirements: 1 2
News stories of up to 120 words.
Player interviews and features
between 550 and 1000 words.
Comments: 'Think pieces' tend to be
rejected immediately.
Approach: By telephone.
Lead time: Two weeks.
Payment: Up to £80.

Norfolk Life

Barn Acre House
Saxtead Green
Woodbridge
Suffolk
IP13 9QJ

Tel: (0728) 685832   **Fax:** (0728) 685842

Frequency: Monthly

Circulation: 15,000

Contact: Kevin Davies, Editor
Profile: A general consumer and
business title for Norfolk. Very
broad in scope, covering a wide
range of subjects.
Requirements: 2 5 6 7 8
Feature articles on local places of
interest, the countryside, historical
matters, etc. Length up to 1000
words.
Comments: All submissions must be
directly connected with the county of
Norfolk.
Approach: By telephone or letter.
Lead time: Four weeks.
Payment: £25 per thousand words.

1/News 2/Features 3/Fiction 4/Letters 5/Fillers
6/B&W Photos 7/Colour Photos 8/Reviews

Northamptonshire Image

Upper Mounts
Northampton
NN1 3HR

Tel: (0604) 231122   **Fax:** (0604) 233000

Frequency: Monthly

Circulation: 16,000

Contact: Peter Hall, Editor

Profile: A county magazine which places a strong emphasis on local events and personalities.

Requirements: 2
Feature articles on food and wine, entertainment, fashion, antiques and travel.

Comments: Writers should look for ideas with a strong local angle.

Approach: In writing.

Lead time: Two months.

Payment: By arrangement.

The Northumbrian

Powdene House
26 Pudding Chare
Newcastle-upon-Tyne
NE1 1UE

Tel: 091-230 3454   **Fax:** 091-232 1710

Frequency: Quarterly

Circulation: 12,000

Contact: Stewart Bonney, Editor

Profile: A countryside magazine concerned with local country news, the environment and historical matters.

Requirements: 2 7
Articles relating to the countryside or the history of the county. Copy must be factual rather than literary, and anything that is easy to illustrate stands a better chance. Length up to 1000 words.

Comments: No poetry or conventional news items.

Approach: By letter with ideas.

Lead time: Two months.

Payment: Negotiable.

Nursery Choice

32 Sekforde Street
Clerkenwell Road
London
EC1R 0HH

Tel: 071-251 2505   **Fax:** 071-251 2709

Frequency: Quarterly

Circulation: 60,000

Contact: Caroline Townley, Editor

Profile: An upmarket lifestyle magazine for parents and parents to be.

Requirements: 2
Authoritative articles on matters such as child development, health, car safety and the organic 'green' side of parenting. Length up to 2000 words.

Comments: No articles on 'how to cure tantrums,' etc.

Approach: By telephone.

Lead time: Two months.

Payment: Negotiable.

Nursery World

The Schoolhouse Workshop
51 Calthorpe Street
London
WC1X 0HH

Tel: 071-837 7224   **Fax:** 071-278 3896

Frequency: Weekly

Circulation: 20,000

Contact: Lindsey Blythe, Editor

Profile: A features-based magazine concerned with the care of children under 8 years of age.

1/News **2**/Features **3**/Fiction **4**/Letters **5**/Fillers
6/B&W Photos **7**/Colour Photos **8**/Reviews

Requirements: 2 8
Features on child development,
health and education. Length 750 to
1500 words.
Comments: Opinion pieces are also
used occasionally.
Approach: Submit complete
manuscript.
Lead time: Two months.
Payment: Negotiable.

Nursing Times

4 Little Essex Street
London
WC2R 3LF

Tel: 071-379 0970   **Fax:** 071-497 2664

Frequency: Weekly

Circulation: 94,083

Contact: Tricia Reid, Features Editor
Profile: Professional journal for
nurses. Includes news, news analysis
and features.
Requirements: 2
General articles on all nursing
specialities, together with historical,
international, political and
sociological articles on health care.
Length up to 2000 words.
Comments: Contributions must be of a
high standard and well-referenced.
Guidelines for contributors are
available on request.
Approach: By telephone with ideas.
Lead time: Negotiable.
Payment: £100-£144 per article.

O

The Observer Magazine

Chelsea Bridge House
Queenstown Road
London
SW8 4NN

Tel: 071-627 0700   **Fax:** 071-627 5570

Frequency: Weekly

Circulation: 500,000

Contact: Simon Kelmer, Editor

Profile: Glossy magazine distributed with the *Observer* newspaper, aimed at an upmarket audience.

Requirements: 1 2
The stories behind the news, in-depth analyses of current issues and profiles of prominent figures. Length between 1000 and 5000 words.

Comments: Welcomes quirky news items about unusual things.

Approach: By letter with synopsis.

Lead time: Six weeks.

Payment: £250 per thousand words.

Odds On

PO Box 10
Oswestry
Shropshire
SY10 7QR

Tel: (0691) 70426   **Fax:** (691) 70315

Frequency: Monthly

Circulation: 20,000

Contact: The Editor

Profile: Aims to highlight the opportunities in betting and the potential profits to be made.

Requirements: 2
Feature articles on anything from horse racing and cards to backgammon and financial investments. Length from 500 to 1000 words.

Comments: Only material of the highest quality and originality will be considered.

Approach: Submit finished manuscript.

Lead time: Two months.

Payment: £100 per thousand words.

Office Buyer

Trade Media Ltd
Brookmead House
Two Rivers
Station Lane
Witney
Oxon OX8 6BH

Tel: (0993) 775545   **Fax:** (0993) 778884

Frequency: Bi-monthly

Circulation: 10,500

Contact: Lucy Sloan, Editor

Profile: Management magazine for purchasers and facilities managers in the UK's top organisations.

1/News 2/Features 3/Fiction 4/Letters 5/Fillers
6/B&W Photos 7/Colour Photos 8/Reviews

Requirements: 2
Feature articles relating to office equipment and services.
Comments: The readers are from a specific clearly-defined group. Establish their needs and write accordingly.
Approach: By letter with ideas.
Lead time: 10 weeks.
Payment: Negotiable.

Office Equipment News

Wilmington Publishing Ltd
Wilmington House
Church Hill
Wilmington
Dartford
Kent
DA2 7EF

Tel: (0322) 277788 **Fax:** (0322) 276474

Frequency: Monthly

Circulation: 50,000

Contact: Richard Davies, Editor
Profile: A magazine for those concerned with the purchase of equipment and products for use in the office.
Requirements: 1 2
News of new products and developments, plus features on the use of office equipment.
Comments: Contributions should not be too technical, and should not use jargon.
Approach: In writing.
Lead time: Six weeks.
Payment: By arrangement.

Office Secretary

Studio A132
The Riverside Business Centre
Bendon Valley
London
SW18 4LZ

Tel: 081-875 0343 **Fax:** 081-875 0344

Frequency: Quarterly

Circulation: 60,000

Contact: Jane Slade, Editor
Profile: Investigates issues affecting the senior secretary and executive PA. Also covers travel, health, food, technology, fashion and books.
Requirements: 1 2
Fresh views of an old problem, or something with a strong European/international flavour.
Comments: Pictures should be included where possible.
Approach: In writing with initial ideas.
Lead time: Six weeks.
Payment: £125 per thousand words.

OK!

PO Box 381
Mill Harbour
London
E14 9TW

Tel: 071-987 5090 **Fax:** 071-987 2160

Frequency: Monthly

Circulation: Not disclosed

Contact: Anne Wallace, Editor
Profile: A glossy monthly that concentrates on celebrities and personalities. Aimed mainly at women aged between 18 and 45.
Requirements: 2
Interviews and profiles based on personalities that are well known throughout the UK.

1/News **2**/Features **3**/Fiction **4**/Letters **5**/Fillers
6/B&W Photos **7**/Colour Photos **8**/Reviews

Comments: Unlike *Hello!*, this magazine focuses on British rather than international celebrities.
Approach: In writing with proposals.
Lead time: Two months.
Payment: By negotiation.

Old Glory

CMS Publishing
Knowle Lane
Cranleigh
Surrey
GU6 8JP

Tel: (0483) 274855   **Fax:** (0780) 65788

Frequency: Monthly

Circulation: 22,000

Contact: Brian Gooding, Editor
Profile: Britain's leading vintage machinery magazine. Covers traction engines, tractors, trams, canals and stationary engines.
Requirements: 1 2 5 6 7
Welcomes articles on the above, plus pieces on relevant museums, personal profiles, etc. Photos are required to accompany material.
Comments: Interested in both steam and internal combustion engines.
Approach: By letter or telephone.
Lead time: Two months.
Payment: £30 per page.

The Oldie

Oldie Publications Ltd
26 Charlotte Street
London
W1P 1HJ

Tel: 071-636 3686   **Fax:** 071-636 3685

Frequency: Fortnightly

Circulation: 35,000

Contact: Isabel Lloyd

Profile: Humorous, general-interest title for the more mature and articulate reader. Not for the fluffy slipper brigade.
Requirements: 1 2 5 8
The magazine is reasonably flexible in terms of requirements. Welcomes snippets for the diary section and personal experiences about 'How I once met...' Length around 600 words.
Comments: Definitely no poetry.
Approach: By telephone, letter or fax.
Lead time: Four weeks,
Payment: From £60.

On Board Surf

Andrew House
2a Granville Road
Sidcup
Kent
DA14 4BN

Tel: 081-302 6150   **Fax:** 081-300 2315

Frequency: Bi-monthly

Circulation: 20,000

Contact: Mark Griffiths, Editor
Profile: The official journal of the UK Boardsailing Association. Covers equipment, event reports and personalities.
Requirements: 2 6 7
Experiences of surfing locations and equipment reports, plus features on beach style. Length 1000 to 1500 words.
Comments: Read by both beginners and experts.
Approach: Submit complete manuscript.
Lead time: Four weeks.
Payment: Negotiable.

1/News **2**/Features **3**/Fiction **4**/Letters **5**/Fillers
6/B&W Photos **7**/Colour Photos **8**/Reviews

On The Edge

PO Box 21
Buxton
Derbyshire
SK17 9BR

Tel: (0298) 72801   **Fax:** (0298) 72839

Frequency: Bi-monthly

Circulation: 7,000

Contact: Gill Kent, Editor

Profile: Covers rock climbing in the UK and overseas.

Requirements: 2
Articles on climbing techniques and training, plus mountaineering and alpinism and mountaineering internationally.

Comments: Contributors should have a good understanding of the subject.

Approach: In writing.

Lead time: Three months.

Payment: Negotiable.

Open Road

100 Bury New Road
Whitefield
Manchester
M25 6AG

Tel: 061-766 1590   **Fax:** 061-766 2497

Frequency: Bi-monthly

Circulation: 140,000

Contact: Hugh Ash, Editor

Profile: A tabloid-style publication distributed through Granada service stations, hotels and travel lodges.

Requirements: 2 6 7
Features on motoring, leisure and travel. Particularly welcomes celebrity interviews with a travel connection. Length up to 2000 words.

Comments: Will also consider proposals for series of articles.

Approach: By telephone.

Lead time: Two months.

Payment: Negotiable.

Opera

1a Mountgrove Road
London
N5 2LU

Tel: 071-359 1037   **Fax:** 071-354 2700

Frequency: Monthly

Circulation: 11,500

Contact: Roger Milnes, Editor

Profile: A magazine for opera enthusiasts. Reviews current events and activities in the world of opera.

Requirements: 2 5
Informed articles about any subject relating to the performance and recording of operas, or features on relevant personalities.

Comments: Contributors are expected to have a good understanding of the subject.

Approach: In writing, with a brief CV and examples of published work.

Lead time: Two months.

Payment: By negotiation.

Opera Now

241 Shaftesbury Avenue
London
WC2H 8EH

Tel: 071-528 8784   **Fax:** 071-528 7991

Frequency: Monthly

Circulation: 15,000

Contact: Graeme Kay, Editor

Profile: News and reviews of events and releases relating to all aspects of opera.

1/News 2/Features 3/Fiction 4/Letters 5/Fillers
6/B&W Photos 7/Colour Photos 8/Reviews

Requirements: 1 2 6 7 8
Reviews of performances, CDs and videos connected with opera music. Length 300 to 500 words.
Comments: The magazine has changed substantially, and writers should be aware of the current format and style.
Approach: By letter.
Lead time: Two months.
Payment: Negotiable.

Options

IPC Magazines
King's Reach Tower
Stamford Street
London
SE1 9LS

Tel: 071-261 5000   **Fax:** 071-261 7344

Frequency: Monthly

Circulation: 150,000

Contact: Maureen Rice, Editor
Profile: A glossy monthly aimed at career women aged between 25 and 35.
Requirements: 2
Good-quality general features and exclusive celebrity profiles, plus exceptional and relevant human-interest stories. Length 1000 to 3000 words.
Comments: New writers with potential are encouraged.
Approach: In writing, with ideas or complete manuscript.
Lead time: Three months.
Payment: Around £250 per thousand words.

Orbis

199 The Long Shoot
Nuneaton
Warwickshire
CV11 6JQ

Tel: (0203) 327440   **Fax:** (0203) 385551

Frequency: Quarterly

Circulation: 1000

Contact: Mike Shields, Editor
Profile: A literary publication that encourages creativity from writers.
Requirements: 2 3 8
Prose contributions of up to 1000 words in length, plus book reviews and poetry.
Comments: Also runs competitions for contributors.
Approach: Submit manuscripts to the above address.
Lead time: Four months.
Payment: Negotiable.

Organic Gardening

PO Box 4
Wiveliscombe
Taunton
Somerset
TA4 2QY

Tel: (0984) 23998   **Fax:** (0984) 23998

Frequency: Monthly

Circulation: 30,000

Contact: Basil Caplan, Editor
Profile: A guide to organic gardening methods for the amateur gardener. Includes techniques, equipment, cultivational methods and wildlife.
Requirements: 2 5 6 7
Problem-solving or 'how-to' articles about organic practices. Length 600 to 1800 words. Photographs or illustrations are useful.

1/News 2/Features 3/Fiction 4/Letters 5/Fillers
6/B&W Photos 7/Colour Photos 8/Reviews

Comments: It is important that the cultivation techniques are based on organic methods.
Approach: By telephone or letter.
Lead time: Two months.
Payment: From £35 per thousand words.

Our Dogs

5 Oxford Road
Station Approach
Manchester
M60 1SX

Tel: 061-236 2660   **Fax:** 061-236 5534

Frequency: Weekly

Circulation: 23,000

Contact: The Editor
Profile: For owners of pedigree dogs of every breed.
Requirements: 1 2 6
News items and feature articles on breeding and exhibiting pedigree dogs. Also show reports and related information.
Comments: Photographs to accompany features are always welcome.
Approach: In writing with ideas.
Lead time: Three weeks.
Payment: NUJ rates.

Outdoor Action

Hawker Consumer Publications
13 Park House
140 Battersea Park Road
London
SW11 4NB

Tel: 071-720 2108   **Fax:** 071-498 3023

Frequency: Monthly

Circulation: 27,000

Contact: Laura McAffrey, Editor

Profile: Everything of interest to the walker, including gear, travel and routes. Also covers other outdoor pursuits from the non-specialist perspective.
Requirements: 1 2 7
Flavour-of-the-area walking articles, rather than blow-by-blow route descriptions. Also introductory pieces on other outdoor pursuits. Length 1000 to 1200 words.
Comments: Aim at the keen walker aged between 14 and 45, and avoid being too earnest or worthy. Copy on Macintosh disk preferred.
Approach: By letter with ideas or complete manuscript.
Lead time: Six weeks.
Payment: By arrangement.

Outdoors Illustrated

PO Box 845
Bath
Avon
BA1 3TW

Tel: (0225) 443194   **Fax:** (0225) 443195

Frequency: Monthly

Circulation: 30,000

Contact: Kate Russell-Cobb, Editor
Profile: A general-interest magazine for those involved in active outdoor pursuits.
Requirements: 1 2 7
News and features about activities such as mountaineering, canoeing, hiking and riding. Also relevant features on health, photography and the environment. Length 1000 to 1500 words.
Comments: The style should be practical and inspirational, rather than folksy.

1/News 2/Features 3/Fiction 4/Letters 5/Fillers
6/B&W Photos 7/Colour Photos 8/Reviews

Approach: Bv letter or fax, with
  examples of previously published
  work.
Lead time: Three months.
Payment: £85-£90 per thousand
  words.

P

Pacemaker & Thoroughbred Breeder

38-42 Hampton Road
Teddington
Middlesex
TW11 0JE

Tel: 081-943 5702   **Fax:** 081-943 5632

Frequency: Monthly

Circulation: 6000

Contact: John Boyce, Editor

Profile: A specialist trade publication for those involved in the bloodstock and breeding side of racing.

Requirements: 1 2 6
News and features relating to horse nutrition, veterinary matters and racing people. Length 1000 to 1200 words.

Comments: The magazine is not concerned with betting.

Approach: By letter with ideas.

Lead time: Two weeks.

Payment: £110 per thousand words.

Panorama

MMP Business Publications
Alexander House
Forehill
Ely
Cambridgeshire
CB7 4AF

Tel: (0353) 665577   **Fax:** (0353) 662489

Frequency: Monthly

Circulation: 9000

Contact: Eileen Martin, Editor

Profile: For professionals in the photographic trade, but aimed primarily at manufacturers and suppliers rather than photographers.

Requirements: 1 2
News and features on technical subjects, products, professional associations and industry issues.

Comments: Writers should have a good understanding of the subject.

Approach: In writing.

Lead time: Six weeks.

Payment: Negotiable.

Parents

Victory House
14 Leicester Square
London
WC2H 7BP

Tel: 071-437 9011   **Fax:** 071-434 0656

Frequency: Monthly

Circulation: 75,000

Contact: Erika Harvey

Profile: Deals with child care from birth through to the age of five.

Requirements: 1 2 6 7 8
Frank, informative articles on caring for young children, aimed primarily at mothers. Length 1000 to 1200 words.

1/News **2**/Features **3**/Fiction **4**/Letters **5**/Fillers
6/B&W Photos **7**/Colour Photos **8**/Reviews

Comments: Also publishes a supplement called 'Your Pregnancy' covering ante-natal care.
Approach: By letter.
Lead time: Two months.
Payment: Around £100 per thousand words.

Parks, Golf Courses and Sports Grounds

61 London Road
Staines
Middlesex
TW18 4BN

Tel: (0784) 461326   **Fax:** (0784) 462073
Frequency: Monthly
Circulation: 6000
Contact: Alan Guthrie, Editor
Profile: For professionals concerned with the construction and care of leisure amenities.
Requirements: 2 6
Features concerning parks, open spaces, golf courses, sports grounds and other amenities. Length 750 to 2000 words.
Comments: Welcomes contributions concerning management, design, construction and maintenance.
Approach: In writing.
Lead time: Six weeks.
Payment: £70 per thousand words.

Past and Present

Unit 5
Home Farm Close
Church Street
Wadenhoe
Peterborough
PE8 5TE

Tel: (0801) 5440   **Fax:** (0801) 5440

Frequency: Quarterly
Circulation: Not available
Contact: The Editor
Profile: A magazine which offers a nostalgic look at five decades of change.
Requirements: 2 6 7
Articles examining the way the world has changed over the last fifty years. In particular, features comparing the past of a certain location to its present, illustrated by historical and current photographs.
Comments: Writers should aim for a nostalgic and reflective style.
Approach: In writing.
Lead time: Four months.
Payment: Negotiable.

PC Answers

Future Publishing
30 Monmouth Street
Bath
BA1 2BW

Tel: (0225) 442244   **Fax:** (0225) 447465
Frequency: Monthly
Circulation: 35,128
Contact: Ian Sharpe, Editor
Profile: A friendly, accessible title aimed at everyone using a PC in a working environment.
Requirements: Articles that will help ordinary users to get more from their PCs. These are commissioned according to an agreed brief.
Comments: Send outline proposals together with a CV and examples of previous work.
Approach: By letter or fax.
Lead time: Two months.
Payment: £115 per published page.

PC Direct

Ziff-Davis UK Ltd
Cottons Centre
Hay's Lane
London
SE1 2QT

Tel: 071-378 6800   **Fax:** 071-378 1198

Frequency: 12xYear

Circulation: 90,000

Contact: Tony Westbrook,
  Editor-in-Chief
Profile: The complete guide to buying
  PCs and PC products by mail order.
  Everything in the magazine supports
  the selection and purchase of these
  products.
Requirements: 2 7 8
  Reviews of hardware, software and
  peripheral products. Technical and
  consumer features, plus 'hands-on'
  features about using hardware and
  software.
Comments: Contributions must be
  aimed at business buyers of PCs and
  PC products.
Approach: By telephone.
Lead time: Six weeks.
Payment: £100-£200 per thousand
  words.

PC Format

Future Publishing
30 Monmouth Street
Bath
BA1 2BW

Tel: (0225) 442244   **Fax:** (0225) 446019

Frequency: Monthly

Circulation: 65,000

Contact: Mark Higham, Editor
Profile: A guide to PC leisure activities
  aimed at the home PC owner.
  Includes news, reviews and features
of low-cost creativity and
entertainment products.
Requirements: 2 8
  Beginners' features, 'how-to' articles
  and hardware round ups. It is
  imperative that copy is entertaining
  and lively. Length 800 words and up.
Comments: Contributors must be
  capable writers.
Approach: By letter with ideas.
Lead time: Six weeks.
Payment: From £70 per thousand
  words.

PC Magazine

Ziff-Davis UK Ltd
Cottons Centre
Hay's Lane
London
SE1 2QT

Tel: 071-378 6800   **Fax:** 071-378 6702

Frequency: Monthly

Circulation: 90,078

Contact: Steve Malone, Editor
Profile: A PC buyer's guide that is
  mainly concerned with comparative
  product reviews.
Requirements: 1 2 8
  News, features and reviews of
  interest to those using or buying
  PCs. Length usually between 400
  and 2000 words.
Comments: All work is commissioned,
  so writers must contact the editor to
  discuss projects.
Approach: By letter with examples of
  previous work.
Lead time: Three months.
Payment: From £120 per thousand
  words.

1/News **2**/Features **3**/Fiction **4**/Letters **5**/Fillers
6/B&W Photos **7**/Colour Photos **8**/Reviews

PC User

EMAP Publications
33-39 Bowling Green Lane
London
EC1R 0DA

Tel: 071-837 1212   **Fax:** 071-278 4003

Frequency: Fortnightly

Circulation: 43,000

Contact: Dave Allen, Editor

Profile: For IT managers in corporate organisations who make buying decisions relating to PC products. Concentrates on reviews.

Requirements: 1 6 7 8
News and reviews of new hardware and software products, etc. All material must be considered from the user perspective.

Comments: No features or case studies.

Approach: By letter with examples of previous work.

Lead time: Two weeks.

Payment: £130 per thousand words.

PC Week

VNU Business Publishing
32-34 Broadwick Street
London
W1A 2NG

Tel: 071-439 4242   **Fax:** 071-734 3789

Frequency: Weekly

Circulation: 50,000

Contact: Julian Patterson, Editor

Profile: Corporate computing from a desktop perspective. The emphasis is on news throughout the magazine.

Requirements: Business aspects of IT and its implementation, plus good independent case studies. Also reviews that are not too detailed technically. Length up to 1800 words.

Comments: News analysis and comment pieces are produced in house. Copy on disk preferred.

Approach: By telephone with ideas.

Lead time: Ten days.

Payment: Negotiable.

PCW Plus

Future Publishing
30 Monmouth Street
Bath
BA1 2BW

Tel: (0225) 442244   **Fax:** (0225) 447465

Frequency: Monthly

Circulation: 24,700

Contact: Martin Le Poidevin

Profile: Offers advice and information to owners of Amstrad PCW computers.

Requirements: 1 2 8
Articles giving useful hints and tips, plus occasional witty pieces and reviews. Also general features giving personal views on relevant subjects. Length 1000 to 2000 words.

Comments: The style needs to be fairly simplistic for a non-technical readership.

Approach: By letter with ideas.

Lead time: Three weeks.

Payment: £140 per thousand words.

Pembrokeshire Life

Old Hakin Road
Merlins Bridge
Haverfordwest
SA61 1XF

Tel: (0437) 763133   **Fax:** (0437) 760482

Frequency: Monthly

Circulation: 30,000

Contact: The Editor

1/News **2**/Features **3**/Fiction **4**/Letters **5**/Fillers
6/B&W Photos **7**/Colour Photos **8**/Reviews

Profile: A light look at country life in West Wales, concentrating on pictorial content.

Requirements: 2 6 7
Articles on subjects that characterise the county. These may be humorous, historical, or concerned with unusual people and pastimes.

Comments: More likely to accept unusual and quirky items.

Approach: By letter with ideas or complete manuscript.

Lead time: Four weeks.

Payment: Negotiable.

Pennine Magazine

Stable Courtyard
Broughton Hall
Skipton
N. Yorks
BD23 3AE

Tel: (0756) 701381   **Fax:** (0756) 701326

Frequency: Monthly

Circulation: 57,034

Contact: David Joy, Editor

Profile: Regional magazine covering matters of interest to everyone in the Pennines region.

Requirements: 2 7 8
Articles on subjects such as local events, regional humour, personalities and history. Length around 1000 words.

Comments: The emphasis is on people rather than places.

Approach: By letter with ideas.

Lead time: Eight weeks.

Payment: Negotiable.

Pensioner's Voice

14 St Peter Street
Blackburn
Lancashire
BB2 2HD

Tel: (0254) 52606

Frequency: 10xYear

Circulation: 7000

Contact: Robert Stansfield, Editor

Profile: Political comment on state pensions, benefits and community care. Of interest to those pensioners without private incomes.

Requirements: 2 5
Articles of up to 1000 words on almost any topic of general interest to state pensioners.

Comments: Although political, the editorial is independent in terms of party.

Approach: By telephone with ideas.

Lead time: Four weeks.

Payment: Up to £50 per thousand words.

Penthouse

Northern & Shell Building
PO Box 381
Millharbour
London
E14 9TW

Tel: 071-987 5090   **Fax:** 071-987 2160

Frequency: Monthly

Circulation: 100,000

Contact: Jonathon Richards, Editor

Profile: Glossy, well-established magazine for men.

Requirements: 2
Feature articles on subjects of interest to male readers. Length up to 3500 words.

1/News **2**/Features **3**/Fiction **4**/Letters **5**/Fillers
6/B&W Photos **7**/Colour Photos **8**/Reviews

Comments: Receives a lot of unsolicited manuscripts that are not suited to the style of the magazine.
Approach: In writing.
Lead time: Two months.
Payment: Negotiable but good.

People Magazine

33 Holborn Circus
London
EC1P 1DQ

Tel: 071-353 0256   **Fax:** 071-822 3829

Frequency: Weekly

Circulation: 2.24 million

Contact: Frank Walker, Associate Editor
Profile: Colour supplement to the *People* newspaper. A TV listings magazine featuring TV-based articles and interviews.
Requirements: 2 7
Feature articles on television celebrities and prominent personalities, or any other TV-related topic. Length up to 1000 words.
Comments: Interested in material that the editorial staff may not be able to cover.
Approach: By telephone or letter.
Lead time: Four weeks.
Payment: £400 per thousand words.

People & the Planet

IPPF
Regent's College
Inner Circle
Regent's Park
London
NW1 4NS

Tel: 071-486 0741   **Fax:** 071-487 7950

Frequency: Quarterly
Circulation: 15,000
Contact: Jeremy Hamand, Assistant Editor
Profile: Development magazine concerned with population and the environment.
Requirements: 1 2 6 7 8
News and features on moves to balance worldwide resources and the global population. Length 500 to 1200 words.
Comments: First-hand reports from third-world countries are always welcome.
Approach: By telephone with ideas.
Lead time: Two months.
Payment: From £70 per thousand words.

The People's Friend

D.C. Thomson & Co Ltd
80 Kingsway East
Dundee
DD4 8SL

Tel: (0382) 462276   **Fax:** (0382) 452491

Frequency: Weekly

Circulation: 500,000

Contact: Sinclair Matheson, Editor
Profile: A fiction-based magazine that aims to provide a good read for all the family. Runs romantic, emotional family short stories and serials, plus general-interest features.
Requirements: 2 3 4 5 7
Short stories and serials about people that readers can identify with. Length up to 4000 words. Also articles on knitting, cookery and crafts, etc.

1/News 2/Features 3/Fiction 4/Letters 5/Fillers
6/B&W Photos 7/Colour Photos 8/Reviews

Comments: This is a traditional magazine, and fiction should be about everyday folk, their problems and family affairs.
Approach: In writing, with ideas for serials or complete manuscripts of short stories.
Lead time: Ten weeks.
Payment: £40-£50 for short stories.

Perfect Home

Times House
Station Approach
Ruislip
Middlesex
HA4 8MS

Tel: (0895) 677677   **Fax:** (0895) 676027
Frequency: Monthly
Circulation: 106,269
Contact: Sarah Gale, Editor
Profile: An inspiring magazine full of ideas for anyone hoping to improve their home. Presents the cosmetic side of home improvement in a bright and affordable fashion.
Requirements: 2
In-depth features on subjects such as converting a loft, tackling home insurance or re-building a room. Maximum length 800 words.
Comments: Targeted at female readers aged between 25 and 45, typically with young children and a part-time job.
Approach: By telephone, letter or fax.
Lead time: Two months.
Payment: £200 per thousand words.

Performance Bikes

Bushfield House
Orton Centre
Peterborough
PE2 5UW

Tel: (0733) 237111   **Fax:** (0733) 231137
Frequency: Monthly
Circulation: 80,061
Contact: Rupert Paul, Editor
Profile: Covers all aspects of performance-oriented motor cycling.
Requirements: 1 2 7
Features on topics ranging from production-bike racing to bikes altered by their owners.
Comments: No touring features or fiction.
Approach: By letter or fax.
Lead time: Four weeks.
Payment: £100 per thousand words.

Performance Car

Bushfield House
Orton Centre
Peterborough
PE2 5UW

Tel: (0733) 237111   **Fax:** (0733) 231137
Frequency: Monthly
Circulation: 66,227
Contact: Paul Clarke, Editor
Profile: A glossy monthly that focuses on all performance-oriented production vehicles.
Requirements: 1 2 7 8
News, features and reviews about high-performance vehicles both in the UK and internationally. Particularly looking for material from overseas. Length up to 2500 words.

1/News **2**/Features **3**/Fiction **4**/Letters **5**/Fillers
6/B&W Photos **7**/Colour Photos **8**/Reviews

Comments: This is a high-quality, well-produced magazine and editorial material must reflect this.
Approach: By telephone.
Lead time: Two months.
Payment: Better than NUJ rates.

Performance Cyclist International

Northern & Shell Building
PO Box 381
Millharbour
London
E14 9TW

Tel: 071-987 5090   **Fax:** 071-987 2160

Frequency: Monthly

Circulation: 40,000 (target)

Contact: Ben Orme, Editor
Profile: For serious cyclists interested in racing and performance products.
Requirements: 1 2 5 7 8
Race coverage, articles on training and products, plus interviews with well-known cyclists.
Comments: Writers will need a good understanding of specialist cycling.
Approach: By telephone with ideas.
Lead time: Two months.
Payment: £85 per thousand words.

Period House

Times House
Station Approach
Ruislip
Middlesex
HA4 8NB
Tel: (0895) 677677   **Fax:** (0895) 676027

Frequency: Monthly

Circulation: 80,000

Contact: Richard Porter, Editor

Profile: About the care and conservation of old buildings. Aimed at a consumer audience.
Requirements: 1 2 7 8
Features on architecture, furniture, bathrooms and kitchens. Length 2000 to 3000 words.
Comments: Colour pictures are always welcome.
Approach: By letter.
Lead time: Two weeks.
Payment: NUJ rates.

Period Living & Traditional Homes

Victory House
14 Leicester Square
London
WC2H 7BP

Tel: 071-437 9011   **Fax:** 071-434 0656

Frequency: Monthly

Circulation: 48,000

Contact: Isobel McKenzie-Price, Editor
Profile: Devoted to the more traditional aspects of home interest and decoration.
Requirements: 2 5
Feature articles on homes, gardens, interior design and collectable items. All material must reflect the values of period living.
Comments: Copy must be about real people's homes, not mansions.
Approach: In writing.
Lead time: Two months.
Payment: £400-£600.

Personal Computer World

VNU Business Publishing
32-34 Broadwick Street
London
W1A 2NG

Tel: 071-439 4242   **Fax:** 071-895 8098

Frequency: Monthly

Circulation: 112,306

Contact: Ben Tisdall, Editor

Profile: A complete guide to all kinds of personal computers aimed at end users.

Requirements: 2 5 8
Proposals for features and reviews of new and popular personal computers. Length 850 to 4000 words.

Comments: Particularly short of good writers on PC networking.

Approach: By telephone with ideas.

Lead time: Two weeks.

Payment: From £130 per thousand words.

Personal Water Craft News

Garden Hall House
Wellesley Road
Sutton
Surrey
SM2 5US

Tel: 081-582 7998   **Fax:** 081-661 1173

Frequency: Bi-monthly

Circulation: 2200

Contact: Neil Asten, Editor

Profile: Covers power-ski watersport. Aimed at both trade and consumer audiences.

Requirements: 1 2
Profiles of personalities connected with the sport, interviews, racing reports and news of products and developments.

Comments: Writers should have a good understanding of the subject.

Approach: In writing.

Lead time: Three months.

Payment: £75 per thousand words.

Personnel Management

17 Britton Street
London
EC1M 5NQ

Tel: 071-336 7646   **Fax:** 071-336 7637

Frequency: Monthly

Circulation: 55,866

Contact: Susanne Lawrence, Editor

Profile: Specialist professional publication for personnel managers.

Requirements: 1 2
Features on industrial relations, training, pay, employment legislation, etc. Length up to 2500 words. Also news of personnel events that would not be covered by editorial staff.

Comments: Contributors need a good knowledge of relevant subjects to write successfully for this publication.

Approach: In writing.

Lead time: Two months.

Payment: NUJ rates.

Pet Dogs

Shires Mace Ltd
PO Box B163
Huddersfield
HD4 7YZ

Tel: (0484) 460372   **Fax:** (0484) 460373

Frequency: Bi-monthly

Circulation: 38,000

Contact: Paula Shires, Editor

Profile: A magazine for anyone who really cares about dogs.

Requirements: 2 5
  Topical features concerning dogs as the family pet, perhaps linked to a certain event or time of the year. Length between 750 and 1500 words.

Comments: Remember that this is a magazine for dog lovers, and articles should reflect a positive, caring attitude.

Approach: In writing.

Lead time: Six months.

Payment: Negotiable.

Photo Answers

Apex House
Oundle Road
Peterborough
PE2 9NP

Tel: (0733) 898100   **Fax:** (0733) 894472

Frequency: Monthly

Circulation: 64,104

Contact: Steve Moore

Profile: Answers the questions raised by the typical amateur photographer.

Requirements: 2 6 7
  Advice on improving photographic techniques, or on solving particular problems. High-quality photos to accompany features are always welcome.

Comments: Short, sharp items have the best chance of success.

Approach: In writing.

Lead time: Two months.

Payment: From £25 per page.

Photo Pro

Icon Publications
Maxwell Place
Maxwell Lane
Kelso
Scottish Borders
TD5 7BB

Tel: (0573) 226032   **Fax:** (0573) 22600

Frequency: Bi-monthly

Circulation: 10,000

Contact: David Kilpatrick, Editor

Profile: Information, instruction and inspiration for the practising photographer and creative enthusiast.

Requirements: 2 6 7
  Original technical and aspirational features and portfolios. Length 800 to 2400 words.

Comments: Each issue has a specific theme, so writers should contact the editor for information.

Approach: By telephone, letter or fax.

Lead time: Two months.

Payment: £50 per page.

PIC

Lingley House
Commissioners Road
Strood
Rochester
Kent
ME2 4EU

Tel: (0634) 291115   **Fax:** (0634) 724761

Frequency: Monthly

Circulation: 25,000

Contact: Maureen More, Editor

Profile: People in Camera — a magazine for all those interested in photography.

1/News **2**/Features **3**/Fiction **4**/Letters **5**/Fillers
6/B&W Photos **7**/Colour Photos **8**/Reviews

Requirements: 1 2 6 7 8
News and features relating to all aspects of photography and photographic techniques.
Comments: The focus of the magazine is on people rather than places.
Approach: By letter.
Lead time: Four weeks.
Payment: £50 per page.

Picture Postcard Monthly

Reflections of a Bygone Age
15 Debdale Lane
Keyworth
Nottinghamshire
NG12 5HT

Tel: (0602) 374079

Frequency: Monthly

Circulation: 4000

Contact: Brian Lund, Editor
Profile: A specialist title for postcard collectors worldwide. Available from specialist shops and on subscription.
Requirements: 1 2
News and features relating to any aspect of postcard collecting. Length between 500 and 3000 words.
Comments: Articles must be well-researched and accurate in every detail.
Approach: In writing.
Lead time: Two months.
Payment: £33 per page.

Pilot

The Clock House
28 Old Town
Clapham
London
SW4 0LB

Tel: 071-498 2506   **Fax:** 071-498 6920

Frequency: Monthly
Circulation: 30,208

Contact: James Gilbert, Editor
Profile: A general aviation magazine, covering the world of private and business flying.
Requirements: 1 2 7
News and features on pleasure flying, air sport and other aviation subjects.
Comments: All material should be concise and succinct.
Approach: With ideas or complete manuscript.
Lead time: Two months.
Payment: £125-£700.

Pine News International

4 Red Barn Mews
High Street
Battle
East Sussex
TN33 0AG

Tel: (0424) 774982   **Fax:** (0424) 774321

Frequency: Monthly

Circulation: 6500

Contact: John Legg, Editor
Profile: Newspaper aimed at the pine furniture and softwoods market. Read worldwide by people in the industry.
Requirements: 1 2 4 5 6 7 8
Interested in articles relating to pine furniture and the softwood market, including antique pine. Also technical articles regarding finishing, etc. Length up to 1500 words.
Comments: Material must be accurate and sympathetic as well as technically interesting.

Approach: By letter or fax.
Lead time: Four weeks.
Payment: From £50 per thousand words.

Planet

PO Box 44
Aberystwyth
Dyfed
SY23 5BS

Tel: (0970) 611255 **Fax:** (0970) 623311

Frequency: Bi-monthly

Circulation: 1350

Contact: John Barnie, Editor
Profile: Concerned with topical affairs in Wales and ethnic minorities internationally.
Requirements: 2 3 6
  Articles on current issues affecting the Welsh community. Short stories and poems. Length up to 3500 words.
Comments: Also welcomes contributions concerning cultural minorities in countries throughout the world.
Approach: In writing.
Lead time: Three months.
Payment: £40 per thousand words.

Plays & Players

18 Friern Park
London
N12 9DA

Tel: 081-343 8515 **Fax:** 081-343 7831

Frequency: Monthly

Circulation: 15,000

Contact: Sandra Rennie, Editor
Profile: Provides comprehensive coverage of the theatre worldwide.

Requirements: 2 6 7 8
  Feature articles and reviews on all aspects of the theatre. Contributors should be well informed, with a good understanding of the subject.
Comments: Photographs to accompany features are appreciated.
Approach: In writing.
Lead time: Two months.
Payment: Negotiable.

Plus

Revenue Buildings
Chapel Road
Worthing
Sussex
BN11 1BQ

Tel: (0903) 214198 **Fax:** (0903) 217663

Frequency: Bi-monthly

Circulation: 7500

Contact: Virginia Symonds, Editor
Profile: Lively comic for under 12s read by children in Sunday schools and church youth groups. Contains bible facts, stories, features etc.
Requirements: 2 5 6
  Humorous fillers, stories about famous Christians, etc. Accompanied by pictures where possible. Nothing 'churchy' is required.
Comments: Test your piece on a child before sending it in.
Approach: By letter with initial idea or complete manuscript.
Lead time: Three months.
Payment: By arrangement.

1/News **2**/Features **3**/Fiction **4**/Letters **5**/Fillers
6/B&W Photos **7**/Colour Photos **8**/Reviews

PM Plus

17 Britton Street
London
EC1M 5NQ

Tel: 071-336 7646 **Fax:** 071-336 7635

Frequency: Monthly

Circulation: 55,866

Contact: Susanne Lawrence, Editor

Profile: A monthly magazine for everyone involved in personnel and human resources management.

Requirements: 1 2
News and features of interest to personnel staff. Also analysis of the background to the news.

Comments: Study the magazine before contributing material.

Approach: In writing.

Lead time: Two months.

Payment: Negotiable.

Pony

296 Ewell Road
Surbiton
Surrey
KT6 7AQ

Tel: 081-390 8547 **Fax:** 081-390 8696

Frequency: Monthly

Circulation: 38,000

Contact: Kate Austin, Editor

Profile: Bright and breezy title for girls aged between 10 and 16.

Requirements: 1 2
Features on riding, pony care, veterinary matters and stable management. Length between 800 and 1200 words. Also fiction of up to 1200 words related to ponies.

Comments: Study the magazine before attempting contributions.

Approach: By letter.

Lead time: Six weeks.

Payment: £60 per thousand words.

Popular Classics

Bushfield House
Orton Centre
Peterborough
PE2 0UW

Tel: (0733) 237111 **Fax:** (0733) 239527

Frequency: Monthly

Circulation: 56,021

Contact: Mark Dixon, Editor

Profile: About buying, driving and restoring affordable classic cars. Covers cars from the 70s and 80s in addition to earlier cars.

Requirements: 1 2
Information on where to find parts and accessories, plus historical and nostalgic pieces. Also profiles of people connected with classic cars. Copy should be matter-of-fact in style and easy to read.

Comments: Aim at a reader aged between 35 and 45 who owns one or more classic cars.

Approach: In writing.

Lead time: Two months.

Payment: Negotiable.

Popular Crafts

Argus Specialist Publications
Argus House
Boundary Way
Hemel Hempstead
Hertfordshire
HP2 7ST

Tel: (0442) 66551 **Fax:** (0442) 66998

Frequency: Monthly

Circulation: 30,122

Contact: Brenda Ross, Editor
Profile: A practical magazine that covers all kinds of crafts. Includes patterns and ideas for various craft projects.
Requirements: 1 2
Instructional features suggesting interesting projects, interviews with craftsmen, personal anecdotes and news items.
Comments: Material should be bright and easy to read.
Approach: By letter with ideas.
Lead time: Two months.
Payment: Negotiable.

Popular Flying

76 Kempe Road
Enfield
Middlesex
EN1 4QS

Tel: (0992) 523879   **Fax:** (0992) 523879
Frequency: Bi-monthly

Circulation: 8000

Contact: Roger Jones, Editor
Profile: For everyone interested in planes and private flying.
Requirements: 2
Articles on re-building and restoring classic or vintage aircraft. Also material on precision flying, aerobatics and touring.
Comments: Articles must be informed and well-researched.
Approach: In writing.
Lead time: Three months.
Payment: Negotiable.

The Post

UCW House
Crescent Lane
Clapham
London
SW4 9RN

Tel: 071-622 9977   **Fax:** 071-720 6853
Frequency: Monthly

Circulation: Not available

Contact: Stan Watts, Editor
Profile: Distributed free to members of the Union of Communication Workers.
Requirements: 2 6
Features relating to communications by post, telephone and telegraph. Also contributions on general trade union matters. Maximum 1000 words.
Comments: Contributors should remember that the publication has an international readership.
Approach: In writing.
Lead time: Two months.
Payment: Negotiable.

Pot Black

Fairwinds
First Avenue
Hook End
Brentwood
Essex
CM15 0HL

Tel: (0277) 823263   **Fax:** (0277) 823266
Frequency: Monthly

Circulation: 30,000

Contact: Terry Smith
Profile: Provides comprehensive coverage of all cue sports.

1/News **2**/Features **3**/Fiction **4**/Letters **5**/Fillers
6/B&W Photos **7**/Colour Photos **8**/Reviews

Requirements: 1 2
  News and features on every aspect of snooker, billiards and pool.
Comments: Material with an original angle has the best chance of success.
Approach: In writing.
Lead time: Two months.
Payment: Negotiable.

PR Week

22 Lancaster Gate
London
W2 3LP

Tel: 071-413 4520   **Fax:** 071-413 4509

Frequency: Weekly

Circulation: 16,000

Contact: Amanda Hall, Features Editor
Profile: A weekly news magazine for the public relations industry.
Requirements: 1 2 6
  Freelance contributions on any aspect of public relations or corporate communications. Must appeal to a well-informed readership. Length 200 to 2000 words.
Comments: Remember that many of the readers are themselves professional writers.
Approach: By telephone.
Lead time: Four weeks.
Payment: £150 per thousand words.

Practical Boat Owner

c/o IPC Magazines
Westover House
West Quay Road
Poole
Dorset
BH15 1JG

Tel: (0202) 680593   **Fax:** (0202) 674335

Frequency: Monthly
Circulation: 70,098
Contact: George Taylor, Editor
Profile: A down-to-earth guide for both the novice and experienced boat owner.
Requirements: 2 7
  Articles on practical projects and restoration. Also features on pleasure sailing and coastal cruising.
Comments: The magazine also publishes supplements on cruising and trailer boating.
Approach: In writing.
Lead time: Six weeks.
Payment: Negotiable.

Practical Caravan

38-42 Hampton Road
Teddington
Middlesex
TW11 0JE

Tel: 081-943 5021   **Fax:** 081-943 5098

Frequency: Monthly

Circulation: 52,566

Contact: Jacki Buist, Editor
Profile: One of the leading titles in the caravan sector, catering for both the novice and the experienced caravanner. Aims to cover lifestyle as well as providing information.
Requirements: 2 5
  Detailed informative features on places to go, sites to use and things to see. The emphasis must be on the practical facts that caravanners need to know.
Comments: Much of the material received is too basic in content.
Approach: By letter.
Lead time: Two months.
Payment: From £70 per thousand words.

Practical Classics

Bushfield House
Orton Centre
Peterborough
PE2 5UW

Tel: (0733) 237111 **Fax:** (0733) 371273

Frequency: Monthly

Circulation: 82,004

Contact: Peter Simpson, Editor

Profile: A practical magazine aimed at owners of cars from the period 1930 to 1980. Covers owning, running, repairing and restoring classic cars.

Requirements: 1 2 5 7 8
Informed coverage of repair and restoration of older cars. Also topical news and stories of DIY restorations. Length no more than 3000 words.

Comments: No fiction. Contributors should understand the subject and must contact the editor first.

Approach: By telephone.

Lead time: Eight weeks.

Payment: Negotiable.

Practical Fishkeeping

EMAP Pursuit Publishing Ltd
Bretton Court
Bretton Centre
Peterborough
PE3 8DZ

Tel: (0733) 264666 **Fax:** (0733) 265515

Frequency: Monthly

Circulation: 41,000

Contact: Steve Windsor, Editor

Profile: Aimed at both the beginner and the experience fishkeeper, covering cold water, marine and tropical fish.

Requirements: 1 2 7 8
Information and ideas on breeding, fish species, projects, etc. Length 1000 to 1500 words.

Comments: Prefers copy on disk, or clear, black print for scanning.

Approach: By telephone.

Lead time: Two months.

Payment: Negotiable.

Practical Gardening

Apex House
Oundle Road
Peterborough
PE2 9NP

Tel: (0733) 898100 **Fax:** (0733) 898433

Frequency: Monthly

Circulation: 111,181

Contact: Gill Crawley, Deputy Editor

Profile: A monthly with high production values, majoring on people, plants and places. Offers fresh ideas for creative gardeners.

Requirements: 1 2
Welcomes features from people who have created a lifestyle from their love of gardening. Length up to 1000 words.

Comments: Look for a practical element which can be used as a panel at the end of the article.

Approach: By fax or letter with ideas.

Lead time: Two months.

Payment: From £100 per thousand words.

Practical Householder

Greater London House
Hampstead Road
London
NW1 7QQ

Tel: 071-388 3171 **Fax:** 071-387 9518

1/News 2/Features 3/Fiction 4/Letters 5/Fillers
6/B&W Photos 7/Colour Photos 8/Reviews

Frequency: Monthly

Circulation: 39,000

Contact: Martyn Hocking, Editor

Profile: A DIY and home improvements magazine for the enthusiast.

Requirements: 1 2 7 8
Examples of successful projects connected with any aspect of improving your home. Advice, information and tips. Length up to 1200 words.

Comments: Particularly welcomes articles on projects which the writer has carried out.

Approach: In writing.

Lead time: Three months.

Payment: NUJ rates.

Practical Parenting

IPC Magazines
King's Reach Tower
Stamford Street
London
SE1 9LS

Tel: 071-261 5058   **Fax:** 071-261 5366

Frequency: Monthly

Circulation: 142,000

Contact: Features Editor

Profile: Concerned with pregnancy, birth, baby care and child care up to school age. Discusses education, health, activities for toddlers and personal parenting experiences.

Requirements: 2 5
Viewpoint articles, personal anecdotes and accounts of parenting experiences. Length up to 1000 words.

Comments: Interested in material from writers who are aware of the magazine's style.

Approach: Send complete manuscript.

Lead time: Five months.

Payment: £100-£125 per thousand words.

Practical PC

Alban House Publishing
Edinburgh House
82-90 London Road
St Albans
Hertfordshire

Tel: (0727) 844555   **Fax:** (0727) 844202

Frequency: Monthly

Circulation: 130,000

Contact: John Taylor, Editor

Profile: A magazine for the personal computer user. Aims to provide the best guides, the best deals and the best reviews.

Requirements: 1 2
News and features of products and developments in the PC market. Covers hardware, software and peripherals.

Comments: Encourages submissions from readers and freelance writers.

Approach: In writing.

Lead time: Two months.

Payment: Negotiable.

Practical Photography

Apex House
Oundle Road
Peterborough
PE2 9NP

Tel: (0733) 898100   **Fax:** (0733) 894472

Frequency: Monthly

Circulation: 110,041

Contact: William Cheung, Editor

Profile: A magazine for photographers ranging from beginners to the semi-pro.

1/News **2**/Features **3**/Fiction **4**/Letters **5**/Fillers
6/B&W Photos **7**/Colour Photos **8**/Reviews

Requirements: 1 2 6 7 8
Feature articles on methods and techniques, plus general features on photography. Length up to 2000 words.
Comments: Photos should be supplied where possible to accompany features.
Approach: By letter.
Lead time: Two months.
Payment: £150 per thousand words.

Practical Wireless

Arrowsmith Court
Station Approach
Broadstone
Dorset
BH18 8PW

Tel: (0202) 659910   **Fax:** (0202) 659950

Frequency: Monthly

Circulation: 28,000

Contact: Rob Mannon, Editor
Profile: Caters for the radio ham and the professional radio and electronics engineer.
Requirements: 1 2
Construction and technical features concerned with radio communications.
Comments: Guidelines for contributors are available on request. Prefers copy on disk.
Approach: By letter, telephone or fax.
Lead time: Three months.
Payment: Up to £70.

Practical Woodworking

IPC Magazines
King's Reach Tower
Stamford Street
London
SE1 9LS

Tel: 071-261 6689   **Fax:** 071-261 7555
Frequency: Monthly
Circulation: 42,000
Contact: Alan Mitchell, Editor
Profile: Directed at people who are enthusiastic workers in wood. Includes projects on furniture making, woodturning, woodcarving and toy making.
Requirements: 1 2 4 5 6 7
Projects, techniques and tips from knowledgeable writers. Text must be technically accurate, with colour transparencies and scale drawings included where possible.
Comments: All projects must demonstrate a high level of craftsmanship.
Approach: By telephone or fax with ideas.
Lead time: Three months.
Payment: £60 per page.

The Practitioner

Morgan-Grampian House
30 Calderwood Street
London
SE18 6QH

Tel: 081-855 7777   **Fax:** 081-855 2406

Frequency: Monthly

Circulation: 40,000

Contact: Howard Griffiths, Editor
Profile: A professional publication covering matters of interest to GPs and others in the medical profession.
Requirements: 1 2
News of current developments in general practice, articles on clinical subjects, case studies and conference reports.

Comments: Contributors must be able to write competently and authoritatively on medical subjects.
Approach: By letter with ideas.
Lead time: Six weeks.
Payment: Negotiable.

Prediction

Link House
Dingwall Avenue
Croydon
CR9 2TA

Tel: 081-686 2599   **Fax:** 081-760 0973

Frequency: Monthly

Circulation: 35,000

Contact: Jo Logan, Editor
Profile: Occult and astrology magazine for the general consumer. Publishes a wide range of new age articles.
Requirements: 2
Feature articles on alternative medicine, divination or other new age subjects. These should be practical rather than theoretical. Length 800, 1500 or 2000 words.
Comments: Contributors should write for the novice or intermediate level of reader.
Approach: In writing.
Lead time: Three months.
Payment: Up to £50.

Prima

Portland House
Stag Place
London
SW1E 5AU

Tel: 071-245 8700   **Fax:** 071-630 5509

Frequency: Monthly

Circulation: 682,191

Contact: Claire Steele, Editor

Profile: A women's consumer title with a strong crafts base.
Requirements: 2 4
Practical features about crafts and other creative activities for women. Also articles on legal and similar consumer issues.
Comments: Aimed at women who enjoy doing things. Unsolicited manuscripts are generally not welcome.
Approach: By letter.
Lead time: Three months.
Payment: £200 per thousand words.

Prime of Life

Burrator House
Sheepstor
Yelverton
Devon
PL20 6PF

Tel: (0822) 833060   **Fax:** (0822) 855365

Frequency: Monthly

Circulation: 55,000

Contact: Brian Doel, Editor
Profile: A magazine for those who wish to make the most of their middle-to-later years. Aimed at men and women aged over 50.
Requirements: 1 2
Features on finance, health, entertainment and holidays. Length from 300 words.
Comments: Always looking for new writers and new ideas.
Approach: By letter with examples of previous work.
Lead time: Four weeks.
Payment: In line with NUJ rates.

1/News 2/Features 3/Fiction 4/Letters 5/Fillers
6/B&W Photos 7/Colour Photos 8/Reviews

Printing World

Benn Publications Ltd
Benn House
Sovereign Way
Tonbridge
Kent
TN9 1RW

Tel: (0732) 364422   **Fax:** (0732) 361534

Frequency: Weekly

Circulation: 10,700

Contact: Gareth Ward, Editor

Profile: A trade publication for everyone concerned with the printing industry.

Requirements: 1 2 6 7
News and features on business and technical matters affecting print professionals, both in Britain and internationally.

Comments: Contributors should have a good understanding of printing matters.

Approach: In writing.

Lead time: Three weeks.

Payment: By negotiation.

Private Eye

6 Carlisle Street
London
W1V 5RG

Tel: 071-437 4017   **Fax:** 071-437 0705

Frequency: Fortnightly

Circulation: 200,000

Contact: Ian Hislop, Editor

Profile: A satirical magazine with a highly individual style.

Requirements: 1 2 5
Welcomes ideas for humorous news stories, features and filler items. Quirky or unusual items have the best chance of success.

Comments: Contributors must be familiar with the magazine's editorial style and format.

Approach: In writing.

Lead time: Three weeks.

Payment: By arrangement.

Professional Engineering

Northgate Avenue
Bury St Edmunds
Suffolk
IP32 6BW

Tel: (0284) 763277   **Fax:** (0284) 704006

Frequency: Monthly

Circulation: 60,000

Contact: Keld Fenwick, Editor

Profile: The official journal of the Institution of Mechanical Engineers. Read by engineering management throughout industry.

Requirements: 1 2
Feature articles alerting engineers to developments in their specialities and in adjacent fields.

Comments: Copy must be topical and relate to trends, tendencies and events.

Approach: By telephone or letter with ideas.

Lead time: Five months.

Payment: £185 per thousand words.

Professional Nurse

Brook House
2-16 Torrington Place
London
WC1E 7LT

Tel: 071-636 4622   **Fax:** 071-637 3021

Frequency: Monthly

Circulation: 45,000

Contact: Ann Shuttleworth, Editor

1/News **2**/Features **3**/Fiction **4**/Letters **5**/Fillers
6/B&W Photos **7**/Colour Photos **8**/Reviews

Profile: A practice-based magazine aimed at fulfilling the continuing education needs of qualified nurses. Keeps them up to date with developments in their profession.

Requirements: 2
Fully-referenced articles of a practical nature, giving nurses information they can use to develop their practice. Length 2000 to 2500 words.

Comments: Features should be well-researched and related to clinical practice.

Approach: Send complete manuscript.

Lead time: Two months.

Payment: £100 per article.

Psychic News

2 Tavistock Chambers
Bloomsbury Way
London
WC1A 2SE

Tel: 071-405 3345

Frequency: Weekly

Circulation: 13,000

Contact: Tim Haigh, Editor

Profile: A weekly newspaper for those interested in spiritualism.

Requirements: 2
Feature articles on subjects such as ghosts, hauntings, spiritualism, paranormal events and life after death.

Comments: Does not wish to receive unsolicited manuscripts.

Approach: In writing with ideas.

Lead time: Three weeks.

Payment: Negotiable.

Public Sector Building

91-93 High Street
Bromsgrove
Worcestershire
B61 8AQ

Tel: (0527) 36600   **Fax:** (0527) 35286

Frequency: 10xYear

Circulation: 11,000

Contact: Romany Quershi

Profile: Covers all aspects of construction in the public sector.

Requirements: 2 7
News and features of interest to those in concerned with public sector building.

Comments: Study the magazine before submitting manuscripts.

Approach: In writing.

Lead time: Two months.

Payment: Negotiable.

The Publisher

Magazine Publishing
Conbar House
Mead Lane
Hertford
SG13 7AS

Tel: (0992) 584233   **Fax:** (0992) 500717

Frequency: Monthly

Circulation: 7250

Contact: Cindy Simons, Editor

Profile: Aimed at those in magazine publishing management.

Requirements: 1 2 6 7
Information that would help a publisher manage a title more effectively. Covers topics such as production, promotion and selling. Length around 1500 words.

Comments: Concerned with the administrative rather than the creative aspects of publishing.

1/News **2**/Features **3**/Fiction **4**/Letters **5**/Fillers
6/B&W Photos **7**/Colour Photos **8**/Reviews

Approach: By telephone, letter or fax.
Lead time: Four weeks.
Payment: £100 per thousand words.

Publishing Magazine

3 Percy Street
London
W1P 9FA

Tel: 071-436 1673   **Fax:** 071-436 1675

Frequency: Monthly

Circulation: 9402

Contact: Adam Leyland, Editor
Profile: A senior management
  magazine for both magazine and
  newspaper publishers. Concerned
  with all aspects of the business.
Requirements: 1 6 7
  Articles on new technologies and
  techniques which help publishers do
  their jobs better. Length 1000 to
  1500 words.
Comments: No puffery. Writers
  should have a vibrant style and
  comprehension of publishing issues.
Approach: By letter with ideas.
Lead time: Four weeks.
Payment: £100 per thousand words.

Publishing News

43 Museum Street
London
WC1A 1LY

Tel: 071-404 0304   **Fax:** 071-242 0762

Frequency: Weekly

Circulation: 12,000

Contact: Fred Newman, Editor

Profile: Provides extensive coverage of
  current affairs and developments
  within the publishing business.
Requirements: 2 6
  News items and feature articles on
  all aspects of book production, the
  publishing industry and the book
  trade.
Comments: Material should be up to
  date and topical.
Approach: In writing.
Lead time: Two weeks.
Payment: Negotiable.

Pulse

30 Calderwood Street
Woolwich
London
SE18 6QH

Tel: 081-855 7777   **Fax:** 081-855 2406

Frequency: Weekly

Circulation: 43,000

Contact: Howard Griffiths, Editor
Profile: A weekly newspaper for
  general practitioners throughout the
  UK.
Requirements: 2 6 7
  Features and general articles on all
  matters of concern to doctors in
  general practice. Maximum length
  750 words.
Comments: Clinical material should
  only be submitted by those who are
  qualified to do so.
Approach: In writing.
Lead time: Two weeks.
Payment: Around £100.

1/News **2**/Features **3**/Fiction **4**/Letters **5**/Fillers
6/B&W Photos **7**/Colour Photos **8**/Reviews

Q

Q

Mappin House
4 Winsley Street
London
W1N 7AR

Tel: 071-436 1515   **Fax:** 071-323 0680

Frequency: Monthly

Circulation: 171,000

Contact: Features Editor

Profile: A high-class, high-quality mainstream rock monthly.

Requirements: Original stories about rock music that are not appearing anywhere else. Length up to 3000 words.

Comments: All submissions are given serious consideration.

Approach: By letter.

Lead time: Six weeks.

Payment: £180 per thousand words.

1/News 2/Features 3/Fiction 4/Letters 5/Fillers
6/B&W Photos 7/Colour Photos 8/Reviews

R

RA

Friends of the Royal Academy
Royal Academy of the Arts
Burlington House
Piccadilly
London
W1V 0DS

Tel: 071-494 5657   **Fax:** 071-287 9023

Frequency: Quarterly

Circulation: 85,000

Contact: The Editor

Profile: A prestigious magazine devoted exclusively to fine art.

Requirements: 2
Articles on art, exhibitions and the Royal Academy. All work is commissioned. Length up to 1500 words.

Comments: Writers should have a good understanding of the art world.

Approach: In writing with ideas.

Lead time: Three months.

Payment: £150.

Racing & Football Outlook

63-67 Tabernacle Street
London
EC2A 4AH

Tel: 071-490 1212   **Fax:** 071-608 3299

Frequency: Weekly

Circulation: 20,000

Contact: Sir Hugh Joseph, Editor

Profile: Covers the world of football pools and horse racing, together with greyhounds and other gambling sports.

Requirements: 2 5
Articles on all aspects of betting and related sports.

Comments: Study the magazine before submitting manuscripts.

Approach: In writing.

Lead time: Two weeks.

Payment: Negotiable.

The Racing Pigeon

Unit 13
21 Wren Street
London
WC1X 0HF

Tel: 071-833 5959   **Fax:** 071-833 3151

Frequency: Weekly

Circulation: 28,000

Contact: Rick Osman, Editor

Profile: News and features covering the world of pigeon racing.

Requirements: 1 2 3 5
Hints and tips on breeding and caring for pigeons, articles about racing and profiles of people who have won races.

Comments: Welcomes material from the wives of pigeon fanciers, etc. Also runs short story competitions.

1/News **2**/Features **3**/Fiction **4**/Letters **5**/Fillers
6/B&W Photos **7**/Colour Photos **8**/Reviews

Approach: Write with examples of previous work.
Lead time: One week.
Payment: Up to £60.

The Racing Pigeon Pictorial

Unit 13
21 Wren Street
London
WC1X 0HF

Tel: 071-833 5959   **Fax:** 071-833 3151

Frequency: Monthly

Circulation: 12,000

Contact: Rick Osman, Editor
Profile: A glossy monthly that reviews pigeon racing and its people.
Requirements: 1 2 6 7
Feature articles on achievements within the sport and similar subjects.
Comments: Writers should consider the visual dimension.
Approach: Write with examples of previous work.
Lead time: Six weeks.
Payment: Up to £60.

RAD

The Blue Barn
Tew Lane
Wootton
Woodstock
OX7 1HA

Tel: (0993) 811181   **Fax:** (0993) 811481

Frequency: Monthly

Circulation: 16,000

Contact: Mark Sturgeon, Editor
Profile: A magazine for boys aged between 12 and 16 interested in skateboarding and other teenage crazes.

Requirements: 1 2 6 7 8
News of what's happening in your local area, specialist features on techniques and articles on international developments. Length 500 to 700 words.
Comments: Concentrates on skateboarding in the UK.
Approach: Send complete manuscript.
Lead time: Three weeks.
Payment: £40 per thousand words.

Radio Control Model Cars

Argus Specialist Publications
Argus House
Boundary Way
Hemel Hempstead
Hertfordshire
HP2 7ST

Tel: (0442) 66551   **Fax:** (0442) 66998

Frequency: Monthly

Circulation: 14,674

Contact: Alan Harman, Editor
Profile: Provides comprehensive coverage of the hobby for enthusiasts.
Requirements: 1 2
News and features about new cars, competitive events, etc. Particularly looking for writers who can provide regional reports from their part of the country.
Comments: All material must be topical and up to date.
Approach: By letter with ideas.
Lead time: Two months.
Payment: Negotiable.

1/News **2**/Features **3**/Fiction **4**/Letters **5**/Fillers
6/B&W Photos **7**/Colour Photos **8**/Reviews

Radio Control Model World

Traplet House
Severn Drive
Upton-on-Severn
Worcestershire
WR8 0JL

Tel: (0684) 594505   **Fax:** (0694) 594586

Frequency: Monthly

Circulation: 25,000

Contact: Simon Rodway, Editor

Profile: For enthusiasts of radio-controlled model aircraft. Includes everything from construction to testing of models.

Requirements: 2 7
Looking for electronic and technical articles from competent writers. Also material of interest to newcomers to the hobby. Length up to 1500 words.

Comments: The readership is of a very wide ability and age range.

Approach: By letter.

Lead time: Six weeks.

Payment: £25 per page minimum.

Radio Controlled Models & Electronics

Argus Specialist Publications
Argus House
Boundary Way
Hemel Hempstead
Hertfordshire
HP2 7ST

Tel: (0442) 66551   **Fax:** (0442) 66998

Frequency: Monthly

Circulation: 33,000

Contact: Kevin Crozier, Editor

Profile: The UK's top-selling model aircraft magazine. Offers advice to beginners and experts alike.

Requirements: 1 2
Welcomes 'how-to' articles, especially those backed up with good step-by-step photographs. Also features on contributor's own designs. Maximum 2000 words.

Comments: Particularly interested in articles that show modelling techniques at all skill levels.

Approach: In writing with complete manuscript.

Lead time: Three months.

Payment: From £30 per page.

Radio Modeller

Argus Specialist Publications
Argus House
Boundary Way
Hemel Hempstead
Hertfordshire
HP2 7ST

Tel: (0442) 66551   **Fax:** (0442) 66998

Frequency: Monthly

Circulation: 18,782

Contact: Alec Gee, Editor

Profile: A specialist magazine appealing to flyers and builders of radio-controlled models. Covers models from gliders to helicopters.

Requirements: 2 5 6 7 8
Kit reviews, model designs, technical advice and practical tips. Length up to 2000 words.

Comments: A well-balanced piece includes photos and simple pencil sketches.

Approach: By telephone or letter.

Lead time: Six weeks.

Payment: £40 per page.

1/News **2**/Features **3**/Fiction **4**/Letters **5**/Fillers
6/B&W Photos **7**/Colour Photos **8**/Reviews

Radio Times

80 Wood Lane
London
W12 0TT

Tel: 081-576 2000   **Fax:** 081-576 3160

Frequency: Weekly

Circulation: 1.9 million

Contact: Nicholas Brett, Editor

Profile: Weekly TV listings guide,
covering broadcast TV and satellite
channels.

Requirements: 2
Interviews and features based on
personalities appearing in
forthcoming TV schedules.

Comments: Talented writers may
become part of the regular team of
commissioned freelances.

Approach: In writing.

Lead time: Three weeks.

Payment: Negotiable.

Rail

Apex House
Oundle Road
Peterborough
PE2 9NP

Tel: (0733) 898100   **Fax:** (0733) 894472

Frequency: Fortnightly

Circulation: 36,000

Contact: Murray Brown, Editor

Profile: A news magazine aimed at the
general rail enthusiast. Readers may
be aged anywhere between 10 and
60.

Requirements: 1 6 7
Newsworthy topical items, covering
developments, new infrastructure or
unusual train movements. Length
500 to 1000 words.

Comments: Items must be submitted
promptly as this is a topical, news-
based publication.

Approach: By telephone or fax.

Lead time: Two weeks.

Payment: £50 per thousand words.

Rail Bulletin

Fourways House
57 Hilton Street
Manchester
M1 2EJ

Tel: 061-237 1007   **Fax:** 061-237 1006

Frequency: Quarterly

Circulation: 5000

Contact: David Honour, Editor

Profile: A professional technical
magazine for all rail managers and
executives.

Requirements: 2
Technical features on all aspects of
railways and railway management.
Length 1500 to 2000 words.

Comments: This is not a train spotters
magazine.

Approach: By fax with synopsis.

Lead time: Three months.

Payment: £90 per thousand words.

Railway Gazette International

Quadrant House
The Quadrant
Sutton
Surrey
SM2 5AS

Tel: 081-652 3739   **Fax:** 081-652 3738

Frequency: Monthly

Circulation: 9363

Contact: Murray Hughes, Editor

1/News 2/Features 3/Fiction 4/Letters 5/Fillers
6/B&W Photos 7/Colour Photos 8/Reviews

Profile: An international publication concerned with the operation of railway networks worldwide.

Requirements: 2
Informed feature articles on railway management and finance. Also material on engineering topics. Length 1000 to 3000 words.

Comments: A number of supplements are also published throughout the year.

Approach: In writing.

Lead time: Two months.

Payment: Negotiable.

Railway Magazine

IPC Magazines
King's Reach Tower
Stamford Street
London
SE1 9LS

Tel: 071-261 5821   **Fax:** 071-261 5269

Frequency: Monthly

Circulation: 32,000

Contact: Peter Kelly, Editor

Profile: News of modern traction and steam preservation for railway enthusiasts.

Requirements: 2 6
Articles on memories of steam, features on steam and modern railways. Length up to 2000 words.

Comments: Has a UK rather than international circulation.

Approach: In writing.

Lead time: Six weeks.

Payment: Negotiable.

Railway Modeller

Underleys
Beer
Seaton
Devon
EX12 3NA

Tel: (0297) 20580   **Fax:** (0297) 20229

Frequency: Monthly

Circulation: 66,421

Contact: John Brewer, Editor

Profile: Concerned with all matters relating to British railway modelling.

Requirements: 2 6 7
Descriptions of model railways in various forms, from particular trains to complete set ups. Also information from clubs, etc. Length from 200 words.

Comments: Some prototype material is included, but the emphasis is on practical content.

Approach: By letter.

Lead time: Six weeks.

Payment: Negotiable.

Rally Sport

Central House
162 Southgate Street
Gloucester GL1 2EX

Tel: (0452) 307181   **Fax:** (0452) 307170

Frequency: Monthly

Circulation: 27,000

Contact: Simon Cooke, Editor

Profile: Covers the world of motor rallying for enthusiasts of the sport.

Requirements: 1 2 6 7
Rally reports, profiles of drivers, interviews with team managers and technical information. Length 1500 to 2000 words.

1/News **2**/Features **3**/Fiction **4**/Letters **5**/Fillers
6/B&W Photos **7**/Colour Photos **8**/Reviews

Comments: Most of the magazine's content is contributed by freelance writers.
Approach: By telephone.
Lead time: Four weeks.
Payment: £50 per thousand words.

Rambling Today

The Ramblers' Association
1/5 Wandsworth Road
London
SW8 2XX

Tel: 071-582 6878   **Fax:** 071-587 3799

Frequency: Quarterly

Circulation: 92,000

Contact: The Editor

Profile: House magazine for members of the Ramblers' Association. Contains articles on walking and the countryside.

Requirements: 2
Articles written to a very high standard about walks or walking, concentrating on rambling rather than environmental issues. Contributions should preferably be based in the UK. Length 900 to 1300 words.

Comments: Writers of successful articles about walking must, in every sense, take the reader with them.
Approach: By telephone.
Lead time: Four months.
Payment: Between £50 and £150.

Reader's Digest

Berkeley Square House
Berkeley Square
London
W1X 6AB

Tel: 071-629 8144   **Fax:** 071-408 0748

Frequency: Monthly

Circulation: 1.5 million

Contact: Russell Twisk, Editor-in-Chief

Profile: General-interest publication that combines light-hearted pieces with in-depth examinations of more weighty topics.

Requirements: 5
Short humorous contributions to regular features such as Life's Like That, Humour in Uniform, All in a Day's Work (laughter in the workplace).

Comments: A booklet on writing for Reader's Digest is available from the above address. Send an s.a.e. with a cheque for £2.50.
Approach: In writing.
Lead time: Three months.
Payment: £150 for up to 300 words.

Record Collector

43-45 St Mary's Road
Ealing
London
W5 5RQ

Tel: 081-579 1082   **Fax:** 081-566 2024

Frequency: Monthly

Circulation: 45,000

Contact: Mark Paytress, Features Editor

Profile: For record collectors and enthusiasts. Also acts as a digest of rock history from Sinatra onwards.

Requirements: 2 5
Features concentrating on the work and careers of particular artists, or the history of a certain genre. The successful contributor will have a good knowledge of the chosen subject. Length 1500 to 9000 words.

1/News **2**/Features **3**/Fiction **4**/Letters **5**/Fillers
6/B&W Photos **7**/Colour Photos **8**/Reviews

Comments: Particularly interested in articles that link recording histories with interviews.
Approach: By telephone.
Lead time: Two months.
Payment: £100 per thousand words.

Recording Musician

PO Box 30
St Ives
Cambridgeshire
PE17 4XQ

Tel: (0480) 461244   **Fax:** (0480) 492422

Frequency: Monthly

Circulation: 15,750

Contact: Paul White, Editor
Profile: Features reviews of recording equipment, as well as providing information and advice for musicians.
Requirements: 2 6 7
Articles on any subject related to professional music recording. These may cover subjects such as individual studios and the people who work in them.
Comments: Reviews of equipment are handled by the editorial staff.
Approach: By telephone or letter.
Lead time: Four weeks.
Payment: Negotiable.

Rendezvous

PO Box 45
Dorking
Surrey
RH5 5YZ

Tel: (0306) 712712

Frequency: Bi-monthly

Circulation: 550

Contact: Carol Andrews, Editor

Profile: Concerned with all matters relating to conferences, venues, incentive travel and destinations.
Requirements: 2 8
Features and reviews concerning individual venues or destinations that are of interest to those in the conference and incentive travel industry. Length up to 1500 words.
Comments: Features must concentrate on the areas of interest to conference and incentive travel organisers, rather than general tourism.
Approach: By letter with ideas.
Lead time: Three months.
Payment: Negotiable.

Report

7 Northumberland Street
London
WC2N 5DA

Tel: 071-930 6441   **Fax:** 071-930 1359

Frequency: 8xYear

Circulation: 139,000

Contact: Julia Hagedorn, Editor
Profile: Published by the Association of Teachers and Lecturers.
Requirements: 1 2
News, features and comment about aspects of teaching or lecturing in primary, secondary and further education.
Comments: No poetry.
Approach: By letter with proposals.
Lead time: Three months.
Payment: From £60 per thousand words.

Resident Abroad

102-108 Clerkenwell Road
London
EC1M 5SA

1/News 2/Features 3/Fiction 4/Letters 5/Fillers
6/B&W Photos 7/Colour Photos 8/Reviews

Tel: 071-251 9321   Fax: 071-251 4686

Frequency: Monthly

Circulation: 19,142

Contact: William Essex, Editor

Profile: A primarily financial magazine which deals with tax and investment issues for British expatriates. Also covers property, education, and the quality of life abroad.

Requirements: 2 5 6 7 8
First-hand accounts of living overseas, whether interviews or the writer's own experiences. These should be useful to people considering a move to the country in question. Include lots of specifics and anecdotes. Length up to 1000 words.

Comments: It is better to cover one aspect of life in a particular country than to try and cram everything into one article.

Approach: By letter with ideas.

Lead time: Two months.

Payment: £100 per thousand words.

Retail Business

40 Duke Street
London
W1A 1DW

Tel: 071-493 6711   Fax: 071-499 9767

Frequency: Monthly

Contact: Nicholas Hall, Editor

Profile: Provides detailed reports on consumer markets for managers of retail organisations.

Requirements: 2
Detailed and informed analysis of particular sectors in the retail trade, or reports of consumer buying trends, etc.

Comments: The magazine has a standard form for all reports, so writers should contact the editor before attempting contributions.

Approach: By letter with CV.

Lead time: Two months.

Payment: Negotiable.

Retail Week

Maclaren House
19 Scarbrook Road
Croydon
CR9 1QH

Tel: 081-688 7788   Fax: 081-688 8375

Frequency: Weekly

Circulation: 14,906

Contact: Elaine Kavanagh, Features Editor

Profile: Trade weekly for all sectors of the retail sector. Concentrates on business issues affecting larger retailers.

Requirements: 1 2
News of developments and events affecting retail businesses. Also in-depth features analysing trends and issues of interest to retailers, plus case studies. Average length 1000 words.

Comments: Contributors do not need to be experts, provided they are able to research their subject effectively.

Approach: In writing with ideas.

Lead time: Three weeks.

Payment: £130 per thousand words.

1/News 2/Features 3/Fiction 4/Letters 5/Fillers
6/B&W Photos 7/Colour Photos 8/Reviews

Retirement Homes

Unit 1
Raans Road
Amersham
HP6 6LX

Tel: (0494) 432433   **Fax:** (0494) 432572

Frequency: Bi-monthly

Circulation: 30,000

Contact: Alan Walsh, Editor

Profile: For people aged over 55 looking to move into a new home for their retirement.

Requirements: 1 2 5 6 7
Articles on home finance, retirement in other countries around the world or spotlights on certain areas in the UK. Length up to 1000 words.

Comments: Concentrates on homes built specifically for retirement.

Approach: By telephone.

Lead time: Two months.

Payment: Approx. NUJ rates.

The RIBA Journal

Builder House
1 Millharbour
London
E14 9RA

Tel: 071-537 2222   **Fax:** 071-537 2007

Frequency: Monthly

Circulation: 27,032

Contact: John Welsh, Editor

Profile: The official journal of the Royal Institute of British Architects.

Requirements: 2
Feature articles on all architectural subjects, including interiors and current issues. Length up to 2000 words.

Comments: Contributors should have a good understanding of architecture.

Approach: In writing.

Lead time: Two months.

Payment: £120 per thousand words.

Ride BMX

PO Box 1300
Dorchester
Dorset
DT1 1FN

Tel: (0305) 263662   **Fax:** (0305) 251263

Frequency: Monthly

Circulation: 21,500

Contact: Mark Noble, Editor

Profile: Covers the sport of BMX racing, from freestyle to ramp riding.

Requirements: 1 2 5 6 7
News of local events and activities, information about competitions and developments within the sport. Length 2000 to 3000 words.

Comments: Covers BMX bikes only. No material on mountain biking, etc.

Approach: By telephone.

Lead time: Four weeks.

Payment: Negotiable.

The Riders

Hopes House
Longyester
Gifford
East Lothian
EH41 4PL

Tel: 062 081 596   **Fax:** 062 081 788

Frequency: Monthly

Circulation: 8000

Contact: Alison Rae, Editor

Profile: An equestrian magazine for riders in Scotland and the North of England.

1/News **2**/Features **3**/Fiction **4**/Letters **5**/Fillers
6/B&W Photos **7**/Colour Photos **8**/Reviews

Requirements: 1 2
News of the equestrian scene, plus features on subjects relevant to horse riders and drivers.
Comments: Writers do not need to be experts to contribute.
Approach: In writing.
Lead time: Two months.
Payment: By negotiation.

Riding Magazine

Corner House
Foston
Grantham
Lincolnshre
NG32 2JU

Tel: (0400) 82032   **Fax:** (0400) 82275

Frequency: Monthly

Circulation: 30,000

Contact: Helen Scott, Editor
Profile: Aimed at the knowledgeable horse owner who is interested in all the disciplines. Includes informative articles, product reviews, competitions, etc.
Requirements: 1 2 6 7
Will consider instructional features and practical tips. Length between 1000 and 1200 words. Photographs to accompany features are always welcome.
Comments: Does not accept show and event reviews from freelance writers.
Approach: In writing.
Lead time: Six weeks.
Payment: £65 per thousand words.

Right Start

71 Newcomen Street
London
SE1 1YT

Tel: 071-403 0840   **Fax:** 071-378 6883

Frequency: Bi-monthly
Circulation: 10,000
Contact: Bernard Hubbard, Editor
Profile: Offers information, advice and guidance to parents of young children.
Requirements: 1 2
News and features on the health, behaviour and education of pre-school children. Length up to 1200 words.
Comments: Also features a section that focuses on children from birth to the age of two.
Approach: By letter with examples of previous work.
Lead time: Four months.
Payment: £150 per thousand words.

Rock CD

United Leisure Magazines
PO Box 3205
4 Selsdon Way
London
E14 9GL

Tel: 071-712 0550   **Fax:** 071-712 0562

Frequency: Bi-monthly

Circulation: 46,000

Contact: The Editor
Profile: Provides coverage of adult rock music, from the 60s through to the present day.
Requirements: 2
In-depth features on new artists, or established artists who are still active. Also articles about the industry behind the music. Length from 700 to 4000 words.
Comments: The editor likes to achieve a balance of serious and light-hearted features.

1/News **2**/Features **3**/Fiction **4**/Letters **5**/Fillers
6/B&W Photos **7**/Colour Photos **8**/Reviews

Approach: By letter with ideas.
Lead time: Three months.
Payment: £120 per thousand words.

Routing

Argus Specialist Publications
Argus House
Boundary Way
Hemel Hempstead
Hertfordshire
HP2 7ST

Tel: (0442) 66551   **Fax:** (0442) 66998

Frequency: Quarterly

Circulation: 38,000

Contact: John Perkins, Editor
Profile: A quarterly title for
woodworkers with a particular
interest in routing.
Requirements: 2 6 7
Practical instructional features on
routing, plus detailed projects for
the experienced woodworker.
Comments: Illustrations and
photographs are always welcome.
Approach: In writing.
Lead time: Two months.
Payment: By negotiation.

Rowing Magazine

PO Box 125C
Esher
Surrey
KT10 0HE

Tel: (0372) 467098   **Fax:** (0372) 469967

Frequency: Monthly

Circulation: 6500

Contact: Peter Ayling, Editor
Profile: Covers the world of rowing,
from coaching to regattas. Aimed at
athletes from school to international
level.

Requirements: 1 2 6 7 8
Looking for material that is more
light-hearted and humorous than the
material that is usually received.
Topics include diets and exercise,
plus general comment and opinion.
Comments: Copy should be written to
interest the people in the boats.
Approach: By fax or letter.
Lead time: Five weeks.
Payment: £25 per thousand words.

Royal Dempsters

The Publishing House
Highbury Station Road
London
N1 1SE

Tel: 071-226 2222   **Fax:** 071-226 1255

Frequency: 2xYear

Circulation: 50,000

Contact: David Hale
Profile: A society magazine that carries
gossip and news about the royal
family and other personalities.
Requirements: 1 2
Humorous features and snippets of
gossip about society figures. All
material must be topical and up to
date. Length up to 1000 words.
Comments: Contributors should be
familiar with the style and content of
the magazine.
Approach: In writing.
Lead time: Six months.
Payment: £130 per thousand words.

Rugby Leaguer

Martland Mill
Martland Mill Lane
Wigan
WN5 0LX

Tel: (0942) 228000   **Fax:** (0942) 214004

1/News **2**/Features **3**/Fiction **4**/Letters **5**/Fillers
6/B&W Photos **7**/Colour Photos **8**/Reviews

Frequency: Weekly

Circulation: 13,000

Contact: John Huxley, Editor

Profile: Provides comprehensive coverage of the sport of rugby league.

Requirements: 1 2
Personality profiles and features on issues connected with rugby league football. Length up to 800 words.

Comments: Does not want to receive reports of rugby matches.

Approach: By telephone or fax with ideas.

Lead time: Two weeks.

Payment: NUJ rates.

Rugby News

24 Notting Hill Gate
London
W11 3JQ

Tel: 071-229 9944   **Fax:** 071-727 5442

Frequency: Monthly

Circulation: 15,000

Contact: David Lawrenson, Editor

Profile: For the serious rugby enthusiast, covering the sport both nationally and internationally.

Requirements: 1 2
News and features on a wide range of rugby topics, from player interviews and overseas news to fitness information and tour details. Length from 800 to 1200 words.

Comments: Looking for unusual feature ideas, targeted at a predominantly male audience.

Approach: By telephone.

Lead time: Two months.

Payment: £70-£100 per thousand words.

Rugby World & Post

Chiltern House
17 College Avenue
Maidenhead
Berkshire
SL6 6BX

Tel: (0628) 776433   **Fax:** (0628) 39519

Frequency: Monthly

Circulation: 50,000

Contact: Nick Cain, Executive Editor

Profile: Coverage of the world of rugby union football in the UK, throughout Europe and worldwide.

Requirements: 1 2 5 6 7
Profiles and interviews with players from local clubs, plus articles on regional teams or divisions.

Comments: Also includes a section on youth rugby.

Approach: Send complete manuscript.

Lead time: Two months.

Payment: Negotiable.

Running

Stonehart Leisure Magazines
67-71 Goswell Road
London
EC1 7EN

Tel: 071-410 9410   **Fax:** 071-410 9440

Frequency: Monthly

Circulation: 16,000

Contact: Nick Troop, Editor

Profile: A magazine for distance runners, covering both road and off-road running, plus orienteering.

Requirements: 1 2 5 6 7
Features on running overseas or competing in unusual locations, plus interviews with well-known runners, etc. Length between 1500 and 2000 words.

1/News **2**/Features **3**/Fiction **4**/Letters **5**/Fillers
6/B&W Photos **7**/Colour Photos **8**/Reviews

Comments: Does not require humour or stories on 'my first marathon'. A package of words and pictures will be well received.
Approach: By telephone.
Lead time: Two months.
Payment: Negotiable.

S

Safety Education

Cannon House
The Priory Queensway
Birmingham
B4 6BS

Tel: 021-200 2461 **Fax:** 021-200 1254

Frequency: 3xYear

Circulation: 17,500

Contact: Carole Peart, Editor

Profile: An official publication of the
Royal Society for the Prevention of
Accidents.

Requirements: 2 6 7
Welcomes contributions on all
matters concerning safety for
children. Particularly interested in
material on the teaching of safety.

Comments: Concentrates on safety at
home, on roads, in the water and
during leisure activities.

Approach: In writing.

Lead time: Four months.

Payment: By negotiation.

Saga Magazine

The Saga Building
Middleburg Square
Folkestone
Kent
CT20 1AZ

Tel: (0303) 711523 **Fax:** (0303) 220391

Frequency: 10xYear

Circulation: 503,000

Contact: Paul Bach, Editor

Profile: A magazine for active
individuals in their later years. Read
by men and women who have some
money to spend and wish to make
the most of their time.

Requirements: 2 4 5
Articles on older people who are
achieving something notable, plus
interesting anecdotes and
recollections of the past. Also filler
items and letters.

Comments: The magazine does not
publish fiction.

Approach: In writing with ideas.

Lead time: Two months.

Payment: £200 for a 1200-word
feature.

Sales & Marketing Management

31 Upper George Street
Luton
Bedfordshire
LU1 2RD

Tel: (0582) 456767 **Fax:** (0582) 453640

Frequency: Monthly

Circulation: 14,000

Contact: Angela Cummins, Editor

1/News 2/Features 3/Fiction 4/Letters 5/Fillers
6/B&W Photos 7/Colour Photos 8/Reviews

Profile: News and information for senior executives involved in sales or marketing. Includes export news, computer updates, sales fleet information and video-selling techniques.

Requirements: 2

Snappy articles offering something new in the way of sales approaches or marketing strategies. Length around 800 words.

Comments: Only pays for commissioned work, so approach with ideas rather than complete manuscript.

Approach: By telephone or letter.

Lead time: Six weeks.

Payment: From £50 per thousand words.

Salmon, Trout & Sea Trout

The Square
Aberfeldy
Perthshire
PH15 2DE

Tel: (0887) 820082   **Fax:** (0887) 829626

Frequency: Monthly

Circulation: 23,000

Contact: David Goodchild, Editor

Profile: For the enthusiastic game angler, covering everything from fly-tying to environmental matters.

Requirements: 2 3

Articles on techniques, locations and types of fly, etc. Also features on associated wildlife and occasional short stories with a fishing angle. Length 800 to 1500 words.

Comments: Welcomes articles that capture the whole experience of game fishing, including the surroundings, the atmosphere, etc.

Approach: Send complete manuscript.

Lead time: Two months.

Payment: £48 per thousand words.

Satellite Times

23 Mitcham Lane
Streatham
London
SW16 6LQ

Tel: 081-677 7822   **Fax:** 081-677 8223

Frequency: Monthly

Circulation: 270,000

Contact: Eric Woods, Editor

Profile: Primarily concerned with satellite TV listings, but also includes TV-related and general-interest editorial.

Requirements: 2 7

Features on forthcoming satellite programmes or their stars, plus articles on video, cinema or women's subjects. Length up to 1000 words.

Comments: Strong material is always welcome, especially if accompanied by good photos.

Approach: By telephone.

Lead time: Six weeks.

Payment: £100 per thousand words.

Satnews

M2 Communications Ltd
184 Brookside Avenue
Coventry
CV5 8AD

Tel: (0203) 717417   **Fax:** (0203) 717418

Frequency: Fortnightly

Circulation: 75,000

Contact: Darren Ingram

Profile: Provides a worldwide
perspective on satellite and
terrestrial broadcasting. Also covers
other satellite communications.
Requirements: 1 2 5 8
News and features of interest to
professionals and management
within the industry.
Comments: This is not a satellite
listings magazine.
Approach: By letter or fax.
Lead time: Four weeks.
Payment: By negotiation.

Scale Aircraft Modelling

Douglas House
Simpson Road
Bletchley
Milton Keynes
MK1 1BA

Tel: (0908) 377559   **Fax:** (0908) 366744

Frequency: Monthly

Circulation: 18,000

Contact: Alan Hall, Editor
Profile: Concerned with the
construction of scale models of
aircraft in plastics.
Requirements: 2 6
Current and historical information
about relevant aircraft, instructional
features, etc.
Comments: Welcomes anything that
will help model builders improve
their skills.
Approach: By telephone or letter.
Lead time: Four weeks.
Payment: £20 per page.

Scale Models International

Argus Specialist Publications
Argus House
Boundary Way
Hemel Hempstead
Hertfordshire
HP2 7ST

Tel: (0442) 66551   **Fax:** (0442) 66998

Frequency: Monthly

Circulation: 9702

Contact: Kevin Barber, Editor
Profile: Worldwide news and
information for the enthusiastic
modeller. Covers all aspects of scale
modelling, apart from trains.
Requirements: 2 6 7 8
News and information relating to
model construction. Details of new
products and instructional articles.
Length 1500 to 2000 words.
Comments: Always check with the
editor before sending material,
especially if this relates to new
products.
Approach: In writing.
Lead time: Three months.
Payment: £30 per page.

Scootering

PO Box 46
Weston-super-Mare
Avon
BS23 1AF

Tel: (0934) 414785   **Fax:** (0934) 820928

Frequency: Monthly

Circulation: 18,000

Contact: The Editor
Profile: A magazine for scooterists,
Mod revivalists and scooter-racing
fans.

1/News **2**/Features **3**/Fiction **4**/Letters **5**/Fillers
6/B&W Photos **7**/Colour Photos **8**/Reviews

Requirements: 2 6 7
Features on vintage scooters and racing, plus practical and technical pieces. Also contributions on the associated lifestyle, music, etc.

Comments: Writers should be familiar with the magazine's style and approach.

Approach: In writing.

Lead time: Two months.

Payment: By negotiation.

Scotland on Sunday

20 North Bridge
Edinburgh
EH1 1YT

Tel: 031-225 2468   **Fax:** 031-220 2443

Frequency: Monthly

Circulation: 92,000

Contact: Nigel Billen, Editor

Profile: A colour supplement to an upmarket Sunday newspaper.

Requirements: 2 6 7
Well-written features on any subject of interest to readers in Scotland. Length 850 to 2000 words.

Comments: As each issue has a particular theme, writers are advised to make contact before submitting material.

Approach: By telephone or letter.

Lead time: Four weeks.

Payment: Negotiable.

The Scots Magazine

2 Albert Square
Dundee
DD1 9QJ

Tel: (0382) 23131   **Fax:** (0382) 25511

Frequency: Monthly

Circulation: 88,000

Contact: John Rundle, Editor

Profile: A regional magazine covering matters of interest to everyone living in Scotland.

Requirements: 2
Feature articles on Scottish history and traditions, wildlife, walking, climbing and the environment.

Comments: Writers should look for ideas with a strong Scottish angle.

Approach: In writing.

Lead time: Two months.

Payment: Negotiable.

Scottish Diver

25 Kingspark Avenue
Glasgow
G44 4UW

Tel: 041-425 1021   **Fax:** 041-632 8982

Frequency: Bi-monthly

Circulation: 2500

Contact: Mick McGowan, Editor

Profile: The official publication of the Scottish Sub-Aqua Club.

Requirements: 1 2
News and features on all aspects of diving north of the border, from wrecks and legends to practical advice.

Comments: Contributions must be well researched and accurate.

Approach: In writing.

Lead time: Three months.

Payment: Negotiable.

The Scottish Farmer

The Plaza Tower
The Plaza
East Kilbride
Glasgow
G74 1LW

Tel: (0355) 246444   **Fax:** (0355) 263013

1/News **2**/Features **3**/Fiction **4**/Letters **5**/Fillers
6/B&W Photos **7**/Colour Photos **8**/Reviews

Frequency: Weekly

Circulation: 23,000

Contact: Angus MacDonald, Editor

Profile: A journal for the farming community in Scotland.

Requirements: 2 6
Features on livestock, arable farming and agricultural machinery. Length 1000 to 1500 words.

Comments: Welcomes photographs to accompany submissions.

Approach: In writing.

Lead time: Three weeks.

Payment: By arrangement.

Scottish Field

The Plaza Tower
The Plaza
East Kilbride
Glasgow
G74 1LW

Tel: (0355) 246444 **Fax:** (0355) 263013

Frequency: Monthly

Circulation: 20,000

Contact: Joe Stirling, Editor

Profile: A full-colour glossy magazine for everyone living in Scotland today.

Requirements: 2 3 7
Feature articles on home interiors, gardening, holidays, fashion and motoring. Length around 1000 words.

Comments: Every story must have a Scottish connection.

Approach: By letter, followed up with a telephone call.

Lead time: Two months.

Payment: NUJ or better.

The Scottish Golf Magazine

113 St George's Road
Glasgow
G3 6JA

Tel: 041-332 5738

Frequency: Monthly

Circulation: 19,700

Contact: Douglas Lowe, Editor

Profile: For golfers of every level, from club players to the professional.

Requirements: 1 2 6 7
News of events and developments, profiles of prominent players and other golf features with a Scottish angle. Length 500 to 2000 words.

Comments: Photographs to accompany features are appreciated when available.

Approach: By letter with synopsis.

Lead time: Two months.

Payment: Negotiable.

Scottish Home & Country

42a Heriot Row
Edinburgh
EH3 6ES

Tel: 031-225 1934

Frequency: Monthly

Circulation: 18,000

Contact: Stella Roberts, Editor

Profile: A magazine aimed mainly at women in rural areas throughout Scotland.

Requirements: 2
Feature articles on subjects concerning the home, family and countryside. Writers should look for an original Scottish angle.

Comments: Study the magazine before submitting material.

Approach: In writing.
Lead time: Two months.
Payment: By arrangement.

Scottish Memories

Unit 26
Clydeway Centre
45 Finnieston Street
Glasgow
G3 8JU

Tel: 041-204 3104   **Fax:** 041-204 3101

Frequency: Monthly

Circulation: 34,000

Contact: Ken Laird, Editor
Profile: Devoted to rekindling interest in Scotland's history.
Requirements: 2 5 6
Welcomes articles on folklore, nostalgic pieces and personal reminiscences. Humorous articles are always in demand.
Comments: Old photographs and illustrations are always appreciated.
Approach: In writing.
Lead time: Two months.
Payment: £150 per thousand words.

Scottish Rugby

113 St George's Road
Glasgow
G3 6JA

Tel: 041-332 5738   **Fax:** 041-332 9880

Frequency: Monthly

Circulation: 17,000

Contact: Alan Campbell, Editor
Profile: A magazine for both players and supporters, covering the game of rugby at all levels.

Requirements: 2 6 7
Off-beat or humorous articles on players, prominent personalities and teams. Also material on regional and schools rugby in Scotland. From 500 to 3000 words.
Comments: Articles should be about the game in Scotland, but written to appeal to an international readership.
Approach: By letter or telephone.
Lead time: Two months.
Payment: Negotiable.

Scottish World

Royston House
Caroline Park
Edinburgh
EH5 1QJ

Tel: 031-551 2942   **Fax:** 031-551 2938

Frequency: Quarterly

Circulation: 10,000

Contact: Archie MacKenzie, Editor
Profile: A quality, lifestyle magazine for Scotland, covering a wide and varied range of subjects.
Requirements: 1 2 6 7 8
Anything with a Scottish flavour will be considered. In particular, nostalgic pieces and features on interesting people or country pursuits. Length 1500 to 2500 words.
Comments: Also interested in the Gaelic language.
Approach: By telephone or letter.
Lead time: Four weeks.
Payment: Negotiable.

1/News **2**/Features **3**/Fiction **4**/Letters **5**/Fillers
6/B&W Photos **7**/Colour Photos **8**/Reviews

Scouting

Baden Powell House
Queen's Gate
London
SW7 5JS

Tel: 071-584 7030   **Fax:** 071-581 9953

Frequency: Monthly

Circulation: 35,000

Contact: David Easton, Editor

Profile: For adults in the Scouting movement, providing a forum for exchange of views and ideas.

Requirements: 1 2 6 7 8
News and features relating to activities within the movement, recent developments and future proposals. Length 750 to 1000 words.

Comments: For scout leaders rather than scouts themselves.

Approach: By letter.

Lead time: Three months.

Payment: Negotiable.

Screen Incorporating Screen Education

Glasgow University
53 Hillhead Street
Glasgow
G12 8QQ

Tel: 041-330 5035   **Fax:** 041-330 5035

Frequency: Quarterly

Circulation: 2000

Contact: The Editor

Profile: A serious journal concerned with the theory of film and television.

Requirements: 2 8
Articles on the academic aspects of cinema and television, reports of events and reviews of relevant books. Length up to 5000 words.

Comments: Writers should have a good knowledge of the subject.

Approach: Send complete manuscript.

Lead time: Three months.

Payment: By negotiation.

Screen International

EMAP Publications
33-39 Bowling Green Lane
London
EC1R 0DA

Tel: 071-837 1212   **Fax:** 071-278 4003

Frequency: Weekly

Circulation: 12,000

Contact: Oscar Moore, Editor

Profile: An international business publication for the film and television industry.

Requirements: 1 2 6 7
News and features on business issues and technological developments affecting the industry. Length up to 1000 words.

Comments: No unsolicited manuscripts.

Approach: By telephone.

Lead time: Three weeks.

Payment: From £142 per thousand words.

Scuba World

18 Market Street
Poole
Dorset
BH15 1NF

Tel: (0202) 682699   **Fax:** (0202) 682987

Frequency: Monthly

Circulation: 14,000

Contact: Nina Pendred, Assistant Editor

1/News **2**/Features **3**/Fiction **4**/Letters **5**/Fillers
6/B&W Photos **7**/Colour Photos **8**/Reviews

Profile: Devoted to diving in the UK. Includes everything from equipment to conservation.

Requirements: 2 6 7 8
Information about holiday locations or UK diving sites, plus profiles of well-known divers. Length 1500 words.

Comments: Guidelines for contributors are available on request.

Approach: By letter with ideas.

Lead time: Two months.

Payment: £100 per piece.

Sea Angler

EMAP Pursuit Publishing Ltd
Bretton Court
Bretton Centre
Peterborough
PE3 8DZ

Tel: (0733) 264666   **Fax:** (0733) 265515

Frequency: Bi-monthly

Circulation: 20,239

Contact: Mark Bowler, Editor

Profile: Covers both shore and boat fishing throughout UK.

Requirements: 1 2 7 8
News and features relating to catches or fishing trips, as well as practical, instructional articles. Length 1000 to 1500 words.

Comments: Colour transparencies are always welcome.

Approach: By letter.

Lead time: Six weeks.

Payment: Around £100 for an 800-word article with colour pictures.

Sea Angling

EMAP Pursuit Publishing Ltd
Bretton Court
Bretton Centre
Peterborough
PE3 8DZ

Tel: (0733) 264666   **Fax:** (0733) 265515

Frequency: Bi-monthly

Circulation: 23,092

Contact: Cliff Brown, Editor

Profile: Covers shore and boat sea fishing. Content includes advice, venue information and readers' experiences.

Requirements: 2 3 7
Instructional material on fishing methods, species and tackle. Also accounts of interesting fishing trips. Length up to 1000 words.

Comments: Welcomes in-depth articles with plenty of advice for readers.

Approach: By telephone or letter.

Lead time: Six weeks.

Payment: From £60 per thousand words.

Sea Breezes

202 Cotton Exchange Building
Old Hall Street
Liverpool
L3 9LA

Tel: 051-236 3935

Frequency: Monthly

Circulation: 17,000

Contact: C.H. Milson, Editor

Profile: Concerned with ships and the sea, both today and in the past.

Requirements: 2 6 7
Stories of ships, sailors and maritime history, written from personal experience or detailed research.

1/News **2**/Features **3**/Fiction **4**/Letters **5**/Fillers
6/B&W Photos **7**/Colour Photos **8**/Reviews

Comments: Accepts material on both merchant and naval ships.
Approach: In writing.
Lead time: Two months.
Payment: By negotiation.

Sega Force

Case Mill
Temeside
Ludlow
Shropshire
SY8 1JW

Tel: (0584) 875851   **Fax:** (0584) 876044

Frequency: Monthly

Circulation: 52,000

Contact: Mathew Yeo
Profile: One of the top-selling Sega console titles. Includes up-to-date news on games, plus hints and tips.
Requirements: 1 2
News on developments within the games market, plus features on interesting software companies. Length 2000 to 3000 words.
Comments: Copy on Macintosh disk preferred.
Approach: Send ideas with examples of previous work.
Lead time: Three weeks.
Payment: Negotiable but good.

Sega Power

Future Publishing
30 Monmouth Street
Bath
BA1 2BW

Tel: (0225) 442244   **Fax:** (0225) 446019

Frequency: Monthly

Circulation: 102,033

Contact: Mark Ramshaw, Editor

Profile: Provides comprehensive reviews of all Sega software for consoles, plus features and news.
Requirements: 1 2
News snippets or features based around Sega consoles and related games, etc. Length 200 to 2000 words.
Comments: Writers should be familiar with the magazine's style.
Approach: By telephone with initial ideas.
Lead time: Two to three months.
Payment: £50 per page.

Select

Mappin House
4 Winsley Street
London
W1N 5AR

Tel: 071-436 1515   **Fax:** 071-637 0456

Frequency: Monthly

Circulation: 95,000

Contact: Hannah Ford
Profile: A contemporary 'indie' rock magazine aimed at those aged between 16 and 24. Covers everything from music to groupies.
Requirements: 1 2 8
News and features on any aspect of contemporary music, etc. Always looking for new writers to add to its established stable of contributors.
Comments: New writers are asked to write reviews initially, progressing to features later.
Approach: In writing with examples of previous work.
Lead time: Four weeks.
Payment: £100 per thousand words.

1/News **2**/Features **3**/Fiction **4**/Letters **5**/Fillers
6/B&W Photos **7**/Colour Photos **8**/Reviews

Serve and Volley

The Lawn Tennis Association
Queen's Club
West Kensington
London
W14 9EG

Tel: 071-385 2366   **Fax:** 071-381 6656

Frequency: Monthly

Circulation: 37,265

Contact: Henry Wancke, Editor
Profile: The official journal of the Lawn Tennis Association. Covers tennis both in Britain and internationally.
Requirements: 2 7
Articles on coaching techniques, plus features on other issues affecting the world of international tennis. Length 1000 to 2000 words.
Comments: Good photographs are always welcome.
Approach: By letter.
Lead time: Six weeks.
Payment: Negotiable.

Shape

Weider Health & Fitness Ltd
Greenroyd Mill
Sutton-in-Craven
Keighley
BD20 7LW

Tel: (0535) 632294   **Fax:** (0535) 634082

Frequency: Monthly

Circulation: 20,000

Contact: The Editor
Profile: A health and fitness magazine for women who want to get into shape. Covers diet, exercise, fashion, beauty, sport and adventure.

Requirements: 1 2
News concerning dieting or exercise methods, aerobics competitions, training techniques, etc.
Comments: Contributors do not need to be experts in this field.
Approach: In writing.
Lead time: Three months.
Payment: Negotiable.

She

National Magazine House
72 Broadwick Street
London
W1V 2BP

Tel: 071-439 5000   **Fax:** 071-439 5350

Frequency: Monthly

Circulation: 293,117

Contact: Linda Kelsey, Editor
Profile: A magazine for 'women who juggle their lives'. Readers are typically aged between 25 and 45, with a busy working and domestic life.
Requirements: 2 4
Original and well-written features for affluent, stylish women who may be playing the roles of mother, career woman and lover.
Comments: Unsolicited material will not be read or returned.
Approach: In writing with ideas.
Lead time: Two months.
Payment: £250-£400.

Sherlock Holmes Gazette

Baker Street Publications
PO Box 221
Alderney
Channel Islands
Great Britain

Tel: (0481) 822137   **Fax:** (0481) 822110

Frequency: Quarterly

Circulation: 8500

Contact: Elizabeth Wiggins, Editor

Profile: A magazine for fans of Sherlock Holmes. Covers anything and everything connected with the character.

Requirements: 1 2

Articles about new Sherlock Holmes films, TV programmes, exhibitions, etc. Also historical pieces on life in the Victorian era and features on the life of Sir Arthur Conan Doyle.

Comments: The magazine is read in the USA, Japan and many other countries, so material should have an international appeal.

Approach: In writing.

Lead time: Three months.

Payment: £35-£50 per thousand words.

Ship & Boat International

10 Upper Belgrave Street
London
SW1X 8BQ

Tel: 071-235 4622   **Fax:** 071-245 6959

Frequency: 10xYear

Circulation: 8000

Contact: Richard White, Editor

Profile: News and feature articles on ships and boats up to 100 metres in length. A technical publication for designers, builders and operators.

Requirements: 2

Detailed and accurate articles on specific matters of interest to boat builders and users. All freelance work is commissioned from initial ideas.

Comments: General interest items on boating subjects are not required.

Approach: By fax.

Lead time: Six weeks.

Payment: By arrangement.

Ships Monthly

Kottingham House
Dale Street
Burton-on-Trent
DE14 3TD

Tel: (0283) 64290   **Fax:** (0283) 61077

Frequency: Monthly

Circulation: 22,000

Contact: Robert Shopland, Editor

Profile: A specialist title for maritime historians and enthusiasts.

Requirements: 2 6 7

Features on merchant or naval ships, concentrating on 20th-century vessels. All material must be accurate and detailed.

Comments: Guidelines for contributors are available on request.

Approach: In writing.

Lead time: Two months.

Payment: By arrangement.

Shivers

PO Box 371
London
SW14 8JL

Tel: 081-878 5486   **Fax:** 081-876 9455

Frequency: Monthly

Circulation: 40,000

Contact: Alan Jones, Editor

Profile: Provides extensive coverage of horror movies for fanatics.

Requirements: 2 6 7

Interviews with stars, producers, directors and other people connected with the production of horror films.

1/News **2**/Features **3**/Fiction **4**/Letters **5**/Fillers
6/B&W Photos **7**/Colour Photos **8**/Reviews

Comments: Contributors should be familiar with the subject.
Approach: Write with ideas and examples of previous work.
Lead time: Four weeks.
Payment: Negotiable.

Shoot

IPC Magazines
King's Reach Tower
Stamford Street
London
SE1 9LS

Tel: 071-261 6287   **Fax:** 071-261 6019

Frequency: Weekly

Circulation: 150,000

Contact: The Editor
Profile: A football title aimed at fans aged between 8 and 14. Focuses on the star players and leading teams.
Requirements: 1 2 7
Informative features on leading names, or human-interest stories on lesser-known players. Length around 400 words.
Comments: Copy should be short and sharp.
Approach: By telephone, letter or fax.
Lead time: One week.
Payment: NUJ rates or better.

The Shooting Gazette

2 West Street
Bourne
Lincolnshire
PE10 9NE

Tel: (0778) 393747   **Fax:** (0778) 425453

Frequency: Bi-monthly

Circulation: 25,000

Contact: Mike Barnes, Editor
Profile: Provides comprehensive coverage of the sport of game shooting.
Requirements: 2
Profiles of prominent people in field shooting, information about locations in the UK and articles on conservation, etc. Length 1000 to 1200 words.
Comments: There is considerable emphasis on the pleasures of being in the countryside.
Approach: Send complete manuscript.
Lead time: Two months.
Payment: By negotiation.

Shooting Times

10 Sheet Street
Windsor
Berkshire
SL4 1BG

Tel: (0753) 856061   **Fax:** (0753) 830370

Frequency: Weekly

Circulation: 36,100

Contact: Tim O'Nions
Profile: A broad-based country magazine that covers everything from game shooting to identifying wild flowers.
Requirements: 1 2
News and features on countryside matters, profiles of personalities in country sport and readers' tales. Length around 1000 words.
Comments: Describes itself as a general country title that happens to focus on shooting.
Approach: By telephone.
Lead time: Three weeks.
Payment: £80 per thousand words.

1/News 2/Features 3/Fiction 4/Letters 5/Fillers
6/B&W Photos 7/Colour Photos 8/Reviews

Shore Link

400 Yorktown Road
College Town
Camberley
Surrey
GU15 4PR

Tel: (0276) 32194   **Fax:** (0276) 600068

Frequency: Monthly

Circulation: 40,000

Contact: Paul Vale, Editor

Profile: A free publication distributed along the coasts of the UK to people who spend their leisure time on the water.

Requirements: 2
Articles about leisure, sport and relaxation on the coast. Material should be informative and entertaining.

Comments: Study the publication before contributing.

Approach: In writing.

Lead time: Two months.

Payment: Negotiable.

Short Circuit Magazine

York House
22 Frederick Street
Birmingham
B1 3HE

Tel: 021-233 3468   **Fax:** 021-236 4230

Frequency: 10xYear

Circulation: 4000

Contact: Mark Haddleton, Editor

Profile: Concerned with stock car racing in the UK, throughout Europe and worldwide.

Requirements: 1 2 4 6 7
Anything from short news items to features on drivers or new cars. Also gossip from the race courses. Length up to 2000 words.

Comments: Concentrates mainly on events in the UK.

Approach: By telephone, letter or fax.

Lead time: Two weeks.

Payment: Negotiable.

Short Wave Magazine

Arrowsmith Court
Station Approach
Broadstone
Dorset
BH18 8PW

Tel: (0202) 659910   **Fax:** (0202) 659950

Frequency: Monthly

Circulation: 18,122

Contact: Dick Ganderton, Editor

Profile: For the hobby radio enthusiast, from broadcast listener to airband and scanner user.

Requirements: 1 2 5 6 7 8
Features of general interest to radio hams, simple constructional articles and reviews of scanners, receivers and accessories. Length about 1000 to 1500 words.

Comments: Copy on Macintosh or IBM disk preferred.

Approach: By letter with ideas.

Lead time: Eight weeks.

Payment: About £60 per printed page.

Shout

D.C. Thomson & Co Ltd
Albert Square
Dundee
DD1 9QJ

Tel: (0382) 23131   **Fax:** (0382) 22214

Frequency: Fortnightly

Circulation: Not available

Contact: Jackie Brown, Editor

1/News **2**/Features **3**/Fiction **4**/Letters **5**/Fillers
6/B&W Photos **7**/Colour Photos **8**/Reviews

Profile: For younger teenage girls, covering music, TV and relationships.

Requirements: 2 3
Features on the opposite sex and emotional relationships. Also fiction appropriate to the readership. Length up to 1000 words.

Comments: Few opportunities for freelances in music, TV or fashion, as this material is sourced elsewhere.

Approach: In writing.

Lead time: Three weeks.

Payment: Negotiable.

Show Jumper

276 Monument Road
Edgbaston
Birmingham
B16 8XF

Tel: 021-456 2344   **Fax:** 021-454 3452

Frequency: Monthly

Circulation: 30,000

Contact: The Editor

Profile: For the enthusiastic show jumper, covering all the year's major competition and events.

Requirements: 1 2
Features on riders and events, plus information on getting started, etc. Both factual and humorous pieces are welcome. Length up to 1000 words.

Comments: Always looking for new contributors, especially those able to offer photographs with features.

Approach: By letter or fax.

Lead time: Two months.

Payment: £90 per thousand words.

The Shropshire Magazine

77 Wyle Cop
Shrewsbury
SY1 1UT

Tel: (0743) 362175

Frequency: Monthly

Circulation: 3500

Contact: Pam Green, Editor

Profile: A general-interest county magazine covering the whole of Shropshire and its people.

Requirements: 2 6 7
Feature articles on subjects such as festivals, events, family histories, local culture and traditions. Length around 1500 words.

Comments: All material must have a local angle.

Approach: By letter.

Lead time: Two months.

Payment: Negotiable.

Sight & Sound

British Film Institute
21 Stephen Street
London
W1P 1PL

Tel: 071-255 1444   **Fax:** 071-436 2327

Frequency: Monthly

Circulation: 30,000

Contact: Philip Dodd, Editor

Profile: International review of the world of film and cinema.

Requirements: 2 6 7 8
Features on subjects relating to the film industry, plus reviews of film and video releases. Length between 1200 and 4000 words.

Comments: Photographs to accompany features are always appreciated.

1/News **2**/Features **3**/Fiction **4**/Letters **5**/Fillers
6/B&W Photos **7**/Colour Photos **8**/Reviews

Approach: By letter with examples of previous work.
Lead time: Six weeks.
Payment: £100 per thousand words.

Signature

Greater London House
Hampstead Road
London
NW1 7QQ

Tel: 071-388 3171   **Fax:** 071-383 7486

Frequency: Bi-monthly

Circulation: 150,000

Contact: Dorothy Stesanczyk, Editor
Profile: An upmarket complimentary magazine for Diners Club card holders in the UK.
Requirements: 1 2
  News and features on leisure, business, travel and related subjects. Length 800 to 1500 words.
Comments: No unsolicited manuscripts.
Approach: By letter.
Lead time: Six weeks.
Payment: Negotiable.

The Skier and Snowboarder Magazine

48 London Road
Sevenoaks
Kent
TN13 1AS

Tel: (0732) 743644   **Fax:** (0732) 743647

Frequency: Bi-monthly

Circulation: 20,000

Contact: Frank Baldwin
Profile: A specialist title for winter sports enthusiasts with considerable experience.

Requirements: 2 7
  Articles on skiing and snowboarding that have a strong story behind them, preferably backed up by colour pictures. 'Off the wall' tales are always welcome, too. Length around 1000 words.
Comments: Not interested in articles on 'oh, what a lovely time I had...'
Approach: By telephone.
Lead time: Six weeks.
Payment: £100 per thousand words.

Ski Special

27 Belsize Lane
London
NW3 5AS

Tel: 071-435 5472   **Fax:** 071-431 3742

Frequency: 2xYear

Circulation: 35,000

Contact: Alan Holden, Features Editor
Profile: Provides information on resorts, tour operators, equipment and fashion for keen skiers.
Requirements: 1 2 6 7 8
  Equipment reviews and informative articles about distant resorts in places such as Japan or South America.
Comments: Looking for original stories that would not otherwise be covered by the magazine.
Approach: By telephone with ideas.
Lead time: Three months.
Payment: £100 per thousand words.

Ski Survey

118 Eaton Square
London
SW1W 9AF

Tel: 071-245 1033   **Fax:** 071-245 1258

1/News **2**/Features **3**/Fiction **4**/Letters **5**/Fillers
6/B&W Photos **7**/Colour Photos **8**/Reviews

Frequency: 5xYear

Circulation: 23,200

Contact: Roland White, Editor

Profile: News and features on all aspects of skiing, plus equipment and resort reviews.

Requirements: 2 7

Ski features, especially about skiing in unusual places or under unusual circumstances. Also resort reports that include lots of practical details and style information. Length around 1000 words.

Comments: Avoid the 'what I did on my winter holiday' approach.

Approach: By telephone with ideas.

Lead time: Five weeks.

Payment: £200 per thousand words.

Skyscene

The Boathouse
Crabtree Lane
Fulham
London
SW6 8NJ

Tel: 071-381 6007   **Fax:** 071-381 3930

Frequency: 2xYear

Circulation: 1.1 million

Contact: Heather Miller

Profile: The in-flight magazine of Britannia Airways.

Requirements: 2

Features on lifestyle, entertainment, sport and destinations. All material should appeal to a broad mix of passengers en route to their holiday destinations.

Comments: Only submissions of the highest standard will be considered for publication.

Approach: In writing.

Lead time: Six months.

Payment: By negotiation.

Slimming

Victory House
14 Leicester Square
London WC2H 7BP

Tel: 071-437 9011   **Fax:** 071-434 0656

Frequency: 10xYear

Circulation: 205,591

Contact: Kandy Shepherd, Editor

Profile: Provides advice and encouragement for those trying to lose weight and get into shape.

Requirements: 2 5

Features on cookery, nutrition and living a healthy lifestyle. Length up to 2000 words.

Comments: Case studies are usually developed in house.

Approach: In writing with a synopsis.

Lead time: Two months.

Payment: Negotiable.

Small Business Confidential

36-38 Willesden Lane
London
NW6 7SW

Tel: 071-625 8656   **Fax:** 071-625 8637

Frequency: Monthly

Circulation: 3000

Contact: Phil Churchill, Editor

Profile: For the small business owner or manager. Runs snappy, jargon-free articles relating to business management.

Requirements: 1 2 5 8

Articles on all aspects of management, marketing, finance, employment, training and information technology. Maximum 750 words.

1/News 2/Features 3/Fiction 4/Letters 5/Fillers
6/B&W Photos 7/Colour Photos 8/Reviews

Comments: Particularly interested in case studies and success stories. Also 'how-to' articles.

Approach: By letter with a brief synopsis.

Lead time: Four weeks.

Payment: £75.

Smash Hits

EMAP Metro
52-55 Carnaby Street
London
W1V 1PF

Tel: 071-437 8050   **Fax:** 071-494 0851

Frequency: Fortnightly

Circulation: 346,148

Contact: Mike Soutar, Editor

Profile: A music magazine for teenagers. Readers are typically aged between 14 and 18, female and very aware of current music and fashion trends.

Requirements: 2 8
Lively features on music, video and film subjects. Also reviews of new releases relevant to the readership.

Comments: New contributors are often asked to write reviews initially.

Approach: In writing with ideas.

Lead time: Two months.

Payment: £100 per page.

Snooker Scene

Cavalier House
202 Hagley Road
Birmingham
B16 9PQ

Tel: 021-454 2931   **Fax:** 021-452 1822

Frequency: Monthly

Circulation: 12,000

Contact: Clive Everton, Editor

Profile: Billiards and snooker news for both the professional and amateur game.

Requirements: 1 2
Topical items and features that will appeal to a wide audience, such as unusual events, significant achievements etc.

Comments: Always talk to the editor before submitting material.

Approach: By telephone or letter.

Lead time: Four weeks.

Payment: Negotiable.

Soccerstars

IPC Magazines
King's Reach Tower
Stamford Street
London
SE1 9LS

Tel: 071-261 5000   **Fax:** 071-261 5007

Frequency: Monthly

Circulation: 80,000

Contact: Peter Stewart, Editor

Profile: A football magazine for readers aged between 5 and 10. Aims to get them interested in football.

Requirements: 1 2 7
Profiles of players and other articles of interest to young readers.

Comments: Keep copy simple and easy to understand.

Approach: By telephone or letter with ideas.

Lead time: Four weeks.

Payment: NUJ rates.

Society Golf

8E Bedford Towers
Brighton
East Sussex
BN1 2JG

1/News 2/Features 3/Fiction 4/Letters 5/Fillers
6/B&W Photos 7/Colour Photos 8/Reviews

Tel: (0273) 325248   **Fax:** (0273) 206047

Frequency: 1xYear

Circulation: 85,000

Contact: Kenneth Wolstenholme, Editor

Profile: A publication for golfers who take the social aspects of the sport seriously.

Requirements: 2 5 6 7 8
Articles on how to run a society more efficiently, how to organise tournaments, etc. Humorous material is always welcome.

Comments: All material is given serious consideration.

Approach: By letter or fax.

Lead time: Two months.

Payment: Negotiable.

Somerset & Avon Life

34 Burlington Court
Redcliffe Mead Lane
Bristol
BS1 6FB

Tel: (0272) 252052   **Fax:** (0272) 252052

Frequency: Monthly

Circulation: 4500

Contact: Neil Pickford

Profile: A monthly regional title covering topics of interest to those in the West country.

Requirements: 2 6 7
Feature articles on lifestyle, historical matters and current events. Length 800 to 1800 words.

Comments: Photographs or advice on illustrations necessary.

Approach: By telephone.

Lead time: Six weeks.

Payment: Up to £40.

The Somerset Magazine

23 Market Street
Crewkerne
Somerset
TA18 7JU

Tel: (0460) 78000   **Fax:** (0460) 76718

Frequency: Monthly

Circulation: 6000

Contact: Jack Rayfield, Editor

Profile: A county magazine that focuses on current events and activities in Somerset.

Requirements: 2 6 7
Features on motoring, fashion, books and cookery, as well as events in the county, etc. Length around 1000 words.

Comments: Illustrations to accompany features are appreciated.

Approach: By telephone or letter.

Lead time: Three months.

Payment: Negotiable.

Songwriting & Composing

Sovereign House
12 Trewartha Road
Praa Sands
Penzance
Cornwall
TR20 9ST

Tel: (0736) 762826   **Fax:** (0736) 763328

Frequency: Quarterly

Circulation: 2000

Contact: Roderick Jones

Profile: Aimed at those interested in writing original songs for professional recording and publishing.

Requirements: 1 2 6 8
News of new opportunities for

1/News **2**/Features **3**/Fiction **4**/Letters **5**/Fillers
6/B&W Photos **7**/Colour Photos **8**/Reviews

songwriters, interviews with songwriters, record companies, and publishers.

Comments: Copy should be targeted at the aspiring songwriter who is hoping to secure a recording or publishing deal.

Approach: By telephone.

Lead time: Four months.

Payment: Negotiable.

Sound on Sound

PO Box 30
St Ives
Cambridgeshire
PE17 4XQ

Tel: (0480) 461244   **Fax:** (0480) 492422

Frequency: Monthly

Circulation: 33,000

Contact: Ian Gillby, Editor

Profile: A practical magazine covering hi-tech music equipment and the people who use it.

Requirements: 2 6 7 8
Artist interviews, features on technology and its applications, etc.

Comments: Concerned with serious music recording.

Approach: By telephone.

Lead time: Two months.

Payment: £50-£100 per thousand words.

Speedway Star

95 Brighton Road
Surbiton
Surrey
KT6 5NF

Tel: 081-399 0012   **Fax:** 081-399 2067

Frequency: Weekly

Circulation: 20,000

Contact: Philip Rising, Editor

Profile: A news-based magazine for enthusiasts that deals with all aspects of Speedway.

Requirements: 1 2
Features on personalities and activities, plus previews of forthcoming events. News of regional results, etc.

Comments: Always pleased to hear from freelance writers who can contribute local news and results.

Approach: By letter or fax.

Lead time: One week.

Payment: NUJ or better.

Sport Diver

Market Link Publishing
Market Link House
Tye Green
Elsenham
Bishops Stortford
CM22 6DY

Tel: (0279) 647555   **Fax:** (0279) 815300

Frequency: Bi-monthly

Circulation: 15,000

Contact: Anne Hamilton, Editor

Profile: The largest-circulation independent diving magazine in the UK. Caters for both divers and non-divers.

Requirements: 1 2 5 6 7 8
Features on UK and exotic diving from amateur or professional divers. Length up to 2000 words.

Comments: The magazine is due to change to monthly publication.

Approach: By telephone with ideas.

Lead time: Six weeks.

Payment: £50 per page.

1/News **2**/Features **3**/Fiction **4**/Letters **5**/Fillers
6/B&W Photos **7**/Colour Photos **8**/Reviews

Sporting Gun

EMAP Pursuit Publishing Ltd
Bretton Court
Bretton Centre
Peterborough
PE3 8DZ

Tel: (0733) 264666   **Fax:** (0733) 265515

Frequency: Monthly

Circulation: 34,500

Contact: Robin Scott, Editor
Profile: A magazine for those
   interested in clay, game or rough
   shooting.
Requirements: 1 2
   Practical, informative features that
   will help readers to acquire new skills
   and knowledge. Also general
   features on related subjects. Length
   up to 750 words.
Comments: Does not require
   superficial pieces on everyday
   experiences.
Approach: By telephone.
Lead time: Two months.
Payment: £80 for 750 words.

Sports Boat & Waterski International

Brinkworth House
Brinkworth
Chippenham
Wiltshire
SN15 5DF

Tel: (0666) 510828   **Fax:** (0666) 510655

Frequency: 10xYear

Circulation: 10,194

Contact: Catherine Gunn-Taylor,
   Editor
Profile: Provides information about all
   aspects of sports boats and
   waterskiing, with coverage split
   equally between the two.

Requirements: 1 2 5 6 7 8
   Waterskiing and boating tips, plus
   news and features relating to
   cruising, holiday hot spots, etc.
Comments: Published bi-monthly in
   winter, monthly for the rest of the
   year.
Approach: In writing with ideas or
   complete manuscript.
Lead time: Two weeks.
Payment: Negotiable.

Sports Quarterly

The Vinegar Factory
20 Bowden Street
London
SE11 4DS

Tel: 071-582 6161   **Fax:** 071-793 1302

Frequency: Quarterly

Circulation: 73,500

Contact: Patricia Halpin
Profile: Devoted to providing coverage
   of all mainstream sports, plus
   seasonal coverage of more
   specialised activities.
Requirements: 1 2 8
   Interesting and unusual features on
   sporting activities. Interviews with
   personalities and original news
   stories.
Comments: Writers who come with
   creative ideas are likely to be taken
   up.
Approach: By letter.
Lead time: Four weeks.
Payment: NUJ rates.

Squash Player International

Stonehart Leisure Publications
67-71 Goswell Road
London
EC1V 7EN

1/News **2**/Features **3**/Fiction **4**/Letters **5**/Fillers
6/B&W Photos **7**/Colour Photos **8**/Reviews

Tel: 071-250 1881   **Fax:** 071-410 9440

Frequency: Monthly

Circulation: 4000

Contact: Ian McKenzie, Editor

Profile: A specialist magazine for the enthusiastic squash player, focusing on instruction and technique.

Requirements: 2
Practical features giving advice on how to improve playing skills. Also relevant health features and personality profiles.

Comments: The magazine aims to appeal to a wide audience, from the average player to the fanatic.

Approach: In writing.

Lead time: Two months.

Payment: Negotiable.

Staffordshire Life

Derby Street
Stafford
ST16 2DT

Tel: (0785) 57700   **Fax:** (0785) 53287

Frequency: Bi-monthly

Circulation: 16,000

Contact: Philip Thurlow-Craig, Editor

Profile: A county-based magazine reflecting the social scene in Staffordshire. Upmarket in approach, including material on both historical and current events.

Requirements: 2 6 7
Any material with a county flavour, plus articles on travel and motoring. Length 1200 to 1500 words.

Comments: Illustrations to accompany submissions are always helpful.

Approach: In writing with synopsis.

Lead time: Four weeks.

Payment: NUJ rates.

The Stage and Television Today

Stage House
47 Bermondsey Street
London
SE1 3XT

Tel: 071-403 1818   **Fax:** 071-403 1418

Frequency: Weekly

Circulation: 40,000

Contact: Jeremy Jehu, Editor

Profile: A weekly newspaper for professionals in the entertainment business.

Requirements: 2
Features on all aspects of stage and television. Copy must be original and informative.

Comments: Considers entertainment from the professional rather than the consumer angle.

Approach: In writing.

Lead time: Three weeks.

Payment: £100 per thousand words.

Stamp Lover

British Philatelic Centre
107 Charterhouse Street
London
EC1M 6PT

Tel: 071-251 5040   **Fax:** 071-490 4253

Frequency: Bi-monthly

Circulation: 1350

Contact: Michael Furnell, Editor

Profile: The official journal of the National Philatelic Society.

Requirements: 2 6 8
Feature articles on stamps and the history of the postal service. Also material on postcards and book reviews.

Comments: Welcomes photographs to accompany articles.

1/News **2**/Features **3**/Fiction **4**/Letters **5**/Fillers
6/B&W Photos **7**/Colour Photos **8**/Reviews

Approach: By letter.
Lead time: Three months.
Payment: By arrangement.

Stamp Magazine

Link House
Dingwall Avenue
Croydon
CR9 2TA

Tel: 081-686 2599   **Fax:** 081-781 6044

Frequency: Monthly

Circulation: 23,000

Contact: Richard West, Editor
Profile: One of the UK's leading
publications for stamp collectors.
Requirements: 2
General features on auctions, new
issues and other philatelic subjects.
Comments: Ensure that any synopsis
you submit gives the editor a good
feel for your writing style.
Approach: In writing with ideas or
complete manuscript.
Lead time: Two months.
Payment: Negotiable.

Stamp Monthly

5 Parkside
Ringwood
Hampshire
BH24 3SH

Tel: (0425) 4723363   **Fax:** (0425) 470247

Frequency: Monthly

Circulation: 22,000

Contact: Hugh Jeffries, Editor
Profile: A magazine for stamp
collectors and enthusiasts.
Requirements: 1 2
News items and feature articles
relating to all aspects of philately

and related subjects. Length 500 to
2500 words.
Comments: It is always advisable to
contact the editor before submitting
material.
Approach: In writing with ideas.
Lead time: Two months.
Payment: Up to £42.

Stand

179 Wingrove Road
Newcastle-upon-Tyne
NE4 9DA

Tel: 091-273 3280

Frequency: Quarterly

Circulation: 4500

Contact: Lorna Tracey or Jon Silkin
Profile: One of the oldest literary
magazines in the country, dedicated
to publishing quality fiction and
poetry.
Requirements: 3
Looking for good original short
stories and poetry. Publishes most
types of work except genre fiction.
Length usually up to 5000 words,
but occasionally longer.
Comments: Do not send more than
three short stories or six poems.
Approach: Send complete manuscript.
Lead time: Six months.
Payment: £30 per thousand words or
£30 per poem.

Starburst

PO Box 371
London
SW14 8JL

Tel: 081-878 5486   **Fax:** 081-876 9455

Frequency: Monthly

Circulation: 40,000

1/News **2**/Features **3**/Fiction **4**/Letters **5**/Fillers
6/B&W Photos **7**/Colour Photos **8**/Reviews

Contact: Stephen Payne, Editor

Profile: Specialist title covering fantasy, science fiction, cinema, video, TV and books.

Requirements: 2 6 7

Interviews with stars, directors, producers and other personalities, plus other features relating to the above subjects.

Comments: Writers should be familiar with the magazine's style before attempting contributions.

Approach: In writing with ideas and examples of previous work.

Lead time: Four weeks.

Payment: Negotiable.

Steam Classic

Argus Specialist Publications
Argus House
Boundary Way
Hemel Hempstead
Hertfordshire
HP2 7ST

Tel: (0932) 225330   **Fax:** (0932) 254639

Frequency: Monthly

Circulation: 15,000

Contact: Peter Herring, Editor

Profile: Devoted to the preservation of steam railways and the design, development and history of their locomotives.

Requirements: 1 2

Anything from the design of particular engines to reminiscences of life working on the railways. Length 1000 to 5000 words.

Comments: The typical reader is aged between 35 and 45 with a considerable interest in the steam era.

Approach: In writing.

Lead time: Two months.

Payment: Around £50 per thousand words.

Steam Days

Ian Allan Publishing
Terminal House
Shepperton
Middlesex
TW17 8AS

Tel: (0932) 851591   **Fax:** (0932) 854750

Frequency: Monthly

Circulation: 19,000

Contact: Rex Kennedy, Editor

Profile: Concerned solely with steam and historical railways. Aimed at those aged 30 to 45 who can remember the steam era, plus younger enthusiasts.

Requirements: 2 6

Detailed features on particular routes, stations or engines, especially articles on working stations. Photos are always welcome but not essential. Length 1500 to 4000 words.

Comments: Does not require superficial or general-interest pieces on steam. Copy on disk preferred.

Approach: In writing.

Lead time: Two months.

Payment: £35 per thousand words.

Steam Railway

Apex House
Oundle Road
Peterborough
PE2 9NP

Tel: (0733) 898100   **Fax:** (0733) 894472

Frequency: Monthly

1/News **2**/Features **3**/Fiction **4**/Letters **5**/Fillers
6/B&W Photos **7**/Colour Photos **8**/Reviews

Circulation: 40,144

Contact: Nigel Harris, Editor

Profile: The largest-selling steam railway title, concerned primarily with preservation.

Requirements: 1 2 6 7
News relating to the railway preservation scene, plus information on steam centres, etc. Length around 1500 words.

Comments: Articles must be well-researched and accurate.

Approach: By telephone.

Lead time: Three weeks.

Payment: Negotiable.

Steam Railway News

Martland Mill
Martland Mill Lane
Wigan
WN5 0ZY

Tel: (0942) 228000   **Fax:** (0942) 214004

Frequency: Weekly

Circulation: 7,000

Contact: John Huxley, Editor

Profile: Provides coverage of the preserved railway scene as well as steam activity on the mainline.

Requirements: 1 2 6 7
News and features relating to all kinds of steam railway throughout the UK.

Comments: Always contact the editor before submitting material.

Approach: By telephone or fax with ideas.

Lead time: One week.

Payment: By arrangement.

Steam World

Apex House
Oundle Road
Peterborough
PE2 9NP

Tel: (0733) 898100   **Fax:** (0733) 894472

Frequency: Monthly

Circulation: 20,000

Contact: Chris Leigh, Editor

Profile: A railway magazine concerned only with historical steam between 1948 and 1968.

Requirements: 1 2
News and features relating to railways during the relevant period. Especially interested in articles on the peripheral areas of steam, or new approaches to established subjects. Length up to 6,000 words.

Comments: Takes a hard, practical view of the subject, concentrating on facts and fine details.

Approach: In writing.

Lead time: Three weeks.

Payment: Negotiable.

Stillwater Trout Angler

IPC Magazines
King's Reach Tower
Stamford Street
London
SE1 9LS

Tel: 071-261 5829   **Fax:** 071-261 6016

Frequency: Monthly

Circulation: 30,202

Contact: Roy Westwood, Editor

Profile: For anyone interested in fishing for trout in lakes and resevoirs throughout the UK.

Requirements: 2
Features on any aspect of stillwater trout angling, from instructional

features and advice to accounts of good fishing locations.

Comments: Contributors should have a good understanding of this particular branch of angling.

Approach: In writing.

Lead time: Two months.

Payment: Negotiable.

The Strad

4th Floor
Centro House
Mandela Street
London
NW1 0DU

Tel: 071-387 3848   **Fax:** 071-388 8532

Frequency: Monthly

Circulation: 60,000

Contact: Helen Wallace, Editor

Profile: A classical music magazine for string players, luthiers and string teachers. Contains news, reviews and features.

Requirements: 2 8
Historical and contemporary profiles, or practical features on string music and the string scene generally. Length up to 2000 words.

Comments: Writers are advised to examine the house style before submitting material.

Approach: By telephone, letter or fax with synopsis.

Lead time: Six weeks.

Payment: £50 per thousand words.

Street Machine

Bushfield House
Orton Centre
Peterborough
PE2 5UW

Tel: (0733) 237111   **Fax:** (0733) 231137

Frequency: Monthly

Circulation: 46,417

Contact: Russ Smith, Editor

Profile: Devoted to custom cars, drag racing and associated wild machinery. Covers the latest cars, what they are like to own and how to build them.

Requirements: 1 2 7
Mostly technical material, preferably accompanied by photos. Anything related to the editorial profile is considered. Relevant news items are often taken from freelances.

Comments: The magazine is Britain's bestselling title in this sector.

Approach: By telephone, letter or fax with ideas.

Lead time: Six weeks.

Payment: £95 per thousand words.

Studio Sound & Broadcast Engineering

8th Floor
Ludgate House
245 Blackfriars Road
London
SE1 9UY

Tel: 071-620 3636   **Fax:** 071-401 8036

Frequency: Monthly

Circulation: 19,114

Contact: Tim Goodyear, Editor

Profile: A professional audio publication circulated to top studios, producers and designers. Read both in the UK and internationally.

Requirements: 2 8
Features on studios, equipment and design, plus other aspects of pro audio. Also reviews of specialist equipment. Length 800 to 3000 words.

1/News **2**/Features **3**/Fiction **4**/Letters **5**/Fillers
6/B&W Photos **7**/Colour Photos **8**/Reviews

Comments: Particularly seeking writers with specialist knowledge of audio-for-video post production.
Approach: By telephone.
Lead time: Four weeks.
Payment: From £100 per thousand words.

Style Magazine

7th Floor
The Plaza Tower
East Kilbride
Glasgow
G74 1LW

Tel: (0355) 246444   **Fax:** (0355) 263013

Frequency: 3xYear

Circulation: 100,000

Contact: Cate Devine, Editor
Profile: A magazine for Style card holders. Aimed primarily at women aged between 30 and 45, typically with two children and control of the household budget.
Requirements: 2 7
Features on homes, interiors, travel, fashion, cookery and film. Length up to 1000 words.
Comments: All material should be geared towards the profile of Style card holders.
Approach: By telephone.
Lead time: Two months.
Payment: £100 per thousand words.

Success

Paper Moon Publishing
2 Holt Cottages
Ashford Hill
Newbury
Berkshire
RG15 8BH

Tel: (0734) 815635   **Fax:** (0734) 810912

Frequency: Bi-monthly
Circulation: 30,000
Contact: Caroline Kirky, Editor
Profile: Designed to help individuals explore and develop their full potential, both in career terms and in their personal life. Aims to raise consciousness to help readers get more from life.
Requirements: 2
Positive, inspiring stories about family subjects such as sports, gardening and travel. All material should provide information that will enable individuals to improve themselves.
Comments: Copy should be lively, upbeat and informative.
Approach: In writing.
Lead time: Three months.
Payment: £100 per thousand words.

Suffolk Life

Barn Acre House
Saxtead Green
Woodbridge
Suffolk
IP13 3QJ

Tel: (0728) 685832   **Fax:** (0728) 685842

Frequency: Monthly

Circulation: 28,000

Contact: Kevin Davis, Editor
Profile: A general consumer and business title for the county of Suffolk. Very broad in scope, covering a wide range of subjects.
Requirements: 2 5 6 7 8
Historical pieces, accounts of walks around interesting areas or buildings, etc. Length around 1000 words.

1/News **2**/Features **3**/Fiction **4**/Letters **5**/Fillers
6/B&W Photos **7**/Colour Photos **8**/Reviews

Comments: Photos to accompany features are always appreciated.
Approach: By telephone or letter.
Lead time: Four weeks.
Payment: £25 per thousand words.

Sunday Express Magazine

Ludgate House
245 Blackfriars Road
London
SE1 9UX

Tel: 071-928 8000   **Fax:** 071-928 7262

Frequency: Weekly

Circulation: 1.65 million

Contact: Jean Carr, Executive Editor
Profile: Colour supplement to the *Sunday Express* newspaper. Aimed at the middle range of the market.
Requirements: 2 6 7
Stylish, aspirational features, international stories and home or fashion articles.
Comments: Material must be considered in terms of the visual dimension.
Approach: By telephone.
Lead time: Four weeks.
Payment: Excellent.

Sunday Mail Magazine

Anderston Quay
Glasgow
G3 8DA

Tel: 041-248 7000   **Fax:** 041-242 3145

Frequency: Monthly

Circulation: 880,958

Contact: Ken Laird, Deputy Editor
Profile: Monthly colour supplement to the *Sunday Mail* newspaper. A general-interest publication aimed primarily at women.

Requirements: 2 3 7
Articles on subjects ranging from pop music to current fashions. Both serious and light-hearted pieces are welcomed.
Comments: Copy should be targeted at a female Scottish reader.
Approach: In writing with complete manuscript.
Lead time: Five weeks.
Payment: Better than NUJ rates.

Sunday Post Magazine

144 Port Dundas Road
Glasgow
G4 0HZ

Tel: 041-332 9933   **Fax:** 041-331 1595

Frequency: Monthly

Circulation: 1.48 million

Contact: Russell Reid, Editor
Profile: A lively colour supplement to the highest-circulation Scottish newspaper.
Requirements: 2 7
Topical, newsy feature articles on subjects of interest to readers north of the border.
Comments: Study the magazine for style and content before sending contributions.
Approach: By letter.
Lead time: Six weeks.
Payment: NUJ or better.

The Sunday Times Magazine

1 Pennington Street
London
E1 9XW

Tel: 071-782 5000   **Fax:** 071-867 0410

Frequency: Weekly

Circulation: 1.15 million

1/News **2**/Features **3**/Fiction **4**/Letters **5**/Fillers
6/B&W Photos **7**/Colour Photos **8**/Reviews

Contact: Julian Brown, Features Editor

Profile: An upmarket, general-interest supplement to the *Sunday Times* newspaper.

Requirements: 2 6 7 8
Profiles of interesting personalities, articles on trends and issues, plus unusual features that would entertain the Sunday morning reader.

Comments: Only material of the highest standard will be considered.

Approach: In writing.

Lead time: Six weeks.

Payment: £250-£300 per thousand words.

Sunrise

9 Wellands Close
Bromley
Kent
BR1 2AQ

Tel: 081-467 8809

Frequency: Monthly

Circulation: 35,000

Contact: Peter Jolly, Editor

Profile: General interest title covering countries in the Middle East.

Requirements: 2 7
Feature articles covering destinations and other subjects of interest in the Middle East. Length up to 1000 words, accompanied where possible by colour photos.

Comments: Contributions from overseas are always welcome.

Approach: By telephone.

Lead time: Two months.

Payment: £100 per thousand words.

Superbike

Link House
Dingwall Avenue
Croydon
CR9 2TA

Tel: 081-686 2599 **Fax:** 081-781 6042

Frequency: Monthly

Circulation: 39,000

Contact: John Cutts

Profile: Aims to promote the pleasures of motor biking while emphasising the need for a sensible approach. Concentrates on the road and racetrack.

Requirements: 1 2 3
News and features on everything except sports events and bike tests. Also accepts original short stories on biking subjects.

Comments: Writers of promise are encouraged, but contributors should be familiar with the magazine's distinctive editorial style.

Approach: In writing with ideas.

Lead time: Six weeks.

Payment: Negotiable.

Superplay

Future Publishing
30 Monmouth Street
Bath
BA1 2BW

Tel: (0225) 442244 **Fax:** (0225) 446019

Frequency: Monthly

Circulation: 60,000

Contact: Matt Bielby, Editor

Profile: A lively magazine for Nintendo console users. For young people aged between 8 and 20, but aimed primarily at 16 year olds.

Requirements: 2 8
Intelligent features of interest to the experienced games player. Also reviews of new products and games. Length 200 to 600 words.

Comments: Contributors do not need to have expert knowledge of the computer games market.

Approach: By telephone with ideas.

Lead time: Six weeks.

Payment: Negotiable.

Surrey County Magazine

PO Box 154
South Croydon
Surrey
CR2 0XA

Tel: 081-657 8568　**Fax:** 081-657 8568

Frequency: Monthly

Circulation: 8000

Contact: Theo Spring, Editor

Profile: A lifestyle magazine for affluent readers throughout the county of Surrey.

Requirements: 1 2 6 7
News and features on life in Surrey, county history, walks and fashion. Length around 1000 words.

Comments: Receives a lot of topical articles which arrive too late for publication.

Approach: By telephone or letter.

Lead time: Six weeks.

Payment: By arrangement.

Surrey Occasions

115 Potters Lane
Send
Near Woking
Surrey
GU23 7AW

Tel: (0483) 750692　**Fax:** (0483) 750692

Frequency: 10xYear

Circulation: 20,000

Contact: Martin Gates, Editor

Profile: A county-oriented lifestyle magazine with an upmarket approach and readership.

Requirements: 1 2 6 7 8
Features on places to visit, local personalities, travel, artists, wine and music. Length from 800 words.

Comments: Articles on places to visit should cover original locations rather than familiar sites.

Approach: By telephone or letter.

Lead time: Two months.

Payment: Negotiable.

Surveyor

Room 1504
Quadrant House
The Quadrant
Sutton
Surrey
SM2 5AS

Tel: 081-652 4881　**Fax:** 081-652 4898

Frequency: Weekly

Circulation: 10,314

Contact: Rick Pendrous, Features Editor

Profile: Concerned with the management and economics of infrastructure and road construction. Read principally by local authority engineers.

Requirements: 1 2 6 7
Technical information on all aspects of highways and waterworks, transport, treatment and urban renewal. Length 1000 to 1500 words.

Comments: Articles tied into the magazine's features list have the best chance of success.

1/News **2**/Features **3**/Fiction **4**/Letters **5**/Fillers
6/B&W Photos **7**/Colour Photos **8**/Reviews

Approach: By telephone.
Lead time: Three weeks.
Payment: Negotiable.

Sussex Life

30a Teville Road
Worthing
West Sussex
BN11 1UG

Tel: (0903) 204628   **Fax:** (0903) 820193

Frequency: Monthly

Circulation: 55,000

Contact: Trudi Linscer

Profile: A county magazine aimed
primarily at women living in Sussex.
Readers tend to be intelligent,
affluent and aged over 30.

Requirements: 2 3 6 7
Features on health, history and
matters relating to Sussex lifestyle.
May consider fiction. Length up to
1000 words.

Comments: Short, concise pieces are
preferred, although the magazine is
very open to ideas.

Approach: By letter.

Lead time: Three months.

Payment: £50 per article.

Swimming Times

Harold Fern House
Derby Square
Loughborough
Leicestershire
LE11 0AL

Tel: (0509) 234433   **Fax:** (0509) 235049

Frequency: Monthly

Circulation: 17,079

Contact: Karren Glendenning, Editor

Profile: Provides coverage of national
and international major swimming
events. Also general articles on the
four main aquatic disciplines.

Requirements: 2
Would consider technical articles on
all aspects of swimming, diving,
synchronised swimming and water
polo.

Comments: Articles should be aimed at
the teaching or coaching level.

Approach: By letter with initial ideas.

Lead time: Two months.

Payment: By negotiation.

T

Take a Break

H. Bauer Publishing
25-27 Camden Road
London
NW1 9LL

Tel: 071-284 0909   **Fax:** 071-284 3778

Frequency: Weekly

Circulation: 1.4 million

Contact: John Dale, Editor

Profile: A women's weekly that aims to involve the reader by running puzzles, crosswords, etc. Currently the best-selling magazine in the UK, aimed mainly at women in the home.

Requirements: 2 3 4 5
Personal experiences of an emotional nature, and dramatic true stories. Short stories with a strong, sharp plot are also used. Length up to 1000 words. Accepts a large number of filler items, and pays for reader's letters.

Comments: Always welcomes unusual or dramatic true-life stories.

Approach: In writing.

Lead time: Four weeks.

Payment: £100 per article, £10 per filler.

Target Gun

Peterson House
Northbank
Berryhill Industrial Estate
Droitwich
Worcestershire
WR9 9BL

Tel: (0905) 795564   **Fax:** (0905) 795905

Frequency: Monthly

Circulation: 22,500

Contact: Richard Atkins, Editor

Profile: A specialist target-shooting magazine that covers all disciplines of the hobby. Caters for both pistol and rifle users, but leans towards hand guns.

Requirements: 2 6 7 8
Practical, technical features that will help readers to improve their skills. Also event reports from those involved, plus articles on gunsmithing, coaching, etc.

Comments: Aims to encourage people to take up shooting. Short, concise pieces are always valuable.

Approach: By telephone or letter with ideas.

Lead time: Ten weeks.

Payment: From £30 per page.

1/News **2**/Features **3**/Fiction **4**/Letters **5**/Fillers
6/B&W Photos **7**/Colour Photos **8**/Reviews

Taste

HHL Publications Ltd
Greater London House
Hampstead Road
London
NW1 7QQ

Tel: 071-388 3171   **Fax:** 071-377 4890

Frequency: 10xYear

Circulation: 35,000

Contact: Emma Bland

Profile: A food and drink magazine for cooks, chefs and others in the trade.

Requirements: 1 2 7
Original and imaginative material on food or cooking styles. Also news of relevant new products and developments. Length up to 2000 words.

Comments: Contributions must be accurate and well-researched.

Approach: By letter with ideas.

Lead time: Two months.

Payment: Around £165 per thousand words.

The Tatler

Vogue House
Hanover Square
London
W1R 0AD

Tel: 071-499 9080   **Fax:** 071-409 0451

Frequency: Monthly

Circulation: 73,000

Contact: Geffany Calkin, Features Editor

Profile: A glossy, upmarket lifestyle magazine. Runs features on important and interesting people, fashion etc.

Requirements: 2 7 8
Ideas for feature articles that will interest the readership. Profiles of national or international personalities, etc. Length around 1500 words.

Comments: Unsolicited articles are rarely used, but promising writers with good ideas will be commissioned.

Approach: By letter with ideas and examples of previous work.

Lead time: Three months.

Payment: Negotiable.

Taxi Globe

59 Reading Lane
Hackney
London
E8 1DY

Tel: 071-275 9846   **Fax:** 071-275 9864

Frequency: Fortnightly

Circulation: 18,000

Contact: Ernest Keates, Editor

Profile: A newspaper for the licensed taxi trade. Concerned with all trade matters plus associated industries.

Requirements: 2 6 7
Will consider all material relevant to the tourist trade, entertainment, etc.

Comments: Especially interested in taxis overseas.

Approach: In writing with proposals.

Lead time: Four weeks.

Payment: Negotiable.

Taxi Newspaper

Taxi House
Woodfield Road
London
W9 2BA

Tel: 071-286 2728   **Fax:** 071-286 2494

1/News 2/Features 3/Fiction 4/Letters 5/Fillers
6/B&W Photos 7/Colour Photos 8/Reviews

Frequency: Fortnightly

Circulation: 25,000

Contact: Stuart Pessok

Profile: Provides information and news related to the licensed taxi trade throughout the UK. Also covers leisure activities, reviews and competitions.

Requirements: 1 2 5 6 7

Articles on the taxi business, especially from outside Britain. Length up to 1500 words. Photographs to accompany features are always appreciated.

Comments: Particularly interested in the political aspects of taxi networks internationally.

Approach: By telephone with ideas.

Lead time: Six weeks.

Payment: From £40 per thousand words.

The Tea Club Magazine

PO Box 221
Guildford
Surrey
GU1 3YT

Tel: (0483) 628888   **Fax:** (0483) 302732

Frequency: 3xYear

Circulation: Not available

Contact: Lorna Swainson, Editor

Profile: Dedicated to the particular interests of readers 'addicted' to tea.

Requirements: 1 2 4 5 6 8

Any material on the history, rituals, customs, growing, blending and distribution of tea. Maximum length 2000 words.

Comments: Also interested in articles on tea 'paraphernalia'.

Approach: In writing with initial ideas.

Lead time: Two months.

Payment: Up to £100 per thousand words.

Team

22-24 Worple Road
London
SW19 4DD

Tel: 081-947 3131   **Fax:** 081-944 6139

Frequency: 2xYear

Circulation: 50,000

Contact: Sharon Watson, Editor

Profile: A women's magazine for trade union members in the food, drink, hotels and leisure industries.

Requirements: 1 2 5 7 8

Food features, consumer articles and people profiles, together with colour transparencies. Length up to 1000 words.

Comments: Copy on disk preferred.

Approach: By letter or telephone.

Lead time: Four weeks.

Payment: NUJ rates.

Team Talk

Football Directories
North Curry
Taunton
Somerset
TA3 6DU

Tel: (0823) 490469   **Fax:** (0823) 490281

Frequency: Monthly

Circulation: 30,000

Contact: Steve Whitney, Editor

Profile: Covers the world of non-league football for players and fans.

Requirements: 1 2 4 5 6 7 8

Articles on the non-league game from grass roots level up to the

---

1/News 2/Features 3/Fiction 4/Letters 5/Fillers
6/B&W Photos 7/Colour Photos 8/Reviews

conference league. Also features on women's football, schools and youth games.

Comments: Profiles of clubs, players and managers are always welcome.

Approach: By telephone or letter with ideas.

Lead time: Two weeks.

Payment: Negotiable.

Television

Royal Television Society
Holborn Hall
100 Gray's Inn Road
London
WC1X 8AL

Tel: 071-430 1000   **Fax:** 071-430 0924

Frequency: 8xYear

Circulation: 4000

Contact: Louise Bishop, Deputy Editor

Profile: Examines current topics of debate in the sphere of television.

Requirements: 2

Feature articles on the art, science and politics of television. All material should be of interest to those working in the industry. Length up to 1000 words.

Comments: The magazine is not read by a consumer audience.

Approach: By telephone with ideas.

Lead time: Six weeks.

Payment: £150 per thousand words.

Televisual

50 Poland Street
London
W1V 4AX

Tel: 071-379 4222   **Fax:** 071-287 0768

Frequency: Monthly

Circulation: 8,000

Contact: The Editor

Profile: A features-based magazine read mainly by executives and broadcasters in independent TV production companies.

Requirements: 2

Features relating to future events and developments in broadcasting, especially programme production.

Comments: Contributors must have a good understanding of the industry.

Approach: By letter or fax with ideas.

Lead time: Six weeks.

Payment: £150 per thousand words.

Tempo

Boosey & Hawkes
295 Regent Street
London
W1R 8JH

Tel: 071-580 2060   **Fax:** 071-436 5675

Frequency: Quarterly

Circulation: Not available

Contact: The Editor

Profile: For performing musicians and serious amateurs. Provides an overview of contemporary, formal music.

Requirements: 2

Informed and informative articles on all aspects of 20th century music. Length 2000 to 4000 words.

Comments: Contributors should study the publication before submitting material.

Approach: In writing.

Lead time: Four months.

Payment: By negotiation.

Tennis World

The Spendlove Centre
Enstone Road
Charlbury Oxon
OX7 3PQ

Tel: (0608) 811446   **Fax:** (0608) 811380

Frequency: Monthly

Circulation: 11,500

Contact: Alastair McIver
Profile: Provides comprehensive coverage of the world of international tennis.
Requirements: 1 2
Tournament reports and interviews with players, plus features on current affairs in tennis.
Comments: The magazine has a strong international flavour.
Approach: By telephone.
Lead time: Four weeks.
Payment: Approx. NUJ rates.

Textile Horizons International

Benjamin Dent Publications
Eastern Boulevard
Leicester
LE2 7BN

Tel: (0533) 548271   **Fax:** (0533) 470194

Frequency: Bi-monthly

Circulation: 10,000

Contact: John Gibbon, Editor
Profile: A magazine for marketing, management, production and design staff in the textile industry. Covers yarns, fabrics, garments, etc.
Requirements: 1 2 6 7
Informative articles on technical or management subjects, accompanied by pictures, tables or charts where appropriate. Length 750 to 3000 words.

Comments: Technical articles on manufacturing are always welcome.
Approach: In writing with ideas.
Lead time: Six weeks.
Payment: From £90 per thousand words.

This Caring Business

1 St Thomas's Road
Hastings
East Sussex
TN34 3LG

Tel: (0424) 718406   **Fax:** (0424) 718460

Frequency: 10xYear

Circulation: 17,503

Contact: Michael Monk
Profile: A trade periodical for those concerned with the private and voluntary sectors of long-term care and short-stay private hospitals.
Requirements: 1 2
Business-oriented articles relating to property, mortgages, operating costs and legislative matters connected with patient care.
Comments: This is a business publication for administrators and managers, not a medical or nursing journal.
Approach: By telephone.
Lead time: Two months.
Payment: £75 per thousand words.

This England

PO Box 52
Cheltenham
Gloucestershire
GL50 1YQ

Tel: (0242) 577775   **Fax:** (0242) 222034

Frequency: Quarterly

Circulation: 172,500

Contact: Roy Faiers, Editor
Profile: For those interested in English heritage, providing a nostalgic and reflective view of all things English.
Requirements: 2 5 6 7
Features on English customs, traditions and history, etc. Length up to 2000 words. Also filler items of up to 300 words, poetry and nostalgic pieces.
Comments: Contributions should reflect the traditional style and content of the magazine.
Approach: In writing.
Lead time: Three months.
Payment: By arrangement.

Titbits

2 Caversham Street
London
SW3 4AH

Tel: 071-351 4995   **Fax:** 071-351 4995
Frequency: Monthly
Circulation: 150,000
Contact: James Hughes, Features Editor
Profile: A general-interest magazine for men, covering show business, leisure, etc.
Requirements: 1 2 3 5 7 8
Exposés and investigative features, plus articles on travel, celebrities and other subjects of interest to men. Maximum length 2500 words.
Comments: Always contact the editor before submitting material.
Approach: In writing with ideas.
Lead time: Ten weeks.
Payment: Negotiable.

Today's Golfer

EMAP Pursuit Publishing Ltd
Bretton Court
Bretton Centre
Peterborough
PE3 8DZ

Tel: (0733) 264666   **Fax:** (0733) 265515
Frequency: Monthly
Circulation: 86,000
Contact: Martin Vousden, Deputy Editor
Profile: A golfing title that concentrates on instruction, star players and courses.
Requirements: 1 2 3 7
General features on golf, especially humorous or off-beat material. Also profiles of players and details of courses to play. Maximum 2500 words.
Comments: Guidelines for contributors are available on request.
Approach: By telephone.
Lead time: Six weeks.
Payment: Around £100 per thousand words.

Today's Runner

EMAP Pursuit Publishing Ltd
Bretton Court
Bretton Centre
Peterborough
PE3 8DZ

Tel: (0733) 264666   **Fax:** (0733) 265515
Frequency: Monthly
Circulation: 28,000
Contact: Allan Haines, Editor
Profile: For both the beginner and the experienced club runner, covering road, fell and cross-country running.

1/News **2**/Features **3**/Fiction **4**/Letters **5**/Fillers
6/B&W Photos **7**/Colour Photos **8**/Reviews

Requirements: 2 3 7

Humorous or instructional features, plus interviews with personalities. Length 500 to 1000 words.

Comments: Copy needs to be topical and easy to read, ideally accompanied by pictures.

Approach: By telephone with ideas.

Lead time: Seven weeks.

Payment: £60-£70 per thousand words.

Top Car

Argosy House
161 High Street
Orpington
Kent
BR6 0LW

Tel: (0689) 874025   **Fax:** (0689) 896847

Frequency: Monthly

Circulation: 40,000

Contact: Tony Middlehurst, Editor

Profile: A light-hearted but authoritative title concerned with modified cars. Aspirational in style.

Requirements: 2 5

Technical material that does not assume a great deal of relevant knowledge. Also general features that would not otherwise be covered by the editorial staff.

Comments: Unsolicited manuscripts will be accepted if submitted on Mac-compatible disk.

Approach: Best to send a synopsis by fax.

Lead time: Six weeks.

Payment: £100 per thousand words.

Top Rail

BLA Business Publications
2 Duncan Terrace
London
N1 8BZ

Tel: 071-833 0519   **Fax:** 071-278 6246

Frequency: Quarterly

Circulation: 200,000

Contact: Andrew Sanger, Editor

Profile: A travel magazine for users and potential users of the French railway system. Distributed to homes and individuals in the UK.

Requirements: 2 6 7

Feature articles about people and places in France, Germany, Italy or Spain. Articles should be between 800 and 1500 words, and photos are appreciated when available.

Comments: Interviews with appropriate celebrities are particularly welcome.

Approach: In writing with ideas and examples of previous work.

Lead time: Three months.

Payment: By arrangement.

Topics

Compass House
80 Newmarket Road
Cambridge
CB5 8DZ

Tel: (0223) 315944   **Fax:** (0223) 322565

Frequency: Quarterly

Circulation: 2000

Contact: Bronwen Rees, Editor

Profile: A specialist title for human resource professionals and general managers.

1/News **2**/Features **3**/Fiction **4**/Letters **5**/Fillers
6/B&W Photos **7**/Colour Photos **8**/Reviews

Requirements: 2 6 8
Feature articles on all aspects of human resource management. Also case studies, training material and book reviews. Length up to 3000 words.
Comments: Study the publication before contributing material.
Approach: In writing.
Lead time: Six weeks.
Payment: Negotiable.

Total Fitness Magazine

260 Great North Road
Woodlands
Doncaster
DN6 7HP

Tel: (0302) 722213   **Fax:** (0302) 725687

Frequency: Bi-monthly

Circulation: 50,000

Contact: Roger Byrne, Managing Editor
Profile: Covers fitness and associated activities relative to an active lifestyle. Includes health, beauty, fashion, holidays, aerobics and careers.
Requirements: 2 6 7
Articles relating to any area of health and beauty. Particularly welcomes features on specific areas such as reflexology, careers, aromatherapy, cycling, etc. Length around 1000 words.
Comments: Articles should be well-researched and authoritative, appealing to the wide 'active lifestyle' market.
Approach: By telephone with ideas.
Lead time: Six weeks.
Payment: £50 per thousand words.

Touchdown

Garnett Dickinson Publishing
Eastwood Works
Fitzwilliam Road
Rotherham
S65 1JU

Tel: (0709) 364721   **Fax:** (0709) 820588

Frequency: Monthly

Circulation: 15,000

Contact: N. Alexander
Profile: Provides coverage of American football, based around the NFL. For readers who are very interested in the sport and associated statistics.
Requirements: 1 2
News and features on subjects relating to the game, its teams and players. Length up to 1000 words.
Comments: Off-beat material is always appreciated.
Approach: By telephone.
Lead time: Four weeks.
Payment: £30 per thousand words.

Toy Trader

Turret House
171 High Street
Rickmansworth
Hertfordshire
WD3 1SN

Tel: (0923) 777000   **Fax:** (0923) 771297

Frequency: Monthly

Circulation: 6500

Contact: Neil Nixon, Editor
Profile: A trade publication distributed to manufacturers, retailers and wholesalers in the toy business.
Requirements: 1 2
News of developments in the toy trade and features of interest to those who produce or sell toy products.

1/News **2**/Features **3**/Fiction **4**/Letters **5**/Fillers
6/B&W Photos **7**/Colour Photos **8**/Reviews

Comments: Deals with trade rather than consumer issues.
Approach: In writing.
Lead time: Six weeks.
Payment: By arrangement.

Trailfinder

9 Abingdon Road
London
W8 6AH

Tel: 071-937 7933   **Fax:** 071-937 6059

Frequency: 3xYear

Circulation: 250,000

Contact: G. Hunt, Editor

Profile: An independent travel magazine covering long-haul destinations. Aims to encourage travellers to visit regions overseas.
Requirements: 2
  Travel articles on destinations in Australia, New Zealand, Asia and North America. Length 700 to 800 words.
Comments: Does not cover adventure travel.
Approach: In writing with ideas.
Lead time: Three months.
Payment: £80 per article.

Trail Walker

EMAP Pursuit Publishing Ltd
Bretton Court
Bretton Centre
Peterborough
PE3 8DZ

Tel: (0733) 264666   **Fax:** (0733) 265515

Frequency: Monthly

Circulation: 24,000

Contact: David Ogle, Editor

Profile: A magazine for the adventurous walker. Covers walking and backpacking both in the UK and overseas.
Requirements: 2 7
  Articles on suggested weekend walks, including route descriptions. Also features on longer, more adventurous walks. Length 750 to 2000 words.
Comments: Concentrates mainly on locations within the UK.
Approach: By telephone or letter with ideas.
Lead time: Two months.
Payment: £40 per thousand words.

Transport

35-39 Castle Street
High Wycombe
Buckinghamshire
HP13 6RN

Tel: (0494) 450054   **Fax:** (0494) 450836

Frequency: Bi-monthly

Circulation: 16,000

Contact: Malory Davies, Editor

Profile: Distributed free of charge to members of the Chartered Institute of Transport.
Requirements: 2 6 7
  Articles on matters concerned with transport of every kind. Length between 1000 and 2000 words.
Comments: Welcomes photographs to accompany features.
Approach: In writing.
Lead time: Three months.
Payment: £120 per thousand words.

Travel & Leisure Magazine

301 Channel Sea Centre
Abbey Lane
Stratford
E15 3ND

Tel: 081-519 8488   **Fax:** 081-555 0061

Frequency: Quarterly

Circulation: 60,000

Contact: Simon Deane, Editor

Profile: Provides comprehensive coverage of travel destinations, holidays and leisure activities.

Requirements: 2 7 8
Feature articles based on unusual or particularly interesting holiday areas or leisure activities. Maximum length 1000 words.

Comments: Study the magazine before contributing.

Approach: In writing with ideas.

Lead time: Four weeks.

Payment: £50 per thousand words.

Travel Club

Morgan Grampian House
Calderwood Street
London
SE18 6QH

Tel: 081-855 7777   **Fax:** 081-316 3938

Frequency: Quarterly

Circulation: Not available

Contact: Howard Carr, Editor

Profile: A magazine for younger travel agency staff, typically women aged between 18 and 35.

Requirements: 2 5
Features on general-interest subjects such as film, TV, pop etc. Length up to 1000 words.

Comments: Bear in mind that this is essentially a trade magazine.

Approach: In writing.

Lead time: Three months.

Payment: Negotiable.

Travel UK

Unit 5
The Edge Business Centre
Humber Road
London
NW2 6EW

Tel: 081-208 2046   **Fax:** 081-208 2058

Frequency: Quarterly

Circulation: Not disclosed

Contact: Alan Jamieson, Editor

Profile: Aims to encourage people to take holidays in the UK. Read by British citizens who would normally travel abroad, but who are now looking to save money or explore territory closer to home.

Requirements: 1 2
News and features on interesting holiday breaks in less well-known parts of the UK, plus interviews with celebrities who holiday at home.

Comments: Aim to write for the 'mum' at home who may be considering a second holiday for the family.

Approach: In writing.

Lead time: Three months.

Payment: By negotiation.

Traveller

45-49 Brompton Road
London
SW3 1DE

Tel: 071-581 4130   **Fax:** 071-581 1357

Frequency: Quarterly

Circulation: 35,000

1/News **2**/Features **3**/Fiction **4**/Letters **5**/Fillers
6/B&W Photos **7**/Colour Photos **8**/Reviews

Contact: Caroline Brandenburger,
Managing Editor
Profile: A wide-ranging travel
magazine which focuses mainly on
areas outside Western Europe.
Requirements: 2 7
Strong material based around quirky
ideas or unusual subjects.
Particularly interested in
ethnographic angles. Maximum 2000
words.
Comments: Does not want accounts of
people's trips or holidays.
Approach: By telephone or letter with
ideas. Alternatively complete
manuscript with pictures.
Lead time: Three months.
Payment: £125 per thousand words.

Treasure Hunting

Greenlight Publishing
Hatfield Peverel
Essex
CM3 2HF

Tel: (0245) 381011   **Fax:** (0245) 381950

Frequency: Monthly

Circulation: 15,000

Contact: Greg Payne, Editor
Profile: Covers all aspects of treasure
hunting, but mainly concerned with
the hobby use of metal detectors.
Requirements: 1 2 5 6 7
Specific features on archaeology,
local history or the use of metal
detectors. Length 1000 to 3000
words. Also news stories of 300 to
1000 words.
Comments: If you are not an
enthusiast, contact a detector club to
acquire the information you need.
Approach: By telephone with ideas.
Lead time: Six weeks.
Payment: By arrangement.

Triangle

Youth Hostels Association
Trevelyan House
8 St Stephen's Hill
St Albans
Hertfordshire
AL1 2DY

Tel: (0727) 855215   **Fax:** (0727) 844126

Frequency: 3xYear

Circulation: 300,000

Contact: Helen Barnes, Editor
Profile: A travel magazine for
members of the Youth Hostel
Association, providing coverage
both in the UK and internationally.
Requirements: 2 5 7
Travel articles on off-beat or
unusual subjects and destinations
anywhere in the world. Length up to
1000 words.
Comments: Aim to emulate the style
generally used for articles in the
magazine.
Approach: By telephone.
Lead time: Four months.
Payment: Negotiable.

Trout and Salmon

EMAP Pursuit Publishing Ltd
Bretton Court
Bretton Centre
Peterborough
PE3 8DZ

Tel: (0733) 264666   **Fax:** (0733) 265515

Frequency: Monthly

Circulation: 50,404

Contact: Sandy Leventon, Editor
Profile: A specialist title for anyone
interested in game fishing.
Requirements: 2
Features relating to any aspect of
fishing for trout or salmon. Material

should be practical and informative in content.

Comments: Contributors should have a good understanding of the subject.
Approach: In writing.
Lead time: Two months.
Payment: Negotiable.

Trout Fisherman

EMAP Pursuit Publishing Ltd
Bretton Court
Bretton Centre
Peterborough
PE3 8DZ

Tel: (0733) 264666   **Fax:** (0733) 265515

Frequency: Monthly

Circulation: 42,000

Contact: Chris Dawn, Editor
Profile: For enthusiasts of stillwater trout fishing, covering both shore and boat fishing.
Requirements: 2 6 7
Articles on techniques, locations and fly-tying, aimed at either the beginner or the more experienced fisherman. Particularly looking for articles that apply a new angle to an old theme, especially if accompanied by pictures. Length up to 1500 words.
Comments: Articles should be broken down with subheads.
Approach: By telephone.
Lead time: Two months.
Payment: Negotiable.

Trucking International

Central House
162 Southgate Street
Gloucester
GL1 2EX

Tel: (0452) 307181   **Fax:** (0452) 307170

Frequency: Monthly
Circulation: 35,897

Contact: Stewart Brown, Editor
Profile: A magazine for lorry drivers, owner-drivers and managers of small fleets of trucks.
Requirements: 1 2
News and features on all subjects related to trucking. Copy must be detailed and accurate yet clear and consistent in style.
Comments: Study the magazine carefully before contributing.
Approach: By letter or fax.
Lead time: Two months.
Payment: By arrangement.

TV Hits

4 Tottenham Mews
London
W1P 9PJ

Tel: 071-436 5565   **Fax:** 071-436 5277

Frequency: Monthly

Circulation: 156,685

Contact: Pauline Haldane, Editor
Profile: A lively magazine for teenagers. Concentrates on music, TV, film, etc.
Requirements: 1 2 7 8
News and features relating to subjects of interest to teenagers. Particularly interested in celebrity-based features.
Comments: Study the style of the magazine before sending contributions.
Approach: In writing.
Lead time: Four weeks.
Payment: NUJ rates.

1/News **2**/Features **3**/Fiction **4**/Letters **5**/Fillers
6/B&W Photos **7**/Colour Photos **8**/Reviews

TV Quick

25-27 Camden Road
London
NW1 9LL

Tel: 071-284 0909   **Fax:** 071-284 4707

Frequency: Weekly

Circulation: 709,000

Contact: Lori Miles, Editor

Profile: A TV listings magazine covering both broadcast and satellite TV channels. Also runs features and interviews.

Requirements: 2 5
Gossip and features relating to TV subjects and personalities, plus very strong stories on personal subjects. Length up to 1200 words.

Comments: Writers with new and original ideas will have the best chance of success.

Approach: In writing.

Lead time: Three weeks.

Payment: Negotiable.

TV Zone

PO Box 371
London
SW14 8JL

Tel: 081-878 5486   **Fax:** 081-876 9455

Frequency: Monthly

Circulation: 30,000

Contact: Jan Vincent-Rudzki, Editor

Profile: Devoted to covering cult science fiction programmes on television.

Requirements: 2 6 7
Feature articles about the stars, producers, directors and others associated with sci-fi on TV. Length according to the importance of the subject.

Comments: Study the magazine before contributing material.

Approach: In writing with ideas and examples of previous work.

Lead time: Four weeks.

Payment: Negotiable.

Twinkle

D.C. Thomson & Co Ltd
Albert Square
Dundee
DD1 9QJ

Tel: (0382) 23131   **Fax:** (0382) 22214

Frequency: Weekly

Circulation: Not available

Contact: David Robertson, Editor

Profile: A picture-story magazine for girls aged between 3 and 7 years old. Also runs competitions, puzzles, etc.

Requirements: 3
Scripts for picture stories based on the established characters owned by the publishers. These should be simple but original, with the text able to stand independently of the pictures. Also brief (up to 400 words) text-only short stories based on animals, etc.

Comments: As a large number of stories have already been written about the standard characters, writers will need to find a different angle.

Approach: In writing with examples.

Lead time: Four weeks.

Payment: Negotiable.

220

Newstead Press
PO Box 613
Swindon
SN1 4TA

1/News 2/Features 3/Fiction 4/Letters 5/Fillers
6/B&W Photos 7/Colour Photos 8/Reviews

Tel: (0793) 533713   **Fax:** (0793) 481103

Frequency: Monthly

Circulation: 10,000

Contact: Janet Smith, Editor

Profile: Covers national and international triathlon and duathlon races. Includes reports of events, training information and reviews of equipment.

Requirements: 1 2
Race and technical features. Also articles on the individual disciplines of swimming, cycling and running. Length up to 1600 words.

Comments: All submissions are given serious consideration.

Approach: In writing with ideas or complete manuscript.

Lead time: Six weeks.

Payment: £50 per thousand words for commissioned features.

U

Under Five Contact

20 Beechwood Crescent
Chandlers Ford
Hampshire
SO5 1PA

Tel: (0703) 254063

Frequency: 10xYear

Circulation: 22,000

Contact: Mrs A. Henderson, Editor

Profile: Offers practical advice and support for people working in pre-school groups. Also read by parents and carers bringing up children.

Requirements: 2 6 7
Features on children's play and learning activities, plus information on child development generally. Maximum 2000 words.

Comments: Material needs to be accessible without being over simplified.

Approach: By telephone with ideas.

Lead time: Three months.

Payment: Up to £50.

Undercover

Unit 5
Shepley Industrial Estate North
Shepley Road
Audenshaw
Manchester
M34 5DR

Tel: 061-337 8995   **Fax:** 061-337 8995

Frequency: Bi-monthly

Circulation: Not available

Contact: Brian Clarke, Editor

Profile: Aims to expose and discuss espionage and covert operations, plus conspiracies and international intelligence.

Requirements: 2
Features explaining the story behind political or international events, exposing intrigue or coverups. Long features can be split over two issues.

Comments: Writers do not need to be investigative journalists to contribute to the magazine.

Approach: In writing.

Lead time: Three months.

Payment: £30 per thousand words.

Used Bike Guide

PO Box 10
Whitchurch
Shropshire
SY13 1ZZ

Tel: 061-928 3480   **Fax:** 061-941 6897

Frequency: Monthly

Circulation: 24,936

Contact: Frank Westworth, Editor

Profile: A practical guide for those interested in second-hand motorbikes. All about buying and running used bikes on a budget.

1/News **2**/Features **3**/Fiction **4**/Letters **5**/Fillers
6/B&W Photos **7**/Colour Photos **8**/Reviews

Requirements: 2 6 7

Riders' personal experiences of owning and riding particular machines. Length from 1000 to 1400 words.

Comments: Photographs to accompany features are always welcome.

Approach: Submit complete manuscript.

Lead time: Four weeks.

Payment: £25 per thousand words.

V

Vanity Fair

Vogue House
Hanover Square
London
W1R 0AD

Tel: 071-499 9080   **Fax:** 071-499 4415

Frequency: Monthly

Circulation: 70,243

Contact: Henry Porter, Editor

Profile: A glossy, upmarket magazine for affluent, intelligent readers.

Requirements: 2
Features on style and fashion, the media and political issues.

Comments: Writers should study the magazine before contributing.

Approach: In writing.

Lead time: Two months.

Payment: By negotiation.

Video Camera

IPC Magazines
King's Reach Tower
Stamford Street
London
SE1 9LS

Tel: 071-261 5633   **Fax:** 071-261 6050

Frequency: Monthly

Circulation: 25,000

Contact: Chris George, Editor

Profile: For the hobbyist and enthusiast, covering all aspects of buying and using video recorders.

Requirements: 1 2
Technical and instructional articles, reviews of equipment, news and information about new products.

Comments: Writers should consider the visual dimension when writing.

Approach: By letter or fax with ideas.

Lead time: Two months.

Payment: Negotiable.

Video Home Entertainment

Strandgate
18-20 York Buildings
London
WC2N 6JU

Tel: 071-839 7774   **Fax:** 071-839 4393

Frequency: Weekly

Circulation: 9500

Contact: Sean King, Editor

Profile: A trade publication for the video rental and retailing business. Also encompasses video and computer games.

Requirements: 1 2 8
News of developments in the video industry, and other features of interest to those in the trade.

Comments: This is a business publication, not a consumer video magazine.

1/News 2/Features 3/Fiction 4/Letters 5/Fillers
6/B&W Photos 7/Colour Photos 8/Reviews

Approach: By telephone.
Lead time: Four weeks.
Payment: £100 per thousand words.

Video – The Magazine

Unit 1
Raans Road
Amersham
Buckinghamshire
HP6 6LX

Tel: (0494) 432433   **Fax:** (0494) 432572

Frequency: Monthly

Circulation: 30,000

Contact: Alan Walsh, Editor
Profile: An informal, chatty magazine that covers all the major video releases, for both rental and purchase. Aimed primarily at the 15 to 35 age group.
Requirements: 1 2
Features on different types of video, ranging from sport to foreign language tuition. Also interviews and profiles with relevant personalities. Length up to 1000 words.
Comments: Does not accept reviews from freelance contributors.
Approach: In writing with examples of previous work.
Lead time: Six weeks.
Payment: £75 per thousand words.

Video World

PO Box 381
Millharbour
London
E14 9TW

Tel: 071-987 5090   **Fax:** 071-987 2160

Frequency: Monthly

Circulation: 32,000

Contact: Alan Bryce, Editor
Profile: Provides comprehensive coverage of the world of film and video.
Requirements: 2 6 7 8
Interviews and features based on film personalities, or articles on any other relevant subject. Length up to 2000 words.
Comments: Photographs are always welcome.
Approach: By letter with ideas.
Lead time: Three months.
Payment: £100 per thousand words.

Vintage Roadscene

40 Fairfield Way
Ewell
Epsom
Surrey
KT19 0EF

Tel: 081-394 1542   **Fax:** 081-394 1542

Frequency: Quarterly

Circulation: 11,500

Contact: S.W. Stevens-Stratten, Editor
Profile: A specialist title for enthusiasts of vintage and veteran trucks and buses.
Requirements: 2 6 7
Articles with a technical bias covering historical lorries, vans, buses, trolleybuses and trams. Also features by old drivers reminiscing on their experiences.
Comments: Does not require reports of vehicle rallies or 'newspaper' type stories.
Approach: In writing with ideas.
Lead time: Six weeks.
Payment: £20 per thousand words.

1/News **2**/Features **3**/Fiction **4**/Letters **5**/Fillers
6/B&W Photos **7**/Colour Photos **8**/Reviews

Visitor

30 Princes Street
Yeovil
Somerset
BA20 1EQ

Tel: (0935) 411030 **Fax:** (0935) 411026

Frequency: Monthly

Circulation: 31,500

Contact: The Editor

Profile: A free-distribution magazine that covers current affairs, news and views.

Requirements: 2 6 7
Features on a wide range of general-interest subjects. Humorous, relevant and topical articles are likely to be well received. Length around 800 words.

Comments: All submissions are given serious consideration.

Approach: By telephone or letter with ideas.

Lead time: Two weeks.

Payment: By arrangement.

Vogue

Vogue House
Hanover Square
London
W1R 0AD

Tel: 071-499 9080 **Fax:** 071-408 0559

Frequency: Monthly

Circulation: 186,126

Contact: Alexandra Shulman, Editor

Profile: An upmarket glossy that focuses mainly on fashion, but also includes some cultural material.

Requirements: 2 6 7 8
Highbrow features on subjects such as art, film, music, actors and design. Also material on travel and home interest topics. Length 500 to 3000 words.

Comments: Does not accept unsolicited manuscripts, but will commission promising writers.

Approach: In writing with ideas.

Lead time: Three months.

Payment: Negotiable.

The Voice

370 Coldharbour Lane
Brixton
London
SW9 8PL

Tel: 071-737 7377 **Fax:** 071-274 8994

Frequency: Weekly

Circulation: 50,000

Contact: The Editor

Profile: A national news weekly for the Caribbean, African and Asian population in the UK.

Requirements: 1 2 5 6 7 8
News and features on any subject of especial interest to the black community. Also welcomes features on art and entertainment for a lifestyle supplement. Length up to 2000 words.

Comments: Covers international as well as UK-based stories.

Approach: By letter with ideas.

Lead time: Two weeks.

Payment: £100 per thousand words.

Vox

25th Floor
IPC Magazines
King's Reach Tower
Stamford Street
London
SE1 9LS

Tel: 071-261 6312 **Fax:** 071-261 5627

1/News **2**/Features **3**/Fiction **4**/Letters **5**/Fillers
6/B&W Photos **7**/Colour Photos **8**/Reviews

Frequency: Monthly

Circulation: 107,000

Contact: Mal Peachey, Features Editor

Profile: A broad-based rock magazine, covering a very wide cross-section of music.

Requirements: 2 6 7 8
Interviews with musicians or bands, plus very strong features on general rock subjects. Length about 1500 words. Also reviews of new releases.

Comments: Readers should enjoy the music they are writing about.

Approach: By letter or fax with ideas.

Lead time: Six weeks.

Payment: £100-£125 per thousand words.

W

Warship

101 Fleet Street
London
EC4Y 1DE

Tel: 071-583 2412   **Fax:** 071-936 2153

Frequency: 1xYear

Circulation: 5000

Contact: Robert Gardiner, Editor

Profile: Concerned with the design, development and service history of warships.

Requirements: 2 6 8
Well-researched historical articles on combat ships, emphasising technical matters. Length preferably under 5000 words, but possibly up to 8000.

Comments: Very little contemporary material used.

Approach: In writing.

Lead time: Nine months.

Payment: Negotiable.

Waterways World

Waterway Productions Ltd
Kottingham House
Dale Street
Burton-on-Trent
Staffordshire
DE14 3TD

Tel: (0283) 64290   **Fax:** (0283) 61077

Frequency: Monthly

Circulation: 23,000

Contact: Hugh Potter, Editor

Profile: Concerned with all aspects of inland waterways, both in the UK and overseas.

Requirements: 2 6 7
Articles on history, cruising and tow-path walking, plus information on hiring and buying boats. The emphasis should be on facts and technical matters.

Comments: No poetry or fiction. Guidelines for contributors are available on request.

Approach: In writing.

Lead time: Six weeks.

Payment: £33 per thousand words.

Wedding & Home

IPC Magazines
King's Reach Tower
Stamford Street
London
SE1 9LS

Tel: 071-261 7471   **Fax:** 071-261 7459

Frequency: Bi-monthly

Circulation: 45,000

Contact: Debbie Djordjevic, Editor

Profile: A glossy, fashion-based magazine for brides to be.

Requirements: 2 6 7
Features on honeymoon travel destinations, emotional matters,

---

1/News 2/Features 3/Fiction 4/Letters 5/Fillers
6/B&W Photos 7/Colour Photos 8/Reviews

wedding cakes, arrangements, etc. Length up to 1000 words.

Comments: Aim for a witty but factual style. All work is commissioned.

Approach: By letter or fax.

Lead time: Three months.

Payment: £150-£200 per thousand words.

The Weekly Journal

370 Coldharbour Lane
London
SW9 8PL

Tel: 071-737 7377   **Fax:** 071-924 0134

Frequency: Weekly

Circulation: 30,000

Contact: Isabelle Appio, Editor

Profile: A broadsheet newspaper for the black community in the UK. Includes current news and lifestyle features.

Requirements: 1 2
News of national and international events of particular relevance to black Britons. Also features on the arts, etc. Length up to 1500 words.

Comments: Aimed at those who find that their interests are not catered for by national newspapers.

Approach: By telephone or letter.

Lead time: Two weeks.

Payment: £100 per thousand words.

The Weekly News

Albert Square
Dundee
DD1 9QJ

Tel: (0382) 23131   **Fax:** (0382) 22214

Frequency: Weekly

Circulation: 487,606

Contact: W. Kelly, Editor

Profile: A lively general-interest title for all the family, although aimed mainly at housewives.

Requirements: 1 2 5 6 7
Anything newsy, but TV-related subjects are of particular interest. Inspiring stories of how individuals have overcome difficulties or achieved their goals. Length up to 1000 words.

Comments: Welcomes filler items such as humorous moments, helpful hints and unusual happenings.

Approach: By letter.

Lead time: One week.

Payment: Around £50 per thousand words.

Weight Watchers Magazine

2nd Floor
175-179 St John Street
London
EC1V 4RP

Tel: 071-490 1166   **Fax:** 071-490 2497

Frequency: 8xYear

Circulation: 175,000

Contact: Harriet Cross, Editor

Profile: For women interested in controlling their weight and improving their appearance.

Requirements: 2 7
Features on all aspects of weight loss, health, beauty and diet. Features should be aimed at wide audience, not just members of weight watchers classes.

Comments: Success stories are usually handled by the editorial staff.

Approach: By letter.

Lead time: Six weeks.

Payment: Negotiable.

What Bike?

Bushfield House
Orton Centre
Peterborough
PE2 5UW

Tel: (0733) 237111   **Fax:** (0733) 231137

Frequency: Monthly

Circulation: 25,241

Contact: Mark Graham, Editor

Profile: For anyone buying a
    motorbike, whether new or second
    hand. Includes riding and touring
    features, plus in-depth surveys of
    related areas such as insurance,
    repairs, etc.

Requirements: 2 5 6 7 8
    Features on owning and riding
    particular bikes. Also stories about
    servicing, touring, etc. Length
    between 1200 and 2000 words.

Comments: Keep copy clear and
    snappy.

Approach: By telephone or letter with
    ideas.

Lead time: Three weeks.

Payment: £100 per thousand words.

What Camcorder?

57-59 Rochester Place
London
NW1 9JU

Tel: 071-485 0011   **Fax:** 071-482 6269

Frequency: Bi-monthly

Circulation: 27,494

Contact: Ian Campbell, Editor

Profile: A glossy title that provides
    information and advice on choosing,
    buying and using video cameras.

Requirements: 1 2 7
    Practical, instructional features on
    camcorder techniques, plus
    equipment reviews and evaluation.
    Length around 800 words.

Comments: The style should be
    approachable and user friendly,
    avoiding technical jargon.

Approach: In writing with ideas.

Lead time: Six weeks.

Payment: £90 per thousand words.

What Car?

38-42 Hampton Road
Teddington
Middlesex
TW11 0JE

Tel: 081-943 5000   **Fax:** 081-943 5659

Frequency: Monthly

Circulation: 145,116

Contact: Ralph Morton

Profile: General-interest motoring
    title, covering the purchase and use
    of both new and second-hand cars.

Requirements: 1 2 6 7 8
    Features about driving or running
    particular cars, plus articles on
    motor finance, insurance, etc.

Comments: Looking for writers who
    can generate original ideas.

Approach: By letter or fax.

Lead time: Six weeks.

Payment: £175 per thousand words.

What Hi-Fi?

38-42 Hampton Road
Teddington
Middlesex
TW11 0JE

Tel: 081-943 5000   **Fax:** 081-943 5098

Frequency: Monthly

Circulation: 68,395

Contact: Rahiel Nasir

1/News **2**/Features **3**/Fiction **4**/Letters **5**/Fillers
6/B&W Photos **7**/Colour Photos **8**/Reviews

Profile: Covers new products and developments in the hi-fi market, including testing, advice and general features.

Requirements: 1 2 7 8
News and features concerning developments in the hi-fi industry of interest to consumers. Mainly interested in the separates market, although midi systems are becoming more important. Length up to 2000 words.

Comments: Keep technical material out of the main body of the text, putting it into a separate panel.

Approach: By letter.

Lead time: Three months.

Payment: £105 per published page.

What Investment?

3rd Floor
4-8 Tabernacle Street
London
EC2A 4LU

Tel: 071-638 1916   **Fax:** 071-638 3128

Frequency: Monthly

Circulation: 25,000

Contact: Keiron Root, Editor

Profile: A magazine for private investors, concentrating on stocks and shares, trusts, pensions, taxation and other aspects of financial planning.

Requirements: 2 6 7
Feature articles dealing with some aspect of finance, including 'alternative investments'. Copy should be simple but not patronising. Length 1200 to 1500 words.

Comments: Copy on Macintosh disk preferred. Technical treatises accompanied by complex tables are not required.

Approach: In writing with ideas or complete manuscript.

Lead time: Six weeks.

Payment: From £150.

What PC?

VNU House
32-34 Broadwick Street
London
W1A 2HG

Tel: 071-439 4242   **Fax:** 071-437 8985

Frequency: Monthly

Circulation: 54,000

Contact: Mick Andon, Editor

Profile: An easy-to-use, no-nonsense guide to buying PCs, software and peripherals.

Requirements: 1 2 8
Exclusive reviews or early product previews, plus group tests of hardware and software. Length 500 to 3000 words.

Comments: Keep it simple and interesting. No 'propeller heads or train spotters'.

Approach: By fax, telephone or letter. Also via Compuserve: 70007, S417.

Lead time: Two months.

Payment: £120 per thousand words.

What Personal Computer?

EMAP Publications
33-39 Bowling Green Lane
London
EC1R 0DA

Tel: 071-837 1212   **Fax:** 071-278 4003

Frequency: Monthly

Circulation: 48,000

Contact: Gail Robinson, Editor

1/News **2**/Features **3**/Fiction **4**/Letters **5**/Fillers
6/B&W Photos **7**/Colour Photos **8**/Reviews

Profile: Aimed at those who have limited experience of personal computers. For both home and small business users.

Requirements: 2 8
Reviews of the latest software and hardware products, plus features about buying and using PCs. Length up to 1500 words.

Comments: No unsolicited manuscripts.

Approach: By telephone.

Lead time: Four weeks.

Payment: Negotiable.

What Satellite TV?

57-59 Rochester Place
London
NW1 9JU

Tel: 071-485 0011   **Fax:** 071-284 2145

Frequency: Monthly

Circulation: 63,000

Contact: Geoff Bains, Editor

Profile: A buyer's guide to satellite TV equipment, with technical tutorials, industry news and programme information.

Requirements: 1 2 6 7 8
User stories, some equipment reviews and background technical pieces. Maximum 2500 words.

Comments: Avoid technical jargon. Photos are appreciated when available.

Approach: By telephone with ideas.

Lead time: Two months.

Payment: £90 per thousand words.

What Video?

57-59 Rochester Place
London
NW1 9JU

Tel: 071-485 0011   **Fax:** 071-284 2145

Frequency: Monthly

Circulation: 42,000

Contact: Steve May, Editor

Profile: One of the leading video magazines for consumers. Covers video recorders, televisions, camcorders and video games.

Requirements: 1 2
Unusual or interesting articles on video-related subjects. Especially welcomes features on novel applications or adventurous videos. Length up to 1000 words.

Comments: Writers should aim to inform as well as entertain.

Approach: In writing.

Lead time: Two months.

Payment: £85-£95 per thousand words.

What's New In Farming

30 Calderwood Street
Woolwich
London
SE18 6QH

Tel: 081-855 7777   **Fax:** 081-854 6795

Frequency: Monthly

Circulation: 49,000

Contact: Don Taylor, Editor

Profile: A digest of new products of value to farmers, including explanations of what their attributes are and how they work.

Requirements: 1 2
Short illustrated items, plus juicy news items of up to 700 words.

Comments: Brevity, clarity and accuracy are essential.

Approach: By telephone with initial ideas.

1/News **2**/Features **3**/Fiction **4**/Letters **5**/Fillers
6/B&W Photos **7**/Colour Photos **8**/Reviews

Lead time: Six weeks.
Payment: £107 per thousand words for features.

What's New in Interiors

30 Calderwood Street
Woolwich
London
SE18 6QH

Tel: 081-855 7777   **Fax:** 081-316 3169

Frequency: Quarterly

Circulation: 22,000

Contact: Derrick Jolley, Editor
Profile: Covers new products and developments relating to interior design.
Requirements: 2
Articles based on press material, written in the magazine's house style. These are written to commissions by prior arrangement with the editor.
Comments: Speculative work is not accepted. Writers should be able to provide copy on disk in Macintosh format.
Approach: By telephone, letter or fax.
Lead time: Three months.
Payment: By arrangement.

What's On In London

182 Pentonville Road
London
N1 9LB

Tel: 071-278 4393   **Fax:** 071-837 5838

Frequency: Weekly

Circulation: 40,000

Contact: Michael Darvell, Editor

Profile: Information and listings covering forthcoming events and activities in London.
Requirements: 1 2 6 7
General features about things to see and do in London and the Home Counties, perhaps tied to a particular event. Length 800 to 1000 words.
Comments: Summer issues cover events and places over a wider geographical area, covering English traditions, etc.
Approach: By telephone.
Lead time: Four weeks.
Payment: £50 per thousand words.

What's On TV

IPC Magazines
King's Reach Tower
Stamford Street
London
SE1 9LS

Tel: 071-261 7769   **Fax:** 071-261 7739

Frequency: Weekly

Circulation: 1.4 million

Contact: Suzy Barber, Commissioning Editor
Profile: A mass-market TV listings magazine. Also runs features and competitions.
Requirements: 2 4 7
Features on programmes, celebrities and other TV-related subjects. Length 450 to 500 words.
Comments: Ensure that copy is concise, clear and easy to read.
Approach: By telephone, fax or letter.
Lead time: Six weeks.
Payment: Around £200.

Which Camera?

60 Waldegrave Road
Teddingon
Middlesex
TW11 8LG

Tel: 081-943 5851   **Fax:** 081-943 5871

Frequency: Bi-monthly

Circulation: 18,300

Contact: Stuart Watts, Editor

Profile: A comprehensive guide for all
those interested in buying a new
camera.

Requirements: 1 2
Features that explain the benefits
associated with particular products.
Length up to 1500 words.

Comments: Study the magazine before
suggesting features.

Approach: By telephone.

Lead time: Two months.

Payment: £120 per thousand words.

Which Computer?

EMAP Publications
33-39 Bowling Green Lane
London
EC1R 0DA

Tel: 071-837 1212   **Fax:** 071-278 4003

Frequency: Monthly

Circulation: 30,709

Contact: David Dobson, Editor

Profile: A business computing
magazine for managing directors
and financial controllers. Has a
management rather than a technical
bias.

Requirements: 1 2 8
Any news or features on large,
corporate solutions and information
technology strategy. Length up to
4000 words.

Comments: Looking for feature
articles rather than product-based
reviews.

Approach: By letter.

Lead time: Four weeks.

Payment: £150 per thousand words.

Which Motorcaravan?

Elm Farmhouse
Epping Green
Epping
Essex
CM16 6PU

Tel: (0992) 578905   **Fax:** (0992) 575380

Frequency: Monthly

Circulation: 10,500

Contact: John Page, Editor

Profile: Provides information and
advice for those interested in buying
and owning motorcaravans.

Requirements: 1 2 6 7
Articles on travelling and touring
with motorcaravans. Also
equipment reviews, and features on
related subjects such as walking and
nature. Length 2000 to 3500 words.

Comments: This is a very pictorial
magazine, so consider picture
opportunities.

Approach: In writing with ideas.

Lead time: Two months.

Payment: Negotiable.

Who Minds?

Greater London House
Hampstead Road
London
NW1 7QQ

Tel: 071-388 3171   **Fax:** 071-387 9518

Frequency: Quarterly

Circulation: 55,000

1/News 2/Features 3/Fiction 4/Letters 5/Fillers
6/B&W Photos 7/Colour Photos 8/Reviews

Contact: Jackie Marsh, Editor

Profile: The official publication of the National Childminding Association. Facilitates contact and communication between registered childminders.

Requirements: 2
Features on issues such as training, regulations, health and safety, etc. Also articles suggesting innovative ways of entertaining or encouraging children.

Comments: Articles that help to establish a sense of identity among childminders are welcomed.

Approach: In writing.

Lead time: Two months.

Payment: Negotiable.

Wild About Animals

40 Grays Inn Road
London
WC1X 8LR

Tel: 071-405 3916   **Fax:** 071-831 5426

Frequency: Monthly

Circulation: 60,808

Contact: Brenda Marsh

Profile: A magazine for all animal and nature lovers. Includes articles and information about animals of every kind.

Requirements: 2 3
Articles from knowledgeable writers on subjects such as biology and zoology. Also fiction which demonstrates a relationship between animals and humans. Length 1400 to 1500 words.

Comments: All material must be accurate and well-researched.

Approach: In writing.

Lead time: Two months.

Payment: Negotiable.

Windows User

Quadrant House
The Quadrant
Sutton
Surrey
SM2 5AS

Tel: 081-652 3662   **Fax:** 081-652 8943

Frequency: Monthly

Circulation: 50,000

Contact: Sean Geer, Editor

Profile: A computing magazine for PC owners who use the Windows interface.

Requirements: 1 2 8
Enthusiastic articles on using Windows and related applications, peripherals, etc. Also news items, reviews and comment.

Comments: Although it helps to have technical knowledge, this is not essential.

Approach: By telephone.

Lead time: Two months.

Payment: Negotiable but good.

Windsurf

The Blue Barn
Thew Lane
Wootton
Woodstock
Oxon
OX7 1HA

Tel: (0993) 811181   **Fax:** (0993) 811481

Frequency: 10xYear

Circulation: 22,700

Contact: Mark Kasprowicz, Editor

Profile: Provides comprehensive coverage of all aspects of windsurfing.

Requirements: 2 6 7
Feature articles on travel and locations for windsurfing in the UK.

1/News 2/Features 3/Fiction 4/Letters 5/Fillers
6/B&W Photos 7/Colour Photos 8/Reviews

Comments: All technique-based articles are written in house.
Approach: By telephone.
Lead time: Two months.
Payment: Negotiable.

Wine

60 Waldegrave Road
Teddington
TW11 8LG

Tel: 081-943 5943 **Fax:** 081-943 5871

Frequency: Monthly

Circulation: 35,000

Contact: The Editor

Profile: For people who love good wine and good food.

Requirements: 1 2 6 7 8
News and features relating to quality food and wine, plus related travel stories. Length up to 1500 words.

Comments: Unsolicited manuscripts are not welcome.

Approach: In writing.

Lead time: Three months.

Payment: £125 per thousand words.

Woman

IPC Magazines
King's Reach Tower
Stamford Street
London
SE1 9LS

Tel: 071-261 5000 **Fax:** 071-261 5997

Frequency: Weekly

Circulation: 716,800

Contact: Carole Russell, Features Editor

Profile: Still one of the leading women's magazines. Read by people of all ages, but especially women in their thirties.

Requirements: 2 4 5
General features on topical issues and matters of concern. Length up to 1500 words.

Comments: Fiction is only accepted from well-known authors.

Approach: By telephone or letter with ideas.

Lead time: Four weeks.

Payment: Negotiable.

Woman Alive

96 Dominion Road
Worthing
West Sussex
BN14 8JP

Tel: (0903) 821082 **Fax:** (0903) 821081

Frequency: Monthly

Circulation: 15,000

Contact: The Editor

Profile: A woman's magazine for Christians. Includes specifically Christian articles plus general articles.

Requirements: 1 2 3 5 6 7
Reports on Christian and social issues, celebrity features and testimonies. Also short stories. Length 750 to 1200 words.

Comments: Articles must be written from a positive Christian perspective.

Approach: By letter with idea.

Lead time: Three months.

Payment: From £50 per thousand words.

1/News **2**/Features **3**/Fiction **4**/Letters **5**/Fillers
6/B&W Photos **7**/Colour Photos **8**/Reviews

Woman & Home

IPC Magazines
King's Reach Tower
Stamford Street
London
SE1 9LS

Tel: 071-261 5000   **Fax:** 071-261 7346

Frequency: Monthly

Circulation: 410,000

Contact: Jackie Hatton, Features
Editor

Profile: A mass-market, general-
interest title for women aged 35 and
over. Concentrates on home and
cookery.

Requirements: 1 2 7 8
Feature articles on ideas for the
home, etc. Also imaginative short
stories appropriate to the readership,
ranging from 2000 to 6500 words.

Comments: This is not a 'snippet'
magazine. Guidelines for fiction
writers are available on request.

Approach: By letter.

Lead time: Three months.

Payment: £180 per thousand words.

Woman's Journal

IPC Magazines
King's Reach Tower
Stamford Street
London
SE1 9LS

Tel: 071-261 6220   **Fax:** 071-261 7061

Frequency: Monthly

Circulation: 150,000

Contact: Jane Miles

Profile: A broad-based title targeting
women aged over 30.

Requirements: 2 3
Feature articles of general interest to
women, covering any subject apart

from children or pets. Length up to
2500 words. Some fiction is used,
but this is often bought from
publishers and agents.

Comments: Most features are
commissioned, but writers are
encouraged to submit original ideas
and proposals.

Approach: In writing with examples of
previous work.

Lead time: Three months.

Payment: Negotiable.

Woman's Realm

IPC Magazines
King's Reach Tower
Stamford Street
London
SE1 9LS

Tel: 071-261 6033   **Fax:** 071-261 5326

Frequency: Weekly

Circulation: 370,000

Contact: The Editor

Profile: A lively, informative weekly
for both working women and
housewives.

Requirements: 2 3 4
Features on showbusiness or travel,
plus 'truelife' experiences. Also
traditional romantic fiction and
stories with a twist. Length 500 to
2000 words.

Comments: Contact the magazine
before submitting fiction
manuscripts.

Approach: By telephone, fax or letter.

Lead time: Three months.

Payment: £50-£500.

1/News **2**/Features **3**/Fiction **4**/Letters **5**/Fillers
6/B&W Photos **7**/Colour Photos **8**/Reviews

Woman's Weekly

IPC Magazines
King's Reach Tower
Stamford Street
London
SE1 9LS

Tel: 071-261 6131　**Fax:** 071-261 6322

Frequency: Weekly

Circulation: 844,000

Contact: The Editor
Profile: One of the best-established
women's magazines in the UK,
concentrating mainly on the home
and family.
Requirements: 2 3 4
Readers' experiences, personality
profiles and nostalgic pieces.
Maximum 1000 words. Also
contemporary short stories, usually
connected with romance. Length
1000 to 4000 words.
Comments: Ensure that fiction plots
are plausible, with independent
heroines and likeable heroes.
Approach: In writing.
Lead time: Two months.
Payment: Negotiable.

Women & Golf

First Floor
Carlton House
Mere Green Road
Sutton Coldfield
West Midlands
B75 5BS

Tel: 021-323 3073　**Fax:** 021-323 2911

Frequency: Monthly

Circulation: 20,000

Contact: Jane Carter, Editor
Profile: A specialist magazine devoted
to covering golf for women players.

Requirements: 1 2 5 7
Features on golf courses,
competitions, beauty and spring
fashions. Length up to 1200 words.
Comments: Articles on regional golf
are always welcome.
Approach: By letter with ideas.
Lead time: Five weeks.
Payment: Negotiable.

Women in Management

64 Marryat Road
Wimbledon
London
SW19 5BN

Tel: 081-944 6332　**Fax:** 081-944 8406

Frequency: Quarterly

Circulation: 2500

Contact: Elizabeth Harman, Editor
Profile: A magazine for all women in
management positions in business,
industry and commerce.
Requirements: 2 5 6 7
Articles on the art and science of
management, plus features which
encourage education in the
principles of management. Length
up to 500 words.
Comments: Articles should
concentrate on management issues
which are of relevance to women.
Approach: By letter.
Lead time: Two months.
Payment: Negotiable.

Women's Art Magazine

Fulham Palace
Bishop's Avenue
London
SW6 6EA

Tel: 071-384 1110　**Fax:** 071-384 1110

1/News 2/Features 3/Fiction 4/Letters 5/Fillers
6/B&W Photos 7/Colour Photos 8/Reviews

Frequency: Bi-monthly

Circulation: 8000

Contact: Sally Townsend, Editor

Profile: Primarily concerned with contemporary women's art, especially with respect to the visual arts.

Requirements: 1 2 6 7 8
Exhibition reviews, profiles of artists and articles which take up current debates. Length 600 to 4000 words.

Comments: Each issue has a specific theme, so contact the editor before contributing.

Approach: By telephone.

Lead time: Four weeks.

Payment: Negotiable.

Woodcarving

Castle Place
166 High Street
Lewes
East Sussex

Tel: (0273) 477374   **Fax:** (0273) 478606

Frequency: Quarterly

Circulation: 25,000

Contact: Neil Bell, Editor

Profile: A specialist title published by the Guild of Master Craftsmen. Covers all aspects of woodcarving.

Requirements: 2 5
Instructional or practical articles on woodcarving, profiles of woodcarvers, etc. Also useful tips and hints.

Comments: The publishers also welcome suggestions for books on woodworking.

Approach: In writing.

Lead time: Three months.

Payment: From £10 for fillers.

Woodturning

Castle Place
166 High Street
Lewes
East Sussex

Tel: (0273) 477374   **Fax:** (0273) 478606

Frequency: Bi-monthly

Circulation: 30,000

Contact: Nick Hough, Editor

Profile: A glossy bi-monthly for enthusiastic woodturners. Published by the Guild of Master Craftsmen.

Requirements: 2 5
Informative features which will help woodturners to improve their skills. Also practical hints and tips.

Comments: Hints and tips must be original and not previously published.

Approach: In writing.

Lead time: Two months.

Payment: From £10 for fillers.

Woodworker

Argus Specialist Publications
Argus House
Boundary Way
Hemel Hempstead
Hertfordshire
HP2 7ST

Tel: (0442) 66551   **Fax:** (0442) 66998

Frequency: Monthly

Circulation: 45,000

Contact: Zachary Taylor, Editor

Profile: A magazine for keen woodworkers, covering techniques, carving, furniture and joinery.

Requirements: 1 2 6 7
Welcomes design-and-make projects, restoration features and instructional articles. Good photographs and diagrams are also

appreciated. Length 2000 words maximum.

Comments: Tends to be more upmarket in approach than competing magazines. Uses a high percentage of material from freelances.

Approach: In writing with a synopsis.
Lead time: Three months.
Payment: £50 per page.

World Fishing

Nortide House
Stone Street
Faversham
Kent
ME13 8PG

Tel: (0795) 536536   **Fax:** (0795) 530244

Frequency: Monthly

Circulation: 6810

Contact: The Editor
Profile: Concerned with commercial fishing worldwide, covering vessels and fishery operations.
Requirements: 2
Articles about commercial fishing, gear, processing and equipment. Length 1000 to 2000 words.
Comments: Concentrates on management and technical issues.
Approach: In writing.
Lead time: Two months.
Payment: By arrangement.

The World of Interiors

234 King's Road
London
SW3 5VA

Tel: 071-351 5177   **Fax:** 071-351 3709

Frequency: Monthly
Circulation: 61,903

Contact: Min Hogg, Editor
Profile: The best in interior design and decoration from around the world.
Requirements: 2 7
Features on interesting, tasteful and imaginative home interiors that have not been featured in any other publication. Length up to 1000 words.
Comments: This is primarily a visual magazine, so there is no point in submitting manuscripts until the editor has seen rough snaps of the interior.
Approach: Send a proposal accompanied by photographs.
Lead time: Three months.
Payment: £400 per thousand words.

World Soccer

25th Floor
IPC Magazines
King's Reach Tower
Stamford Street
London
SE1 9LS

Tel: 071-261 6821   **Fax:** 071-261 5007

Frequency: Monthly

Circulation: 50,000

Contact: Keir Radnedge, Editor
Profile: Foreign football for the serious student of the game.
Requirements: 1 2 6 7
Personality features and profiles, plus general features concerning football around the world. Length 400 to 900 words.
Comments: Discuss ideas with the editor before submitting any material.
Approach: By telephone.
Lead time: Two months.
Payment: £40-£100.

World Sports Cars

Hyde Park House
5 Manfred Road
London
SW15 2RS

Tel: 081-877 1080   **Fax:** 081-874 2150

Frequency: Monthly

Circulation: 55,000

Contact: Richard Holloway, Editor

Profile: An upmarket magazine covering the latest sports car models internationally.

Requirements: 1 2

Articles on the sports side of the motor industry, about anything from new cars to tyres, and from car security to people in the industry. Length 500 to 5000 words.

Comments: Always looking for something fresh and exciting.

Approach: In writing with ideas or complete manuscript.

Lead time: Six weeks.

Payment: £200-£250 per thousand words.

World's Fair

PO Box 57
2 Daltry Street
Oldham
Lancashire
OL1 4BB

Tel: 061-624 3687   **Fax:** 061-665 1260

Frequency: Weekly

Circulation: 25,000

Contact: Andrew Mellor, Editor

Profile: Covers the leisure and entertainment business, from circuses and fairgrounds to coin-op machines and amusement parks.

Requirements: 2 6 7

Articles on subjects of concern to those in the entertainment industry. Topics could include new shows, site problems, council bye-laws etc. Length up to 3000 words.

Comments: Considers leisure activities from the trade rather than the consumer point of view.

Approach: By letter.

Lead time: One week.

Payment: Negotiable.

Writers' Monthly

29 Turnpike Lane
London
N8 0EP

Tel: 081-342 8879   **Fax:** 081-347 8847

Frequency: Monthly

Circulation: 10,000

Contact: Shirley Kelly, Editor

Profile: Offers practical advice on all kinds of writing, from novels and short stories to articles and scripts.

Requirements: 2 6

Practical, 'how-to' articles or market surveys, preferably drawing on the writer's personal experiences. No fiction or poetry. News and author interviews handled in-house. Length 1200 or 2200 words.

Comments: Does not want articles about the number of rejection slips received, or false optimism about a particular market.

Approach: In writing with synopsis, sources and ideas for illustration.

Lead time: Three months.

Payment: £35-£50 per thousand words.

1/News **2/**Features **3/**Fiction **4/**Letters **5/**Fillers
6/B&W Photos **7/**Colour Photos **8/**Reviews

Writers News

PO Box 4
Nairn
IV12 4HU

Tel: (0667) 54441   **Fax:** (0667) 54401

Frequency: Monthly

Circulation: 11,000

Contact: Richard Bell, Editor
Profile: For aspiring and professional
    writers, providing market news,
    advice and inspiration. Covers all
    kinds of writing for publication,
    broadcasting, etc.
Requirements: 1 2 4 8
    Practical, instructional articles on
    the craft of writing, especially
    anything with an interesting or
    innovative angle. Also suggestions
    for new markets and opportunities.
    Length 900 to 1800 words.
Comments: Incorporates the quarterly
    newstand magazine *Writing*.
Approach: In writing with ideas.
Lead time: Two months.
Payment: £40 per thousand words.

X

XYZ Direction

38-42 Hampton Road
Teddington
Middlesex
TW11 0JE

Tel: 081-943 5035   **Fax:** 081-943 5639

Frequency: Monthly

Circulation: 20,000

Contact: Sue Weekes, Managing
  Editor
Profile: A magazine for the creative
  industry, concerned with the use of
  technology in design, etc.
Requirements: 2
  Articles on desktop publishing or
  related technologies, and their
  implementation and use in creative
  work. Length up to 1800 words.
Comments: Articles should be up-to-
  date and topical.
Approach: By letter or fax with a
  synopsis.
Lead time: Six weeks.
Payment: Negotiable.

1/News 2/Features 3/Fiction 4/Letters 5/Fillers
6/B&W Photos 7/Colour Photos 8/Reviews

Y

Yachting Life

113 West Regent Street
Glasgow
G2 2RU

Tel: 041-226 3861   **Fax:** 041-248 5311

Frequency: Monthly

Circulation: 10,500

Contact: Alastair Vallance

Profile: A magazine for yacht owners
and users, concentrating on
Scotland, the North of England and
Northern Ireland.

Requirements: 2
Articles and reports on yachts and
yachting, with a firm emphasis on
the above regions.

Comments: Study the magazine before
contributing.

Approach: In writing.

Lead time: Two months.

Payment: By arrangement.

Yachting Monthly

IPC Magazines
King's Reach Tower
Stamford Street
London
SE1 9LS

Tel: 071-261 6040   **Fax:** 071-261 6704

Frequency: Monthly

Circulation: 43,000

Contact: Paul Gelder, Features Editor

Profile: A monthly title for yachting
enthusiasts. Provides international
coverage, but concentrates on waters
closer to home.

Requirements: 2 5 6 7
Practical and technical articles on
seamanship, navigation, the
handling of small craft, design,
construction and equipment. Also
cruising narratives, and pilotage
articles.

Comments: Think of a fresh, well-
thought-out idea or re-work an old
idea from a new angle. Ensure that
technical articles are
well-researched.

Approach: In writing with 150-word
synopsis.

Lead time: Two months.

Payment: £113.40 per thousand words.

Yachting World

IPC Magazines
King's Reach Tower
Stamford Street
London
SE1 9LS

Tel: 071-261 6800   **Fax:** 071-261 6818

Frequency: Monthly

Circulation: 29,000

Contact: Andrew Bray, Editor

Profile: The most international of the
UK yachting magazines in both

1/News **2**/Features **3**/Fiction **4**/Letters **5**/Fillers
6/B&W Photos **7**/Colour Photos **8**/Reviews

coverage and circulation. Covers yacht racing and cruising.

Requirements: 1 2 7
Technical articles about yachting and good sailing narratives.

Comments: In writing with a one-page synopsis.

Approach: By letter.

Lead time: Six weeks.

Payment: £100 per thousand words.

Yachts and Yachting

196 Eastern Esplanade
Southend-on-Sea
Essex
SS1 3AB

Tel: (0702) 582245   **Fax:** (0702) 588434

Frequency: Fortnightly

Circulation: 22,500

Contact: Frazer Clark, Editor

Profile: Covers racing and performance sailboats, including dinghies, keelboats and offshore racing.

Requirements: 1 2
News and features relating to yacht racing. All material should be topical and relevant. Length typically 1500 words.

Comments: Does not require material on cruising.

Approach: By letter or fax.

Lead time: Two weeks.

Payment: Negotiable.

Yorkshire Life

Oyston Mill
Strand Road
Preston
PR1 8UR

Tel: (0772) 722022   **Fax:** (0722) 736496

Frequency: Monthly

Circulation: 8500

Contact: Brian Hargreaves, Editor

Profile: A county magazine covering society events, fashion, country sport and other subjects of local interest.

Requirements: 2 6 7
Feature articles on antiques, motoring, the arts, gardening, etc. Also profiles of villages and towns in Yorkshire.

Comments: Aims to be 'provincial but not parochial'.

Approach: In writing.

Lead time: Three months.

Payment: Negotiable.

Yorkshire Ridings Magazine

33 Beverley Road
Driffield
Yorkshire
YO25 7SD

Tel: (0377) 43232   **Fax:** (0377) 43232

Frequency: Bi-monthly

Circulation: 10,500

Contact: Winston Halstead, Editor

Profile: A traditional county periodical, including a mixture of historical and contemporary material.

Requirements: 2 6 7
Looking for material with a strong regional flavour. Topics could include fashion, furniture, gardening and antiques. Length up to 1000 words.

Comments: Photographs and illustrations are always welcome.

Approach: Send complete manuscript.

Lead time: Four weeks.

Payment: £35 per page.

1/News 2/Features 3/Fiction 4/Letters 5/Fillers
6/B&W Photos 7/Colour Photos 8/Reviews

You and Your Wedding

Silver House
31-35 Beak Street
London
W1R 3LD

Tel: 071-437 3493　**Fax:** 071-287 8655

Frequency: Bi-monthly

Circulation: 70,000

Contact: Ramune Burnes, Editor

Profile: A lively magazine for women planning to get married, similar in style and approach to *Cosmopolitan*.

Requirements: 1 2 7 8
Features on wedding preparations and arrangements, concentrating on hair, dresses, honeymoons and setting up home. Length up to 2000 words.

Comments: Study the magazine before contributing.

Approach: By letter.

Lead time: Two months.

Payment: £100-£200 per thousand words.

You Magazine

Northcliffe House
2 Derby Street
Kensington
London
W8 5TS

Tel: 071-938 6000　**Fax:** 071-937 3829

Frequency: Weekly

Circulation: 2 million

Contact: The Features Editor

Profile: A glossy colour supplement to the *Mail on Sunday*. Includes fashion, travel and general features.

Requirements: 2 7
Profiles of people with interesting jobs or hobbies, plus articles on unusual holidays.

Comments: Looking for features that can be illustrated easily, and which have some topical connection.

Approach: In writing with a synopsis.

Lead time: Four weeks.

Payment: £450 per thousand words.

Young People Now

17-23 Albion Street
Leicester
LE1 6GD

Tel: (0533) 471200　**Fax:** (0533) 471043

Frequency: Monthly

Circulation: 40,000

Contact: Jackie Scott, Editor

Profile: For everyone working in the field of personal and social education, including youth workers, teachers, etc.

Requirements: 2 6 7
Features on subjects such as homelessness, drugs and unemployment. Length 1000 to 1500 words.

Comments: Guidelines for contributors are available on request.

Approach: By telephone.

Lead time: Four weeks.

Payment: £45 per thousand words.

Your Choice

HHL Publications Ltd
Greater London House
Hampstead Road
London
NW1 7QQ

Tel: 071-388 3171　**Fax:** 071-387 9518

Frequency: Monthly

1/News 2/Features 3/Fiction 4/Letters 5/Fillers
6/B&W Photos 7/Colour Photos 8/Reviews

Circulation: 3.5 million

Contact: Dorothy Stesanczyk, Editor

Profile: A magazine for Co-op shoppers, similar to *Bella* and *Best* in style. Mainly food based, but also runs general features.

Requirements: 2
Articles on travel, gardening and personalities. Length 1000 to 1500 words.

Comments: Features that tie in with the editorial schedule are most likely to be accepted.

Approach: By telephone with ideas.

Lead time: Three months.

Payment: £250 per thousand words.

Your Classic

60 Waldegrave Road
Teddington
Middlesex
TW11 8LG

Tel: 081-943 5955   **Fax:** 081-943 5877

Frequency: Monthly

Circulation: 40,252

Contact: Robert Coucher, Editor

Profile: A hands-on classic car magazine for enthusiasts.

Requirements: 1 2
Detailed features on re-builds and restorations, plus general articles on popular, affordable classics.

Comments: All material should be practical and informative.

Approach: By fax or letter.

Lead time: Six weeks.

Payment: By arrangement.

Your Garden

Westover House
West Quay Road
Poole
Dorset
BH15 1JG

Tel: (0202) 680603   **Fax:** (0202) 674335

Frequency: Monthly

Circulation: 140,000

Contact: Graham Clarke, Editor

Profile: A magazine for gardeners who are enthusiastic, but who may not have much experience. Aims to give readers a greater understanding and more pleasure from their gardens.

Requirements: 2 6 7
Readers' success or failure stories, 'how-to' instructional features and articles on growing particular plants.

Comments: Copy should be targeted at a readership that is younger and more upmarket than that of *Amateur Gardening*.

Approach: In writing with ideas.

Lead time: Two months.

Payment: NUJ rates.

Your Health & Lifestyle

Silver House
21-35 Beak Street
London
W1R 3LD

Tel: 071-437 3493   **Fax:** 071-287 8655

Frequency: Bi-monthly

Circulation: 40,000

Contact: Heather Kirby, Editor

Profile: A health, beauty and fashion magazine for women aged between 25 and 40.

Requirements: 2 7
Features with a health bias, covering

both mind and body. Also relevant material on fashion and beauty.

Comments: Contributors should be familiar with the magazine's style and approach.

Approach: In writing with a synopsis.

Lead time: Four months.

Payment: By arrangement.

Your Home

995 High Road
North Finchley
London
N12 8QX

Tel: 081-343 9977   **Fax:** 081-343 7831

Frequency: Monthly

Circulation: 110,000

Contact: Ros Dunford, Editor

Profile: A magazine for anyone interested in improving their home environment.

Requirements: 2
Feature articles on possible ways of enhancing a house. Material must be concise and detailed, including plenty of hard facts.

Comments: Submissions should aim to give readers 'hindsight in advance'.

Approach: In writing.

Lead time: Two months.

Payment: £70 per thousand words.

Your Horse

EMAP Pursuit Publishing Ltd
Bretton Court
Bretton Centre
Peterborough
PE3 8DZ

Tel: (0733) 264666   **Fax:** (0733) 265515

Frequency: Monthly

Circulation: 42,881

Contact: Lesley Eccles, Editor

Profile: One of the leading horse titles, aimed mainly at horse owners. The average reader is aged 29 and fully committed to horses.

Requirements: 2
Off-beat articles, perhaps on riding in an unusual or exotic location. Also humorous pieces and original workings of well-worn themes.

Comments: Concentrates on down-to-earth advice for owners who do not have too much money to spend.

Approach: By telephone or letter with ideas.

Lead time: Two months.

Payment: £50 per thousand words.

Yours Magazine

Apex House
Oundle Road
Peterborough
PE2 9NP

Tel: (0733) 555123   **Fax:** (0733) 312025

Frequency: Monthly

Circulation: 149,407

Contact: Neil Patrick, Editor

Profile: A bright, informative and entertaining colour monthly for those aged over 55. Many of these are pensioners, and almost 80 per cent are women.

Requirements: 1 2 3 4 5 6 7
News about elderly people and their achievements, plus humorous articles of interest to retired people. Also shared experiences, short stories and opinions.

1/News **2**/Features **3**/Fiction **4**/Letters **5**/Fillers
6/B&W Photos **7**/Colour Photos **8**/Reviews

Comments: Contributions should be bright, optimistic and sensitive. Complicated things must be explained in simple terms, and writers should not be afraid to show their feelings.
Approach: By letter or fax with ideas.
Lead time: Seven weeks.
Payment: By arrangement.

Youth Clubs Magazine

Youth Clubs UK
11 St. Bride Street
London
EC4A 4AS

Tel: 071-353 2366   **Fax:** 071-353 2369

Frequency: 5xYear

Circulation: 8500

Contact: The Editor
Profile: A magazine for youth workers and others involved with young people. Distributed to groups affiliated to Youth Clubs UK.
Requirements: 1 2 6 7
News and features on youth work issues, and in-depth analyses of current topics such as young people and alcohol, crime, etc. Length around 2000 words.
Comments: The magazine aims to share examples of good practice. Guidelines for contributors are available on request.
Approach: By telephone or letter.
Lead time: Two months.
Payment: £75 per thousand words.

1/News **2**/Features **3**/Fiction **4**/Letters **5**/Fillers
6/B&W Photos **7**/Colour Photos **8**/Reviews

Part 3

Index of Subjects

Index